D0461659

Her Dream of Dreams

Her Dream of Dreams

The Rise and Triumph of Madam C. J. Walker

Beverly Lowry

ALFRED A. KNOPF · NEW YORK 2003

This Is a Borzoi Book Published by Alfred A. Knopf

Copyright © 2003 by Beverly Lowry

Grateful acknowledgment is made to Hill and Wang for permission to reprint excerpts from
The Big Sea *by Langston Hughes. Copyright © 1940 by Langston Hughes. Copyright renewed
1968 by Arna Bontemps and George Houston Bass. Reprinted by permission of Hill and Wang,
a division of Farrar, Straus and Giroux, LLC.*

Library of Congress Cataloging-in-Publication Data
Lowry, Beverly.
*Her dream of dreams : the rise and triumph of Madam C. J. Walker /
Beverly Lowry.—1st ed.*
p. cm.
ISBN 0-679-44642-7 (hc : alk. paper)
*1. Walker, C. J., Madam, 1867–1919.   2. African American women executives—
Biography.   3. Cosmetics industry—United States—History.   I. Title.*

HD9970.5.C672 W3558 2003
338.7'66855'092—dc21
[B]   2002027494

Manufactured in the United States of America
First Edition

In memory: Polly and Dora, mother and daughter, fire and ice

Contents

Prologue: Who She Was

There has never been anyone like her. This is an extraordinary statement to make, but I believe it. And when you hear what she did, the impossible leap she made against such odds, maybe you will too.

Her name when she was born, or so we are told, was Sarah Breedlove. There is no birth certificate, no family Bible or church record, and "Sarah Breedlove" does not appear on any census record in any state until 1900, and by then she had married twice and changed her surname. Unable to document even this most basic clue to her whereabouts and existence, we have to find her in stories and legends, in marriage certificates, deeds, interviews, insurance maps, city directories. We have to put these scraps of information alongside allegations and patently untrue tales, paste them together, see what we come up with.

On her tombstone she is called Madam C. J. Walker. That for the historical record there is no "Sarah" or family name makes sense. She is a woman remembered by who she became: a product, an icon, a legend and an exemplar. Whoever visits her grave does not come to remember Sarah Breedlove; they are there to pay respects to her creation, who was often called, simply and grandly—as became appropriate to her demeanor—Madame, often with a culminating *e* when used, almost as a title, without the initials or the last name.

Names are labels, and sometimes, like Post-its, they come unstuck. When my mother died, my father proposed that we carve MRS. DAVID L. FEY into the Austin marble that would mark her grave, since—he reasoned—she hated her name. I knew he was right, but suggested that we had to consider the connections her marker established for later generations, one death to the next birth. So we put her legal name, Dora Smith Fey, on the top line and after that, the ones she liked better: PRECIOUS HENRI, her marker reads. BELOVED MOO.

Madam Walker's only child, a daughter, is buried beside her, and the name carved on the left-hand side of the marble is A'Lelia, also a chosen name. Born Lelia McWilliams, Madame's daughter claimed the surname of her mother's third husband for business purposes and added the A-apostrophe after her mother's death. Neither woman felt bound to a destiny restricted by biology; they made their lives up as they went, and in time became, by name, the chosen, dreamed-of self. The two of them lie side by side in a shady spot up in the Bronx in Woodlawn Cemetery, not far from the much grander digs of J. C. Penney and F. W. Woolworth. The tombstone is modest, with "WALKER" across the top. There is a blank place on Madame's right, and so far as we know, no one is buried there. Had one of A'Lelia's husbands chosen to lie in the Walker plot, Madame would've separated him from his wife for eternity.

It's beginnings I'm after, the rising arc of how Sarah Breedlove became Madam C. J. Walker. I want to try to understand how a child born to former slaves in a sharecroppers' cabin went on to sell the fire out of a hair-care product she'd invented for African-American women in a city she had only just moved to, then have the gumption required to turn that homemade preparation—not to mention herself—into a signifier of national renown, then found a business empire the likes of which no one had ever yet seen, and to renovate a Harlem town house in high style and build a mansion on the Hudson River and fill it with antiques and books, Persian rugs and works of art, and there entertain politicians, statesmen and classical musicians.

The girl born Sarah Breedlove will become a woman of great reserve and dignity who travels all over the country to sell her product and make speeches. She will live in St. Louis, Denver, Pittsburgh, Indianapolis. She will wear imported lace dresses and Tiffany diamonds and fancy feathered hats, and drive newfangled cars before others dare. She will give money to worthy causes and stand up to Booker T. Washington when he refuses to acknowledge her at the National Negro Business League convention—and within two years will be photographed standing next to him. You can see how far she has come by taking a quick look at her in the picture taken in Indianapolis: in a wide-brimmed hat and lacy black dress, her chin lifted, she looks very settled, very calm and utterly unimpressed, as befits a woman who knew she deserved to stand there in that outfit right next to the most famous black man in America.

Yet the question remains: how? It is a miraculous transformation, from obscurity and poverty to wealth, leadership and fame, particularly in light of the barriers of race, gender and literacy, all the more so given the mind of the South, which during her young womanhood had hardened itself into the post-Reconstruction terrorism we call Jim Crow. It makes Abe Lincoln's trek from log cabin to White House look easy by comparison, since if Abe had had the money to pay for first-class railroad accommodations, he would have *ridden* first-class; and at least he could *vote*.

As for the official versions of the story, there are plentiful discrepancies, omissions and cagey manipulations of the truth. No, to find Sarah Breedlove we must begin even before her birth and then jump ahead, consider how she turned out then fold back to where she started, applying what we know to that which we can only suspect or surmise and finally making the case for what *seems* to have occurred. We have to focus on the person she became—the interviewed, remembered, photographed, documented Madame—and, like a wily shrink with a famous couched patient, jump abruptly back, to *here* when she was seven or *there* at thirteen, in order to creep forward in painstaking pursuit of the most nearly possible truth.

But the living soul is wily, and the heart eludes discovery. And we will never know it all.

I · *Where She Came From, 1867–1878*

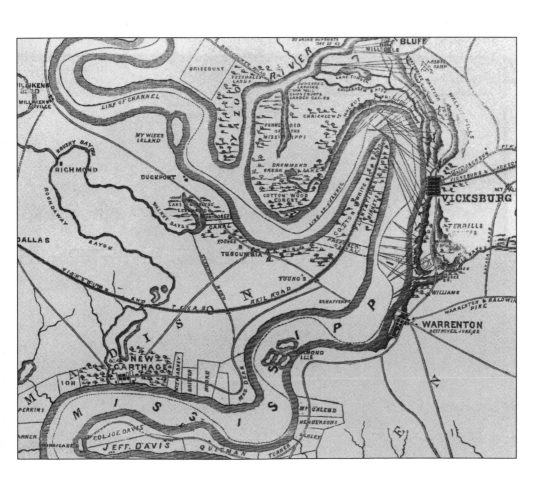

Croppers' Child

The year is 1874, and in flat wet country located in what was then regarded as the semi-barbaric Southwest there is a small cabin I want to enter, a sharecroppers' dwelling on the edge of a cotton field, inside of which a woman lies in a deep sleep on a narrow wooden bed. Between chills and fever, she breathes evenly, a quilt from the old days tucked firmly under her chin.

Dying is no mystery once it begins—it is as dutiful as a clock—and this woman is now into the process. A child is also in the house, a girl, and I will place her at the foot of her mother's bed: her high wide forehead, strong set jaw, brown skin and dark burning eyes, her hair tied up in strings.

From outside, if the water is back within the banks, come the sounds of early summer: hoes scraping at weeds in the cotton rows, railroad tracks being repaired, a depot under construction and, beyond it, a wharf boat that will rise and fall with the river, to facilitate the transfer of railroad cars from land to water and vice versa. A mule might bray or some far-off rooster let go as if dawn had just cracked. There is a blast of a boat's whistle, either passing by mid-river or stopping to pick up freight and passengers. These are the sounds of summer in this particular Louisiana river town. Year to year, only the nature of the construction changes. Everything else is repetition, ritual, more of the same.

Water is the story of the dying woman's life. Water, hard work and scraps of paper, one declaring her sound of body and a slave for life, the other proclaiming her to be now and henceforward forever free. Having lived on this patch of ground as far back as she can remember, she can identify by the number of hoots and the pitch of the whistle what boat is going which way, the ferryboat *P. F. Geisse* making one of its four daily trips between Delta and Vicksburg sounding nothing like the steamboat *Pelican* passing down to New Orleans or the *Albatross* going upriver to St. Louis.

Where does this scene come from, history or the imagination? Some things we can reckon precisely enough to construct a reasonable set of probabilities. To begin with what perhaps matters most, in time we are in the post–Civil War period and some ten years into Reconstruction. Geographically, we are in northeastern Louisiana, not far south of the Arkansas line and as far east as Louisiana reaches to the Mississippi. And while Reconstruction is on its last legs in this particular state, its effects—and those of the war—are still a part of everyday life. When Andrew Johnson, raised poor and white in Tennessee, took his seat in the White House, he promptly gave white Southerners every reason to believe that life would soon snap back to normal with only one exception: they would have no slaves. And so these people—having experienced the early stages of humiliation and defeat—are on their feet again, nail-spitting mad and armed to the teeth.

The one-room cabin is constructed of cottonwood logs collected in the surrounding countryside, then chinked with rocks and daubed with clay to hold them in place and keep out rain and wind. There is no floor except the ground. A fireplace for warmth and cooking takes up most of one wall, but no fire likely burns now, for in all probability we are in the sickly season, either well into or entering the summer months, when in nineteenth-century Louisiana disease goes on an annual tear.

Because black people are not allowed to congregate socially with whites, even posthumously, they often bury their loved ones in the levees and along the riverbanks. They know that the ground will turn wet and sucky when the water rises, that the dead will be washed downstream past New Orleans into the Gulf of Mexico, where their bones will drift and roll with the tide and eventually become one with salt, sand and fish eggs. But there is nothing else to do. And perhaps, these families reason, in the end the river is an apt tomb for those who lived by its whims and occasional blessings their entire lives.

Stiff ropes knotted at the corners hold the bedstead snugly together and cradle the woman's mattress—a sack of homespun cloth stuffed with Spanish moss which has been scalded and then buried for a time to soften its threads and kill off the fleas. Moss is easy to come by in Delta, Louisiana, where it hangs in mournful swags from the willows and the sycamore and swamp ash, dense as a curtain out in the swamps and bottoms.

The mother slips beyond thought as the alert, big-boned girl at the foot of the bed maintains her watch. Single-mindedness, stubborn focus and wind enough for the long haul are part of her nature. She is seven years and some months old. Her parents have been croppers since before she was born, and she has spent pretty much every minute since with them. When she was a baby, her mother either strapped her to her back while she worked the fields or sat her on a long burlap bag and pulled her along the rows, keeping a sharp eye out for copperheads and moccasins. By the age of four, a croppers' child had a job drilling holes for cotton seeds and dropping them carefully in.

Long after Sarah Breedlove's death, a woman from Delta will say that she and Winnie (as some people there called Sarah) were the best pickers of all the children, and I believe this. Later, as Madam C. J. Walker, Sarah Breedlove is demonstrably tireless. No one can match her capacity for work, whether younger or fitter and no matter from what kind of background. Work is what she knows, as deeply ingrained as a heartbeat.

Louisiana is a state so divided in its geography and culture that natives can know close to nothing about those who live only miles to the north or west. Where, then, are we exactly—where this woman is dying? Using a map from the early 1870s, find Vicksburg, Mississippi, then move your finger across the river. There, in northeastern Louisiana, is a town called Delta, on a wickedly narrow peninsula that until 1876 extends into the Mississippi like a lifted pinkie finger, forcing the river to veer from its natural course and flow briefly almost due north before looping around and crashing furiously southeast again.

The woman, who wears a loose dress made of heavy cotton, has been sick for longer than she knows. Here, where frost touches down like a quick kiss and lingers only briefly on its way to someplace else, sickness sleeps in the system all year round. One reason Southerners have the reputation of being sleepy and slow is that they are, many of them, sick deep down, all of the time. Fever, general malaise, a spleen so tender people call it an ague cake.

Let me tell you her first name: Minerva. For years she had no officially documented last name, but in an 1869 Madison Parish marriage certificate, the only Minerva on the Burney place—where Sarah Breedlove's parents were owned like mules and she herself was born and grew up—is called Minerva Anderson. Since the bride cannot read or write, she signs the certificate with an X, as does her husband, Owen Breedlove. There is an accepted way of doing this. "Minerva" is written, presumably by someone else, and then there is a big X penned, presumably by the bride herself, and finally the surname: Owen X Breedlove and Minerva X Anderson.

In time, their youngest child will be interviewed by newspaper reporters, and large crowds will come to hear her speak, and they will want to know where she came from and how she managed to hack her way through poverty and oppression to become a woman in a full-length fur coat who can conduct audiences with politicians and interviews with reporters from the *New York Times*. And while Madame herself will rarely speak directly or publicly about her parents, many stories will be told about them in press releases she authorized and in accounts whose details she approved.

In 1874 disease is thought to be as free-floating as ghosts and memories, alive in the air and damp enough to soak like milk into paper and clothes. When epidemics hit, mail delivery halts; boats don't stop for passengers; even newspapers aren't printed. People live in dread of the night mist, when pale clouds of what are called *miasmata* move invisible through the river bottoms. Minerva Breedlove may think she became ill walking barefoot on the cool ground or from the air that sneaks through the chinking, or she may remember a night when, after the hogs were called up from the brakes, she and her daughters sat on the front porch and listened to a neighbor play the banjo, unmindful of the passing mist creeping down her unsuspecting throat.

Madison is a parish of bottomland, with only an occasional undulation to break the flatness, and is rimmed by rivers: the Ouachita to the west, the Arkansas and the Yazoo to the north, and to the south the less significant Tensas, which flows through a channel created by the Mississippi known as a meander scar. The Tensas—named for Indians, pronounced "Ten-saw"—drains Madison Parish, or tries to, through a maze of bayous to the north, south and west: Bayou Macon, Joe's Bayou, Roundaway and Brushy Bayous, the Bayou Bonne Idee.

We are, of course, west of the Big Daddy of rivers, actually *on* the Mississippi. In deeds and contracts, the property on which the dying woman's cabin is located is invariably described as "bounded on the East and West side by the Mississippi River, on the North by the old

Hoffman tract, on the South by the Frederic Smith tract, now owned or occupied by Nicholson Barnes."

The town of Delta was improbably carved out of swampland in the 1830s by hopeful, upstart white men hot to fill their pockets with revenues from cotton, of course, or from ferryboats running east-west or steamships working north and south or, eventually, railroads headed west. In the nineteenth century, railroads turned the entire nation into a veritable money park. And because Delta is situated on the thirty-second parallel—which constitutes the shortest route between oceans from Savannah to San Diego—planters were hoping to claim and colonize territory as the tracks moved west. Before their spree was busted up by Lincoln and the Union Army, they had hoped to provide even the labor system for this enterprise; by 1874, now that slavery's disallowed, they'll settle for the real estate profits.

A short walk from Minerva Breedlove's cabin there is a smart new restaurant, and the railroad speculators have made Delta the parish seat. An engineer from the North Louisiana and Texas Railway Company has even marked off blocks and squares in preparation for the building of a whole new town around the projected depot. The ballyhoo never stops. Asked about the inflated property values in Delta, a participant said in 1874, "Well . . . we was booming the town."

When the sun goes down, Minerva Breedlove can see from her cabin the gaslights and lanterns of Vicksburg, where on the landing there are bars and cafés and a famous whorehouse. Vicksburg is the city Delta yearns toward, and its white citizens shop, pray and marry there, and they bury their dead in a cemetery on a hill east of the city. For black people, there are jobs, churches where they are welcome, schools for their children, a life beyond cotton fields and tree stumps.

Now we do not historically *know* that in 1874 a young girl stood at the foot of her mother's bed and attended her dying. We don't know exactly when Minerva Breedlove died or from what or, for that matter, when or where she was born or who, if anybody, owned her before Robert Burney did. Until 1913, neither death nor birth certificates were required by the federal government. And earlier, since slaves were considered property—classified, in Louisiana, as real estate—they were not counted as people in either U.S. Census or parish records.

What we do know is that within three years, when the little girl is ten years old and is said to have left Delta, she is— *has to be*—a fully formed person. This certainty is based on hard study, extended thinking and what feels like rock-bottom necessity, considering the woman she turned into; based too, in general, on what I have learned, lived and come to believe if not always, that is, on verifiable *fact.*

A mother who'd been born a slave would necessarily pass on hard-won information to her children. Lesson one is a commandment every bit as non-negotiable as those of Moses: *Learn to read.* Not especially for self-improvement or even education but as strategy. As long as the other race reads and you don't, they get to make the rules, interpretations, decisions and laws. Rules two and beyond are less predictable. *Never mind business that's not yours,* perhaps. Maybe, *Stay out of white people's way.* And again: *Learn to read.*

To create the scene of a mother's death—her very bed and fire-place—and then boldly assert that this was possibly the moment at which that particular daughter marshaled her strength and began becoming the girl who would become the woman we know as Madam C. J. Walker is, of course, a brash assumption. But let us do just that, without apology, and go on.

Minerva Breedlove

Many versions of the same story are always possible, racial or political interpretations, economic or religious. Sometimes people who have known water and cotton and a flat, hot, mosquito-infested world from their earliest days are prone to dream up, even consort with, the same desires. Whether black, white, rich, poor, Asian, Jewish, third-generation Italian or first-generation Lebanese, we share the same appetites for food, dance, music, stories, drink, a ceiling fan, sweet iced tea, a cool breeze. At other times the differences among and between us can seem infinite and scalding, dividing us inalterably.

It's a fantasy of mine to stand magically mid-river and hold out my arms, touching Louisiana and Arkansas, where my parents grew up, with the fingertips of one hand and, with the other, Mississippi, where I did. I'd like to be able to imagine the lives of all the people who grew up and have a history in that place, and then feel in these same electric fingers what we share and know and dream in common, regardless of differences. But knowing a place takes a great deal more work than that simple desire, and to fully imagine it requires not just hope and fervor but thought.

If the disease killing Minerva Breedlove is swamp fever—malaria—it might have been in her system for a year or longer, leaving her sporadically achy and exhausted. If she has contracted one of its more catastrophic versions, in its final stages she will experience intermittent sieges of chills, and a deep quietude that edges close to paralysis and is followed by racking chills, high fever, then peace and chills once again. Who, if anyone, diagnosed and treated this very ill woman and prescribed whatever medicine she took?

During slavery times and especially afterwards, black people had their own doctors who prescribed cures often unknown to whites. Because they believed more in roots and herbs than in treatments favored at the time—which included purging, bleeding and blistering—their healer was called the root doctor. To cure swamp fever, a root doctor commonly used the bark, pulverized to a powder, of the chinchona tree, which is high in quinine. And if malaria was indeed the disease from which Minerva Breedlove suffered, quinine could possibly have cured her, but only if she continued to ingest it long after her symptoms had disappeared, which neither root doctors nor physicians with college degrees realized then.

For years, black people were considered immune to the fatal version of malaria—because they were indelicate and brutish, white people said, less susceptible to heat and disease. But even they had to admit that slaves newly arrived from West Africa had to go through a period of "acclimation" to the American version of the fever, a process of sickness and recovery through which they built up a resistance.

There is no way to know how far Minerva Breedlove—and therefore Sarah—is from her African ancestors. In the Madison Parish Courthouse in an 1848 property contract, Robert Burney states that he owns a young slave woman named Minerva and that she is nineteen, sound of mind and body and a slave for life. There is no reason why he would've been precise about her age, but let's assume he was and that indeed Minerva Breedlove was born in 1829, by which time the African slave trade to the United States had stopped. While legally banned since 1808, it had persisted afterwards, particularly in New Orleans, where the pirate Jean Lafitte ran a cash-only slave trade in a blacksmith shop; but by 1820, slavers were no longer openly taking the Middle Passage across the Atlantic direct to North America. And Minerva Anderson was therefore almost certainly born on these shores. But, to take the story back a generation, where then did her people come from?

The state of Louisiana has a special history. If Minerva Anderson's ancestors were brought into the U.S. *before* the Louisiana Purchase of 1803, they most likely came directly from West African Senegambia, where the French had exclusive rights to purchase and ship all cargo headed for Louisiana. If, on the other hand, her people were brought first to one of the older seaboard states, such as Virginia, and then to the new Southwest—as were most of the slaves in Mississippi and Louisiana—their ancestral home might have been any one of a number of West African countries. In the 1900 U.S. Census, Owen and Minerva Breedlove's daughter Sarah reports that both her parents were born in Louisiana, which she might have known for a fact or merely repeated from family legend. Perhaps she was simply providing an easy answer; no one now can say. In any case, by 1874 Minerva Breedlove would have had decades in which to lose any resistance to the New World's fatal diseases.

In the South, mosquitoes determine architecture and decide summer plans. People long to sit out on open, unscreened porches and watch the sun set, but don't dare. Dusk is the worst, when, in the evening sop, insects attack in clouds. Unable to keep from scratching, children come in from play with long lines of blood running down their legs.

Before the Civil War, a farming ritual was to drain the land for planting; but by 1874, with the levees caved in and the ditches and fences still down, the water flows in and just stands, a stagnant scum in which mosquitoes—including the deadly *anopheles* and the *aedes aegypti*—breed in skittering profusion. There is no insecticide to kill them, and nobody has a clue to what they're up to.

The Breedlove cabin is dark; their candle—more reliable than tree knots—is not lit. There are no windows, and so the only illumination comes in crooked spikes through gaps between the logs. Although daytime is fading, the sun's heat burns well past suppertime and does not let up until an hour before dawn, when the frailest whisper of a breeze might ruffle the grass.

And surely, when Minerva Breedlove rallies slightly, she sits up a little and beckons her daughter closer. Lifting herself up out of this sickness, yielding health, life and desire for the benefit of the child, she says, *Learn to read.*

Burney, the Planter

Whirl . . . was its king. Life simply could not be—not yet—a
certain, settled thing.

W. J. CASH, *THE MIND OF THE SOUTH*

O ne way to find out how black people lived under
slavery is to explore the lives of their owners,
what kind of land they owned and how much accumulated in what
way, what they planted, who they married, how they died.

Robert W. Burney, owner of Minerva and Owen Breedlove, was
born on November 23, 1819, or so say the burial records of the Christ
Episcopal Church of Vicksburg, Mississippi. According to the 1870
U.S. Census, his birthplace was South Carolina. Beyond statistics,
who was he? In 1792, a land grant was issued to a William Burney in
South Carolina, where Birneys and Barneys lived at that time; and in
Cincinnati, a well-known abolitionist was named James G. Birney.
William may have been related to our Burney, and "Birney" may or
may not have been a variant spelling of the same family's name—it certainly recurs throughout Robert Burney's life. I have no idea what the
W. in his name might stand for. William, perhaps—or nothing: people
weren't shy about name altering in those years, and a middle initial,
among ambitious men, seems to have been considered almost a
necessity.

Since the invention of the cotton gin, the South had been supplying
cotton for the industrial North and England in staggering quantities,
with swampy, fertile South Carolina one of the prime producers. But

by the time Robert Burney is eighteen years old, the cultivated land in the seaboard states has been worked to exhaustion. And when the first Great Depression spreads across the country, those people take to the waterways, heading west and south toward new country and the Mississippi. Only those well enough fixed to ride out the downturn remain; one such South Carolina planter opines that Louisiana is "sickly and lacking good society" and declares he's not about to take his family "into the savage and semi-barbrous Southwest."

Burney, since he can't afford that planter's attitude, sets his sights south and west, probably on Texas, after living for a time in Tennessee, with kin. And if he's anything like the majority of white men who come to Mississippi and Louisiana, he has little knowledge of farming and no idea what he will find or how he might succeed. All he knows is, life might be better out there. There's a chance he can become a planter! And for the man with a gambling turn of mind, chance turns to a sure thing as quick as the thumb flicks on a light switch.

In Mississippi and Louisiana in the 1830s and '40s, paper floated from town to town like mimosa blooms on a windy day. Friends signed for friends. Banks issued their own notes. Reckless lending was a given when nobody had actual cash. A Vicksburg speculator named Chewning bought the entire town of Pine Bluff, Arkansas, using notes signed by himself and his friends.

By the time Burney arrives, Vicksburg is awash in easy money and good times. A railroad line to Jackson is being built, and the first steam locomotive has come to town, the Commercial, weighing seven tons, with a megaphone-shaped smokestack and no headlight, bell or cowcatcher. Railroads are the next hot thing. They will link disparate regions of the country, and whoever develops the railroad to serve this new territory will also get to decide whether or not it will be a slaveholding society.

The year Burney turns twenty, the state of Louisiana carves a new parish—named in honor of the third president—out of a jungle of hardwoods, alligator backswamps and bog. The woods are impenetrable, and no land is open or cleared; it is basically uninhabitable. The parish's early population is drawn mostly from Mississippi and is primarily black, at a ratio of six to one, and within twenty years the figures will grow even wider apart, nine to one. There are no roads for horseback travel between Madison and the next parish to the west, Ouachita. Henry Clay Lewis, a doctor who moved here from the Northeast, describes it as a "quagmire, never thoroughly dry and almost impassable nine months out of the year" and reports that he found, on arrival, only one frame house in the settlement, the rest being made of logs, many with the bark still attached. He also tells of two woodsmen—hired at a thousand dollars apiece to mark out a road through the swamps—become so "embarrassed in the thick cane brakes and swamps" that they were trapped for weeks between Bayou Macon and the Boeuf River, surviving on alligator and wildcat meat. The Yankee doctor's life will end in the swamps when, having drunk heavily and played poker into the early morning hours, he steers his horse in the wrong direction. Both rider and mount will drown. Today, some claim, his ghost rides the night mist.

When Madison Parish is created in 1839, Minerva Anderson and Owen Breedlove are both ten years old—the age when legally they can be separated from their mothers—but we do not know who owns them. Some Breedlove family stories hold that Minerva was born in Delta, but the town did not exist in 1829. And while Breedlove is a common name in Louisiana—a distinguished one in New Orleans—there is no indication how Owen came by it.

Courthouse documents place the intrepid Robert Burney in Madison Parish in 1845, buying and selling property. A bachelor, he keeps circling the land he lusts after, that rich, risky pinkie finger of bottomland reaching brazenly into the Mississippi. He might well be acting as an agent for other men, using their money; nonetheless, whatever the details, he is buying and selling.

But what the land requires is money and Negroes. And until 1846, Burney has neither.

The year after Minerva Anderson's birth, on April 3, 1830, Mary Fredonia Williamson is born in Vernon, Mississippi, a town located just above Jackson, in the black-earthed Yazoo River Valley. A breathless local newspaper account describes it as a "colony of men and women of high breeding," primarily three clans who operate large estates with many slaves and live "like landed gentry of the British Isles." Most go to the Methodist church—some prefer the Episcopal—and own, in addition to the manor house, a summer home on the Gulf. The most distinguished of these families are the Kearneys, and Mary Fredonia is the second daughter of Sarah Lindsay Kearney and Russell McCord Williamson (called simply McCord). The Kearney family, the newspaper further reports, are of "noble lineage," traceable to twelfth-century Ireland, their history complete with a castle and a count. Not to be outdone, the Lindsays can trace *their* lineage back to William the Conqueror. When these clans joined together in matrimony, the offspring arrived owning family crests, lace dresses and slaves. Whereas all that can be said of Mary Fredonia's father is that he was born in North Carolina and attended an "institution of higher learning in Raleigh." In Mississippi, he served as a state representative and helped write the 1832 constitution.

In 1840, while Robert Burney is making connections in Vicksburg, Mary Fredonia Williamson, now ten, and her older sister, Almedia, are being sent to Nazareth Academy in Bardstown, Kentucky. Their mother died when Mary Fredonia was barely a year old, and their father has subsequently married a woman named Eliza, who bore him another daughter, Octervine.

The two motherless girls are given a classical education at Nazareth Academy: Latin, some Greek, sewing, manners, dress, music. They will have read Homer and certainly Sir Walter Scott. Upon graduation they will be proper young ladies, able to converse skillfully, do needlepoint and, probably, play the piano for their father's enjoyment. By the time the girls are sent off to Kentucky, McCord Williamson owns at least forty-two slaves and some eleven hundred acres of land. But in April of 1844, the girls are summoned back to Vernon. Their father is ill and will die the following March in Tennessee, after what an obituary describes as "a long and painful illness." His brief will leaves equal shares of his estate to his widow and three daughters, although the girls, of course, cannot claim their inheritance until they either marry or attain adulthood at twenty-one.

So it is not surprising that sixteen-year-old Mary Fredonia is married on October 21, 1846, at the oldest and most socially prestigious church in Vicksburg, Christ Church Episcopal. The groom? Our swift-heeled opportunist, twenty-seven-year-old Robert W. Burney. While appropriately impressive, the wedding perhaps is not as lavish as it would have been when the fortunes of McCord Williamson were riding high.

And Burney's surely a smug and happy groom, congratulating himself as he stands at the altar watching his bride come down the aisle, a dowered girl of prominence and noble lineage.

When Burney marries Mary Fredonia Williamson, James Polk is president and Manifest Destiny, the right of Americans to usurp any country they take a shine to, is in full swing. Texas has been annexed as a slave state, and Dred Scott has appealed to a court in St. Louis for his freedom. Frederick Douglass has published his eponymous *Narrative* and in 1847 will put out the first issue of his abolitionist paper, the *North Star*. In the Northeast, women are starting to agitate about voting rights; and Joseph Cinque and the other African captives who commandeered the slave ship *Amistad* have been cleared of murder charges by the U.S. Supreme Court.

In every session of Congress there are rumblings of discontent and threats of secession, the "gag rule" preventing discussions of slavery having been abolished. South Carolina Senator John C. Calhoun makes fire-breathing speeches warning of anarchy if Northern industrialists try to strip Southerners of their economic power. Henry Wadsworth Longfellow has published a poem called "Anti-Slavery Melodies for the Friends of Freedom." Abraham Lincoln of Illinois has been elected to the House of Representatives.

A man from Vermont, Ezra Blake Towne, has moved to Madison Parish, where he founds a newspaper and also buys two plantations, one of which—Wilderness Place—lies directly on the Mississippi, just south of where the Burney place will soon become a reality.

National and state politics seem irrelevant to the man with a mission, and besides, white people in the South assume slavery is not only their natural right but an inherent part of their interior lives. Nobody's got secession or war in mind at this point, and Robert Burney has his eye fixed on the rich bottomland on that finger of land across from Vicksburg, and not just for planting. He imagines a ferryboat landing and, in time, a railroad depot. He may be planning trips in the future, promising his educated wife that someday they'll take a train all the way to the Pacific Ocean.

They won't make it, of course, not even as far as Texas. The war will commence a year after he and some associates incorporate and begin planning a town called De Soto Point, which will be situated on the Burney place and will include a depot and ferryboat landing. And though all their bright plans will come to nothing, someone else on that plantation will someday see the Pacific—the youngest child of a slave couple, our own Sarah Breedlove.

Doubtless a guest at Burney's wedding is Oliver O. Woodman, a sharp dealer who lives in Vicksburg and is listed in the 1843 Warren County tax rolls as a druggist. Advertisements for his business suggest a combination bookstore, newsstand, drugstore and music establishment. Woodman's an Easterner, born in Maine, and Caroline, his wife, is from Washington, D.C. The year of Burney's nuptials, Woodman buys at least two more slaves: an aging couple named George and Vinny Kitteral, who once belonged to McCord Williamson.

Since Burney's the only man in his father-in-law's family—albeit by marriage—he has been appointed executor of the estate, and so, armed with power over his wife's inheritance, he now burns the midnight oil with Woodman. Pooling their assets, the two men form, in January of 1848, a three-year partnership, called R. W. Burney & Co., "for the purpose of cutting cord wood for Steam Boats &tc. and to clear up and cultivate the land as fast as the timber is taken off." Woodman transfers a 50 percent interest in his property—"sections 11 and 15, more or less bounded on the east and west side by the Mississippi River," etc.—to Burney, in return for which Burney will provide Negroes and live on and work the land. During the first year, Burney's services are to offset the value and interest of three promissory notes of $1,000 each, written to Woodman and signed over to Burney. A contract called an "Indenture Act and Agreement" stipulates that he will have three saddlehorses for his own use free of charge, and will provide Woodman with a monthly accounting of expenses and disbursements. Mary Fredonia Burney is granted an acre or more for a vegetable garden, from which to feed both her family and Woodman's. The second year of the contract, Burney can either hire a manager or receive a salary for his services.

After the three years are up, Woodman has the right to buy Burney out for $3,000 plus one-half the value of whatever improvements Burney has made, such as slave quarters, a gin, a cistern, cribs, a mill house. If, on the other hand, Woodman wishes to sell, Burney has the right of first refusal. If the partnership ends and the two men divide up the assets, those slaves originally owned by Burney will be his sole property, their worth to be determined by their age and the number of children they have produced, including those still in the womb.

And here is the information we are looking for: The slaves Burney currently owns and will place on the land are Israel, a "good carpenter," twenty-five years old, valued at $1,000, and his wife, Harriet, twenty-two, at $800; Solomon, twenty-two, at $900; Billy, nine—who by Louisiana law should not have been separated from his mother until he was ten—at $300; Jinny, twenty-two, at $700 and her children, Barnes, four, at $200 and Frederick, two, at $100. And, of course, Owen, nineteen, who weighs in at $700, and Minerva, also nineteen, at $600. Clearly they had not yet married or Burney would have said so, as he did with Israel and Harriet. Not that slave marriages had any legal standing; while respected among the slave community, they were strictly plantation rituals, performed by the owner, his wife or the overseer. Some slave couples jumped over a broom backwards to denote their betrothal. Others threw a rope over the house. The master might come out on a Sunday and bless multiple unions. And sometimes marriage was enforced, a male slave foisted on a female for breeding purposes.

For a nineteen-year-old man, $700 isn't a particularly high estimation; nor is $600 for a woman the same age. For Louisiana at that time, they're about average. One of the accounts of Madam Walker's life claims that her father, Owen Breedlove, was a blacksmith purchased by Robert Burney for $2,000. The Owen Breedlove owned by Burney may well have been a blacksmith, but the contract mentions no trade, nor is there any record of Burney purchasing a slave at anything near this extremely high price. But in the 1890s, a New Mexico newspaper reports that a Negro blacksmith named Owen Breedlove—almost certainly Sarah's brother—is living in Albuquerque, where indeed Sarah's sister-in-law, Lucy, lives with her four daughters. Among slaves, blacksmithing was a highly regarded skill, which a father would certainly pass on to his son, and perhaps Owen Sr. did just that.

There is no written record of how Burney came by nine slaves, the Burney place having burned to the ground during the war; but we have to assume they were dowry, and that Burney then moved his wife and his property over to Delta, Louisiana, on the finger of land where Sarah Breedlove's life began.

Death and Babies

According to numerous biographical accounts, Madam Walker was born in 1867 at "Grand View, Robert W. Burney's thousand-acre plantation overlooking the Mississippi."

Since most of the time the only things to see there are mud, junk trees and brown rolling water, Grandview's a misnomer. And while Burney's surely optimistic enough to have come up with it, there's no evidence he did. Madison Parish diarist Kate Stone mentions "the depot at Mr. Burney's," and everybody else calls the spread simply "the Burney place." When Union officers confiscate the property after capturing Vicksburg, they officially rename it the Burney (old) Home Place. Finally, as for Sarah Breedlove being born on his plantation, by the year of her birth Robert W. Burney is dead, as is Fredonia, and ownership of the land her parents are working is up for grabs.

In the fall of 1862, with Union soldiers by then occupying most of Madison Parish, Robert Burney packs up his family, his goods and his chattel and rolls them on to the ferryboat, headed for the Mississippi piney woods around Morton, where his partner, the now-deceased O. O. Woodman, owns property. Though General Sherman soon torches the area, Burney will remain until the end of the war, and so, presumably, will his slaves, including Minerva and Owen. Minerva might have given birth to children in Mississippi. By the time they all return to Delta, in the spring of 1865, the Emancipation Proclamation has been in effect for two and a half years, but Burney's workers may not have received the word. In the interior counties of Mississippi, according to a local diarist, "freedom came in a slow and capricious fashion."

A few months later, in October 1865, Fredonia gives birth to her sixth daughter, Minnie Agnes, and the following spring, right around planting time, her forty-seven-year-old husband is struck down by apoplexy (what we now call cerebral hemorrhage, stroke or brain attack). And on April 12—six days after the Civil Rights Bill is passed over Andrew Johnson's veto, and nine days after Fredonia's thirty-sixth birthday—he dies, leaving his widow in debt to the eyeballs and with six young girls to raise. Fredonia buries her husband in what will become the family plot in Vicksburg's Cedar Hill Cemetery, and the funeral, including ten hacks for mourners, sets her back $175.

She then returns home to cope, but "home," at this point, is not much. Either Union or Confederate troops have burned the house and taken the fences for fuel. The Bureau of Refugees, Freedmen and Abandoned Lands (BRFAL) has confiscated the property, on which freed men and women are now camped, some of them planting crops, others sick and sitting on the broken-down levee, looking at the river.

Then come the creditors. A lawyer writes to say that his client, Ivory Fenderson Woodman, Oliver's brother, is pressing a claim for owner-ship of the land. A Vicksburg plantation supply store asks Mrs. Bur-ney to please cover the debt accumulated by her husband since the end of the war, a whopping $24,000 in little over a year; and because the plantation store is in turn seriously in hock to its own suppliers, they will push hard for the money.

Spring is a time of new birth and bloom. In the South, spring comes early and settles its lush greenness on the countryside for more than half the year. But in the spring and summer of 1866, hope comes hard. Since nobody's had time to drain the land, stagnating floodwaters provide ground for mosquitoes to breed in clouds, and crops go unplanted. Local opportunists join up with rascals and gamblers. For those without homes, money or credit, help is nonexistent. The rest of the country is bored with Southerners, black or white, and is already looking to the West, where the news is happier. Now that the Thir-teenth Amendment, abolishing slavery, has been ratified, people want to move on. Those newly freed people, the thinking goes, must make their own way, without expecting to be coddled; they have to learn to swim by being thrown into the water and there discover what one observer calls "the necessity of swimming." The Louisiana legislature rules that freedmen must support their own schools. In Memphis, white Democrats and policemen—crazed by the thought of a black man voting—attack freedmen and their white Republican friends. Forty-six blacks and two whites are killed, seventy others wounded. Officially this slaughter is called a race riot, the first of many to be thus titled in the next one hundred and some-odd years. And, in Pulaski, Tennessee, six bored former Confederate soldiers meet and form a knockabout terrorists' organization they call the Ku Klux Klan.

Under these conditions, Minerva and Owen Breedlove are quietly constructing a life, presumably raising their children and leasing land on shares from the Burney estate. Sharecropping contracts varied, but in many cases the owner provided a house and the land, sometimes mules and sacks, in return for which tenants worked the land and shared whatever money their crops fetched at the end of the year, giving the owner anywhere from a quarter to a half of the profits. But to farm, a family needs tools, seed, a plow; and without money or government assistance, the only way to pay for these essentials is with credit, using the next crop as collateral. Some planters have the assets to operate their own store, but the Breedloves' account is with Delta store owner Moses Feibleman, their credit tied to their contract with Burney's estate. Whatever they owe at the store will be taken directly out of their share of that year's yield. And so, inevitably, sharecroppers start every new year deep in the red. Even if they have a good crop, debts from the year before will yank them back down into the vicious cycle. As one farmer explains, "We were poor, had nothing to go on, had no collateral, and we just had to plant the crop that would bring the money right away. We did not have time to wait."

The Breedloves have stayed put because the land is what they know and growing cotton on shares is their only hope. Freedpeople want three things: to own land, enjoy mobility, and educate their children. Owen and Minerva are not thinking in terms of mobility or education for themselves; they are aiming at owning land, so that their children might enjoy both.

Concerning freed slaves living in the river parishes, Philip Sheridan, the head of the Louisiana BRFAL, writes: "The Negroes as a class have not yet learned that their labor is their capital and are therefore too ready to quit for trivial reasons." He goes on to register the general hostility among whites to colored schools, as proved by the burning of schoolhouses and the beating of teachers and students.

Life in the swamps goes dark and inward. After the floods, a drought. Everybody's crop is thin, and the cotton market is down.

People working the land have no time to think about politics or cattle drives or even the vote. They are too busy bailing water and worrying about starvation, wet cotton and money.

So much for "Grand View" in the spring and summer of 1866.

A parish judge appoints Mary Fredonia Burney natural tutrix to her children. To no one's surprise her neighbor—the newspaperman Ezra Towne—is named undertutor and will watch over Fredonia's affairs. If something should, God forbid, happen to Mrs. Burney, Towne will see to the girls' education.

A cholera epidemic erupts at the end of August 1866, four months after Burney's death. In New Orleans, 569 people have died, and by early fall the epidemic is moving upriver. People die quickly of cholera, often in less than a week. In contrast with yellow jack and malaria, black people and white die from it in equal numbers. And because it is a disease spread by contaminated water and food, in flood-ridden spots like New Orleans, Vicksburg and Delta, it can quickly become endemic, as contamination seeps into cracked cisterns, and people drink as much water as they can, especially in August and September when the temperature and humidity soar into the nineties every day. And given her emotional and physical debilitation—the recent birth of her sixth child, the sudden death of her husband, the onslaught of suits and claims, the lack of any security for herself and all those daughters, the constant pressure of worry and more worry—Fredonia goes down fast when cholera hits Delta.

Cholera is insidious and creepy, its first sign a watery flux that will not stop. Health drains by the cupful from its victims, who are removed so gradually from life that death is the gentlest liquid descent, hardly noticeable to a thin, exhausted woman lying with her hips raised over the bedpan. On November 14, 1866, seven months after her husband's burial, Mary Fredonia Williamson Burney dies—even as cholera is being controlled in Boston, New York and most European cities. Health officials and scientists don't yet understand its causes, but they do know that the disbursal of clean water will keep the disease from spreading. But in the ruined South, once cholera strikes, the only treatments—blistering and quarantine—are at once hysterical and hopeless. There are no disease-control programs. Nor is there any clean water.

Ezra Towne, who in time will become known as "Colonel" and "the

Patriarch of Delta," makes the arrangements and accompanies the older Burney daughters to the funeral. This service, with only six hacks, costs $135. Robert W. and Mary Fredonia's headstones, installed many years later by their children, are identical, respectably tall marble spires with decorative urns on top.

Less than a month later, at another family meeting, Towne is appointed temporary guardian of the children and formally requests that he be officially appointed to that position. He quickly makes bond, takes oath and, in December, is named administrator of the Heirs of Burney estate and guardian of the six daughters and is given permission to do what he thinks best "for the Burney babes and the land."

By the winter of 1867, Minerva and Owen Breedlove have harvested their first crop. And even though 1866 was a disaster, they ride the same dream as the white farmers, of a better crop next year—and if not that one, the next. For sharecroppers, even though the land doesn't officially belong to them, because they farm it themselves and because the chance for a bigger yield is, if unlikely, at least possible, the land at least *seems* like theirs. Most of them don't talk, or even think, about how hard they have to work; they just go out and do it.

Now that the Freedman's Bill has been passed, black people are hoping that the federal government will finally come to their aid, providing them with schools for their children and the forty acres and a mule that Sherman promised them in Field Order #15. There is rumor, too, that the U.S. government is planning to give them the entire South.

Meanwhile, Ezra Towne is laying plans. Friends of his have bought up rights to a railroad company, and he's got control of the land. Their depot will span Burney's boundaries and his own, but he assures the politicians that he controls both, and a deal is struck. He hires an engineer to map the new town, which is shaped somewhat like a triangle and will have 325 blocks, each measuring three hundred feet by three hundred feet, with named avenues, numbered streets and six public squares, one of which will be reserved for the parish courthouse (located, until then, in his own house).

In the midst of all this hubbub, thirteen months after Fredonia's death, another daughter is born on the Burney (old) Home Place. In

December of 1867, the last Breedlove baby arrives, possibly named Winnie. Or maybe her parents added a middle name, Sarah, or maybe this very strong-willed girl eventually decided the matter herself, because she will be listed as Sarah in city directories by the 1890s and later in the 1900 census. On July 13, 1877, the *Vicksburg Herald*'s Sexton Report will note the death of a "Sarah Breedlove, Colored," of consumption, at the age of twenty-eight. This, of course, is a different Sarah, but she is surely kin, either by blood or marriage, and perhaps when she moved to Vicksburg the next year, the ten-year-old daughter of Minerva and Owen took her name. Who can say?

She is born on the twenty-third, two days before Christmas, when the crops are in and the farming year is all but over and people are getting ready to celebrate the holiday—or not, because the croppers and planters who ended 1866 hoping for better in 1867 have suffered another grim comeuppance. In April, the river had risen to an all-time high. When it finally receded, farmers put in their seeds and built new levees. Then the water came back, destroying the levees, washing the seeds away. The Louisiana delta was inundated for thirty miles in every direction, and there was nothing to do but look at the water and wait it out. When the overflow settled back within the banks, they started over, but the summer brought searing drought. Lack of rain created puny cotton stalks, yet at least they were up. Then, just as the bolls opened, so did the skies. Sheets of rain blanketed the fields; sodden bolls drooped in the mud; floods followed. And when the sun finally emerged, the army worm appeared and—rapacious, farmers said, as Sherman—often chewed its way through three acres of cotton in a night.

Field reports sent to the BRFAL testify to the chaos among croppers and freedmen. Morals, they conclude, have disappeared. Starving people cheat and kill one another over a chicken. Since the army worm had no taste for corn, that crop came on strong, but in the night, swampers stole unripe ears off the stalk. No corn meant no cornshucks to weave into halters and hats, no meal to grind for bread, no feed for hogs and mules. Even the marketplace participates. By the end of the year cotton has plunged to fifteen cents a pound while the price of a mule has rocketed to $250.

In the Louisiana river parishes, according to a BRFAL official, "freedpeople poverty-stricken, without homes or supplies . . . seldom receive the protection state laws should guarantee. . . . Yellow fever prevails. The worm prevails. . . . Freedmen are working diligently, despite discouragement. . . . But their patience ought to merit better results." The report also notes the political "excitement consequent upon the enfranchisement of the colored race," once the Fourteenth Amendment is ratified, guaranteeing the freedman citizenship, due process and the right to vote.

Manhood suffrage must seem like a distant notion to Owen Breedlove, who likely does what he has to. A newspaper story from that time says that colored men living on the Louisiana side of the river "prey on Vicksburg" for jobs and money, so perhaps he takes the ferry across the river to get day work. And when the river rises so high that the ferry can't operate, he chops wood and waits.

The birth of a freeborn child deserves celebrating. And perhaps Minerva Breedlove has saved up enough energy to lavish a little on her new baby. Perhaps from her first breath this daughter hears her mother's whispers telling her that she's special, free, a citizen of a better world. Telling her that she is born for greatness and must step into it like a new dress.

There is no record of Winnie Breedlove's birth, or of Sarah's, or of brothers and sisters. There is only the 1848 contract listing Minerva and Owen among Robert Burney's possessions and the 1869 certificate legalizing their marriage, in a ceremony conducted by Rev. Curtis Pollard. The notoriously suspect 1870 U.S. Census lists no Owen and Minerva Breedlove as citizens of Louisiana, even though all the evidence we have indicates they are there, presumably farming on shares.

As the 1868 election approaches, black and white men are registering to vote all over the South. Andrew Johnson's presidency is in disgrace, and the impeachment proceedings against him have begun. Southern Democrats think they have a lock on power and will soon be in charge. And while they generally support colored manhood suffrage, the Radical Republicans of Louisiana warn against going too far, fearing "negro supremacy."

Chaos and trouble, hope and disappointment mark the year of Sarah Breedlove's birth.

By order of the first Reconstruction Act, in 1868 Louisiana approves a new constitution, Article 13 of which bans racial segregation in public accommodations. The carpetbagger Henry C. Warmouth retains his seat as governor, while a Negro and former housepainter, Oscar Dunn, is elected lieutenant governor. In June, the state is readmitted to the union. Ulysses S. Grant becomes the Republican candidate for president. The slogan of his opponent, Horatio Seymour, is, "This is a White Man's Government." When the election is held in November, Grant is not credited with a single vote in all of northeast Louisiana.

In June of 1869, Ezra Towne holds a sale. There are no advertisements, no bids are taken, and at the last minute the date is changed. And because he has arranged to sell the Burney place as a plantation, *not* a potential town, his associates get it for a song. Everybody knows the land's in no condition to be farmed and that Towne and his cohorts—including Louisiana Supreme Court Justice John T. Ludeling and Congressman John Ray—are going to build a depot and a town there, and that if the Burney place had been sold as such, its value would have jumped sevenfold.

A photograph of the Patriarch of Delta shows a lean, wiry man with a narrow gray beard, large round ears and a significant, aristocratic nose. Flat eyebrows bear down on beady eyes that burn with rectitude and certainty. He is wearing a dark three-piece wool suit, its loose-fitting jacket adorned with fashionable piping outlining the lapels and breast pockets. His hair, parted low, lies flat across his wide pate. He looks fierce and resolute, a Vermonter to his bones.

Five months later, in November, Curtis Pollard joins Minerva Anderson and Owen Breedlove in matrimony. In their own eyes and those of their community, they have been married for many years, but now they have the piece of paper making their union legal. Unable to read the certificate, they depend on the Reverend to tell them what it says and to bless them with prayer and the assurance that they have done the right and Christian thing by themselves and their children. Their baby daughter is almost two years old, and their work for the year is finished except for the picking.

To further boom the new town, Towne and his cronies shamelessly use their influence to move the parish seat to Delta. Public records are taken out of what's referred to as a "Negro shack," where they have been kept since the Yankees burned the courthouse, and are moved to Towne's home—onto which he has built a brick addition to be used as a clerk's office. The parish pays for the addition, naturally, and purchases a large iron-barred cage, used for transporting prisoners to jail, that also finds its way onto the Colonel's property.

As to Grandview, among those present at the family meeting held in November of 1866 just after Fredonia Burney's death was J. A. McDonough, who happened to be serving as sheriff during the incumbent's illness. During the year he held office, McDonough became familiar with the Burney girls and their situation, and early in 1868 he married the eldest, Almedia. She was nineteen years old at the time, still a minor, but with marriage she became independent of her legal guardian. No way to know whether Almedia chafed under Towne's tutelage but certainly she might have. And soon afterwards, in a ledger entitled "Record of Supplies furnished planters for the subsistence of employed freedpeople issued under the provision of Circular #1 of 1865," J. A. McDonough of Madison Parish applied to the U.S. government for assistance, his profession given as "Planter" and the name of his plantation—located on the river near DeSoto Point—"Grandview." The petition asked for rations for fourteen women, six men and no children, amounting to 960 pounds of cornmeal and 400 of pork. The request is denied because of an excess of hands. And only here, in this ledger book, is the Burney place called Grandview until seventy or eighty years later, when stories about—but not by—Madam C. J. Walker state that she was born "at Grand View." (On the same page as McDonough's request, another is recorded for one E. B. Towne, asking for rations for fourteen men and twelve women on the Wilderness plantation. His request is also denied, for the same reason.)

Meanwhile, Towne and his cronies pass bills and bond issues funding Delta's railroad tracks and depot without paying a cent of interest. And as one disastrous agricultural year follows another, the news of coming prosperity provides no comfort at all to the sharecroppers living at "Grandview."

All local histories require careful vetting. For the most part they are town-proud documents given to self-congratulation and puffery, but sometimes they are all we have. There is such a history of Madison Parish, written in the late 1920s and early '30s by William M. Murphy, a lawyer from Tallulah. After spending many years in Baton Rouge as a state senator and representative, he left Louisiana in 1904 to work as an attorney for a land company, a job that took him to Chicago, Kansas City, St. Louis and New York. On one of his trips to New York, the widowed Murphy met and married Minnie Spann, who had grown up on Milliken's Bend in Madison Parish and was at that time a staff writer for the *New York Times.* But in 1927, when William became ill, the childless couple moved back to Tallulah, where Minnie tended to his needs and contented herself by reading, gardening and writing the occasional feature article. And after her husband's death, when the WPA began recording local histories, she anonymously submitted a number of stories. Like her husband, Minnie Murphy's aim was to praise Tallulah, and on racial matters she's unreliable, her attitudes and perceptions having been formed at a time when white superiority was taken for granted. She writes of "the terrible Reconstruction years" and concludes that black people didn't fear yellow fever because of an immunity "handed down from jungle ancestors." Nonetheless, among her stories are ones about the little girl who became Madam C. J. Walker.

Without noting her sources, Mrs. Murphy reports that Winnie Breedlove was an industrious and honest little girl, open-faced and well thought of "by her white folks," but that there was nothing about her to indicate that in time she would become a millionaire. "Her and me was friends," she quotes Celeste Hawkins, an African-American, as saying. "We played together and cotch crawfish in de bayous; we went to fish frys and picnics; we sat side by side in the old Pollard Church house on Sunday." Nobody, she says, could beat either one of them at chopping cotton or picking the bolls clean, and she says they both wore their hair twisted and wrapped in strings, like "any right-minded nigger chile." Celeste then wonders if it wasn't right then and there, when she was out in the cotton fields with her hair wrapped, that little Winnie started conjuring up ways to straighten her hair.

Now, Celeste Hawkins may or may not have picked cotton with Winnie Breedlove, or called her Winnie or a "nigger chile." She may have decided to tell Mrs. Murphy the tale she wanted to hear, in the language she knew the lady preferred. But it is undoubtedly true that the young Sarah Breedlove worked hard, because by all accounts Madam Walker could outwork any of her employees, and it makes sense that this habit would have been ingrained at an early age. Unquestionably, a young black girl living on this stretch of the river would have picked cotton and fished in the bayous. She would certainly have worn her hair twisted up tight and held by strings all week long, until her mother, on Sunday morning, took the strings out and furiously brushed and greased her hair so that she would look presentable at church. Monday, or perhaps Sunday night, the strings went back in, sometimes pulled so tight, black children said, it hurt to blink, until the strings stretched out a little; it was as if their hair were being jerked out at the roots, especially at the temple.

A serious child, she turns four, five, six. She is growing, studying, paying close attention to the people around her. I imagine her spending a great deal of time either alone or hanging by Minerva's side, nagging her with questions. And so by the time she's of an age when white children are just starting school, young Winnie has begun to consider a larger range of possibilities than other little girls might imagine. People who leap from obscurity into widespread renown are usually on their way before they know it. Sarah Breedlove must have absorbed her mother's experience and understood that she was the family's representative, the culmination of all their years of hope and pain and pure determination.

Once she becomes wealthy and famous, reporters will constantly ask about her early life, and Madam Walker will say that her mother and father died the same year, when she was seven years old. But that's not exactly how she puts it. "Orphaned at seven," she says. The story is not her parents', then, but hers, Madame's, and she will do this consistently, to bring the story close and make it her own. Nor is it true that Minerva and Owen Breedlove died the same year. On August 26, 1874, Owen Breedlove, now forty-five years old, will take a new wife, Mary Jane Lewis, who in the census taken four years before her marriage is listed as twenty-five years old, black, born in Louisiana, her profession, "Keeping House." Edward Troy—who leased land on the Burney place after the government confiscated it and has become assistant pastor of the New Hope Church—performs the ceremony. Both Mary Jane and Owen sign the marriage certificate with X's.

And so we come back to where we started, to the ill woman lying still and breathing deeply on the homemade bed, the young girl at its foot watching hard. By August 1874, Minerva Breedlove will be dead. Three years later, in 1877, Mary Jane Breedlove will rent a mule to Ike Moseley for six hundred pounds of lint cotton. A married woman would not rent out a mule on her own; her husband would have signed the contract. And so in the space of three years, Sarah's father has died as well. In 1877, a smallpox epidemic raged through northeastern Louisiana and proved particularly devastating to black people. Perhaps he died from that. Or, possibly, he one day up and left. But would he have, after all those years staying put? Emancipated, stays put. Hard times, stays on. Worse times, still there. Widowed, with two daughters to take care of, he remarries and soldiers on. Then, with the girls growing up with a new mother, he leaves? It doesn't make sense. Holding to the probabilities of character and constancy, I believe he never left, but died and was buried in the colored cemetery.

At any rate, however it goes, by 1877 Mary Lewis Breedlove's husband, Sarah's father, is not in the picture. And I have calculated Minerva Breedlove's death as falling in early summer of 1874, during the fever months but before Owen's remarriage on August 26. Sarah sees her mother go, then watches as the women on the Burney place bathe her, wrap her body in a shroud and lay it in a wooden casket, following along as the men carry the casket from the small cabin to where she will be buried, near the Pollard church, in a garden of graves for people of her race.

Learn to read.

A big child, a smart girl, she will make her own life, form her own thoughts, grieve in her own way. Perhaps she *feels* orphaned when her mother dies and that's where her later phrasing comes from. With Minerva gone, her youngest child—her baby—finds herself abandoned. Alone.

N ot far away, in Colfax, Louisiana, some sixty black people are slashed to death in a riot, after which the perpetrators walk over the dead men's bodies and beat out the brains of those not quite dead. Later, one of them will boast, "We shan't have no more trouble with the niggers in Grant Parish. When as clean a job is made in every parish in the state, we shall begin to have some quiet and niggers will know their place." Statements such as these are common as dirt.

Because it doesn't consider itself a benevolent institution, the federal government has turned education over to the states. "Public assistance to the poor," declares O. O. Howard, the former head of BRFAL, "is abnormal to our system of government."

Reconstruction is holding on. After Henry Warmouth is impeached, the mulatto lieutenant governor of Louisiana, P. B. S. Pinchback, serves a short stint as governor and then, after he is replaced, is elected to the

U.S. Senate. (In the early 1920s Pinchback's grandson, the writer Jean Toomer, will move to Harlem and become a friend of Madam Walker's daughter.) John Roy Lynch, a former slave from Mississippi, has been seated in Congress.

In the face of these facts, the White League in Louisiana declares itself dedicated to the violent restoration of white supremacy, vowing that "the niggers shall not rule over us." And in Mississippi, Democrats develop a strategy designed to overthrow Republican rule, oust carpetbaggers and rid themselves of Reconstructionism. The Mississippi Plan—also called, more pointedly, the Shotgun Plan—will begin in Vicksburg, where during elections the White Man's Party will patrol the streets, assassinating and terrorizing. "Couple of years," one planter declares, "and the niggers will be ours again."

"Tell me this," a white woman challenged New York journalist Whitelaw Reid, when he asked about the freed Negroes who had once worked her land. "If they aren't mine then whose are they?"

"Reconstruction," a former slave said, years afterwards, "was a hard pull."

The big dark-skinned girl with the wide forehead and strong jaw knows politics and injustice in the most basic ways: because they inform her life and make it what it is. Because she cannot make a safe life without taking politics into consideration.

A s a child, she "craved the beautiful," an unnamed person supposedly said of Winnie Breedlove. But this was some forty or fifty years after Minerva Breedlove's death, after the girl Winnie, or Sarah, was living in Indianapolis and had become Madam C. J. Walker. And this person is being quoted in a story about a celebrity, a black woman who dresses in fine silks and brocades and lavishly decorates her mansion. But let's assume the remark is truthful. How does a girl in those circumstances reveal her craving for the beautiful? What does she look for and bring home, to save in a secret place of her own? A length of red ribbon? Mulberry blossoms, clover chain, a rock washed smooth by the river? A blue-black tailfeather from a squawky grackle or a scrap of cloth dyed hackberry-mauve, found on the steps of the Pollard church?

We decipher one childhood year from the next by meaningful events and recurring rituals: school, teacher, illness, death, the year the mule died or the depot was finished. But young Sarah will not go to school. In Delta, Negro children receive no public education. As for missionaries from the North, they never spent much time in backwater Louisiana. Some ventured in, but they didn't stay long—only until disease sent them elsewhere. And by now, they are all long gone.

So instead of school projects or favorite teachers, the recurring rituals of Sarah Breedlove's young life are the larger ones, which the Rev. Curtis Pollard has told them come from God: the river; the sun, stars and moon; the rain.

II · *Vicksburg, 1878–1887*

On the P. F. Geisse

Early summer, 1878, Sarah and her sister Louvenia are striking out, taking the ferryboat across the river. No Breedloves remain in Delta except their stepmother. *Those Breedloves,* someone will say years and years from now, *they're hot-tempered.* Maybe Louvenia doesn't get along with Mary Jane, who has signed a new lease—on *their* shares—with the Burney daughters and their husbands. And she rented that mule to Ike Moseley. Mary Jane Lewis Breedlove seems to have taken over their whole world, and that may be why the two young girls have left.

Besides, another yellow fever epidemic has struck the northwestern parishes of Louisiana, especially around Shreveport, and it is creeping eastward. Soon all traffic to and from Delta will cease. There will be no mail. No boats will stop, so no one will be able to leave. The girls are getting out while they can. They will become washwomen in Vicksburg. Though the work is hard, it has its advantages. A washwoman is a kind of freelance contractor, who doesn't have to work by somebody else's clock. And as everyone knows, washerwomen are in demand all over the South.

A little over two years ago, the prediction made in 1853 by the renowned river engineer Charles Ellet finally came true. The Mississippi chopped off the tip end of that delicately raised pinkie finger of land which Robert Burney had coveted, claimed and lost. Because it occurred in 1876, the event was called the Centennial Cutoff, and afterward the finger looked as ragged and ugly as a tree stump cut with a dull saw.

In the early spring of that year, the overflow was the only news anybody paid attention to. In March, the rains came as usual, but this time they didn't stop, and the river level rose and rose until the end of the story was a foregone conclusion. All Vicksburg and Madison Parish waited and watched as the Mississippi nibbled away at the land. Day by day, newspapers tracked crevasses in the levees. The first one happened at Milliken's Bend, above Delta, and the river roared on through, caving in many acres, taking at least three entire farms. Engineers made predictions not on whether there would be a cutoff, but when.

More land floated away throughout the month. In April, sightseers rode the tug *Bigley* out to the middle of the river, hoping to be there at the moment when the water came through. In the stillness of the night, Vicksburgers from any part of town could hear water washing over the peninsula.

There had been a forewarning two years earlier, when in the spring before Minerva Breedlove died, the river had hacked off a big hunk. A map drawn the next summer shows how much land had been lost between 1828, when the shortest distance across the peninsula was 6,100 feet, and 1875, when the narrowest point measured only 650 feet. In less than fifty years, almost two thousand acres had been lost, and 161 million cubic yards of sand and earth dumped into the Mississippi.

On April 26, 1876, from a high point on Burney's levee, Sarah must have been watching at 2:00 p.m. when the foaming, hungry Mississippi breached the peninsula and casually devoured the land. Maybe her friend Celeste Hawkins was with her. Wherever she was, she will never forget the sounds of the flood: trees snapping in two, the land groaning like an animal caught in a trap, water roaring like a factory that never shuts down. The sights will be harder to accommodate, and later she will go back over the whole thing again and again, wondering, Did I actually *see* that, or was it a dream? The air darkens, the sky turns yellowish, the wind stops and in the stillness, new birds appear as, all up and down the Mississippi, giant white cranes track the first sign of extra water and, lifting themselves on broad wings, skim like outsized handkerchiefs over what used to be rows and rows of cotton, dipping their beaks in the crashing brown water for grain, insects, small bits of sweet refuse.

Finally the last levee started to go. Measuring a hundred fifty-three feet long, from one side of the peninsula to the other, it sank out of sight within minutes. Then whole tracts of land—entire plantations, with all their mules, barns and gins—tumbled in. "The river went after them," the *Vicksburg Daily Commercial* reported with a shrug. "They became submerged." In less than two hours, the land was gone and driftwood was already floating down the new channel the river had cut. Over the next month, more land disappeared, and people talked about the overflow as if it had its own life. By the end of May, the hotly touted new Delta was ruined. The railroad landing, where trains were supposed to stop en route to the Pacific, had turned into swamp and sandbars. And with the water still lapping at their doors, the inhabitants were advised to move to Vicksburg.

Most stayed. Another Burney daughter, Anna, had married George Long, a farmer who took advantage of Ezra Towne's financial devastation and was renting parcels of the Burney place and clearing the land himself. Moreover, the Burney sisters and their husbands were taking legal action against Towne, filing suit to get their property back. In four massive volumes of case history and legal briefs, *The Heirs of Burney Against E. B. Towne, J. T. Ludeling, et al.* carefully chronicles the actions of the failed boomers. The suit won't be settled for more than twenty years, by which time many of the litigants are long dead.

A one-way passage from Delta to Vicksburg costs twenty-five cents, and the *P. F. Geisse* makes four trips a day. Because of erosion and overflow, the old landing has become too sandy to use anymore, and so the girls would have walked a half-mile to get to the new landing on the other side of the peninsula. They carry their personal belongings in a piece of cloth tied up in a bundle, maybe a skirt, and it's possible they've come by some washtubs and scrub boards. They will have to share, borrow or buy the laundress's biggest investment, a boiling pot, which at forty pounds or more is too heavy to carry.

The white citizens of Vicksburg will not welcome our two young girls. By now the Mississippi Plan has become so obnoxious that the U.S. Congress has held hearings to investigate what is called "the Vicksburg Troubles" of 1875, when as many as three hundred African-Americans were killed and many more wounded or forced from their homes. When Governor Adelbert Ames requests help from Washington, he is told that the nation is tired of "these annual autumnal outbreaks" when Negroes try to vote in the South. And it isn't until the death toll rises above the two hundred mark that President Grant finally sends troops. Nonetheless, black people keep steadily moving to Vicksburg. However dicey life seems in the hill city, it's even worse in the rural parishes of Louisiana and the piney woods country of Mississippi.

I imagine Sarah Breedlove shouldering her own bundle. Cotton chopping has made her strong, and though still a child, she has the swooping stride and erect carriage of a young woman. Madam Walker will be a stately woman, with broad shoulders, a full chest and lush rounded hips. She will carry herself taller than she is and be said to "unfold" as she moves in your direction, gaining in size and stature with every step.

At ten Sarah is sturdy, and walks apart from her big sister, keeping her thoughts to herself the way children do when dreams of the future are a steady presence in their everyday life.

"Madam Walker could be," recalls a friend of hers, pausing in search of the correct word, long after her friend's death, "*reticent.*" She articulates each syllable with great precision as she remembers once walking into a room and—finding Madame standing at the window, lost in thought—withdrawing quietly, knowing that she was busy thinking of how she might make her business even more successful. Because, she explains, what you have to understand is that Madam Walker was *always* thinking about business.

Anyway, by the time the sisters leave Delta, Louvenia has married a man named Jesse Powell, and so she probably seems different now, less attentive to Sarah, having taken her husband's name, moved into his bed and life, having become somebody Sarah doesn't exactly recognize, almost as if she's just plain vanished.

Madam Walker will be distinctly unsentimental regarding residence. In time, she will live in many cities and will consistently remember the places that have been good to her with money, presence and her time. But once she has lived a place out and done her work there, she doesn't moon over leaving, she just packs up and goes. Even in her last days, when she is bedridden and dying in a palatial mansion she adores, she will write a letter promising to buy her daughter the chateau she wants, so that the two of them can move to Paris.

In a way, race is all the city, state or country a Madam Walker—or a young Sarah Breedlove—needs. For a black person, writes James Weldon Johnson, education means "preparation to meet the tasks and exigencies of life *as a Negro,* a realization of the peculiar responsibilities . . . and a comprehension of the application of American democracy to Negro citizens." In this respect, Sarah Breedlove carries her residence within her.

The ferryboat is jammed with people, hogs, cows, horses and mules, with bags and crates and makeshift suitcases filled with everything poor white and black people might own. In the fall, the ferry will transport thousands of bales of cotton across the Mississippi, stacked higher than it seems the boat can safely bear. At about this time, Martin Kearny, owner of the *Geisse,* figures his boat carries a good fifteen hundred people east across the river every day.

The *Geisse* advertises a clean cabin reserved for ladies, but it is restricted to *white* ladies and so, following the unwritten rule, Sarah finds her place on the open deck. The trip takes about half an hour, but for a child, terror won't measure. Blades of water lap and coat the edges of the deck as the boat cuts through the current. The water licking at young Sarah's toes could knock her down and whisk her away on a whim. She has seen it happen to houses, trees, mules, one time an entire levee. Who will come to her rescue if the river decides to take her, a small brown girl of no use or value to anyone? Who would care enough to try?

Looking back toward Delta, all she can see is trees. Louvenia might point things out as they go, maybe the new levee, the Burney place or the gin house. But there are so many trees and tangled vines between the river and the land that Sarah might just nod and say yes without really being able to make anything out, as a child will often say "Yes, I see" to make the other person, usually an adult, quit insisting. Meanwhile, her birthplace is shrinking before her eyes, and she is on her way to becoming a citizen of a larger world than her ancestors could have imagined. Her mother is buried over there, possibly on a plot of ground newly set aside as the colored cemetery, next to the New Hope Baptist Church; and so, probably, is her father.

"Used to be a colored cemetery," a current Delta resident told me, pointing toward a stock pond surrounded by a thatch of trees. "When they dug that pond, bones and bodies started floating up out of the ground. Those fellows dropped their shovels and tore out of there." He was white, and when he laughed at the thought of men running in fear, I knew the men he was describing were black.

There is a piece of one gravestone on the north side of the pond, but most of it is buried, seized by tree roots. One corner pushes out of the ground like the tip of a dead man's toe. THOMAS, it says.

At ten, Sarah does not feel she is abandoning the sacred ground where her parents are buried. Visiting a cemetery means close to nothing to a child, except maybe pulling weeds to keep the grave clean. *Presence* is what children long for, and since that's the one thing she cannot have, what's the use in crying over a mound of dirt?

Sarah Breedlove can't read or write. She's seen dogs swim but has no idea of how to do it herself. Is she fearful, crossing the river on the *Geisse?* Does she wish her mother were with her? Of course. "Fearless" is a word which will be applied to Madam Walker many times, but given the kinds of danger she will face, fearlessness is not only impossible, it's foolhardy. To be without fear means not paying attention to history, observation, experience, to what simply *is.* Sarah Breedlove's afraid, all right; she needs to be. But she's learned how to hide it, set it aside, turn it into something else. Children who know how to gather and make use of courage don't even think of themselves as children, and later, when others marvel at the discipline and fearlessness they showed at such an early age, they will look—and feel—puzzled and calm, never having considered themselves either young or remarkable.

Nettie Johnson, who owned a beauty shop in Indianapolis during Madam Walker's years there, tells the story of how Madame had come onstage to give a speech to a large group of people, wearing a full-length fur coat. As the applause died, she slipped the coat from her shoulders and reached to place it on a nearby chair, but the heavy coat slid to the floor. When someone raced from the wings to pick it up, she waved him away. "Oh, that's all right," Nettie Johnson quotes her as saying, then imitates Madame by lifting her hand palm-out in a stop gesture and shaking her head. "Because a mink coat falling to the floor didn't matter to Madam Walker. It didn't matter." Nettie Johnson holds her chin high, and the look on her face is of perfect triumph. And that same attitude is present in ten-year-old Sarah Breedlove.

E xactly two weeks after the Centennial Cutoff of the Mississippi, the bell in Philadelphia's Independence Hall chimed out the opening of the U.S. Centennial Exposition. Inspired by Queen Victoria's Jubilee, the $10 million exhibition covered 236 acres and celebrated "the Progress of the Age." Ulysses S. Grant and Dom Pedro II, the emperor of Brazil—the first major foreign potentate to visit the U.S.—attended the July 4 festivities, during which the mournful president bestirred himself to give a cheerful talk about technical progress and material abundance, ignoring both the great depression that gripped the country and the continuing scandals of his administration.

Grant's attitude reflects current thinking. Machines, it is believed, will remake society and usher in an era of new prosperity. Alexander Graham Bell's first telephone was on display at the exposition, as were a typewriter, an electric light, packaged yeast, ice cream sodas, bananas packaged in tinfoil, hot popcorn and a 700-ton Corliss steam engine. As if in deference to new times and the "redemption" of the South, the Southern Restaurant featured a band of "oldtime plantation darkies." In the agricultural competition, a bale of cotton raised by Benjamin Montgomery—a former slave now living and working on Jefferson Davis's former plantation, Davis Bend—won the first-prize medal, defeating entries from as far away as Brazil and Egypt, but this feat went mostly unnoticed by the nation's press. As for Reconstruction, one of Grant's staffers is quoted as having said, "By the summer of '76, there was no one around the White House who gave a damn about black people."

The West continues to hold people's attention, even though some of the news from out there is puzzling. Grant heard about the Battle of Little Big Horn while he and Dom Pedro were still in Philadelphia at the fair. Believing that if a thing can't happen, it won't, a lot of white people still think that General Custer's defeat and death were cooked up.

White supremacists have a different take on the Indian wars. When federal troops go after Sitting Bull, night riders hope he and Crazy Horse will keep the soldiers busy until after the fall elections. "Nothing intimidates a Negro," one participant in the terrorist campaign states, "as much as mystery and seeing armed men riding around at night." In Louisiana and some parts of Mississippi, night riders are known, appropriately enough, as bulldozers.

The following winter, in 1877, the Ohioan Rutherford B. Hayes becomes president by gaining the electoral votes of three Southern states—including Louisiana—in exchange for his promise to withdraw all federal troops from the South and permit many hardline Democratic claimants to take office. To maintain his Republican support, Hayes appoints a presidential commission to investigate racial outrages—but at the same time has the Secretary of the Army announce that federal troops will not be used to prevent armed revolt, even if requested by a state government.

Hayes's policies, as one writer put it, abandon Southern Republicans to the "tender mercies of the KKK." Noting this on the occasion of abolitionist Gerrit Smith's death, an editorial in the *New York Times* declared the end of an "era of moral politics."

Reconstruction, as W. E. B. DuBois described it, was a period when "the slave went free; stood a brief moment in the sun; then moved back again toward slavery."

The *Geisse* approaches a piece of property familiar to the Breedlove girls, and perhaps Louvenia points it out to her little sister: De Soto Island, which two years ago the river broke loose from the riverbank at Delta. The excised tip of the peninsula had then drifted across the racing current—taking the same route as the *Geisse*—and come to rest at the Vicksburg levee, snugly cozied up to the place where steamships, barges and the ferryboat once docked. This allowed the Mississippi to straighten its path and slide past Vicksburg altogether, leaving the Hill City high and dry and without its main source of access and income, much as Generals Williams, Sherman and Grant envisioned back in 1862 when they dug a canal meant to redirect the river. The former busy Vicksburg landing has now gone to sand and silt. And De Soto Island belongs to Louisiana, even though it's lodged against Mississippi. So when Louisiana votes wet, whiskey can legally be sold on De Soto Island to Mississippians.

It must be odd for the Breedlove sisters to see this chopped-off piece of Delta, as if it had gone across first to show them the way.

Right about now, the former slave Booker T. Washington, having graduated from Hampton College, returns home to West Virginia. Here he begins teaching school and launches his campaign for acknowledgment and power by preaching the value of accommodation, cleanliness and patience, as well as the necessity of a purposefully slow march to progress, including the acceptance of a gradual and "earned" suffrage. But many disagree with his philosophy, and for other blacks, colonization becomes a more attractive possibility. Henry Adams, who claims to have a list of sixty thousand people willing to emigrate to Liberia, describes Shreveport and northern Louisiana as a horrible part of the country, where black people cannot find a way to live with former slaveholders and enjoy the same rights they enjoy.

In this climate, who will help Louvenia and Sarah Breedlove when they arrive in the hot, bright and dangerous city of Vicksburg? Who might have gone along to look after them, or meet them when they dock? Church people, most likely. And perhaps Louvenia's new husband, Jesse Powell, is either with them on the *Geisse* or awaiting their arrival at Kleinston's Landing, the new dock, located a mile and a half south of the city. The 1877 Vicksburg city directory lists an "Alex Breedlow" living on Crawford Street near the river; surely this is Alexander, Sarah's older brother, who will offer Sarah refuge in St. Louis and would certainly feel obliged to do the same now, when his sisters are so young. Regardless of who helped or from which church, I find it near impossible to believe that members of Vicksburg's black community aren't there to welcome these two girls from Delta into their hearts and lives.

Vicksburg

The streets are wide stretches of rutted dirt, the sidewalks planks laid end to end alongside. On rainy days, the planks sink into the mud and serve no further purpose until long after the sun comes out and the water has drained down side streets to the river. There are stepping stones for ladies to use when crossing the street, and their long dresses with starched crinoline petticoats underneath require them to make some very tricky maneuvers when negotiating the stones. During the mud seasons they sometimes shop only on one side of the street rather than risk a crossing. The narrow boardwalks make for other hazards as well, including mud splashed from wagons and splats of tobacco juice launched by the men lining the storefronts all day long, leaning back in their chairs doing nothing except chew, carp, spit and fulminate.

Called the Hill City, Vicksburg is situated on high red-brown loess bluffs, and from the main street—Washington—you can look down over the levee and see the sandbar where the river used to run. And located on the corner where it intersects China Street is the best hotel in town, the Washington, where Oscar Wilde will stay when he lectures here in 1882, and which boasts a hairdressing parlor, bathing rooms and shops selling foreign and domestic perfumes, cosmetics, brushes and combs. Directly behind the hotel is the most famous address in town, number 15 China Street: a three-story frame building in which, for a price, women in satin dresses light men's cigars and indulge their pursuits of fleshy pleasure. Well known throughout the South, 15 China has been in business for some fifty years, and will prosper for fifty more. Because there is a business called Baer Brothers around the corner, local wits sometimes call 15 China the Bare Sisters.

Vicksburg has heard all about the Centennial Exposition and the popcorn and bananas and the telephone, but the Progress of the Age seems as far away as the icebergs of Alaska. Its white citizens have not yet recovered from the malaise which has held them by the throat since July 4, 1863, when the Hill City surrendered to the Yankees. Newspapers have tried to stir up civic pride, politicians make speeches, but nothing works. According to a Northern newspaper, the town is still crushed, wretched and bemoaning its war wounds.

By 1878, the black population has increased fivefold, so they are now greatly in the majority. There is a school for black children, which white people don't officially object to, but they will tell you at the drop of a hat that if there isn't enough work for either race and with the price of cotton down 50 percent, what good is education anyway, for white or black? And they lean back in their chairs along Washington Street, riding the same excoriations over and over again.

At least, they sigh, Reconstruction is over. When Hayes was elected, the *Vicksburg Daily Commercial* ran a simple headline—T H E E N D !— and reported only elation among its constituency. Even so, most white people believe that because of the cutoff the city is ruined and might as well be given to the Negroes. Others propose petitioning Congress for money to cut a new canal to divert the Yazoo River, which runs north of town, through Chickasaw Bayou, which would then create a lake to restore the Mississippi to its original path. But even though the Vicksburg harbor has fallen from fifty feet in depth to five, the general mood of the town runs against asking the federal government for help, a tactic that intransigent, old-line Democrats—the so-called Redeemers— consider akin to asking for foreign aid. Besides, back before the war, New Orleans had asked the federal government to help open up the river, and the money had yet to arrive. By the time any cash arrived from Washington, Vicksburgers figure, their city would be as vacant and useless as a dried-up locust shell.

I nto this mood of pouty cynicism strides the future Madam C. J. Walker, barefoot—as all black children went about in summer—and in a loose cotton dress, her hair up in strings.

If there is a delegation, from a local church or perhaps the Golden Rule Society, it will hustle Sarah and her sister off the gangplank and away from the river. While yellow fever—also called Yellow Jack,

Bronze John and the Scourge of the South—has not yet hit Vicksburg, it has savaged Shreveport and has moved east across northern Louisiana, into Monroe and beyond.

A number of independent colored churches have settled in Vicksburg. From the end of Reconstruction through the Jim Crow era and straight into the twentieth century, the church will be the most important institution in Negro life throughout the country, providing sanctuary and hope, as it did even in slave times, when religion sanctioned the belief in a power and life beyond and outside the control of white people. In this shelter black people can speak without fear of reprisals, hold classes ranging in subject from finance and management to parenting and hygiene. Most importantly, churches are where black people organize.

In her grown-up life, whether in St. Louis, Indianapolis or New York, Sarah Breedlove will belong to the African Methodist Episcopal Church. In Vicksburg, the AME Bethel was formed in 1867 on the cusp of Reconstruction, and its original minister, Hiram Revels, went on to become the first black state senator in the nation's history. In an account of the church written by one of its members, the AME Bethel's congregation is said to include the city's "best" colored citizens.

But Sarah Breedlove is not yet concerned with who the best people are or which church they go to. Vicksburg's churches are mostly Baptist, regardless of race, and the black ones include Holly Grove, Mount Heroden, and King Solomon. Since Sarah attended Rev. Curtis Pollard's Baptist church in Delta, it's likely she follows his faith into Vicksburg. The first pastor of King Solomon was Randall Pollard; by 1878 he is dead, but perhaps he was kin to Curtis Pollard, and his congregation knows that the two Breedlove girls are coming. A member of their Delta church might even be taking the trip with them.

This could be Sarah's first trip to Vicksburg, and she may well clap her hands over her ears, it's so noisy. With the cries of beggars, stevedores and prostitutes, the grain elevator pounding and the cotton-mill engines grinding, the city might seem as frightening as the river. She will take some comfort in the people she sees pushing carts down the street, selling soap, calling to potential customers, trying to get a jump on business, because they are mostly like her, dark-skinned. Otherwise there is nothing familiar about this place she has moved to, nothing at all.

During Reconstruction, a black man, Peter Crosby, was elected sheriff of Warren County. In those years, the Vicksburg police chief was also black, as was half of the force; but when Sarah and Louvenia arrive, those amazing days of possible racial realignment have disappeared and will not resurface for at least a hundred years. During the 1874 vigilante episodes that forced Crosby to resign, an estimated three hundred black men and women were murdered. And the local branch of the Freedman's Bank is out of business and available for rent.

Most accounts of Madam Walker's life—found in Walker Company manuals and in speeches, interviews, biographical sketches and obituaries—state that she came to Vicksburg when she was about ten years old, with her sister Louvenia, who was about fourteen; and that Louvenia married a man named Powell and the three of them lived together, but that Sarah's brother-in-law was cruel to her and so, at fourteen, she married Jeff—or Moses—McWilliams. Some of this story is doubtless true.

Upstairs in the county courthouse in Vicksburg, the walls are lined with shelves of black leather ledgers that record marriages performed in Warren County. Because they are large and tend to buckle if set upright, they lie on their sides. To find a particular year, you have to crane your head to the side and work down the rows, studying labels. These ledgers, during the 1870s, are separated by race. The ones labeled "White" are indexed; those "Colored" are not. And so to find the marriage record of a particular African-American individual, one has to thumb through ledgers page by page, two certificates to a page.

When I was there, most of the employees on that floor of the courthouse were women: old, young, thin, fat, black, white. A fellow employee had just given birth, and everybody was talking about what to buy for the baby. A very large woman was having a long telephone call with a female friend who, as became clear from the conversation on my end of the line, was complaining about a man who'd betrayed her. On a table at the end of the room were open boxes of doughnuts, and the large woman kept breaking off bits of stale pastry as she doled out advice.

Sarah Breedlove turned fourteen on December 23, 1881. I lifted down book 3 (marriages of African-Americans between early 1881 and

February 1882) and flipped through maybe a hundred pages without finding anything. Book 4 took me up to May 8, 1883, at which point I'd been at it several hours. The courthouse was about to close, so I went back the next day and worked my way through 1883 and 1884 and into early 1885. Since Madam Walker's daughter was born on June 6, 1885, that seemed far enough, so I went backwards to 1880. Still nothing. After double-checking a few months later, I concluded that no African-American bride named Breedlove had received a Warren County marriage certificate in any of those years—not Sarah, not Louvenia, nor anyone else with that name. And no Jeff, or Moses, McWilliams. The closest I came was the marriage of a "Moses Williams, Colored" to "Lucy Mathews, Colored" on December 19, 1881. Right age, groom's name close enough, but there was no plausible reason that Winnie or Sarah Breedlove should be recorded as Lucy Mathews.

I did find Louvenia's marriage certificate, but not in Vicksburg. Louvenia Breedlove married Jesse Powell in Madison Parish on July 30, 1872—*before* her mother died, before her father's remarriage and before the cutoff. Curtis Pollard, who later officiated for Owen Breedlove and Mary Jane Lewis, also married Louvenia Breedlove to Jesse Powell. This, no doubt, is the correct Louvenia. Madam Walker refers to her brother-in-law by name, and in her will she'll include as beneficiaries her sister, Louvenia Powell, and her nephew, Willie Powell. And as for the date, the certificate is clearly recorded and filed among many other marriages performed during the spring and summer of 1872.

And so the received truth that Louvenia was about fourteen when she and her sister crossed the Mississippi (Sarah being ten) simply won't wash. While Louisiana was a backward state in many respects, its laws were originally written by Catholics, and a lot of that religiosity still obtained in the 1870s, and I don't believe for a minute that an eight-year-old girl would've been issued a marriage certificate, or that Minerva and Owen Breedlove would have allowed any such thing. Even at that time, marriage at twelve is one thing, but quite another at eight.

Which can mean only that Louvenia's older than accepted versions of the story claim.

For other kinds of information, we look to city directories, which—published annually as a commercial enterprise—predate telephone books. A city directory records businesses, churches, schools, city services and civic clubs, and it lists inhabitants of the city, their professions and home addresses, sometimes their race and marital status. Only two Vicksburg city directories survive from these years, one published in 1877, the other in 1886. In the earlier one, black people are designated as "Col" (and, curiously enough, widows by "Wid"). And while the African-American population is estimated to be approximately 5,000, the directory lists only 887 "Col." Jesse Powell is not among them, but the Moses Williams from the marriage records in the Warren County Courthouse appears as "Moses Wms Col." He works for Charles Peine at a livery stable at China and Walnut, close to the old landing where many black people live. The stable later became a car repair and tire shop, and like many buildings in downtown Vicksburg, it now stands empty, its paint faded and peeling.

There are "Col" draymen, waiters, laborers, coalmen, ferryboat workers, a blacksmith, butcher, grocer and one lawyer, Robert Brown, whose office, at Washington and Grove, is in the heart of downtown. The directory also lists a great number of African-American barbers. This was a time when barbering was considered a Negro profession; and in the 1886 directory, eleven out of fifteen Vicksburg barbers are black. Barbers also give shaves, trim beards and do massage, but their services are only for white men. The treatment and dressing of black people's hair was done at home and often outdoors, where women especially gathered to oil and brush one another's hair. Often this was done on Saturday, in preparation for church the next day, and the women sometimes lined themselves up in chairs positioned one behind the other, train style, and did one another's hair while telling stories and laughing, making an occasion of it.

The directory provides no street numbers, giving such addresses as "Upper End of Monroe" or "Cherry bet Clay and China." And the 1886 one does away with the "Col" designation by placing all African-American citizens in a "Colored Department."

We can also get an idea of the part of town Sarah, Louvenia and Jesse might have lived in by studying a fire-insurance map printed a few years after they arrived. White people lived in a "Dwg" (Dwelling), while Negroes occupied a "Shanty," or sometimes a "Dwg-Col." Most shanties are located on the river, either along the levee down by the old landing or south of there in an area called Catfish Row, where there is also a string of bars and restaurants and snack houses. But others are scattered around town, in alleys and vacant lots between white dwellings, where there might even be a cistern for the shanty dwellers to share. And there is the section of Cherry Street called "The Bottoms," a few blocks below the bluffs, which floods often.

It's my guess that the newcomers from Delta set up housekeeping close to downtown, so that Sarah and Louvenia can stir up business, somewhere near the levee.

These shanties are grouped tightly together, whether for protection, such communal activities as the raising of animals—chickens and, if they're lucky, hogs—or general mutual support. As slaves, black people were accustomed to living in close proximity, and perhaps they find comfort in establishing a similar life now that they are free. Since there are no cisterns atop the levee, shanty dwellers scavenge for receptacles to hold rainwater and men walk down the levee to haul water back up. Their toilet is the outdoors.

Unemployment among black men is high, and with the three of them living cramped up in a small house, the cruelty Madam Walker was said to have suffered is not hard to imagine. Indeed, it could easily become a part of everyday life, as Jesse takes out his frustrations and boredom on his wife and her little sister. And Louvenia might turn bossy as well, as older siblings often are, just because they can.

Washerwomen work six days a week and take Sundays off. To get to church, Sarah has maybe twelve or fourteen blocks to walk, but why would long walks bother her? Church is exciting, a place where she can learn and be listened to. And at least she's out of the house.

Summer

Soon after Sarah and Louvenia arrive in Vicksburg, yellow fever slips in on their heels. Doctors share the news in whispers and hope summer passes quickly. By July, hundreds of cases a day are reported in Memphis, New Orleans and Grenada, Mississippi. BRONZE JOHN MARCHING! a Vicksburg newspaper announces in a story about the Memphis siege, while another front-page article—GRENADA THE DOOMED CITY— describes that town's distress as being too fearful to contemplate.

Vicksburg keeps the river running—so barges still stop at Kleinston's Landing, mail is posted, people come and go—but takes other precautions. One theory about yellow fever is that once its seed is planted—who knows how?—it waits for rot and heat to encourage its showiest bloom. Because the Grenada epidemic is thought to have germinated in the foul air of an open sewer, a chain gang is brought into Vicksburg to make a pass at sanitizing the levees. They give the streets a stringent cleaning, then scour the persistently filthy alleys, shoveling up countless wheelbarrow loads of human waste and discarded animal carcasses, dumping the fetid mess into the river.

By then, cases of Yellow Jack—so called because infected boats are required to fly a yellow flag—have appeared all over town. But local newspapers downplay the increasingly glum possibilities by running stories in which doctors deny there is anything to worry about and the mayor reiterates these assurances. Dr. William Balfour—the city's health officer and second in importance only to the mayor—insists there is not a single case. And the suggestion is made that if Vicksburg musters a muscular response, they might stave off the disease. The alarmists up in Memphis are sniggered at as "shriekers."

Into this situation, we bring our two young African-American laundresses. Orphans, with nothing to call their own beyond each other, a talent for work, maybe a washtub or two and one husband, Jesse Powell. Illiterate girls on the hopeful lookout for a new, more independent life.

On the Fourth of July, only black people celebrate. Believing that to mark a federal holiday is to acknowledge that, as one Meridian resident put it, "nigger power is in the ascendance," white Southerners hunker down and sulk. And because Vicksburg surrendered to the Union on this day in 1863, its white citizens feel especially sour about the holiday.

So African-Americans get to claim the main street of town as their own, and behind a brass band playing "The Battle Hymn of the Republic," lines of "colored people in handsome costumes" march and dance down Washington Street in a winding parade, and everybody is joyful, even a ten-year-old washerwoman. King Solomon Baptist Church hangs a new bell, and Jefferson Thomas, its pastor, pulls the rope to begin the ringing, which parishioners will line up to take turns doing all day long. Every African-American club and church in the city organizes an outing, and hundreds of people sign up for boat and train excursions, the most popular forms of social activity for Southern black people at the time.

Even though Reconstruction is officially over and black Americans have already suffered a number of political reverses, on a day like the Fourth they can enjoy themselves fully and without fear, and even in a Deep South town like Vicksburg are able to imagine a time when this is what life will be like. In the exclusive company of their own race, they are free to think of themselves as people who make decisions based on their best interests, not out of fear of some other man's reactionary response. And standing on the deck of the *P. F. Geisse* looking out at the brown smooth water—midsummer, the river's as tame as it gets—they can bask in the hot expanse and for the duration of the trip feel like full-fledged citizens of the nation.

These excursions will pretty much come to an end in the 1890s, when Jim Crow laws clamp down. But on Independence Day of 1878—after Hayes has used black people as currency with which to purchase the presidency, but before the fall elections—the boats are jammed: the *Geisse,* the *Kate Dickson,* the *Fair Play* and the *Josephine Spengler* roaming up and down the mighty river from the cutoff to Davis Bend, a favorite spot for picnics. People bring tubs filled with food: whole hams, fried chicken and cornbread, pans of sweet potato pie. Everyone shares and nobody holds back.

Sarah's going on eleven, and even after only a short while, she would be stronger in her legs from walking Vicksburg's hills. Accustomed to running fast and free across fields that reached to the edge of the sky, a child at first would resent the boredom of constant ups and downs, but she's strong and young and by now must be used to the hills. She may even like them, especially zooming down.

From the *Geisse,* Madison Parish looks scary. A scraggly curtain of junk trees obscures the sandbars and swamps beyond, and the snakes and other creatures hiding in them. Bronze John walks the swamps. The disease is called that due to the yellowish-brown skin color of its victims, but children imagine a person, Bronze John, huge as Goliath, immune to alligator bites and snake venom, clomping through the swamps in his enormous black boots. The excursioners marvel at the transformation of the De Soto peninsula, but the boat doesn't stop on the Louisiana side. Nobody does. And whoever is there will stay, including the dead, who are buried quickly, the hasty graves covered with lime so the corpses won't contaminate the soil.

What her friends in Vicksburg tell Sarah is that she's lucky to be gone from over there, not just because of Yellow Jack, but because not one thing is working out for black people in Madison Parish. The black man can't vote, has no money, no refuge, no land. In other northern parishes, one Negro out of twenty owns land, while in Madison the statistic falls to one in fifty. Lost waist-high among the people crowding the rail, our young Sarah watches with a closed-off expression as her former home recedes in the distance and the boat pulls away from Louisiana and moves east and south through the cross channels to dock at Davis Bend.

Perhaps a church elder pulls her close and tells her the story of this place, where black people led by Benjamin Montgomery—winner of the cotton award at the Centennial Exposition—have been farming on their own since Emancipation, when Jefferson Davis's brother Joseph signed the plantation over to the slaves who'd worked the land. Now that Joseph is dead, his more illustrious brother is suing to get his property back—and will of course eventually succeed, until the river wipes the question of ownership off the books forever. But for now, the dream is still alive, and the holiday makers disembark in high spirits. Another boat is right behind them, excursioners who've come all the way from Birmingham.

The first move away from home is hard on a child, who will always miss the life she was used to: fishing in the bayous for crawfish, running from snakes, chasing lightning bugs, playing tag with friends. In Sarah's case she must miss simply being looked after by those who'd known her since she was born. And because children never completely trust the reassurances of adults, she has to wonder if the people telling her how lucky she is really know.

They find a picnic spot. A preacher reads the Emancipation Proclamation and children recite Bible verses; then another preacher asks the blessing and everybody eats. Afterwards they sing songs, hymns and "The Battle Hymn of the Republic." P. B. S. Pinchback makes a speech. The governor-turned-senator has also become a conservative, and he reminds the picnickers that white Southerners are their friends and tells them to forget about the promise of forty acres and a mule because the Republicans have neither power nor mules, money nor land. He says that Gabriel will blow his horn before the stillness of the air is broken by the braying of even one of those mules.

Some of the picnickers take naps. In a baseball tournament, the Vicksburg team beats the locals and takes home a silver cup and a prize bat and ball. In the early evening the boat's steam whistles summon the excursioners back and they reboard. By the time they dock in Vicksburg, darkness has moved across the river like the onset of new weather. The following day, the newspaper will report on the occasional black eye resulting from drunken altercations and on a fight between two women. But the article grudgingly admits that the Fourth of July excursions were basically orderly.

That same day's paper announces the arrival of the season's mosquito crop, which is late but enormous. On the twenty-ninth, there is a total eclipse of the sun. And on the thirtieth, Dr. I. R. O'Leary, the mayor of Vicksburg, officially acknowledges what the city has long known by issuing an ordinance of quarantine, though he still claims that an incursion of the dread illness is only a remote possibility. Nonetheless, no mail will be coming in or out and no boats allowed within ten miles of Vicksburg. Captains who violate this cordon sanitaire will be fined $1,000, imprisoned in the workhouse or put on a chain gang. People from infested cities are banned, and quarantine stations are set up north, east and south of the city. When boats come by, they stop in mid-river, blow a whistle and wait for barges to lumber out and provide whatever supplies are needed.

Vicksburg falls into a state of diminishment and dread. Doctors' horses break down from overwork. Newspapers cut their size, and on some days skip publication altogether. The Howard Society, a white philanthropic organization, joins forces with their colored branch, the Golden Rule Society, to aid victims and educate families, to pass out supplies for treatment and disinfection and to make sure the dead are buried quickly. Newspapers assure readers that if every household takes proper precautions, their city will almost certainly escape an epidemic. "Almost" is the key. Everyone knows it's coming, and the only hope is to stave off panic and perhaps limit its scope and toll.

In early August, a letter signed by businessmen and doctors states that the only incidence of yellow fever in Vicksburg involved three people who disembarked from passing boats, and the newspaper reports on the second week that the scare has practically passed. But by the third week of that month, this charade is over. On the twenty-eighth there are seventy-one burials in just one night. Mayor O'Leary dies. The death lists lengthen, and panic creeps block to block. When people nap with a cloth over their eyes, family members start to worry; and when their skin and the whites of their eyes turn yellow, hope dwindles. The onset of Bronze John is sudden, its course rapid and awful. A victim bleeds from the nose, mouth, eyes, rectum and any open wound. Within a week, fever spikes to new highs and delirium sets in. When the aching, crazed patient vomits blood as black as coffee grounds, death is a welcome certainty.

Once doctors and nurses arrive from Shreveport, where the epidemic has peaked, panic covers Vicksburg like a bedsheet. Friends eye one another for symptoms, and no one escapes suspicion. The newspaper reports that the disease is increasing by the hour. The newly dead include Martin Kearny, owner of the *Geisse*. After tending and burying many family members, one woman writes to a relative that she has completely exhausted her budget of nerves. At night, the bobbing light of lanterns jags into the black air as beleaguered families swiftly deposit their loved ones in shallow backyard graves. Men who once worked the docks as stevedores and roustabouts stand as grim sentries around homes where known cases are in the last stages. Sometimes a doctor will ride by and call out a name, so that one or two of the men can rush over and possibly gain an hour's worth of work carpentering a casket or, if there's no time or money, digging a grave.

As protection, towns close themselves off. Galveston, Texas, still clean, quarantines itself against boats and travelers from Memphis and New Orleans. Meridian bans visitors from Vicksburg and imposes a $500 fine on hotel keepers who don't comply. After Holly Springs, Mississippi, decides not to shut its doors to Memphians, over half of its 3,500 citizens flee; of those who stay—mostly the poor, who have no place to go—304 die. For the moment, politics go tame, bulldozing ceases and members of the Ku Klux Klan and the White Brotherhood spend their nights at home.

In the Deep South, summer heat drags on well into October. Dampness hugs the face like a wet scarf. Fleas and mosquitoes travel in packs. Downtown Vicksburg is deserted, and in the evenings, because the gaslights go unlit, Washington Street turns pitch-black. An occasional policeman makes his lonely rounds. A doctor's buggy grinds slow tracks in the dust. When seventeen Negroes living on Levee Street are stricken, the black churches warn their members to stay at home, take precautions and pray.

Where is Sarah? Hiding out, like everybody else. Holding a scrap of flannel over her mouth when she leaves the house, she must wonder what would happen if Louvenia and Jesse were to catch the fever and die as suddenly as her parents and others did. By now she knows grief all too well, and the swift, sure methods death will come up with when it sets its mind to it. A mixture of lime, tar and carbolic acid is poured from buckets and sprayed from sprinklers on sidewalks and streets, and barrels of this mixture burn on every street corner. Young Sarah tightens the cloth over her nose to filter out the acrid smell. The sidewalks are black with carbolic acid, which mats up dogs' hair and ruins whatever clothing it touches. People take off their shoes before going indoors, so as not to track in clumps of tar. Children are warned that if they walk barefoot, their feet will burn up, but Sarah knows what not to do. Still, people repeat the lessons and she listens anyway, not so much out of well-mannered obedience but because she is a child who keeps her own counsel and finds her own way. Listening not for lessons but strategies.

Weekly arrivals of fresh supplies of orange leaves, quinine and morphine—used to treat the disease—are announced in the newspaper. Daily warnings are tacked up on trees, storefronts and fence posts, urging people to stay away from the river and to place bowls of turpentine in every room, exhortations that have an "if only" quality, as if to suggest that if only people would do these simple things, we wouldn't have to worry about yellow fever at all!

We know, of course, how useless are these precautions and instructions and in hindsight imagining can see it all: a female mosquito cutting away from the pack and—sensing heat, movement and lactic acid—zooming down to sink her pointy proboscis into exposed skin, feasting on blood to mature her eggs. Once the sting registers, she may be smacked by her host into a bloody pulp, but her work might already be done, and it will not be undone by orange leaves, lime, tar, turpentine or quarantine. She is the vector, not the air or the river, ill people or corpses. But no one knows this, and the Pandora's box of pestilence remains open.

When Mrs. B. Bionda, a snack-house keeper, takes sick on a Friday and dies the following Monday, a doctor describes the place as reeking, and blames the disease on New Orleans riverboatmen who have illegally been allowed to bring in supplies of Goyers sugar. "Let no man enter the block. . . . The river is at hand and the snack-house . . . a place of resort for the river men." And then he attacks the victim: "Mrs. Bionda lived in a snack house, drank hard, lived among fumes of food and debris and trash. If a boatman . . . carried a spot of contagion in his clothes, the seeds of disease could not help but germinate." If only Mrs. Bionda had lived a decent Christian life.

What a terrible time for Sarah Breedlove and Louvenia Powell: people sick and dying; the town in a deadlock of fear; the laundry business, like all business, down to nothing, with everyone too worried, tired and busy to think of such things as clean clothes. Any washerwoman lucky enough to be given infected linens—handkerchiefs, bedsheets—to wash uses lime and kerosene to boil the fever out. Restaurants, which a young washerwoman could scavenge for food scraps and fat drippings to make soap, are closing due to lack of customers, business and foodstuff. One of Sarah's jobs would be to scour the town for leftover cinders, but in summertime nobody keeps a stove going except for cooking, and they don't seem to be doing much of that anymore.

When white people look out their windows, they invariably see blacks and poor whites in their yards and on the street, begging for work or food, but they shoo them all away. They don't have anything to give. Those better off always blame the unwashed poor for the onset and spread of disease, and because yellow fever strikes most readily in cities on the water, they believe the fever floats off the river at night to roam at will through shanties on the levee, infesting the unwary sleepers' clothes. Since African-Americans predominate in those shanties, they are particularly suspect. Sometimes people leave a little scrap of something on the back porch, or collect their garbage in a barrel and leave it for scavengers willing to run the risk of infection. Then they close the barely cracked door and shutter their minds against the miasma and those it has infected.

The church is the one place open to a young girl's needs. Black people all over the country are forming benevolent and missionary societies, and in Vicksburg the Women's Aid Societies from the churches in town—having received food and supplies from such national societies as the Daughters of Zion and the Daughters of Samara—have pooled their resources. At her church, Sarah might receive food enough for a meal, and she can stock up on turpentine and fresh drinking water. The Golden Rule Society also hands out turpentine, which people like Jesse and Louvenia then pour into broken bits of crockery or cleaned cans and place throughout the house.

White people are more fearful than blacks, since they are known to be more vulnerable, but by late August Negroes, too, are getting sick in droves. Jefferson Thomas, who only a few weeks ago gave thanks to God for the new bell in King Solomon's steeple by ringing out its first chimes at the Fourth of July festivities, dies of the fever, and the black community grows almost as terrified as the white. Live-in servants move out, and their white employers' resentment of this "betrayal" makes them feel even more helpless than before.

The summer ends with a solid week of rain—more mud, less work—but the epidemic holds on. Robert and Fredonia Burney's fourth daughter, twenty-year-old Mary Ella, a new bride, dies in October. (Her body, stashed in a temporary grave in Delta, will be reburied in the family plot in Vicksburg after the first frost, when the quarantine is lifted.) Both parents and a younger brother of Ida B. Wells, the future newspaperwoman and fierce anti-lynching lecturer, die of the fever in Holly Springs, Mississippi, up in northern Mississippi. Against everyone's good advice, she leaves college to come home and tend to her siblings. This is worth noting because Wells, while working for the Equal Rights League, will spend at least one night in Madam C. J. Walker's Harlem brownstone in 1918, and although not previously a fan of the door-to-door entrepreneur, she will afterwards extol the former washerwoman's virtues and call her a woman of vision and ambition. During this terrible summer and fall of 1878, Wells and Sarah Breedlove are less than two hundred miles apart.

Halloween passes, Bronze John still holds the fort. By the end of November, 1,138 people will have died in Vicksburg, nearly 9,000 in New Orleans and another 4,200 in Memphis—where a yellow-fever cemetery will be built and a book thick as a Bible will chronicle the progress of the disease and list the citizens who died of it. In the aftermath of the epidemic, Memphis will lose its charter due to unpaid and unpayable debts, and its large, relatively prosperous German population will relocate to the healthier St. Louis. To help stanch future episodes, Memphis will install the first municipal sewer system in the country.

Meantime, the gods of agriculture continue toying with the hearts and fortunes of those who live by the soil. Cotton needs hot nights, especially in late summer and early fall, when bolls are setting bloom; and the mild early spring and long late summer of 1878 have made this the most bountiful cotton crop in years. Not that planters and croppers will prosper much from it. Because the South had already seceded when new banking laws were passed, there are no local banks, and farmers are forced to pay exorbitant interest rates to institutions up north. And because they are traditionally disinclined toward developing their own marketing systems, to find buyers they have to rely on wholesalers and factors in New Orleans, who enrich themselves at the farmers' expense.

When people in the river towns of Louisiana and Mississippi wake up one November morning to find a killing frost blanketing the countryside, they draw a collective breath of relief. The frost, they believe, chills the fever where it lies breeding on the land, shrinking it until the infected miasma finally curls up, frozen, and dies. Wigglers no longer jitter on the murky surface of ponds, marshes, swamps and lakes. The water turns cold. Thready mosquito larvae stiffen and do not hatch.

As soon as Bronze John goes down, old habits return, stubborn as a stray dog refusing to be pitched out. Since this is an election year, a lot of squirrelly white people are ready to go at it once again, and men in white masks and capes are soon showing black men what will happen if they try to vote. Hearing of a white campaign to terrorize and kill them, the colored people of Madison Parish organize, meet with a parish court clerk and vow not to vote Republican. Isn't there some way they can settle the problem among themselves, black and white? The clerk says no. "There is more eloquence in double-barreled shotguns to convince niggers," he tells them, "than there is in forty Ciceros." In the end, in a parish containing 2,700 registered Republican voters and 238 Democrats, the latter return a majority of 2,300, firearm eloquence having done its work.

The old dream of land ownership slips away, since when the men in power are the very ones who burn their homes and murder them in the night, people start thinking that anyplace else has to be better. They keep hearing about Kansas, home of old John Brown, where it is said property comes free for the working of it, where a black man can own his own home, vote and send his children to school. Where there are no White Knights or Ku Kluxers.

A schoolteacher who has moved from Mississippi to Kansas writes President Hayes asking him to help bring other black people there. Nothing happens. In Shreveport, the Negro migration apostle Henry Adams writes asking the president to provide protection for black voters, but Hayes does nothing. When the 1878 elections are over and old-line Democrats have been voted into office overwhelmingly throughout the South, Hayes finally acknowledges that black voters' rights might indeed have been compromised, especially in Louisiana and South Carolina, so he appoints a committee to investigate.

As the weather cools and the docks open and cotton is ginned on the river once again, Vicksburg comes alive in every way. In late November, the *Commercial* estimates a murder a day and graphically reports each one. CRAZED SON-IN-LAW, INTENT ON MURDER, HAS HEAD POUNDED TO JELLY, reads one headline. After reading a number of these accounts, even the casual peruser has no trouble discerning the race of those involved, since crimes committed by black people are reported with casual condescension. One describes a row that required the presence of the sheriff, at whose arrival "darkies scattered . . . and one ran into a lamppost and another slammed into persons promenading Cherry," and one fellow "stepping high and fast" came to a dead fall, after which he ran "like greased lightning." Another, about the hanging of three black men in Franklin County, Louisiana, is headlined, THE DANCE OF DEATH!

Cheered by the elections, white Mississippi goes for broke. A "pig law" passed by the state legislature makes the stealing of swine a grand larceny punishable by a five-year prison term. Planters are allowed to lease convicts for twenty-five cents a day, no questions asked, no conditions imposed; the convicts are overwhelmingly African-American, and any who are sick one day have to work two to make up for lost time. Sometimes the men form chain gangs supervised by an overseer wielding a whip or a shotgun and who moreover keeps a pack of "nigger hounds" close by. If a convict tries to escape, the dogs will run him down, at which point he is usually killed.

The state cancels the school tax, leaving education up to individual communities. A Vicksburg newspaper suggests reintroducing the whipping post for acts of petty larceny, basing this on the theory that the black man has "no fear of the workhouse or jail and no sense of shame," but that his "Ethiopian soul would shrink from a whipping post as from a guillotine."

The dream of flight starts to seem like the only possibility worth imagining, and the dream is always the same. *Kansas.*

On December 23, 1878, Sarah Breedlove turns eleven. With so much fear in the air and her birthday so close to Christmas, she and her family may not do much celebrating. They may wait. Since the cotton crop is excellent and steamboats are back in business, any man strong enough to lift a bale can get day jobs down at the landing; and like most men, Jesse would pose less of a threat when he's working. On Christmas Day, the sisters may collaborate with other washerwomen and wring the necks of a chicken or two and make cornbread and pie.

I see young Sarah marking her eleventh birthday in her own way, in whatever secret place she has managed to mark out as her own. There she might keep the company, in advertisements, of ladies in fancy hats and fur-collared ulsterettes, and perhaps study a piano with curvy legs or a horse-drawn carriage pulling up to a fine house, astonished to imagine people owning such things. Because they appeal to the prevalent dreams of their times, ads provide a glimpse of how other people live or would like to, much as mail-order catalogues will in coming years. Here, Sarah might not only discover the current fashions but also come to understand, if vaguely, the shifting dreams which feed and change them.

When she came to Vicksburg, Sarah Breedlove couldn't read and it's likely Louvenia, having signed her marriage certificate with an X, couldn't, either. According to the accounts of those who knew her, Madam Walker never let up in her pursuit of the two things she valued most, respectability and education. Believing that if she focused on the latter, the former would follow, the grown-up Madame hired women to teach her vocabulary, to correct her grammar and broaden her horizons. Mornings she demanded serious readings of the newspaper, and if a word nobody knew came up, somebody had to go look it up in the dictionary then and there.

Of course I have no proof of how young Sarah spends what little free time she has or what she does for fun. But I like to think of her tearing pictures out of discarded newspapers, poring over them for clues. It is a way of understanding how, when the time came, she was able to make the leap she did. At home, out back in the alley where Louvenia can't see, perhaps she makes a glue out of water and what tiny amounts of flour she can scrounge and pastes these pictures into a discarded wallpaper sample book.

National advertising and name brands bring the wider world into closer focus. In the *Vicksburg Herald,* whose circulation is the largest of any newspaper in the state, J. J. Weimar's Hair Invigorator guarantees hair growth, while Tuts Pill—endorsed by doctors and clergymen—cures everything from piles to female irregularities. Davidson and Co. advertises a sure cure for lost manhood, nervous debility, premature decay and all disorders brought on by excess. In the *Concordia Eagle,* David Young's African-American newspaper from across the Mississippi, Vegetine promises a speedy cure for opium and morphine addictions. Cure-alls are endemic, like the fever. To change your life, swallow this draught.

There are also local ads offering escape and adventure—the Cole Circus coming to town; the Parisot (or "P") Line working the Yazoo and Sunflower Rivers; steamboats on the Anchor Line, the *Colorado* or the *Belle of Shreveport,* traveling from Vicksburg to St. Louis and New Orleans; train schedules featuring excursion trips—as well as a range of goods and services including bars, grocery stores, undertakers, plantation supplies and the newest ladies' fashions.

The washerwoman's biggest rival, Chinese laundries, advertise low prices and excellent service, while America Brown (Col) on Veto Street names herself Prize Medal Washerwoman. Within a year there will be advertisements for the Vicksburg Soap Works at the corner of Glass Bayou and Cherry Street, in the Negro section, which prides itself as the only soap manufacturer in the entire state and exhorts people to buy local instead of choosing such national brands as Colgate and Procter & Gamble. But for now, a man named Amos drives a soap cart, and his employer's classified ad assures readers that he is very polite and will promptly answer any question having to do with soap grease.

Even if Sarah can't read, the pictures deliver a clear message on their own. And in time, the young girl begins to match the pictures with the letters. Even though she might not always get the exact meaning, she manages to create a kind of code that passes for reading. And alongside the ingrained habit of work, she acquires another: that of learning.

Once the fever has passed, Sarah goes back to her jobs: scavenging, drumming up business, doing laundry pickup and delivery. These jobs are not unpleasant. A girl can go as she likes down alleys and through back lots, and no one will bother her. Holding her nose against the stench of garbage and raw sewage, even on the gloomiest winter day young Sarah would not feel crushed by her circumstances. It is not in her to let herself be brought down. Because if she allows hardship to stomp out her spirits or other people to determine the limits of her life, Sarah Breedlove will never grow into the woman she became.

Wash

I am not ashamed of my past. I am not ashamed of my humble beginning. Don't think because you have to go down in the washtub that you are any less a lady!

MADAM C. J. WALKER, 13TH ANNUAL CONVENTION,
NATIONAL NEGRO BUSINESS LEAGUE, AUGUST 1912

In nineteenth-century America, nothing comes clean easily, but of all soap-and-water jobs, the one housewives dread most and save their pennies to hire out is laundry. The work is long, tedious, and requires enormous strength; it wrecks the back and turns soft young hands into rough red paws. One week's batch is barely finished before the next one's piled up and ready. New devices are supposed to help, or so the makers claim: wringers to attach to washtubs, washtubs with built-in levers to agitate the clothes and get them clean without scrubbing. The advertisements for these tubs show a smiling white woman dressed in fine clothes either standing or leisurely sitting by the tub, her hand lightly resting on the lever. If, however, the woman doing laundry is black, she will be dressed in traditional colored-lady clothes: a white rag covering her hair, gaudy hoop earrings dangling to her chin, a flashy striped or polka-dot blouse, dark skirt, fluffy white apron. Her smile will show a lot of teeth and her eyes will be bulging. She won't be washing her own clothes, a fact that will go unremarked for a simple reason, because the advertisement isn't designed for black people. The laundress will be posed outside in her employer's backyard, exclaiming how easy washing has become now that she's using the Eclipse Wringer! The white lady who engaged her services is impeccably dressed and holds an equally stylish little girl by the hand, and both are smiling sweetly.

For most of their first two years in Vicksburg, Sarah's main job brackets the work week: Mondays she goes to pick up the laundry, and on Saturday delivers it clean, starched, ironed and folded. Some laundresses carry their bundles on their heads, and so, possibly, does Sarah; but probably not, since she's far removed from African ways. However she manages it, delivering clean clothes requires particular balance and skill. She has all those muddy streets and hills to negotiate, and now that the fever is gone, the new year has blown in another kind of problem. January 1879 is unusually cold in the South, and nobody has wool coats, hats and stockings for ice and snow. That kind of cold never lasts long in Mississippi, but warmer temperatures bring only rain and more rain, so the levee soon is mostly slush. People are cold and wet all the time. To save their shoes, they leave them in the house and go barefoot, even though the mud is cold and their toes freeze.

She maneuvers through the rutted, mucky streets, being particularly careful on Saturdays not to drop a newly starched and ironed white shirt or linen tablecloth. She might use a wheelbarrow or wagon borrowed from one of the other washerwomen, most of whom live in communal-type settlements, so they can share washpots and clotheslines and help one another out in times of sickness and trouble; but a wagon doesn't help much in the rain. The shacks where they live are arranged in a kind of circle: the girls and women do laundry in the center and those too sick or old to participate sit on the front porch, take care of the babies, watch and supervise. Even white ladies' household-hints books hold that laundry should not be a one-woman job.

Because white people traditionally change their clothes and linens on Sunday, they like to send their dirty things out by Monday morning, before the stains set. Mondays, while Sarah's doing pickups, Jesse and Louvenia are hauling gallon after gallon of water up the levee to use for boiling, soaking, washing, bluing and rinsing. They carry the buckets up, empty them into the pots and tubs, go back down again. At the cistern, the washerwomen chat but the men helping out say nothing—sullen from having to do what is essentially women's work, even if their wives' income is the only money coming into the house.

From the old days in Delta, Louvenia may have learned how to make soap from fat drippings and wood ashes. Most women add lye to the mixture, which burns their arms and hands and sometimes eats holes into delicate shirtwaists or hankies. And if the proportion of ashes to grease isn't exactly right, homemade soap can stain clothes or turn them yellow. So when they can afford it, laundresses make deals with Amos, the soap-cart driver, buying ready-made cakes at a discount, in exchange for drippings they've collected.

Louvenia and Jesse may have hauled the water on Sunday. If so, they would've laid the fire that evening and set it going very, very early Monday morning. Sarah may wake up and see the blaze flaming up in the dark and lie in bed and watch as, under her sister's careful tending, the fire dampens down to a soft, burning glow. The young Madam Walker takes note of every detail, including the importance of heat in the entire laundering process: making soap, cleaning clothes, starching and ironing.

Louvenia might not realize how fast her sister's mind is clicking. A family is often blessed with only one child who escapes, whose imagination can expand beyond familiar expectations.

Other washerwomen are in on the fire building. They may chat a bit, eat a little something or drink some coffee, then fold back into their beds for an hour or so while the water warms. By the time Sarah sets off to collect wash, barely past sunrise, steam is rising from the pots in great curling drifts. These iron boiling tubs are the heaviest and costliest of the washerwoman's trade. By now, women in other parts of the country have advanced to copper, which conducts heat more quickly and evenly, but not in the South. By contrast, the washtubs—used for soaking, washing, rinsing and bluing—are considerably lighter. Often made of wood reinforced with iron staves, some of them have been fashioned from beer barrels scavenged from snack shops and bars on Catfish Row. Once scalded and cleaned with kerosene to eliminate the smell, they serve as well as store-bought.

While Sarah is gathering laundry, Louvenia prepares a thin starch for aprons, blouses and the trimming on underclothes, and a thicker one for heavier men's clothing, bed and table linens. The starch has to be brought to a boil, then allowed to cool. In ladies' magazines, Glenfield Starch is advertised as having been applied to Queen Victoria's laundry, and is pronounced by Her Majesty's laundress the finest starch she ever used, now available at grocers' and druggists' throughout the Union.

Finished with the starch, Louvenia gets out soap, kerosene, vinegar, salt and the scrub board.

When Sarah gets back, she and her sister sort the laundry according to fabric, color and dirtiness. Sarah goes for another order while Louvenia and the other women begin dropping the sorted laundry into soapy water. After the clothes have soaked in separate tubs for at least an hour, the women wring out each piece by hand, using a powerful twisting movement in the wrists. Some clothes need more than one soaking; others have to be scrubbed on the washboard long and hard to erase soiled spots, but carefully enough not to tear the fabric. Young girls are filled with admiration at how the women's strong hands mash the fabric against the zinc ripples of the board, their deft fingers manipulating and gathering the fabric as they scrub, so that the cloth is reversed as it's scrubbed and thus gets clean on both sides. It looks easy, but a beginner invariably lets the cloth slip and rubs a knuckle raw. And if a particularly stubborn spot demands kerosene, afterwards the tub has to be rinsed several times to get rid of it. Lamp cloths have to be washed separately. Handkerchiefs get a special borax treatment that dispels germs. The women use salt or vinegar for spot removal, and have to beat out some spots with a batting stick.

After the soaking and scrubbing, the clothes are boiled for ten minutes. It is best to put them into a pot of cold water and let the water come to a slow boil, but this takes too much time; if a white housewife wants her clothes put in a cold pot, then she can do it herself. After boiling, the clothes are pulled out with a stick, then wrung out piece by piece and rinsed two or three times—the water emptied, refilled, emptied—then wrung out again, shaken and put through the trickiest phase of the washday, the bluing process.

In slave days people made their own bluing, but it is now sold in small balls that come apart in the water without dissolving completely. The laundress usually ties the bluing ball into a bit of flannel cloth then swirls it in the pot until the hot water turns exactly the right color. Working against the yellowing that comes from harsh soaps, bluing makes white shirts white and is especially necessary on days when the best bleaching agent of all, the sun, is hidden behind clouds. The younger girls, not trusted to do the actual bluing, stir the pots and watch the water change. Sarah's big, strong and good at whatever she does. Her focus is always the job at hand, whatever it may be. She stirs.

After the bluing pots are emptied and their contents rinsed and wrung out once more, the women lift the laundry onto clotheslines, fences, tree limbs and bushes. Still wet, the tablecloths and bed linens are particularly heavy to hang. But first, those items needing starch must be separated from the rest, then transferred to tubs which, now having been emptied of bluing and soaking water, contain the two kinds of starch mix.

When they can't work outdoors, the women spread the chores among different houses, and stretch clothesline ropes throughout each one. Since the water will slop all over the floor, they have to be careful not to step barefoot in any soap or kerosene; and there's barely room to move with all the equipment and white people's laundry. Jesse, Louvenia and Sarah sleep with it hanging over their beds like frozen ghosts.

The process is repeated all over again for every household they work for, and can run well into Wednesday. That night, Sarah and Louvenia sprinkle the clothes, using a whisk brush made from dried grasses to fling drops of water across the fabric. Some women are adept enough to do it with just a flick of their fingers. The dry clothes lose their stiffness as the water hits them. Linen is particularly cranky and must absorb a great deal to come out smooth.

Ironing begins once the clothes have been set aside to dampen, usually overnight. Sarah's job is to keep the triangular, weighted inserts of several sadirons heating in progression on the stove, so that by the time one cools, another one is ready and her sister can release the cold insert and attach the handle to the next without waiting. They need at least three bases to each handle, though five or six would be better. She is also responsible for keeping the bottoms of the irons free of starch and dirt by wiping them and then rubbing them with paraffin or beeswax wrapped in a scrap of flannel. Sometimes, if the cloth is worn too thin, she'll burn her hand.

To test an iron, Louvenia may lift it to her cheek; if it feels too hot next to her skin, it's too hot to use and she'll let it cool. Or she may simply touch the bottom with a wet finger and listen: the shorter the hiss, the hotter the iron. To prevent scorching, some women try the iron first on a piece of paper or scrap material, for a washerwoman knows that any time she scorches a fine shirtwaist, she loses a customer.

One popular sadiron, called the Mrs. Potts Cold Handle, has a detachable walnut handle which is guaranteed not to burn the hand. There are also specialty irons for fluting, crimping and ruffling. A hopeful girl like Sarah must dream of someday owning a Mrs. Potts and of buying specialty irons for Louvenia, who might well scoff at her little sister's foolish ideas.

Ironing is hard on the back, but most women find it soothing. Sarah and the other girls watch as their sisters, aunts and mothers turn balled-up wads of fabric into tablecloths and pillow slips, blouses with ruffled necklines and bosoms, or handkerchiefs whose lace must be treated with care. Both hands work in a graceful choreography, one working the iron while the other arranges the fabric.

When Madam Walker gives demonstrations of her hair products, people will marvel at her ability to make waves and soft curls with the hot comb. In one of the Walker Company instruction manuals, there is a photograph of a woman having her hair arranged. Nothing of the beautician can be seen except her hands, which belong, the caption notes, to Madam Walker herself. They are rather big hands, the fingers a little plump, but delicate, precise, skillful.

Laundresses iron on tables covered with a woolen blanket and then a cotton sheet, or the surface might be boards laid across upside-down washtubs. When an article is smooth, they fold it according to its nature and then, careful as a mother with her baby, place the finished piece in a basket with the fancy side up.

Saturday is Sarah's delivery day—a happy occasion, when the hard work is done and the white women pay. Sometimes they even give Sarah a penny tip for a sweet. Triumphantly, she brings the money home. Washerwomen earn about a dollar a week for one household's laundry.

There is, however, a bonus to this profession. Laundresses spend their days and nights at home with their families, without white people constantly breathing down their necks telling them what to do and how to do it. While they wash, they can take care of their babies, cook or do their own housework. From Atlanta to Philadelphia, for a majority of black women it is the chosen occupation, far preferable to living in and wearing a uniform.

When Madam Walker first went into the hair-care business in Indianapolis, she carried a square black bag wherever she went. The bag contained her hot combs, the small kerosene stove used to heat them and various other supplies. People made fun of her for carrying it, but Madame held her head up and went on. Sarah Breedlove had given her a wealth of experience at carrying products through busy streets and at selling door-to-door.

A Dream of Kansas

> We looked around and [saw] that there was no way on earth . . .
> that we could better our condition. . . . The men that had held us
> slaves was holding the reins of government over our heads. . . .
> [So] we said there was no hope for us and we had better go.
>
> HENRY ADAMS, 1879

In the late fall of 1878, what night riders call "timely killings" enable Democrats in Louisiana and Mississippi to win every contest. During the congressional hearings President Hayes subsequently orders, Senator William Windom of Minnesota suggests that in the face of these shocking reports of racial terrorism during the elections, perhaps Congress ought to promote a migration of freedmen away from the South, maybe west, to Kansas. "The black man," Windom explains to his colleagues, "does not excite antagonism because he is black, but because he is a *citizen.*"

Windom's pleas accomplish nothing, but news between Washington and the South travels a slow, winding path, and many black people have heard otherwise, and believe that the federal government will help them resettle elsewhere. They have also heard that in Louisiana the legislature is writing a new constitution which will return them to slavery. Their best hope is that Grant will again become president, but the combination of his frail health and his scandalous political reputation make that unlikely, so they start selling possessions and packing up.

Transportation companies tout migration and offer cheap tickets. Their salesmen call Kansas "God's country," promising balmy weather and land that's rich, ripe and ready for cultivation. No pig law or Shot-gun Plan, no planters to steal their crops or burn their children's schoolhouse down. When warned that in Kansas the winter wind blows fierce and ceaseless until late spring, one black migrant retorts: "We believe life, liberty and happiness to be sweeter in a cold climate than murder, raping and oppression in the South."

In his sermons, the Shreveporter Henry Adams vows that God has a place for his people, and wouldn't they rather go into the open prairie and starve than stay in cotton parishes living under the thumb of the very people who once held them in bondage? And then there's Benjamin "Pap" Singleton, a tall, thin, light-skinned man who will come to refer to himself as the "Moses of the colored exodus" and claim to have "fetched out" 7,432 people. Born a slave in Tennessee, he now travels the cotton states handing out circulars and exhorting black people to sell what they can and leave.

Migration fever hits Vicksburg in the frigid January of 1879 and remains a constant presence for its African-American residents until the following autumn. The first migrants—who will become known as Exodusters—are from Madison Parish, and in Vicksburg they will board a steamboat bound for St. Louis, a journey that takes about a week and costs four dollars. In St. Louis, they have been led to believe, government and railroad agents are waiting to transport them to Kansas. The hopeful migrants have passed amongst themselves a pamphlet entitled "A Freedman's Home," with a chromolithograph on the cover depicting fields of grain and a picturesque home, a black man reading the newspaper on the front porch, his children playing at his feet, his wife inside overseeing preparations for the evening meal. Anyone who studies this beautiful picture will rightly feel exhilarated, inspired and ready to go.

Black well-wishers gather at the docks to watch the steamboats depart. A child Sarah Breedlove's age would wake up excited since, these days, anything seems possible. And the hours at the boiling pots and tubs pass more quickly as the younger washerwomen listen to sto-ries of St. Louis and Kansas. At night, a girl might fall asleep wonder-ing whether any of her friends from Delta are moving west. At the landing, she looks for familiar faces and thinks about going herself. In Kansas, no telling what might happen: she might go to school, read books, listen to music, be a child.

Black people argue for and against the exodus in about equal num-bers. Many preachers and trusted leaders are dead set against it.

P. B. S. Pinchback calls the exodus a wild goose chase. Newspaper editor David Young meets would-be migrants at the levee in Vidalia, Louisiana, where he reads a speech by Frederick Douglass admonishing them to take their stand in the South. An AME bishop advises them that "whoever this white race does not consort with they will crush out. Social equality is as necessary to our existence . . . as air to breathe and water to drink." But too many people have been too badly mistreated, and the present is saturated with wrongs of the past. Nobody, not even Frederick Douglass, can convince people not to go.

After those from Madison Parish, migrants come down from the Yazoo Valley and up from Grand Gulf and Port Gibson. Muddy plantation roads are filled with rickety sharecropper wagons and people on foot carrying babies and makeshift suitcases. Black churches in Vicksburg ask their congregations to provide shelter while migrants wait for a boat.

By the first of March, a combined total of some five thousand laborers have fled Madison Parish and Vicksburg, and one of them may have been Sarah's big brother Alexander Breedlove, who shows up in the St. Louis city directory in early 1881. Despite David Young's eloquence, almost the entire black population of Concordia Parish, just south of Madison, has left—a significant depletion, since African-Americans outnumbered whites there by a margin of nearly ten to one. Some white planters recommend a rope slung over the nearest lamppost for migration agitators and, short of that, begin spreading rumors. "Jeff Davis is in Kansas," they claim, and they tell the potential migrants stories of Rebel soldiers in the Memphis harbor, waiting in gunboats to take them back into slavery; of smallpox, armed locals and snow.

S itting unnoticed in a corner, Sarah might hear that in February the migrants disembarked in St. Louis, thinly dressed and barefoot, to a winter much colder than Vicksburg's, onto a cobblestoned levee of soot-speckled ice, with nobody there to help them, no food and Kansas still impossibly far away. Even so, when offered free passage home, the migrants refused to go. Once again Vicksburg churches organize, and send boxes of food and clothing upriver. On the receiving end are churches in St. Louis, particularly the St. Paul AME, a gathering place for rallies, celebrations and conferences.

A child such as Sarah Breedlove goes very still during important adult conversations, noticing names, places and attitudes. Such as Charleton H. Tandy, a schoolteacher who paid his way to Washington to ask for government help for the migrants and, when he was brusquely turned away, came home to convene a mass meeting at St. Paul's "to solicit funds to aid the colored stampeders" and, that very night, created the Colored Relief Board. Or his colleague Moses Dickson, a minister who'd worked on the Underground Railroad. Or, for that matter, St. Paul's Church itself. For when Sarah Breedlove moves to St. Louis, this is the church she will attend. Charleton Tandy and Moses Dickson will speak there. Later, Madam Walker will buy a plot in a private graveyard in St. Louis, in the Moses Dickson Cemetery.

Coincidences occur in life but maybe not that often; maybe hardly ever.

By late March, Southern whites are desperate to hold on to their labor force. In May, at a convention in Vicksburg, planters from all over Mississippi consider the feasibility of importing "coolie" labor but decide that the Chinese can't bear the climate. "Give me the nigger every time," one planter says. "He will live on less and do more hard work, when properly managed, than any other class, or race, of people."

Once this situation is explained to steamboat owners, when a captain sees black people lined up along the riverbank, he passes them by. Ship companies working the Red River announce that colored migrants will have to *walk* to Kansas. And indeed, some people set off on foot, heading vaguely north. Others camp on the riverbank, waiting for two weeks or more as boat after boat goes by, and only then—starving, destitute—trudge back to where they came from.

Some stay in St. Louis, and others actually get to Kansas, where at first they're welcomed. But as the influx mounts, newcomers are forced to continue down the Missouri. At Topeka, newly built shacks are destroyed; and at Atchison, city officials pass an ordinance prohibiting paupers from entering. Yet the Negroes keep coming.

It's cold in Kansas, like the planters warned, and stays so through the spring. The wind's pesky, and doesn't let up. Still, some migrants hang tough for a few years, working for white farmers and living in sod houses; then they either move farther west—some to Colorado, where there are silver-mining jobs—or are recruited by the Army as Buffalo Soldiers.

By 1880, forty thousand are reported to have arrived in Kansas. Meanwhile, the U.S. Congress decides that since the Negro has quite a nice life in the South, there's no reason to help him resettle elsewhere. Senator Daniel Voorhees of Indiana attests that *his* studies show they're leaving only because white Republicans are spreading lies, to snare them into moving about. Indiana no more wants the Negro brought in, "by the regiments, divisions and corps," than Californians want the Chinese.

By Sarah's birthday on December 23, the exodus has passed its peak, and the only excitement on the levees is of cotton bales being loaded and shipped off downstream to New Orleans. Sarah's old enough now to have progressed from laundry pickups and deliveries into real work at the tubs. Louvenia has given birth to a baby boy called Willie. Because work is scarce and the shanty overcrowded, Jesse often gets into ugly moods, stirring up trouble and making dark threats he sometimes carries out. Possibly in response, Sarah and Louvenia, both hot-tempered, unleash their frustrations on one another. Spats between sisters tend to be nasty, and don't end well, and theirs are no exception, especially considering the circumstances. There is never enough food or money, and the tension does not die down until everyone is deeply, safely asleep.

Choice

I wish now to make the case—speculative, to be sure—for young Sarah's departure from her sister's home, sometime, say, after the end of the migration in early 1880. Madam Walker says she married at fourteen in order to have a home and because of her brother-in-law's cruelty, and this rings true. But would she, given any cruelty, not to mention the uneasy relationship with her sister, have stayed any longer than was absolutely necessary? By the age of thirteen she's big enough to scrub and wring, and might well have experienced her first menstrual period. She may not be a full-fledged adult yet, but she's clever, does not take well to bossing, and knows when the wind has turned.

Behind the conjecture are two statements, the first by Violet Davis Reynolds, who says that Sarah Breedlove made a living by working "on farms" in Vicksburg. Reynolds's statement derives from a story told by no telling whom, but the other was made by Madam Walker herself, in a 1912 interview with the *Indianapolis Freeman*. Taking in the elaborate furnishings at her home in Indianapolis, the reporter asks how she had acquired such fine tastes. And Madame looks around and says, "I owe it to the white people with whom I formerly lived."

Which white people? Some relatives, and the Walker Company, would have us believe it was the Burneys, but as we know, they had died before she was born. It could have been some other family in Delta, before she and Louvenia left; or Sarah might have moved into the home of a white Vicksburg family who needed a young girl to do domestic work.

In that same *Indianapolis Freeman* interview Sarah Walker also states that she is not ashamed to admit that at one time or another she worked at every possible kind of domestic service—cooking, cleaning, washing—because it was the only work available to a young black woman.

Some laundresses did their washing at white people's homes but returned home at night rather than living in, which smacked of slavery. But Sarah has no firsthand experience of bondage, and if Jesse's giving her a hard time, let's say she agrees to do it—if for no other reason than to move out of Louvenia's house and on her own. Perhaps in her deliveries and pickups she meets a white woman who takes to her and they cut a deal, her first as an independent contractor.

Living in has its rituals and rules. In exchange for domestic work Sarah would be provided meals, lodging and a small salary. She is too young to cook, but she will dust, change bed linens, clean, scrub, mop, wash dishes, lay fires, scour pots and pans, possibly help take care of a baby. She starches and irons linen cuffs and collarettes, polishes boots spattered with red Vicksburg mud. In WPA slave narratives recorded in the 1930s, people state that when living in, their work was never over, that there was always a fire to be laid or a hearth to be cleaned. Though they weren't slaves, they worked all the time, and because they didn't go to their own homes at night, white people thought of them as *theirs.*

I imagine a curious Sarah in her employers' parlor, studying the artwork, the china, the rugs. She asks questions but mostly listens and watches, learning to distinguish mahogany from lesser woods and silver from plate, to recognize the ping of genuine crystal. She wears a starched white apron over a dark fitted dress buttoned to the chin. Living in entails discretion and encourages intimacy. When Sarah is in her mistress's bedroom, dusting or making the bed, she watches the white woman brush her long hair, then gather it up and plump the back part forward in a high pompadour, noticing that the fringe of curls along the top edge of her forehead softens and improves her looks. Perhaps the woman asks for help when inserting a wire hair-roll into the coil she's making on top of her head or inside the French twist at the back. And at night, a proper white girl needed her hair either braided or rolled up in rags. The next morning, when the rags are removed, the crimped waves are tied back with a ribbon.

Such white people's magazines as *Godey's Lady's Book* and *Blackwood's* and the new *Ladies' Home Journal* advise young women to dress practically and quietly instead of resorting to glaring colors and tinseled rubbish, and to marry for love and avoid the class of men termed "dudes." *Ladies' Home Journal* carries ads for a scalp invigorator and hair-producing remedy called Danderine, which "Grows Hair and we can PROVE IT!" There are testimonials—the new form of authentication—from ladies in St. Paul and Newark, and an illustration featuring a young woman in a high-necked blouse who looks perfectly ordinary except for two wavy manes of hair, which fall from a center part down past her chest, all the way to her knees.

Another notice is for Madame Rowley's Toilet Mask, which is worn overnight to preserve and bleach the complexion; the product's logo features Cleopatra in profile, holding up a mask that replicates her face. Beneath this ad is one for Dr. Scott's Electric Crimper and Curler, for ladies who prefer their hair loose and fluffy. Hair and beauty tricks, once secrets, are now advertised conspicuously.

A young girl learning to read on her own won't find it easy, and the process will take longer than if she were enrolled at Vicksburg's First Street colored school; but Sarah's discovering how to turn letters into words, and after a while the words will become ideas and concepts that help her understand how the world works, at which point she won't be at the mercy of guesses and other people's explanations. She studies notices tacked up on fence posts and Bible verses handed out at church. She can't write—at any rate not well—and can't imagine signing her name, not even knowing exactly how it's spelled. Writing will have to wait. Reading's the main thing.

Her white employers give her Sunday afternoons off, after the big noon meal. Sarah visits her sister and other laundresses, goes to evening church services, returns to her little room. After a couple years of this, she might be ready to move again. She meets a man, perhaps at church. Perhaps the man called Moses McWilliams stirs her heart, courts her, and they team up. While that sounds more like a business partnership than a romance, two lonely people joining up to ease life for each other can be seen as a kind of love. And Moses McWilliams might have his own reasons. After emancipation, many freedmen claimed, they married so they'd have a woman to wait on them and make them feel manly. As for Sarah, whatever her reasons and regardless of her attitude toward romance or sex, no young woman of that time didn't want to be married and have babies.

Sarah McWilliams will become pregnant in approximately November 1884, when she is sixteen. Though there is no trace of the marriage certificate, there are a number of possible explanations for its absence.

Perhaps the ceremony was performed in a church and the minister neglected to register it. Perhaps the certificate was lost to bureaucracy. Or maybe the man Sarah marries is in fact the Moses Williams I found in the ledger at the Warren County Courthouse. While the clerk might easily have skipped the "Mc," deciding that Williams, which was a favored surname for freedmen after emancipation, was good enough, there's no explanation for how Sarah could be the "Lucy Mathews" recorded as his bride. Conceivably the clerk got the names mixed up and Sarah, who was just about to turn fourteen, was too terrified to correct him. The 1886 Vicksburg city directory lists no Moses Williams, but there is a Sarah Williams (Col) who lives at 137 Monroe, which is very close to the livery stable where in 1877 Moses worked.

Maybe, maybe not. Who knows?

Machines are taking over the laundry business, even in Vicksburg. A new commercial laundry downtown, Wah Sing, advertises the newest vacuum-type washing machines, plus wringers, mangles and irons for every purpose. The Chinese don't consider this women's work, and everyone—aunts, uncles, fathers, mothers, children—stays busy in the shop.

Married, Sarah McWilliams has left the white people's home and resumed work as a laundress, but without Louvenia. No more business partners; she's on her own. And since there is no way she can compete with the productivity and speed of a commercial operation, Sarah will sell what she does have: reliability, skill and herself. She will find ways to make white women believe she's the best laundress in town. She'll dress and behave as *Ladies' Home Journal* advised, not because she wants to look white, but as strategy. She'll hold herself high and be staunch and upright. White women will trust her *before* she washes the first shirtwaist.

At fourteen, the emerging Madam Walker has made her first marketing decision: *I was a good washerwoman and laundress. I am proud of that fact.*

In early 1882, the Mississippi goes on another rampage and caves in the levees from Memphis to Vicksburg. Afterwards come the mud, the trash, the dead dogs and mules, the horrible smells. Vicksburg is still a mess that summer; all the streets from Washington to the levee are rivers of mud, and when the steamer *Issaquena* puts in, mule teams are unable to haul even half a load from the wharf up to the main street.

Despite the damage, the Floweree Ice Factory opens and distributes flyers proclaiming, NO MORE ICE FAMINE! Oscar Wilde comes to town wearing a floppy velvet flower in his lapel. Telephones appear in more and more businesses and a few homes, some of which also have musical instruments. When she is grown and can afford it, Sarah will never not have music in her life. When she is dying, Madam Walker will request that music from her gold-encrusted organ be played nonstop throughout every room in her house. She will also take particular pride in her American-made Chickering grand piano, and they are popular all over the U.S. in the 1880s. So the young bride and laundress might have heard one played during this time in her life, and remembered. But music must remain on a wish list for now, and Sarah focuses instead on dailiness, puts on her clean white blouse and plain dark skirt and does her job: greets her customers and delivers her clothes.

The winter of 1881, in his inaugural address, the Republican James Garfield announces that under the U.S. Constitution there is no middle ground for the Negro between slavery and equal citizenship, and that he will not allow there to be a "permanent disenfranchised peasantry in the U.S." There are more Negroes at his inauguration than at any other, and it is a great day for black Americans. Then Garfield is assassinated, and his successor, Chester Alan Arthur, quickly issues the warning that if the Negro doesn't learn to read he may be disenfranchised. The U.S. Supreme Court declares the Civil Rights Act of 1875 unconstitutional and sanctions racial segregation in all states.

Given Arthur's persistent unpopularity, the Democrat Grover Cleveland warms up his presidential ambitions, and by the summer of 1884 Negroes are hearing rumors that he has plans, if elected, to re-enslave them. Pap Singleton develops another migration plan; this time he wants to help his people move to Cyprus. He also inveighs against immigrants and claims that steam laundries and Chinamen have forced three thousand Negro women and children into idleness and prostitution. But it turns out that nobody's much interested in going to Cyprus.

By this time, the schoolteacher and lecturer Booker T. Washington has moved to Alabama, where he has been hired to run an industrial school—not yet constructed—meant "for the rural Negro": the Tuskegee Institute. He and his students raise money for the land and build the school themselves. Washington's aim is to help the students learn "to do a common thing in an uncommon manner." He stresses cleanliness and good habits of personal hygiene.

Meanwhile, Tennessee kicks off the modern segregation era by enacting the first Jim Crow law segregating railroad coaches.

Marriage might prove a disappointment for Sarah, but on June 6, 1885, she satisfies one great desire and has a baby. Sarah McWilliams is a wide-hipped young woman, and so it's likely she doesn't have much trouble giving birth. Women friends help calm her worries and give her small sips of whiskey during labor. That her husband is nowhere in sight is a given. Any husband, black or white, would stay away until the blood is mopped up and the afterbirth buried, and the baby has made her first squall and suckled several meals. Sarah names her baby girl Lelia. Though not particularly uncommon, it is an exotic, fanciful name and exactly right.

At the time of Lelia's birth, *Harper's Weekly* publishes an essay on "Manifest Destiny" praising the ability of the Anglo-Saxon to conquer darker peoples from Mexico to Africa and beyond. Sitting Bull tours with the Buffalo Bill Wild West Show. The Lydia Pinkham Co., makers of a vegetable compound designed to cure every female malady from fallen womb to monthly headaches, runs advertisements in both Negro and white newspapers. These take the form of personal testimonials and letters written to Mrs. Pinkham—who answers every letter personally, even though she has been dead for a number of years. Ulysses S. Grant dies. Grover Cleveland has been inaugurated as president. Jim Crow clamps down; excursions dwindle—by 1890 they will have all but disappeared from African-American life.

In a widely quoted speech to the New England Society in New York, the publisher of the *Atlanta Constitution,* Henry Grady, defines "the New South" for rich and prominent Northerners like J. P. Morgan, Charles Tiffany and other millionaire businessmen. Grady, a businessman himself, knows that in order to raise capital for the South, he has to pacify the rich Northerner's conscience with respect to the black man. And so he makes an eloquent case for the "chivalric grace and strength" of Southern white society and its desire that the Negro should prosper and become educated.

As black people gradually disappear from public life, their leaders negotiate with reality and focus on economic activity, racial solidarity and self-help. The 1886 graduating class of Tuskegee Institute adopts the motto "There Is Room at the Top," and one Negro newspaper urges on its readers the gospel of "real progress: moneymaking." Even the *AME Review* advises church members to concentrate on acquiring wealth, the assumption being that if the Negro prospers materially, he will gain the respect of the white man and be accorded full citizenship rights. Surely the young entrepreneur Sarah McWilliams is paying attention, and telling herself, *I will get my start by giving myself a start.*

I n other states it may be different," declares the *Jackson Weekly Clarion,* the best-known newspaper in Mississippi. But "in this State for some time to come, there is but one issue. All know what it is." When I was growing up in Mississippi, the *Jackson Weekly Clarion* had become the *Jackson Clarion-Ledger,* and it was still the paper of record and it still espoused a white-supremacist philosophy. And even those eighty-odd years later, there was still but one issue, and though many of us either didn't realize that or couldn't bear to acknowledge it, everybody still knew what it was.

III · St. Louis, 1887–1905

Departure

Sometimes people just vanish: there one day and gone the next. Other times they don't so much disappear as get lost in the bookkeeping. This hardly ever happens anymore—what with government computers tracking us by the numbers and genetic thumbprinting to identify us even long after we're dead—but it used to.

In the rote litany of her early years—born in Delta, orphaned at seven, moved to Vicksburg at ten, married at fourteen—the official Madam Walker story closes out the Mississippi chapter with *widowed at twenty with a daughter to raise, moves to St. Louis.* Beyond the surname he passed on, Moses McWilliams's only role is that of a bit character who appears in the first act and then dies offstage. Later accounts of his life further confound a realistic accounting with speculation. One story suggests he might have been lynched or perhaps killed during a race riot in Greenwood. And didn't somebody else hear that he was crushed beneath a wagon wheel?

Lynching's unlikely. To get full value from their actions, mobs wanted their killings publicized, and white newspapers had a field day with the grim details, right down to the distribution of bones, internal organs, fingers and toes. Around the time of McWilliams's disappearance, there was a hellacious slaughter of Negroes in the county courthouse in Carrollton, which is only a day's buggy ride from Vicksburg, but he is not named among the murdered men.

Another possibility is that Moses McWilliams got up one morning, went out the door and never came back, leaving his permanently abandoned wife the opportunity to become that choicer thing, a widow. In any case, whatever happened, the only person who knew the truth never said—not for public consumption, at any rate—because by the time Sarah McWilliams had become Madam C. J. Walker, her first husband's death didn't matter: not to the widow, her interviewers or her public, much less to history. And so, whether orchestrated or experienced, "widowed at twenty" becomes a casually accepted fact of the Madam Walker story.

We can, however, catch one possible glimpse of this forgotten man. In the 1920s, his daughter will become a well-known woman in her own right, much photographed, and she does not bear any particular resemblance to her mother. There's no softness about her, nothing round; instead, she's angular and packed and her gaze—in contrast to Madame's fierce, wary intelligence—reveals a certain lush laxness, a bold sexuality, an inclination toward boredom, even cynicism. The grown-up Lelia will be described by black newspapers as statuesque and grand, like an African queen, and in some pictures her almond eyes have a slightly Asian cast. In these details, and—in a different way—in Lelia's occasional taunt to her mother that she is not a Breedlove but a McWilliams, we find traces of Madam Walker's first husband.

Lacking further facts, let us honor the man by leaving him in peace and assume that he did, in fact, die, and that it was his sudden and perhaps violent death which precipitated Sarah's decision, in about 1887, to leave Vicksburg. The year is approximate, of course, and we don't know how she travels, by boat or train. We know only that around this time she gathers her daughter up and moves to the next river city of her life. Why St. Louis? is a question that need not be asked. Sarah has had that city on her mind at least since the great migration, if not before.

Possibly she takes the train, since so many steamboat lines have disappeared. The Anchor Line has cut its passenger service between Vicksburg and St. Louis from several boats a day to one a week. With more track being laid year after year, trains can go where boats can't; they're faster and more comfortable. Inclines have been installed at Kleinston's Landing and across the river on the De Soto peninsula, so railroad cars can be rolled down them onto a steamer. And the last rail has been laid along the thirty-second parallel, connecting the coasts, an idea first proposed in 1836 and Robert Burney's avid desire in the fifties. There is a line on the Illinois Central that goes north to Memphis, and another from Memphis to St. Louis's Union Station, the country's busiest train station. Sometimes colored porters are given free excursion tickets, which they can hand on to relatives or friends. If Sarah knows a porter, she might get a free ride.

On the other hand, steamship fare is cheaper, and she wouldn't have to transfer in Memphis, a difficult proposition at best, considering the boxes and bags she's carrying, in addition to the baby. Moreover, Jim Crow laws assign colored passengers to the forward car, in which there is no food and no ladies' section. White men wander in to play cards, smoke cigars and eye attractive black women. Vendors— called news butchers—stack magazines, gum, candy and papers on the seats and don't remove them even if passengers have to stand. Men and women share the toilet, if there is one. Sleeping-car porters have reported that white mobs are rampaging through the cars, tossing off any colored passenger who has taken the wrong seat. At the depots, or train sheds, vigilantes position themselves in the waiting rooms to make sure colored travelers don't step out of line.

Say the steamboat wins out. She can leave Vicksburg the same way she arrived, on the river. Remembering the *Geisse,* the *Albatross,* the *Pelican* and all the other boats Sarah Breedlove McWilliams has either ridden or watched come and go, let's place her and her daughter on the *Belle Memphis,* one of the last steamboats plying the river between Vicksburg and the city named for a French king. She would have packed enough food and water for the entire journey, since even if there is no Whites Only or No Colored sign, unwritten assumptions make the rules of exclusion clear. Everybody pays the same four dollars for a ticket, but colored people are assigned to the bottom deck, close to the engine room, where cinders fly and clouds of smoke sting their eyes. The only seating is on hard wooden benches, so most people sit on their own boxes and trunks.

Madam Walker is a precise woman who leaves little to chance and no detail unnoticed, and Sarah McWilliams would have arrived at the wharf early, to find a decent spot and set herself up for the trip, placing her boxes where she and Lelia could take in the sights. Corseted, wearing a fitted jacket buttoned to the chin, I picture the young mother sitting tall. She has certainly seen to it that she and her daughter are dressed in presentable fashion. Her dress, hand-sewn either by herself or another woman, is dark, with a slim skirt that has very little flare. The sleeves of her bodice hug her muscular arms. She won't be comfortable on this trip, but in Victorian America no woman of any class or station expects comfort from her clothing. Lelia wears a loose short dress and a pair of lace-up boots. Both mother and daughter have straw hats perched like plates on top of their heads. Lelia's is held on with strings knotted at the back.

From her seat, Sarah can see the two places she's spent her entire life, the flat swamps of Delta and the red bluffs of Vicksburg. Relief trumps fear. Anticipation cancels exhaustion. Sarah McWilliams doesn't expect St. Louis to be paradise, but she believes that life will be better there, especially for her daughter. There are free schools for colored children, starting with kindergarten, and the classes are taught only by black teachers, something of a small miracle. "I'd rather be a lamppost on Targee Street," one newcomer commented, "than be the mayor of Dixie."

She talks to the baby, as mothers will, telling the little girl to take one last good look at home, then reties Lelia's bonnet strings and holds a cloth over her face to protect her from the sooty air. And if she silently swears by all she holds sacred that her baby will never live in Mississippi or Louisiana, that vow will hold. As an adult, Lelia McWilliams will refer to any state west of the Hudson River as "the interior," and will never live longer than a crazily conceived month or so in any Southern state. There won't be a trace of Southernness in her, no false gentility, no flutter and dip, no need to see herself as a repository of piety and moral rectitude, as do many respectable Southern women of both races.

She has dark skin, angular features, long legs and wide shoulders which quickly strain the seams of her dresses. She will grow up to be a large woman, several inches taller than her mother, maybe five feet nine or ten, and a hundred ninety pounds. She will change her given name on a whim, and alter her surname three times by marriage and once for business purposes. She will travel and live on the far edge of a defining culture, where new ideas about art, music and fashion are born, and will be neither Southern nor Midwestern but urban. A night creature who frequents bars where female performers wear black tie and tails and sing like men and who takes her friends to whites-only Harlem jazz clubs that bend the rules for her. A woman who prefers playing cards and drinking with friends to selling beauty products. Privilege will see to it that Lelia McWilliams becomes a woman not of a particular place but of the times.

For Sarah, leaving Delta was complicated, but moving from Vicksburg is not. By the time the *Belle Memphis* blows its whistle, she is already gone. All that's left is the wait between now and what in her mind has already been accomplished, the beginning of a new life in a new place.

With great iron shovels, the black men in the engine room jab at mounds of coal behind them to feed and stoke the fires; each man takes a ninety-minute shift at the ovens, then they switch places. The boat pulls away from Kleinston's Landing. Louvenia might have come to see her little sister off, but more than likely she has left Vicksburg herself, gone maybe to St. Louis, or Ohio. Sarah knows where. She always keeps up with her kin.

Madam Walker will be a trendsetter and a genius at marketing, every bit as sharp at looking into the future as the fortune-teller and phrenologist Madam L. E. McNairdee, who passed through Vicksburg during her time there and whose path will cross with Sarah's again, some twenty-five years from now. Having consulted her own crystal ball, Sarah would have foreseen a hopeless future for those who stayed in Mississippi. Grover Cleveland is giving Confederates back their war booty, including their flags, and there is no telling what else he will do or how far he will go. To obliterate black people's hope of living autonomous, meaningful lives, white men in the South are making up new racial codes by the day, leading Frederick Douglass to wonder in print whether American justice, liberty, civilization, law and Christianity can be "made to include and protect alike and forever all American citizens in the rights which have been guaranteed to them by the organic and fundamental laws of the land. . . ." Not much help is coming from the North. A New York newspaper reports that the Northeast has given up on the Negro because "as a race they are idle, ignorant, and vicious."

The situation is, of course, trickier for women than for men. In 1905, the magazine *The Voice of the Negro* will publish an article which cautions young African-American women moving from the South to plan ahead and to stay vigilant and suspicious of agencies and individuals promising high wages and easy work. It also advises them that without money, friends or an assured job, they will be safer and more prosperous where they are. Assuming they have the money for lodging and food, they should attach themselves to a church as soon as they arrive, in order to make contact with "the best of [their] race and not those who will lead [them] astray."

Wayward temptation is not a problem for Sarah McWilliams, but lodging and money are. She has never been incautious, and now that she has a child she pays even more attention to warnings and advice. Without question, Sarah's headed to St. Louis not only because she's been hearing about it since she was twelve, but also because she has family there—Breedloves she can stay with, her brother Alexander and others—until she gets herself established. When she dies, one of the obituaries will mention a brother still living in St. Louis.

But how to send word? The minister of Holly Grove Baptist Church, Kelly Rucks, born a slave and uneducated, is known throughout the Baptist grapevine as an eloquent, passionate preacher. A funeral oration he gave in 1887 at the Pleasant Green Baptist Church in St. Louis was so memorable that the congregation invited him back, and then offered him a pastorship. A choice opportunity, but Rucks remained loyal to Vicksburg and refused. Still determined to have him, Pleasant Green offered to pay him a handsome salary as well as railroad fare between the two cities for an every-other-month residency. Rev. Rucks accepted the offer, and for the next twenty years he will commute between the churches. Since the Reverend gave his impressive funeral oration the same year she left, Sarah McWilliams might easily have gone to Holly Grove Church to ask him to tell her family she's coming. It might take several weeks, even months, but because the churchgoing African-American community always maintains close ties, in time one of her relatives would receive the word and pass it on to the rest. Others would be doing the same thing. Because of the Cleveland panic, black people are leaving the South in droves, a kind of floating proletariat that moves from field to town to city to bigger city, searching for anonymity and sanctuary.

The boat stops at Greenville, Helena and Arkansas City. At Memphis, some black people disembark but most stay put, having heard terrible things about the city. The cobbled levee is steep, and people on board can see nothing beyond it. Then the *Belle Memphis* steams back into the center of the river. By Cairo, the captain is starting to pay particular notice. From here to St. Louis is known as the graveyard stretch, where boats can get caught in treacherous currents and run into other boats or slam into obstructions and sink like a stone. And the black passengers take notice too, since this is where the Ohio joins the Mississippi and even those who have never seen it recognize its significance to their race's history and the boundary it marked, between the slave and free worlds.

Night. The boat negotiates the swift currents of the inflowing Ohio and moves steadily north.

And what of the baby lying deadweight in her mother's arms, shushed to sleep by the rhythm of the sluicing water and the turn of the paddlewheel? When do we hear from the child?

We do not hear the daughter's voice because she will never, even after her mother dies, publicly explain how these hardships were for her. She is neither quiet nor submissive by any means, but she can be shrewd. Whatever benefits the Madam C. J. Walker Co. also benefits her, so she takes any personal complaints to the grave. The daughter receives, inherits, accepts and takes advantage, but she does not *create,* the way her mother did. And so she remains the Daughter of Sarah Walker, for life. No wonder her eyes reflect inertia, boredom, the curse of cynicism.

Does she, in time, forget the truth? No, but perhaps she sets it aside so carefully, thoroughly and conveniently that she begins to lose track.

Right now, as the *Belle Memphis* approaches the city in which she will grow up, go to school and become a young woman, Lelia McWilliams may already have lost the sharpest memories of her father, and the clearest pictures of what he looked like. But he still has his place in the quiet part of her mind, and if suddenly he reappeared and touched her cheek, she would know him. A lost parent is always there, no matter how dim his light flickers. And sometime in her life, she must surely ask questions. What happened to Moses McWilliams? What did he look like? Is my father dead? Whether it was the truth or not, she had to have been told *something.* But whatever that was, she kept it to herself.

Mound City

A t St. Louis, the Mississippi is wider than at Vicksburg, the banks low. This is called the Mound City, not because of hills but for some two dozen Indian mounds which for hundreds of years loomed over the city's north side. Once known as the Barn of the Earth, the temple and burial mounds have been crushed, scooped out and carted away as fill dirt in the name of progress, and now they are simply gone.

From miles to the south, the steamboat passengers can see signs of the city ahead: barges harbored in the river, a steady movement of boats, a flat, shelflike cloud of black—smoke, grit, particles of coal—layered across the western sky. When they get a little closer the Eads Bridge comes into view, connecting Missouri to Illinois, and a burble of worry passes among them because of all the accidents, sinkings and drownings. Boat pilots wish bridges across these big rivers had never been dreamt up, much less built. The Eads is a simple structure, spanning the river in three wide, graceful arches with neither girders nor beams, three separate streams of traffic—wagons, pedestrians, trains—moving across it before vanishing into a narrow crack between dark red buildings.

S arah McWilliams draws a quick breath as the *Belle Memphis* turns hard toward the levee. A thriving city like St. Louis has a life beyond what she has experienced or has any way of imagining. She will have to learn new manners, language, dress, food, how people walk and sit and greet one another, what songs they sing, the complicated general patterns people develop as they come together and move apart. She will learn to go for weeks without the South's one saving grace: the nurturing landscape of trees, grass, wild-flowers, honeysuckle, wisteria, natural lushness and odors of the earth. Here, her lungs must accustom themselves to the constant presence of smoke and soot.

Divisions among people will be unfamiliar. In Mississippi there is no immigrant culture to speak of, no newly arrived groups of Irish, Germans, Italians; the races there are divided simply into black and white. She has no idea how it will be to adapt to new forms of racism, the fiery hatred of an Irishman, the cold disdain of a German. Even though church ministers will have advised her on these matters, this is a big city of many parts, at once a river city, a railroad city, the gateway to the West, nonetheless also a city with a Southern ethos, where Jim Crow rides the trolleys and makes his presence known in every facet of daily life.

The steamboat sounds its whistle and begins its slow, crablike swing to the western bank.

By the summer of 1887, a number of Breedloves are living in St. Louis, and some of them are black. Two of them—James and Alexander—are barbers. One is a woman named Samara—variously spelled Semira, Samarah and Samira—who, since 1885, has been identified in city directories as "Widow of Owen." Another, Solomon, will have moved to town before January 1888, when the St. Louis directory does its counting, to work as a waiter, and he, too, may well be there when Sarah arrives. Alexander, James, Solomon and Samara will play a big part in Sarah's St. Louis life.

Some Madam Walker stories give her one brother, named either Tom or Alexander, but most accounts, some of them provided by descendants (including A'Lelia Bundles, her adoptive great-great-granddaughter), suggest there were more. Alexander Breedlove (who we surmise is the selfsame "Alex Breedlow" who lived in Vicksburg in 1877) arrived in St. Louis in time to be listed in the 1881 city directory, which suggests that he might well have come during the great migration. Samara's "dead" husband, Owen, will soon show up in Albuquerque, married to another woman, whom Madam Walker will identify as her sister-in-law. Things add up. And by studying where-abouts, professions and marriages—with the added advantage of their unusual surname—we can determine with more than a little certainty that the four African-American Breedloves living in St. Louis in 1888 indeed are kin. And that they are *our* Breedloves, being Sarah's.

When Alexander first came to St. Louis, he continued working as a porter, as he'd done in Vicksburg. For an uneducated black man in the nineteenth century, this is a respected profession. Working on railroads or in saloons and hotels, porters quickly learn how to deal with white people with humor and grace. The work changes from one day to the next, isn't physically risky, doesn't require overalls or dirty hands, since porters usually wear a white jacket, a tie and a cap. But within a year, Alexander Breedlove has moved up to barbering, a profession that still belongs to Negro men and won't change until the races grow even farther apart at the turn of the century and the Germans and Italians take it over. Within the race, barbers have status. Some are proud family men, churchgoers who may go on to become newspaper editors and teachers, while others conform to the image of the sharp-dressed dandy headed for a crap game on Targee Street. They are often, but not exclusively, light-skinned, and can be snooty toward those with a darker complexion. A book called *The Colored Aristocracy of St. Louis* is written by a mulatto barber, Cyprian Clamorgan.

By 1884, Alexander Breedlove had moved up another step by going into business with a partner, John Welker, and together they opened their own barbershop, Breedlove and Welker, at 616 North Eleventh Street. Alexander will continue to work at this address for the next five years, even after Welker dies, and is clearly an ambitious, responsible, hardworking man.

The next Breedlove, James, arrived sometime in 1882. St. Louis city directories do not list residents by race, but in the 1900 U.S. Census he is identified as a black man born in 1861 in Civil War Mississippi, perhaps in piney-woods Morton, where his family had been moved by Robert Burney. After spending a year as a laborer—which could mean anything from a bricklayer to an elevator operator to a hod carrier—he, too, became a barber, perhaps under the tutelage of Alexander. That same year, Owen Breedlove also came to town, to work as a porter and live very near where Alexander worked. But Owen soon vanished, leaving his wife, Samara, behind. These Breedloves move often, sometimes together and sometimes not, but always within a few blocks of one another in the same neighborhood, Mill Creek Valley. In the years to come the pairings will switch. Sometimes Solomon will live with

Alexander, sometimes James with Samara, sometimes Alexander with James. Sometimes they live in the same house and James and Alexander work at the same barbershop, James often living there as well.

Another group of Breedloves—Cameron, Lillian and Mary—live a good distance north of Mill Creek in a more prosperous part of town where the sky is blue and the air almost clear. Cameron and Lillian are both clerks, a profession open only to white people.

When the steamboat bumps up to the wharf at the foot of Chestnut Street, the passengers on the *Belle Memphis* breathe easier. Sarah McWilliams stands, and after four days and nights in the damp air she's bound to be stiff and the child, cranky. Sarah puts the baby down and looks up the levee at the city above. She will be here for eighteen years. They will be hard years, and neither she nor her daughter will speak much of them. Some experiences are discoverable, others buried under blankets of a heavy silence that delivers its own message.

St. Louis is, however, an essential step in the creation of Madam C. J. Walker, and Sarah McWilliams will not regret coming here. Her daughter will go to school. St. Paul's AME Church and the 1904 World's Fair will bring many important colored people to St. Louis— Booker T. Washington, Emmett Scott, W. E. B. DuBois, Margaret Murray Washington, Ida B. Wells, Josephine Silone Yates, Hallie Q. Brown. These people will make important speeches, and by their example provide light for a young woman to see by. She will begin a new career. Many things will happen that in Mississippi would have been not just difficult but unimaginable.

Still, the road to 1905 will be long, dark and hard.

The year before, Alexander and James Breedlove lived at the same address, 1306 Gay, but since then both have moved, James a few doors up—to 1310—and Alexander about five blocks away. Owen has disappeared, Samara's at 1706 Gay and all of them are within a few blocks of Colored School No. 1, one of the schools Lelia will probably attend (and, incidentally, only eight blocks from Targee Street, where Frankie Baker killed the two-timing Albert Britt, inspiring pianist Bill Dooley to write the ballad "Frankie and

Johnny"). Since the city directory does its counting in January, it's hard to say where the peripatetic Breedlove clan is living by summer, when Sarah arrives, but let's assume it is in these particular residences.

When the gangplank is lowered, colored passengers exit first, so the whites won't have to walk among them. As Sarah files up the levee toward the railroad tracks, roustabouts unloading the boats shout to one another over the din of the whistles, steam engines and grinding factories. This profession runs from generation to generation, so most of these men have been at it their entire lives, having learned to get by on twenty-five cents a week. The barechested rousties haul, load, eat, drink, take the occasional woman, sleep and start over, and are the kind of riffraff Sarah's been told to avoid.

Men selling whiskey at ten cents a shot work the arriving crowd, but she pushes on. All levees look the same, lined with cheap boarding-houses and dingy, jammed-up bars. On the other side of the railroad tracks, dark-red mills and factories line the street, giving the appearance of a walled city. Though a pall of smoke hangs over downtown, nobody complains; smoke and soot are signs of industry and prosperity, of "progress." Even blacker smoke pours from the factories across the river. East St. Louis burns soft coal day and night.

Sarah McWilliams lifts her skirts, crosses the tracks, and turns right to walk the five blocks between Chestnut and the main street, Washington, recognizably the same name as Vicksburg's. She does not concern herself with smokestacks. Since mills don't hire Negroes, soot to her means only filthy clothes in need of washing. Business means money. Money means a better life for her and her baby.

She turns down Washington Avenue. From the river to her destination is not far, a half-mile or so, but she is carrying all her possessions. Maybe to rest her back she lets Lelia walk a few steps, but a two-year-old is short-limbed and dawdles, so she lifts her once again. Stopping occasionally to catch her breath, she invariably begins to cough. When she looks around, other people, too, are covering their mouths, hacking, hawking and sneezing. Downtown St. Louis is so thick with smoke and dust that one visitor described the air as meaty enough to chew, and claimed that an afternoon walk left him as satisfied as if he'd eaten a heavy dinner.

The streets are packed and in flux. Cables are being installed to power trolleys and streetcars, but presently, horse-drawn trolleys and the smaller mule-drawn bobtails do the job. They ring insistent bells, warning slower wagons and pedestrians to move aside. Even though conductors have been instructed to pick up *all* passengers, they often turn blind when a black person tries to hail a ride or hop on.

The horses and mules drop manure onto the macadam streets, sometimes directly onto piles deposited there the day—or week—before. Factory whistles shriek. The city grinds, pumps, screams, smells. People jostle one another and move on. Children dash in and out looking for handouts or something to steal. Most of them are thin as a cane stalk and ash pale. Everyone who lives downtown, black or white, has one thing in common: they are all poor. Irish and Germans—and some African-Americans—set up housekeeping in shacks on Clabber Alley (named when waste milk was poured down the alley, providing "Negroes and low whites" with their primary food source) and in the bigger tenements like the four-story one on Broadway north of the Eads Bridge, and black people mostly live in Mill Creek Valley, which remains theirs for many years. As late as 1954, when the city begins an urban-renewal plan, that neighborhood is still almost 95 percent African-American.

The streets are numbered, and since Sarah is headed for Alexander's barbershop on Eleventh Street, all she has to do is count. But one corner is impassable because of construction, and there's yet another building site on the next block. Within the next two years, some 2,600 buildings will be erected, one of them—the Singer Building—an incredible eight stories tall. St. Louis is set on becoming the Fourth City and will do whatever it takes to beat out Chicago in population, businesses, electric railways and train lines. Some people have proposed that the nation's capital be moved here, to pretty much the exact center of the country. But the Windy City's keeping its lead. And no matter how St. Louis boosts its population figures, Chicago finds a way to win out and now is planning a huge exposition to celebrate the four hundredth anniversary of Columbus's discovery of America, set to open in 1892.

When she looks up, all Sarah can see is one high black wall after another and, at the top, a cap of black smoke. The streets are narrow, and the buildings are made of dark-red brick from local brickworks and so covered with grime that any windows are barely distinguishable. There is a meat-canning factory, a shoe factory, several breweries and a number of tobacco-processing plants. Gaslights flicker in the dark daytime air.

Mill Creek Valley used to be the bottom of a lake, Chouteau's Pond, created when early settlers of the city dammed La Petite Rivière and redirected it to run in front of Gabriel Chouteau's gristmill. Two miles long and shaped like a half-moon, for years the pond occupied a huge part of central St. Louis. Described as a magical fairy lake, residents went there to fish, swim and picnic. Winters, they ice-skated there. Preachers from the first black church in St. Louis, the First African Baptist, conducted wholesale baptisms even when they had to crack open the ice before immersing converts. When the mill closed, the pond remained and, for a while, the baptisms and the fishing continued.

But St. Louis kept booming, and by the end of the 1840s Chouteau's Pond had become everybody's dumping ground, rank with household garbage, human waste, offal from butcher shops and scummy industrial chemicals that floated on its surface like expanding cells of a new disease. After the 1849 cholera epidemic, in which some 4,500 people died, the pond was drained as a menace to public health.

Opened to development, the vast, flat lake bottom became quickly jammed with train yards, factories and cheap tenements. Honky-tonks thrived in nearby Chestnut Valley, and at night Targee and Market Streets jumped with stomp piano beats and trouble, as bars and pool halls stayed open late; the two-step and then ragtime drew people from their tenements into joy spots like Turpin's Rosebud Café, the Four Deuces, the Gilt Edge and the Hurrah Sporting Club, not to mention the boardinghouse where Frankie Baker killed Albert Britt or Bill Curtis's place, where, legend has it, on Christmas night in 1895, "Stack Lee" Shelton shot Billy Lyons for stealing his lucky hat. Mill Creek Valley also comes alive at night. Black women in tight satin dresses patrol the streets; macks in Prince Edward coats and mirror-toed shoes flash their pinkie rings; touts push hot horses, dice and faro; girls sit in lace-curtained windows showing off their lush, inviting bosoms.

Ragtime won't be officially introduced to white America until some five years from now, at Chicago's Columbian Exposition, but its syncopations are already echoing in the alleys and backstreets of St. Louis. From time to time, the composer and piano player Scott Joplin makes his itinerant way from Texarkana to Honest John Turpin's Silver Dollar Saloon, and his complicated rhythms make a new beat for people downtown to dance, walk, sleep and make love to. Joplin and John Turpin's son Tom have taken the march music everybody's so crazy about and messed up its one-two steadiness, "ragging the beat" by pounding out the old-fashioned time with the left hand while letting the right go crazy, sometimes in syncopation with the beat, often not. This new music gives some people the jitters, and others just laugh; a great many think it's appropriate only for whorehouses. Hot pianists are ragging everybody, even John Philip Sousa, and their fans have revived an old slave dance, the cakewalk, to keep up.

Sarah's sleep will be punctuated by this strange, unsettling beat. As a parent, she may disapprove. When Ferdinand "Jelly Roll" Morton played ragtime or jazz on the family piano, he was shooed out of the house and told not to come back until he was ready to play nothing but church music. W. C. Handy's father told him he'd rather see him lying cold in a hearse than playing in a dance band. For parents with racial uplift on their minds, secular music is considered a one-way ticket to the gutter.

No matter how carefully she has dressed, Sarah's clothes give her away as a country girl. Nobody likes ignorant newcomers from the South, and local native blacks are particularly condescending. Her Louisiana accent is so thick that some might have a hard time understanding her; others, even if they do, may pretend not to.

St. Louis is trying to become a more palatable place to Easterners, but when Ida B. Wells comes here to give an anti-lynching lecture she will pronounce the city too Southern in attitude to care. And with more Irish and German immigrants pouring in every day, the situation is not likely to improve. The Irish despise black people. So do the Germans, and they control the unions and keep a lock on skilled positions. Though the immigrants don't exactly work together, they do what they can separately to keep black people down.

Young Sarah senses enough of this to be wary. She will, of course, continue to be a laundress, mainly because essentially it's her only choice. St. Louis, no different from Vicksburg, offers black men and women jobs only at the lowest levels of salary, mobility and educational opportunities. Few skills are required, fewer still accumulated. The year Sarah arrives, a survey of children in St. Louis public schools shows that out of a total of 5,079 Negro parents, 22.6 percent are laundresses and 46.2 percent are laborers. As late as 1920, nationwide, 80 percent of African-American women not tilling the soil will still be maids, cooks or washerwomen.

Black people aren't allowed to work in department stores or factories except as janitors or stokers. In the tobacco mills, roasting leaves is the only job available to black men, a process whose brutally high temperatures will—so it's thought—cause a white man to pass out; Continental Tobacco employs about 350 Negroes in this capacity. At the White Lead Company, to make paint, lead plates are placed in ceramic pots of vinegar, then covered with stable manure for several months, the manure accelerating the reaction between the lead and the vinegar. Black men are hired to pile the horse droppings on and, later, to shovel them off again.

"Nigger work," the Germans call it, and to a great extent, they're in charge. Prosperous families won't allow black women in their homes, even to do the lowest kind of scut work, and they specifically advertise in the classifieds for good German girls.

In no case are the races allowed to mix on the job, and union rules ban black men from membership. Negro bricklayers, carpenters and plumbers can get work only from Negro contractors, of which there's only one in all of St. Louis.

Therefore, a black man working as a porter, a waiter or a barber is either lucky, smart or both. Alexander and the other Breedloves may be poor, but they are hardly lacking in self-respect, drive and intelligence.

Eventually Sarah McWilliams comes to Eleventh Street and turns right, to number 616. She knows not to enter by the front door—the barbershop is a white man's establishment—and goes around to the back, knocks and waits for somebody to open the door.

Let's say it's James, since he works for Alexander and is probably younger. He's six years older than Sarah, and since he says he was born in Mississippi, the possibility exists that they have met there, and are cousins, or even brother and sister. If they have, he would talk about how much she had grown and marvel at her baby; even if they haven't, they would certainly exchange warm family greetings. Still, since her presence in the barbershop is inappropriate, James will quickly direct her to where Alexander lives, given that he's her most established kin and perhaps one who even prepares his relatives for new, more respectable professions.

Four blocks west of the barbershop, Sarah turns west on Fifteenth, then walks seven blocks, past a line of two-story tenements interspersed with a lard refinery, soap works and streetcar stables, to get to Alexander's building. His apartment is small and dark, with a stove in the middle of the one room serving as kitchen and sleeping room. For modesty's sake she will hang an improvised curtain around the space she and Lelia will occupy. That privacy and delicacy promote virtue is a lesson widely taught by the African-American educator Anna Julia Cooper. Through newspapers and church networks, Cooper is telling black women that they are responsible for the management of the race's "primal lights and shadows" by working within the domestic sphere to uplift the family and improve the moral fiber of the race. Sarah hangs the curtain.

There is no electricity and no running water. The only homes likely to have indoor plumbing—one out of five—are almost certainly located west of downtown, where rich people have built gated enclaves for themselves, complete with paved streets and a private sewer line that empties into La Rivière des Pères. Most tenement dwellers use a makeshift toilet called the school sink—a long board with seat holes cut out, laid over a trench—or else outhouses. Landlords are supposed to regularly flush the trenches into the nearest open sewer, but they rarely do. Such civic inequities find ready support in the Gilded Age philosophy, with Andrew Carnegie, for example, cheering poverty for siring greatness and millionaires for being the heroes who produce employment, the food of the human race.

Behind Alexander's building, she can see the school sink, the trainyards and the factories. Only blocks away, hard by the railroad terminals, the steam presses of the St. Louis Compress Company smash five-hundred-pound bales of cotton into nine-inch pancakes, and Mill Creek residents sleep by this fierce rhythm—the machine taking a beastly breath, whooshing down, clanking, whooshing up, taking another breath, whoosh, clank. In this city there is no escaping the crowds or the noise and stink and constant motion.

If Sarah goes out back for a cup of water, she will pump a muddy burst followed by a thin, silty stream. Officials assure people that this water is healthful, restorative and even helps prevent disease, but she has to swipe her tongue across her teeth to loosen the grit.

Perhaps she can find work at one of the commercial laundries until she gets money together for tubs and boiling pots, but if she has to work away from home, who will care for Lelia? She will have to find St. Paul's AME Church right away or hope that Rev. Rucks is arriving shortly. Maybe somebody at the church will know an established laundress she can hire out to or she can find work as a washwoman in white people's homes. In a rich, modern city like St. Louis, some people even own their own washing machines, mangles and wringers. The newfangled, gasoline-powered washers heat up on their own, so there's no need for boiling pots, and the ringers come with white rubber rolls that squeeze the water out without tearing the clothes. In the white people's houses, she can take the baby with her. But she might have to cook in a restaurant while Lelia is sleeping, or she could go back to being a maid, maybe in one of those hotels being built downtown.

Sarah Breedlove McWilliams is twenty years old and has no clue what will happen next. Alone again, she had not realized how dark a city could be, with so little sky and the sunlight tamped down to a pale shimmer.

She keeps names of important people in mind. *Moses Dickson. Charleton Tandy. George Vashon. James Milton Turner. Holly Grove Baptist. St. Paul's AME. Pleasant Green Baptist. Rev. Rucks.* They will help her. They have to. *James, Alexander, Samara, Solomon.*

She unpacks.

Standing Up to Say So

Many stories claim that Madam Walker's sense of charity began when she read an article in the *St. Louis Post-Dispatch* about a blind colored man responsible for the care and financial support of his disabled sister, and then conducted a fund-raising campaign among the membership of St. Paul's. Some of the stories reverse the situation, making the man disabled and the sister blind, but we won't quibble.

Newspapers print sad stories everyday, and usually we read them, cluck in despair and then go on with our lives, but occasionally one takes hold. During the hard Jim Crow days, for striving African-Americans "uplift" was the order of the day, emphasized by educators and ministers alike, and perhaps this particular story led Sarah to understand that in order to maintain her integrity and move up from where she was, she needed to acknowledge that, hard as her life was, others had it worse. This story also suggests that by the time she gets to St. Louis—or soon afterwards—Sarah knows how to read. Looking for work, then, she can cover the classifieds in all the newspapers, including the white *Post-Dispatch* and *Globe Democrat,* whose ads make no bones about race: "A neat white girl to assist in light housework." "A good colored woman." "Small German girl." "A neat white girl to assist in light housework and care of baby."

She might have read about the struggling brother and sister at the end of a particularly hard day doing laundry. And even if she's now traveling out to the suburbs to use white people's fancy new machines—the Acme, say, which claims to do all the work itself and to be easy enough for a child to use—she still has to load the wash, then stand there moving the handles back and forth, pushing and pulling, agitating the water and watching the clothes move against the paddles as the hot water froths and bubbles. And nothing in the Acme ads describes how heavy the clothes are when you lift them sopping wet out of the tub, wringing that load out before moving on to the next, your feet worn out and your back on fire.

Maybe it is on one of those bone-exhausted nights that Sarah McWilliams reads the story about the man and his sister and wakes up the next morning still thinking about them, finally deciding that she can shake loose from this tragedy only by doing something to help. And so on the following Sunday, probably during the afternoon Sunday-school session, Sarah takes another leap. When the teacher offers other people in the class a chance to speak, she pulls herself together and raises her hand.

Sunday school has separate classes for men, women and children. At a time when women practically never speak in public, this makes her task somewhat simpler. But for a Southern country girl and wash-woman, to address a class at St. Paul's is no small thing.

Called upon, she rises. Imagine the whispering, the wonder, the nervous coughing. The knotted fist of her own heart.

Women are just beginning to work within church structures, and missionary societies—the Mite Missionary is one—are forming under the auspices of the AME and other denominations. The idea of a women's organization with no man to run it is new and startling, a notion most men think is doomed to silliness and failure; but the women who lead the missionary societies are determined, and they are all married, and their husbands are more often than not bishops, deacons, or a pastor. Yet Sarah McWilliams is widow of a nobody and a washwoman. Why should refined ladies pay attention?

She moves to the front of the room and, despite her anticipatory jitters, when she faces her Sunday-school class, she finds herself strangely at ease, as if born to public speaking.

Here we ought to look forward a moment to 1912 when, as Madam C. J. Walker, Sarah faces down Booker T. Washington at his own National Negro Business League convention. By then, the extremely influential Washington has toured the Walker Company factory and offices, and he knows that Madame has made a large donation to the YMCA building fund. But he refuses to acknowledge her, even briefly, and so from her place in the audience, before hundreds of conferees, Madam Walker stands and interrupts the proceedings to confront the man affectionately known as the Wizard, the Doctor and the Chief.

"Surely," she begins, "you are not going to shut the door in my face . . . ," and she goes on to chronicle her rise from the cotton fields and to list her current assets and the number of black people she employs. Her impromptu confrontation first shocks the delegates, but in the end they reward her with a healthy round of applause. Washington does not respond, but in 1913 Madam C. J. Walker is a featured speaker at this convention.

Over two decades earlier, at St. Paul's, Sarah McWilliams confronts her Sunday-school class with a copy of the *St. Louis Post-Dispatch*.

She may read the story aloud or else tell it in her own words— probably the latter. She might not yet feel sufficiently confident about her reading to do it in public. And since crying is considered a woman's weakness, if her voice starts to break, she takes hold.

Madam Walker will be famous as an orator whose magisterial presence and resonant voice command attention to the last row. For young men in the nineteenth century, oratory is a highly valued skill that can pave the way to renown, as it did for Booker T. Washington. But women don't make speeches, and they don't debate. The articulate and richly voiced among them become elocutionists, who are envied and respected, their classes and private instruction advertised in every city newspaper, black or white. They often call themselves Madame, and in photographs or drawings are dressed in highest fashion, as regal as Victoria Regina.

And here is Sarah McWilliams standing up in front of women she has only just met, older women, *wives,* wearing the fine kind of clothes she washes and irons. These are the "representative colored women" of St. Louis and they belong not to just any church but to St. Paul's, the most elite black church in the city. But once she goes up in front of them, she's relaxed and adroit and—as she couldn't have known until afterwards—unsurprised that they're listening. Performers of all kinds—actors, singers, politicians—speak of this moment, when in their youth they are called onstage and feel immediately at home there, even as their audience is astounded at their skill. But Sarah's inauguration is more complex, with so many prejudices and preferences running against her. On top of everything else, she's dark-skinned. And while such young African-American women as Ida B. Wells, Mary McLeod Bethune, Anna Julia Cooper, Hallie Q. Brown and Mary Church Terrell will soon become even more famous by writing essays and editorials, giving speeches and lectures, running national organizations, women's clubs and schools, they all have skin color like milk with a little tea in it. Their noses are aquiline, and some have soft hair. But when this dark-skinned, swamp-accented washwoman winds up her story and the plate gets passed, money is collected. Sarah McWilliams's first public moment is a triumph.

That night in her narrow cot behind the curtain, curled up beside Lelia, she's bound to be stark awake and unable to close her eyes, for all the possibilities buzzing in her head. What else might she do? How far might she go?

Does she deliver the money herself? In all likelihood she hands it over to the minister, Rev. E. T. Cottman, because she knows it's expected and that it will bring her more favor within the church than if she took the credit and even though she would've enjoyed seeing the blind man's face when he was presented with the money.

All in good time.

September 22

On Sunday a Catholic city shuts down. Factories and the compress doze, the smog lifts; even locals turn into rubes, craning their necks in the empty streets to catch sight of a sliver of blue jagging through the smoke and specks. Along Targee and in the Chestnut Valley, saloons are open but the hum is hushed and the beat drags. The racetrack's closed, and the backroom crap games have temporarily shut down. Only the staunchest sweet men linger outside on the sidewalk, leaning against doorframes in embroidered silk shirts, waiting for nightfall, when the gamblers and sports greet one another like long lost friends and women change back into jet-beaded silk and piano players roll garters up their shirtsleeves and flex their fingers. And farther downtown, the levee gins on, since the rousties have no intention of giving up Saturday night until they either pass out or are called back to heaving and lifting come Monday morning, still drunk, before daylight.

Sundays, Sarah McWilliams rises slowly. Her weeks are long and Saturday a regular workday, but one day of late sleeping doesn't help and church service sends its own alarm, so she's up and behind the curtain, using the tin can they'd have set aside for a chamber pot. And Lelia? The wakened child stirs but will not rise. Swaddled in a mother's unconditional love, sucking on sleep like a forbidden sweet, she will leave her bed when she chooses, or when her mother's tone turns serious.

St. Paul's is only a block and a half away. Sarah will attend the morning service at ten-thirty and Sunday school at three, but the evening service is probably out. A religious woman would not like working at all on the Sabbath; but as the Bible says, when the ox is in the ditch, the main necessity is getting him out, and as far as she can tell the ox simply will not keep to the road, however hard she drives him, however many hours she puts in during the week. "If I have accomplished anything in life it is because I have been willing to work hard," Madam Walker tells a reporter from the *New York Times Magazine,* who has come to ask about the mansion she's building on the Hudson River. "I never started anything doubtingly and I have always believed in keeping at things with a vim." And it is with vim, and will, that she prepares for church behind a homemade curtain in a St. Louis tenement.

She might set some food on the fire while she dresses, perhaps a pot of greens and meat for the midday meal. As far back as she can remember, everyone she knew, no matter how poor, had Sunday's main meal after the morning service, and everybody ate well.

The AME denomination is both proud of its reputation as the church of choice for "the best people of the race" and demanding as well of its members, expecting their full attention from opening prayer to closing benediction. White Methodism, from which it sprang, emphasizes pietism, as does the written philosophy of AME, but African-Americans have worldly needs that cannot be ignored; so like other black churches it addresses matters not only spiritual but also political, financial, educational, moral and cultural. And in return, the church requires equal commitment from its congregation, and whatever the occasion—whether business meeting, musicale or funeral—their steadfast presence is mandatory.

Getting there isn't easy. The next job is dressing Lelia—bloomers, polished shoes, hat, gloves—rushing, as always, to get ready, to get there, to get finished, to get back, to start over. The child—thoroughly spoiled by now—wants to eat, stay home, go back to bed; but her mother will brook no resistance. They have to save time for hair. She plunks Lelia down and unwraps the threads she tied the night before, then divides her daughter's scalp into squares and begins the painful process of dragging a comb through each section. When Lelia squeals, her mother clamps a hard hand on the top of her head and keeps yanking, using grease for a tamer. This is routine stuff. "Born unruly" is how hairdresser and Walker Company employee Margaret Joyner will describe black women's hair in those days.

The main Sunday service is never short, but nobody expects or even wants it to be, and by the time people get home and have their meal, it's nearly time to go back for Sunday school. But today is not just any Sunday. For African-Americans, next to Christmas, September 22 is the most important day of the year.

"The Negro Fourth of July," one black man calls September 22, the date when in 1862 Abraham Lincoln sat his cabinet down and read them the Emancipation Proclamation and then announced his non-negotiable resolve to put the document into effect. Later that same day, the presidential seal was placed on the proclamation, and he signed it. The next morning, newspapers all over the country announced that the slaves in the states remaining in rebellion would be free as of January 1, 1863.

Emancipation Day is celebrated in most states either on the twenty-second or twenty-third or on January 1. In Washington, D.C., April 16 is the chosen date, because that's when, in 1862, slavery was abolished in the District of Columbia by an act of Congress. In the Northeast, and in certain parts of Missouri and Tennessee, the event is commemorated in early August, some think because slavery was abolished in the British Empire on August 1, 1834, marking "the first dawn of freedom for the colored race." This year the Negroes of St. Louis have shifted their celebration from early August to September 22, despite the coincidence that this is also German-American Day. If the Germans are hostile to begin with, consider how patriotism and beer might fire up their mood. But in 1889 the twenty-second falls on a Sunday, so Emancipation festivities will be delayed until the next day. The opening parade usually sets off at the crack of dawn but won't commence until noon this year, so that children can watch during their lunch hour. Though preachers and principals had requested that colored children be excused for the day, the school board—which includes many Germans—refused.

If, when she arrived two summers ago, Sarah McWilliams moved in with the barber Alexander, then in all probability she's still there. It would be nice to think she'd done well enough to have set up on her own, but for a destitute widow with laundry to do and a little girl to raise that would mean moving into an Irish enclave on Clabber Alley or Wildcat Chute, and nothing in Sarah Breedlove's past or future suggests that she'd degrade herself and her child in that way. Breedloves don't accept life submissively or assume that what little they can afford is all they'll ever get. They are a proud family that, when circumstances become untenable, moves on. By 1896, when *Plessy v. Ferguson* sanctions separate-but-equal accommodations and gives the nod to Jim Crow, they will have abandoned St. Louis.

Solomon no longer waits tables, having become the third barber in the family. He is living with Alexander on Eleventh Street, and soon will move with him to a new address, as Alexander shepherds the younger members of his family from place to place until they can set up on their own. Samara, Owen's "widow," lives only a few blocks away from Alexander and Solomon. James isn't listed in the 1889 city directory, but the year before, he and Samara lived together, and may still.

Another new arrival, Kate Breedlove, had first lived two doors down from James and Samara, but she has moved to a rougher part of town, only two blocks from the notorious Bucket of Blood saloon. And in a few years, the directory will refer to *her* as yet another widow of Owen Breedlove. How many African-American men of that name can live and die in the same city at the same time? People hide from history's grasp, move from one apartment, home or city to the next, take new names, fall through the cracks. Kate Breedlove's name shows up a couple of times and then disappears, and as we shall see, Samara's husband, Owen, has remarried and is starting a new family of daughters in Albuquerque.

In September 1889, Solomon's twenty and Sarah's not much older. Let's say the two get on. And we know he's living with Alexander, so why not Sarah as well? By 1894 Alexander will have died of an intestinal ailment, but perhaps in 1889 they're all together: Solomon, Sarah, Lelia, Mary and Alexander as well as any other children they might have. And now Sarah's settled in fully—working, paying rent, doing her share of the housekeeping and cooking, finding behind the curtain a refuge against intrusion, indelicacy and hopelessness.

R ev. E. T. Cottman has been minister at St. Paul's for only a year, but he's young and a powerful speaker and is already conducting a fund-raising drive. He's determined to build a new church away from downtown, in the neighborhood around Lawton and Leffingwell favored by upstanding black educators, ministers and postal workers. He's after a new building, not another white discard; brick, like that of the Baptists. Indeed, within a year he will have sold the current St. Paul's and preside over the laying of a new one's cornerstone. Soon afterwards, he will leave, and the congregation will be hounded by the debt he incurred for another two decades.

Rev. Cottman will not fail to mention the fund drive today, but the main focus of his message—and of the Sunday-school program at three—will be emancipation. Many times over, Lincoln and the proclamation will be compared to Moses and the tablets. "I, Abraham Lincoln, president of the United States," will be recited, again and again, often by children who have committed it to memory, "do order and declare that all persons held as slaves within said designated states, and parts of states, are, and henceforward forever shall be, free."

Alexander Breedlove is still cutting hair on Eleventh Street near Washington in the shop he used to share with John Welker. The location is excellent, close to hotels and office buildings full of prominent white men, and everybody knows this stretch of Eleventh is practically a barbershop colony, where a white man can choose from any number of tonsorial establishments.

Barbershops also serve as news agents for African-American weeklies, including the *Indianapolis Freeman,* which the National Negro Protective Alliance of St. Louis has labeled "the truest Negro journal in the world," and which will play an important role in the life of Madam C. J. Walker. At the base of its editorial page is a list of addresses where the paper can be purchased in various cities; in St. Louis, three of the agents are barbers on Eleventh Street, one of whom is Alexander Breedlove.

St. Louis has its own Negro newspaper, the *Advance,* but it's poorly financed and enjoys neither the respect nor the circulation of the *Freeman,* which in these years calls itself "An Illustrated Colored Weekly" and features numerous photographs and drawings and is probably the leading African-American newspaper in the West. Alexander almost certainly brings copies home, where Sarah can use them to work on her reading and widen her view of the world.

A recent issue of the *Freeman* featured a two-part political cartoon. In the left panel, an immaculately dressed barber stands decisively in front of his chair, facing a black man nattily attired in a dark cutaway coat, striped trousers, polished shoes and top hat. Caption: "Intelligent Colored Minister—Can I get a shave, sir? Colored Barber—No sir. We don't keep black soap." In the right-hand panel, a white customer has come into the same shop, dressed in patched, ragged clothes and a torn straw hat, his beard scraggly and hair unkempt. The barber stands to the side of the chair, shaking out the starched cloth cover to crisp it. Caption: "Colored Barber—Right this way, Boss." Beneath the diptych is the moral: "The colored people can not hope to obliterate color prejudice so long as they discriminate against themselves."

The editor of the *Freeman,* George Knox, runs a barbershop himself. In 1913, Sarah will be photographed standing next to him on the front steps of the newly opened Indianapolis YMCA, along with Booker T. Washington and five local businessmen, all equally prominent, each looking extremely elegant, Madam Walker the only woman among them.

Studying the *Freeman,* does Sarah imagine herself in Indianapolis, as she had called up the vision of St. Louis in 1879? Even now, in 1889, is she dreaming of moving on? And more importantly, is she paying special attention to the ads, noting marketing techniques that she herself will use someday: the currently popular before-and-after layout, the increasing use of mail order and selling agents, those personal messages ("Is your hair falling out?") from a company's proprietor?

Madam Walker will confess that by the time she began using Wonderful Hair Grower in 1905, she had been having trouble with her hair—dandruff, dryness and, worst of all, alopecia areata, or bald spots—for at least fifteen years. She lays most of the blame on poor diet and stress, but she was also probably experimenting with concoctions to tame her natural frizz so that she could style it however she wished. Most of these substances contain either sulfur or lye, often mixed with capsicum—red pepper, or cayenne—and anybody who's ever rubbed an eye with a cayenne-tipped finger knows how badly it can burn. Sarah McWilliams lives with barbers, who know about hair and experiment with various treatments to make it look sharp, always discussing new theories. And while she stands there ironing and listening, watching the creases in a shirtwaist flatten, she might well wonder if some other kind of heated instruments might not do the same thing to hair.

Not that she doesn't wish to look black, as white women and some African-Americans often suggest. She just wants options, to be able to fix herself up however she pleases and in the styles of her time. Not simply for vanity but also for purposes of confidence and practicality, so when she walks into a room she knows and likes how she looks, and can put that one small worry aside and go on to what *is* important.

When Booker T. Washington was barely into his teens, a white woman he worked for observed that he "was ever restless, uneasy, as if knowing that contentment would mean inaction." And later in his life, a former pupil told him, "You always appeared to be looking for something in the far distant future." It's not hard to see that same look in Sarah's eyes as she fills the Breedlove apartment with the stink of sulfur and fumes of cayenne and packets of strange dark herbs bought from door-to-door root peddlers. Or when, on her way to work, she has to cover embarrassing bald spots with a scarf or a hat. In African-American and hair-care history, the name Rebecca Elliott rarely surfaces. But she is among the first to produce products for that market, and by the late 1880s is on the cutting edge of marketing, using repetitive slogans and illustrations to reach a national audience, promoting and selling her goods by mail order and through her own agents. Her strategies also include "selling the category," as advertising people call the idea of creating a need for the product before pushing a particular brand. To bring high-mindedness to the table, she quotes Scripture—"The glory of woman is her hair"—and then implies that her hair system can help a woman achieve biblical glory.

Rebecca Elliott's System of French Hair Care is based in Indianapolis, where her offices are alongside those of George Knox at the *Freeman.* Her connection with Knox, featured in her advertisements, gives her product a useful imprimatur. Unlike most businesswomen of the time, she does not call herself Miss, Mrs. or Madame. She is—remarkably—R. E. Elliott, Originator and Sole Proprietor. R. E. Elliott lectures and gives demonstrations across the country, actively engaged in what will come to be known as the direct-sales technique, used by such companies as Avon and Mary Kay.

Elliott herself is featured in some advertisements. Stern of demeanor, her shoulders and chest draped in lace, her neck banded by a velvet ribbon, the Anglo-featured entrepreneur offers trips and cash prizes to agents whose orders "foot up the greatest amount of cash," and states that her formulas have been in her family for thirty-five years and were handed down to her as an heirloom. But she cannot, she declares, be responsible for other, "spurious preparations . . . imposed upon the public by outside parties."

To push her Nutritive Pomade, which is said to render hair glossy, pliant and healthy, Elliott uses a drawing of a woman (before) with pom-poms of hair front and back and a frizz across the crown, then another (after) of the same woman transformed, with a cascade of waves lying docile and lustrous on her forehead, a smooth crown, hair wound into a tight chignon in back. "Soft, straight and silky," the caption promises. Elliott's Medicated Hair Grower is said to promote hair growth, even on the temples, where "the hair is ofttimes scant." She also sells a product called Cheveline, "the only true and original preparation that has ever been placed on the market for straightening the hair." The value of Cheveline is reflected in its price, a whopping ten dollars when most of her other formulas sell for around a dollar.

Meantime, postage has gone down to a penny a pound, and as a direct result the Montgomery Ward catalogue is up to 416 pages. Believing that mail order is the future, Richard W. Sears, the founder of Sears, Roebuck and Co., starts test-selling watches by mail and COD at rock-bottom prices and will soon develop the "Send No Money!" campaign that rockets his company past his more conservative competitor. Department stores like John Wanamaker's and R. H. Macy's have entered the game as well, and their catalogues feature fine china, imported clocks, corsets and baby clothes. By now, farmers can buy almost anything by mail: a windmill, feed cutter, thresher, even a dog-powered butter churn.

But word must be spread, through advertisements in magazines and newspapers. And Rebecca Elliott's "scheme" will become standard practice when Madam Walker and her biggest competitor, Annie Turnbo, enter the market some fifteen years in the future.

The *Freeman* runs a regular column called "Prosperous Afro Americans," which reports that in a community of five thousand in Denver, many are lawyers and doctors, some worth as much as $50,000. Is Sarah keeping tabs on possibilities and markets, perhaps looking beyond St. Louis to Indianapolis and Denver? She has family connections in the West, the Owen Breedlove who once lived in St. Louis and now is in Albuquerque.

And the Mound City is not only racially prejudiced, it is struggling. The economic depression has not abated, and farmers are taking the brunt of it. In rural southwestern Missouri, to vent their frustration, night riders called Bald Knobbers are burning, whipping, killing and dispensing vengeance. And since two of St. Louis's industries are cotton and wheat processing, the city also feels the pinch. As life tightens up, social and class distinctions grow sharper among and within all ethnic groups: light-colored local blacks hold migrants from the Deep South in greater disdain; Germans bear down on everybody; Irishmen focus on the only people below them on the socioeconomic ladder.

S arah's life has found its rhythm. Work, Lelia, work, church. Rehang the curtain in another dark, smelly apartment with a school sink and muddy drinking water. Work, Lelia, work, church, move.

But on this particular day she takes her daughter firmly by the hand and explains to her what emancipation meant to her grandparents, and how important it was for Minerva and Owen Breedlove to farm their own land.

W hen the Democrat Grover Cleveland was elected president in 1884, Emancipation Day took on even greater importance. Five years later, even though a Republican, Benjamin Harrison, is in the White House, black people are still feeling jittery. Cleveland and his young wife are waiting to run again. Frances Cleveland's at once pretty—with pale skin some say she eats arsenic to maintain—and fiercely ambitious. While packing to leave the White House, she asked a servant to take care of the furniture because in four years she and Mr. Cleveland would be back.

In general, African-Americans support Harrison. After all, he fought side by side with Sherman in Atlanta, and praised the Negro's progress at his inauguration. But nine months into his term, he hasn't done anything except make speeches and shilly-shally, even after the unspeakable violence against black people during the 1888 elections. When Henry Cabot Lodge introduces a bill requiring supervision of federal elections and one senator after another gets up to spout racist objections, Harrison makes no response. Even if he favors the bill, as reported, he does nothing to press it through—even when Senator George Vest of Missouri attributes, admiringly, the white man's dominance to the "tiger blood in his veins which cannot be tamed or chained."

Later today, John Roy Lynch, a former Mississippi congressman currently holding appointive office in Washington, will make an Emancipation Day speech in Springfield, Illinois, Abraham Lincoln's hometown. Asked why violence against Negroes seems even more prevalent now than during Cleveland's obviously bigoted administration, he will suggest that it is because with Harrison's election, "colored people took courage again, and made some feeble efforts to exercise their rights and in proportion with those efforts the outrages upon them . . . have increased." Lynch ends the interview with the ironic observation that if the colored man in the South forgoes the exercise of his rights altogether, he can have peace.

Arriving at St. Paul's, Sarah settles her daughter beside her in a pew. Church is in every way a sanctuary, the only time a washerwoman has off. On Friday, she will have finished the previous week's work by delivering clean, ironed laundry. In 1912, she will tell Booker T. Washington that she promoted herself from the cotton fields to the washtub to the kitchen, so on Saturday perhaps she washes dishes or cooks at a café or hotel. Tomorrow she will make her collections earlier than usual, or else do some tonight. She's hoping to get downtown in time to watch the parade and the decoration of the Ulysses S. Grant statue at Lucas Market, then go to the festivities at Central Turner Hall; but between work, Lelia and notoriously undependable trolleys, she'll once again be rushing, pressed for time.

The familiar music rises and the congregation stands, joining in song. Rev. Cottman reads the Emancipation Proclamation and might describe that great day in 1862 as one newspaper does, as "the first peep of the sun over the hills . . . certain assurance that day has come as a full view of the orb." He will offer gratitude and thanksgiving to the throne of God for the priceless boon of his people's liberation. He will announce the schedule of events for the following day, and stress that his congregation is *expected* to participate in every facet of the celebration—just as they are expected to contribute to the building fund.

Monday's festivities go off without a hitch, and even a white newspaper is moved to call it an exceptional event. The parade kicks off at noon with lines of carriages bearing ward clubs, lodges, officers of societies and tabernacles, pastors and their guests, and even though the school board has refused to give black children the day off, large groups of them move through the crowd, trying to find a good viewing spot. There are floats on which ride the young ladies representing all the states and territories in the country. The Goddess of Liberty rides in a special four-horse carriage with uniformed Knights of Pythias marching alongside as honor guard. Boys and men from the ward clubs walk the parade route carrying banners

that proclaim: OPEN THE WORKSHOP TO OUR BOYS . . .
WE ARE FOR PRINCIPLES, NOT MEN . . . VIRTUE IS THE
ONLY TRUE NOBILITY . . . WE EXPECT NOTHING FROM
THOSE WHO PROMISE MUCH.

Afterwards, some two thousand people gather at Central Turner
Hall, where the band plays "Nearer My God to Thee." There are
many speeches. Ministers pray, choirs sing. The nighttime activities,
for which a twenty-five-cent admission fee is charged, start around
nine o'clock, when there are more speeches, some by state and city
officials, including the governor of Missouri, all of whom, of course,
are white men. A resolution decrying the outrages on Negroes in the
South is adopted. The cantata is sung by a women's chorus, the Goddess of Liberty is crowned and then the floor is cleared for dancing.

The festivities continue until the early hours of the morning, by
which time Sarah McWilliams is sound asleep in preparation for an
abbreviated and especially hectic wash week. But her exhaustion has
been earned, worthily, happily, on a great, great day, and perhaps she
dreams.

Telling the 1917 *New York Times* reporter about this period of her
life, Madam Walker will say, "When, a little more than twelve years ago,
I was a washerwoman, I was considered a good washerwoman and
laundress. I am proud of that fact. At times I also did cooking, but
work as I would, I seldom could make more than $1.50 a day."

The reporter has come to ask Madam Walker about Villa Lewaro,
the mansion she is building in Irvington Village, the most exclusive
part of Westchester County and a stone's throw from where the Rockefellers and the Tiffanys have country homes. Because its construction
is not finished, the interview takes place at her exquisitely refurbished
three-story brownstone in Harlem, on 136th Street just west of the
broad and bustling Lenox Avenue. The drawing room where Madame
entertains guests is decorated in pale blue and gold, and protected
from harsh sunlight by velvet curtains drawn securely in the fashion of
the day, making the interior an ornate, shady refuge.

And here she speaks of her emergence as what another reporter will
call "the principal figure in the negro colony of upper New York" and
"the richest negress in New York." She has real estate investments in
Indiana, Michigan, Los Angeles and Oklahoma and has bought and
sold an apartment building on Central Park West. Before resolving to
build her own mansion, she considered buying Bishop's Court, the
home of the late AME bishop William B. Derrick in Flushing, Long

Island, but decided against it, partly because the house was surrounded by tenements, inhabited mostly by poor Irish.

After Madame concludes the interview, her secretary, "a young man of pleasing address," takes the reporter on a tour of the Harlem house. Lelia's ivory-colored bedroom is decorated in the style of Louis XVI, at a cost of $4,500, whereas Madame's is primarily mahogany. The dining room is furnished in walnut and cut glass. The kitchen is "dazzling with white tiles, walls and floor." And then her chauffeur drives the reporter north to Irvington in one of her automobiles to see the new house.

Her sleep in Mill Creek is jangled, filled with snores and groans and the strangled night cries of too many people in too little space. Outside, the cotton compress whooshes up and clanks down. On the streets there is laughter and shouting and perhaps a gunshot. Trains coming and going. A policeman's sharp whistle. And behind the nonstop noise of pleasure and rancor and commerce is always music, the offbeat strangeness of the new songs. To Sarah, ragtime doesn't make sense, doesn't soothe or uplift as do marches or church music. Instead, it jabs at the night and tickles the nerves. When one piano player takes a break, there is another to slide in his place. Would-be sleepers rise from their beds. They have to get up and . . . they don't know what. Dance, run wild, *something*.

But an exhausted washwoman sleeps through anything, while her daughter, unawares, absorbs the wildness of the cockeyed beat.

They lie there, fire and ice. Inseparable.

Quaker Oats

Breaking into the darkness of Sarah's early years in St. Louis is one lucky flash: the opening of the St. Louis Colored Orphans' Home. Located nearby on land purchased after the Civil War by black veterans who'd intended to build a soldiers' home there, it provides shelter not only to children without parents, sometimes called "drifts," but also to "half-orphans," who stay at the orphanage on a by-the-day basis in an early version of day care, and whose working mothers can petition the city for a monthly five-dollar stipend to pay for the service.

This being a time when the most popular schoolbook, *McGuffey's Eclectic Reader,* characterizes prolonged poverty as a sign of God's disapproval and wealth as an outward sign of inner salvation, no government assistance is forthcoming. Drifts wander the streets, panhandle, go hungry, get sick. Most die young. Booker T. Washington insists on the validity of the bootstrap philosophy and tells his people if they aren't progressing it's their own fault, and plenty of others agree. Individualism is sacrosanct, and self-help the answer to every problem.

In St. Louis, the Harper Union, the colored chapter of the Women's Christian Temperance Union, approached the People's Theater in 1887 about holding a benefit performance to raise money for the proposed orphanage. The theater manager, however, regretted to inform the women that while they were welcome to rent the theater, colored people would as usual be relegated to the galleries, even if not a single white person attended and all the good downstairs seats remained empty. The benefit didn't take place.

In general, St. Louis doesn't enact laws blatantly hostile to blacks because they constitute only 6 percent of the population and live mostly in the river wards and downtown fringes where no respectable whites want to be. The attitude—now and for some decades to come—is one of "patient endurance toward an inferior but necessary creature."

But the Harper Union keeps at it, and in 1889 the St. Louis Colored Orphans' Home opens. Sarah may or may not have been granted the $5 monthly stipend, but in any case, Lelia becomes a half-orphan while her mother works, and in March 1890 she is escorted to her first day at school by Maggie Rector, matron of the home and one of its founders. The Walker Company will acknowledge this in years to come, saying that Madame was so hard up in St. Louis that she was forced to leave her daughter in an orphanage. And in 1911, when she incorporates her business, one of the first charities she gives money to is the St. Louis Colored Orphans' Home, which she also includes in her will, citing kindnesses shown to her daughter there.

There are twelve schools for black children in St. Louis at this time, each intended originally for white students, then passed down, when their families moved to better neighborhoods or the building became run-down. Unlike their white counterparts, the colored schools are known by numbers—Colored School No. 1 and so on. For twelve years, the Colored Education Association has been petitioning for the right to name their schools for prominent Negroes, such as Crispus Attucks, reportedly among the first to be killed by the British during the Boston Massacre; Benjamin Banneker, astronomer and architect; and Toussaint L'Ouverture, leader of the Haitian revolution. But the school board rejects their requests, countering year after year with the names of white men, from Wendell Phillips to Ulysses S. Grant, who have "distinguished themselves in the cause of the colored race."

When Lelia McWilliams enters the first grade in 1890, St. Louis is home to the High School for Colored Students, the only one of its kind west of the Mississippi. A twelve-room building where white children once attended elementary school, the school is unfortunately located in plain view of a prison. Students on their way to school can glimpse corpses awaiting identification, and on execution days the scaffold's in plain view; so it's no wonder the school board relocated the elementary school. The high school has no library, no gym, no assembly room, no band, no clubs, but since St. Louis public libraries have never been officially segregated, its principal, Oscar Minor War-ing, is quick to take advantage. A gifted linguist who speaks fluent German, Latin, French, Spanish and Italian, he personally organizes reading clubs, and through them he creates his own library.

That same year, the Board of Education finally approves the request of the Colored Education Association: Colored School No. 1 becomes Dumas Elementary, for the French writer Alexandre Dumas; Colored School No. 2 is renamed Dessalines for General Jean-Jacques Dessalines, who took control of the Haitian army after Toussaint L'Ouverture's death; the High School for Colored Students becomes Sumner High, for the Massachusetts abolitionist Charles Sumner. Other elementary schools will honor Banneker, L'Ouverture and Martin Delany, the emigrationist and hero of the Underground Railroad.

In March 1890, Lelia starts school at the former Colored School No. 2, which by then has become Dessalines. She is not yet five years old and might have qualified for kindergarten but goes straight into first grade instead, perhaps because of her size and bearing and maybe because her birthday is less than three months away.

S olomon and Alexander Breedlove have moved again, but only a few blocks. While no Sarah McWilliams is listed, a "Sallie" lives only a half-block away from them at 1316 Wash Street, which is only one block north of the third Breedlove barber, James. Samara is still on Eleventh Street. Seven other McWilliamses are in St. Louis, but most of them are men and none live in a black neighborhood.

Is Sarah starting over yet again, as Sallie, and if so, why? Or is this just a printer's error? We will let those questions linger, for the name Sallie McWilliams will recur.

O n her way to work, Sarah drops Lelia off at the orphanage, confident that Maggie Rector will see to it that she gets to school on time and in the afternoon is safely returned to the orphanage, where she waits for her mother to fetch her.

St. Louis is known for its rigid school system. To bridge the gap between what educators call indulgent family life and responsible citizenship, kindergarten is offered to every child, whether black or white, rich or poor. And since the educators think of children as small savages, early schooling is a kind of boot camp. Games are played not for fun but to develop specific skills. Rote learning is required, and all schools are expected to teach the same set of lessons, so that if the superintendant pops in, he can easily rate the performance of both students and teachers. When reciting, kindergartners stand side by side in a precise line, and the punishment for a small wayward foot is instantaneous and harsh. Thus will children learn punctuality, silence, self-control, cooperation and obedience. They learn to read from *McGuffey's Eclectic Reader,* whose lessons tend to sermonize. One ends by declaring the main business of government to be the protection of private property. Few girls are pictured in the reader and, of course, no black children at all.

As an adult, Lelia will scoff at social rules that require the repression of instinct in favor of manners and decorum. As a child she must chafe under these Teutonic strictures. According to her friends, the woman they knew as A'Lelia Walker was endlessly stylish and engaging, but not overly bright. And if her mother lectured her on how lucky she was to be going to school at all, she would have responded, in time-honored daughterly fashion, by rebelling.

The Supreme Court has not yet given its approval of what will be called separate-but-equal public accommodations, but education in St. Louis exemplifies the philosophy. Black teachers receive half the white salary; black schools are relocated often, and none are newly constructed. Still, the bootstrappers would admonish, Lelia's learning, and at least her teachers are of the same race. But "still" is an amelioration, and time and again people use "at least"s to convince themselves that things are either better than before or not as bad as they could be.

In all likelihood, Sarah's no longer washing at home—for one reason, because she and the barbers move almost every year and her heavy equipment isn't easy to transport. Also, most of her customers live west of downtown, where the water is less polluted, and their own gasoline-powered, heated washing machines can get the clothes cleaner. They might also own a self-heating iron, and custom irons for particular articles. There's an advantage, too, to keeping their precious linens and silks at home, rather than having them carried off in a basket.

Streetcar lines run only in daylight hours between the business district and the western suburbs. Sarah and other domestic workers ride the cars from downtown out west to gated islands of luxury like Compton Heights and Vandeventer Place; winters, when days are short, she has to start home by four. The ride takes thirty, forty minutes, sometimes more. As the streetcar rocks from side to side, Sarah might well ignore the brimming hostility from across the aisle to concentrate on other things.

When she sees the poster featuring the smiling man with white hair wearing a long black coat and a wide black hat and buckles on his shoes, she knows he's selling Quaker Oats, even if she doesn't know anything about his religion. (She might've heard of the Quakers' anti-slavery stand, but what would that have to do with cereal, or anything else?) A woman with the soul of a seller understands quickly that advertising is built on trust, and that even though the Quaker in the black hat isn't a real person, just a picture on a cardboard box, people are being asked to trust his word and buy what he recommends. Other streetcar placards advertise Pearline soap ("Use Pearline and take the drudgery away from housework") and Schilling tea in Perfection cans. Sapolio has begun its Spotless Town bus-card campaign, featuring a sequence of cartoon-type drawings of a dirtless, stain-free town dedicated to this scouring cleanser.

Advertisements appear everywhere: in newspapers and magazines, plastered on wagons and tree trunks, hanging in retail stores. Full-color trade cards come packaged in boxes of tea, coffee and soap, and drummers also distribute them among retailers to pass along to their customers. Each package of Arbuckle Brothers coffee contains one of a fifty-card set, on themes of animals and American history. Some have movable parts, such as the one for Kirkman's borax soap, which features a laughing girl in a bathtub. The girl is blond, with bright red lips, and she is covering her breasts with her arms. When you pull at her head the rest of her body pops tantalizingly up, covered from waist to thighs by a card hawking Kirkman's for laundry and bathroom use. Having a child gives a loving mother something to look forward to, and Sarah may gather these cards for Lelia to play with, like paper dolls.

Advertisements are as big a part of Sarah's life as smokestacks and hot water. The *St. Louis Post-Dispatch* daily runs an ad for Rough on Dirt soap and ironing powder: "The most inexperienced girl can, with Rough on Dirt, do as nice washing and ironing as . . . in any laundry." And Gold Dust soap, formerly used only by millionaires, supposedly, is now within the reach of all, manufactured right there in St. Louis.

The *Ladies' Home Journal* carries ads for womb supporters, bile flushers and products like Magnolia Balm, which promises to lighten skin color. Designed primarily for Caucasian complexions, these whiteners contain arsenic, lead or bismuth; when those substances react with the natural sulfur in the air, they sometimes have an effect opposite to the one desired, and turn a woman's skin as yellow as, according to one beauty manual, a dingy mulatto. Now and again, perhaps Sarah spends a little more money on the Octagon brand of soap, and if she saves up twenty-five of the trademarked Octagon wrappers, she can send off for a free book—*Through the Looking Glass* or *Jane Eyre*—that Lelia might read one day.

By now the idea of "trust" is old news to Sarah McWilliams. She knows how to make her reputation work for her, and help her compete with other washwomen, the big commercial laundries and the pesky Chinese. (The latter have their own schemes, slips of paper with Chinese characters that each week bear the name of a different god, goddess or celestial object—sun, moon, heaven or stars.) Sarah presents herself in such a way that her customers are convinced of her uprightness. "Have the goods," the mail-order genius Richard Sears will advise. "Then advertise." She has the know-how and the reputation, and these are her goods. And, as she learned in Vicksburg, her best advertisement is herself: how she looks and speaks, the authority in her voice assuring moneyed white ladies that she is trustworthy, a hard worker, the real thing.

When she goes to the suburbs she dresses simply, corseted, belted and buttoned to the chin, and in the warm months might wear a light-colored cotton print dress, unbustled now that those bothersome embellishments have gone out of style. Finishing out her ensemble are black leather side-button boots and maybe a leghorn hat or a small poke bonnet crowned with decorative ribbons. Her spine is straight, her head high.

In its instruction manuals, the Madam C. J. Walker Company advises its agents to wear spotless clothing, use zinc to control body odors, keep their fingernails clean and, if the salon is in the home, to dress not in a housecoat but as if going to a job downtown. Its workers are required to wear starched white blouses and dark skirts and conduct themselves like ladies at all times.

On the way home, Sarah is too tired to pay the placards much attention. The walk from the streetcar stop to the orphanage is not far, but blocks quickly turn into miles after a long day. Lelia's often crotchety and wild with restlessness as they walk home. But "home" is a fluid concept. They're always moving, the Breedloves; they find some better place, or the landlord wants them out for his own reasons. One of them lives with this one, then that one, and relationships grow or falter; but though the patterns change, the circle never tears.

In 1892 Grover Cleveland defeats Benjamin Harrison, fulfilling the promise of Frances Cleveland to return to the White House and confirming the fears of African-Americans. Migration talk heats up again. An AME bishop says that he doesn't see "any manhood future in the country for the Negro," and concludes that Africa is a place where his people will gain status and respect. Since Harrison has nothing to lose, in his final speech to the nation—by which time the black man is all but completely disfranchised in the South—he calls for legislation against lynching. When he opened the Oklahoma Territory for settlement in 1889, at least seven thousand African-Americans went there, and some are still going; there is talk of turning the whole of Oklahoma into a Negro colony. But droves of black Southerners are moving to cities: Chicago, Indianapolis, St. Louis.

In 1893, W. C. Handy brings his Lauzetta Quartet from Birmingham to St. Louis only to find the city overrun with musicians. Every pool hall and saloon has its piano player and resident composer, and others waiting their turn. Tom Turpin returns from a gold-mining trip out West and opens his own place not far from Sarah. The Rosebud Café has a gambling parlor in back, a bordello upstairs and, on the street level, a saloon where ragtime pianists like Scott Joplin, Joe Jordan and Turpin himself pound away. If a musician has to look for other work, Handy says, he will find St. Louis a brutal place of violence and need. He describes people sleeping on the levee by the thousands, and policemen routinely bopping them awake with sharp blows of their nightsticks. Pool halls stay open all night, but anyone who tries to sleep there will get the same rough treatment.

The economy grows even more depressed. Ellis Island opens and immigrants flood into the country, twenty million over the next sixty years. Historian Rayford Logan calls the last decade of the nineteenth century the "nadir of the Negro's status in American society." In South Carolina, the white demagogue Ben "Pitchfork" Tillman is elected governor, and declares in his inaugural speech that all men are not, in fact, created equal. And in 1900, when he's elected senator, he will tell a congressional committee that in South Carolina, "we have done our level

best. We stuffed ballot boxes. We shot them. We are not ashamed. . . ."
Since the Southern mind cannot bear the sight of a successful Negro, in
Memphis three respected grocers are taken away and killed. After-
wards, other whites return to shoot every black man in sight.

This outrage provokes—on May 31, 1892—a National Day of
Lamentation, Prayer and Fasting. Protest meetings are conducted in a
number of cities, including Chicago, where an estimated one thousand
people show up. Services are held in black churches throughout St.
Louis, and later in the afternoon a mass meeting draws some fifteen
hundred black citizens to St. Paul's, to hear speeches by James Milton
Turner, Moses Dickson, and George Vashon.

Late in her life, Madam Walker will take part in a silent anti-lynching
parade down Fifth Avenue, and will join a delegation to the White
House in the same cause. One of her final acts of charity is the sponsorship of an anti-lynching campaign, announced at a meeting at
Carnegie Hall. In 1892, Sarah McWilliams has little time and no
money for any cause, but she certainly would know about the meeting
on the thirty-first, and perhaps she attends, in hopes of catching a
glimpse of the truly remarkable Ida B. Wells, who, having given up her
career in print journalism, is making speeches all over the world, giving—as the *Indianapolis Freeman* puts it—"sledge hammer blows to
lynching." She is unmarried and rides the railroads alone, even won a
discrimination suit against one company—only to lose on appeal.
Wells is educated, light-skinned, speaks beautifully, has never dipped
her hands into a tub of scalding water laced with skin-blistering soap
and chemicals. But she is from Holly Springs, Mississippi, and is
probably the most inspiring role model Sarah McWilliams might find.

Other dissatisfactions and platforms for change are announced at
meetings in St. Louis. The People's Party, a populist movement primarily of farmers, holds its convention there, and chooses Tom Watson, a
white Georgian, as its presidential candidate. A black man is seated
next to him on the dais. Populists preach an equality of want, and Watson tells them that skin color should make no difference. "You are kept
apart," he declares, "so that you may be separately fleeced." African-
Americans, he says, are "in the ditch just like we are," and he promises
that the People's Party will wipe out the color line forever.

Not long afterwards, in Homestead, Pennsylvania, a bloody steelworkers' strike ends with sixteen union men dead and thirty-five others
charged with treason. But despite the nation's deepening despair, in
Chicago, the long-anticipated Columbian Exposition opens on sched-

ule to showcase America's amazing technological discoveries. Francis Bellamy writes the Pledge of Allegiance so that schoolchildren across the U.S. can recite it together and thus participate in the dedication of the fair. From Washington, President Cleveland presses a button that sends electricity coursing through the 686-acre fairgrounds, and as the band plays "America the Beautiful," the fair lights up.

A huge national event, it is heavily covered in the black press. Still, many object to the fact that only one day is set aside for "distinguished race visitors," Colored-American (Negro) Day, and are offended by a *Puck* magazine illustration in which big-lipped, spear-wielding Africans and black Americans in band uniforms line up for watermelon at "darkies' day at the fair."

In the midway, people can gawk at unfortunates in the "freak show" or amble through a tropical forest or an African village, where "real savages" from Dahomey prance about in thrillingly few clothes. For a dime they can watch the immigrant Erich Weiss, now known as Harry Houdini, Handcuff King and Escape Artist, do twenty-eight sleight-of-hand, rope-tie and card tricks. "The Creole Show" features sixteen beautiful Negro singing and dancing girls. Fahreda Mahzar—"Little Egypt"—introduces the belly dance to America, and her sinuous movements and dark skin drive people crazy with thoughts of foreign places where sin takes place day and night. And every day, at the nearby band shell, John Philip Sousa plays "After the Ball," the first song in history to sell a million copies. Scott Joplin also plays, and the music that has been stirring the soul of St. Louis for years finally gains a name that white people can call it by, even as black musicians and composers are moving beyond ragtime. The exposition is an ideal occasion to launch new products. Richard Sears unveils his first five-hundred-page catalogue and his company's new slogan, "The Cheapest Supply House on Earth" (only a few words and one large concept removed from Montgomery Ward's "The Cheapest Cash Supply House in America"). Other new items include *McClure's* magazine and an onsite demonstration of Aunt Jemima pancake mix, with a former slave named Nancy Green cast in the title role. Dressed in kerchief and kitchen-slave garb, during the course of the fair she flips thousands of pancakes while telling jolly stories about the good ole days in Dixie. At the close of the fair, she receives a medal for showmanship and is proclaimed the Pancake Queen. Nancy Green then quits her job as a domestic, and for the rest of her life will travel the country as Aunt Jemima, flipping pancakes and spinning yarns.

Science is another theme and it, too, supports the stereotyping of the races. In living ethnological shows, a "sliding scale of humanity" puts Teutons and Celts at the top, Muhammadans and Asians somewhere in the middle; then, according to one observer, "we descend to the savage races, the African of Dahomey and the North American Indian, each of which has its place."

The Columbian Exposition will last a little over a year and cost the city of Chicago $27,245,566.90. During its run, in April 1893, Henry Ford displays the first gasoline-powered automobile, and in May the stock market collapses, triggering the failure of 8,000 businesses and 360 banks across the country. The Chicago exposition closes in October in an atmosphere of hopelessness and panic, the day after the mayor is shot and killed.

Back in February of that same year, in Paris, Texas, after a black man was hauled from jail and lynched, the mob fought over "souvenir" bones, teeth and hair. This is only one of 118 lynchings reported in the year of 1893.

Marriage

By the beginning of 1894, Sarah McWilliams is living at 1615 Linden Street, not far from the dividing line between Mill Creek Valley and the Grand Street suburbs, but still in the all-night saloon district. If any other Breedloves are with her, they've either skipped the official counting or were overlooked. The father figure of the family, Alexander, has been dead since April of the year before. In a few years, "Mary Breedlove Widow of Alexander" will appear in the directory, but we don't know where she is now—perhaps living with Sarah and Lelia. The itinerant James has moved again, closer still to the barbershop, where he might have taken Alexander's place. There's no trace of Solomon or Samara—whose nine-year-old daughter, Onee, is presumably Owen's child—but by 1900 Samara will have married a minister, Walter Harris.

The family adjusts to new circumstances, realigns, holds on.

The economic depression has deepened further, and a large segment of the industrial workforce is unemployed. But the government makes no move to help, and when wealthy businessman Jacob Cox marches with his fifteen hundred supporters from Missouri to Washington, D.C., to publicize the need for an unemployment bill, he is arrested in the nation's capital for walking on the grass. When the Chicago railroad magnate George Pullman cuts his workers' pay without reducing their rents and then refuses to bargain, a strike is called. Faced with the prospect of widespread railroad shutdowns, President Cleveland threatens to send in troops. The governor of Illinois protests this, and the mayor warns that if troops arrive, Chicago will be "spattered with blood, brains, hair, hide, livers and lights," but

Cleveland doesn't relent. Some fourteen thousand police, state militia and Army soldiers are mustered, and at that point the workers' mood turns ugly. They burn the railyard and seventy Pullman cars, but when the air clears the strike is broken and so is the union, with thirty-four members dead. "The workers," George Pullman declares, "have nothing to do with the amount of wages they shall receive."

Many millionaires and others agree. As Henry Demarest Lloyd writes in *Wealth Against Commonwealth,* dreams of wealth run so strong in the U.S. that no home is too poor to hope that "out of its fledglings one may grow the hooked claw that will make him a millionaire."

In such an atmosphere, an intelligent but destitute black woman might sit down and do some figuring. If what Sarah McWilliams makes in a day is the $1.50 she reported to the *New York Times,* and she averages that for six days of every week, she brings home a total of $468 a year. Deduct $8 a month for rent and $3 a week for food and she's left with $216 for fuel, medicine, transportation, clothing, church, bleach, bluing, soap and incidentals. If Sarah's great desire is to provide for her daughter what her own mother gave her— hope and a shot at a better life—this income won't support it. She can't work more hours or find a more lucrative job, because there aren't any.

What she can do is take a partner. Black men and women earn about the same daily wage, so if she meets a man who makes the same $1.50, their net income would increase by approximately a third.

In 1919, about six months after Madam C. J. Walker's death, a man named John Davis claims, in a back-page article in the *Indianapolis News,* to be her surviving husband. They married in St. Louis, he says, and were never officially divorced, even though she subsequently married again.

John Davis? Company accounts present only two husbands: Moses McWilliams, who died and made her a widow at twenty, and Charles J. Walker, who gave her a name and a "push." So who is John Davis?

In response to this article, Madame's business manager, Freeman Ransom, writes a letter to the *Indianapolis Recorder,* an African-American newspaper, acknowledging that a marriage between Madam Walker and a John H. Davis of St. Louis did in fact occur, but that a legal divorce had been subsequently granted Mrs. Davis because of her husband's failure to support and provide for her. Ransom asks the *Recorder* to ignore the story, "in justice to Madam C. J. Walker's memory" and "in consideration of the business relation" between the newspaper and the Walker Company. To further stave off the claim, he collects affidavits from two women who knew Sarah when she lived in St. Louis, friends who swear that not only was Davis unwilling to provide for his wife, he parceled out some of his wages to another woman. They also testify to Davis's habitual drunkenness and his violent behavior toward Sarah, characterizing him as "fussy, mean and dangerous." But Freeman Ransom's request is honored and none of this will make the papers in Indianapolis, so the story remains under wraps and John Davis continues to go unacknowledged in Walker Company literature.

Several men of this name live in the Mill Creek Valley in 1894, and one of them, at 1607 Gay Street, is only a block away from Sarah, on Linden. The John Davis Sarah marries turns out to work at a steam laundry, where it's possible Sarah might also work. Or, living that close together, they might meet in the neighborhood, or at St. Paul's.

Washers stand over boiling tubs all day, poking at laundry with long wooden sticks. They lift the sticks up high and stab them into the water to move the clothes and linens through the soap. This takes strength, and steam-laundry owners consider it a job suitable only for blacks, given the enervating heat. The men wrap rags around their heads to keep sweat from running into their eyes, and their hands are perpetually red and raw from overflow and spills. There is a porter called John Davis in St. Louis in 1890, and a janitor of that name in 1891. Laundry work would be a step down from either of those jobs, but work is scarce in 1894 and laid-off men accept whatever work they can find.

The hopelessness and low wages take their toll. Humiliation and shame may push John Davis over the edge, and he turns on the people nearest him, his family. Like Jesse Powell, he becomes dangerous. He lashes out. Sarah has been here before.

B ut as to the marriage itself: At the St. Louis City Hall, an archivist escorted me downstairs to where the older records are kept. There were no microfilm machines. As in Vicksburg, indexes to marriage licenses are handwritten, in large Morocco red bound ledgers that rest on rollers. They are dusty, heavy, unwieldy and thrilling to handle. Looking for a McWilliams bride who married between 1890 and 1910, we found only one, in the 1894 book. We flipped to the record itself, which showed that on August 11, John Davis indeed married a woman named McWilliams, but her given name was Sallie and there was no small *c* beside their names to indicate they were colored. A search for Sarah Breedlove revealed nothing at all. When I sighed in frustration over these inconsistencies, the archivist gave me a look. "I've done this for a long time," she said. "I don't believe in coincidence." Busy clerks make mistakes, she reminded me, and I should keep my eye on the main event. If there are enough facts to support a theory and the only contradiction is possibly a bureaucratic slip-up, the wisest course is to consider the theory valid, because odds are, it is. And sometimes you can verify it otherwise. She retrieved the actual records, and returned and pulled the original marriage application and certificate from a large envelope.

In Application #57142 for License to Marry, John Davis of DeSoto, Missouri, states his desire to procure a license to marry Miss Sallie McWilliams of 1517 Linden Street. He swears that he is twenty-five years old, and Miss McWilliams that she is twenty-six. Both vow that they are single and unmarried.

John Davis's signature is labored and shaky, the hand of a man uncomfortable wielding a pen, whereas the bride's is a little more relaxed, the *S* and *M* and *W* practiced and even slightly swirly. The license was issued the same day as the application, and the wedding itself was conducted by the justice of the peace in his office.

These documents fail to resolve three problems: the bride's given name, the "Miss" instead of "Mrs.," and the missing "c." The archivist asked if Sarah McWilliams was light-skinned, perhaps enough to pass for white. No, I said, she was dark; and while I didn't know about him, the 1900 census had him as "B" for black, not "M" for mulatto. Well, she said with some finality, because of a Missouri prohibition against mixed marriages, you only have to prove the race of one to know the other. I left City Hall with copies of the application and marriage license.

Back to numbers, and the city directory. The street address given by Sallie McWilliams, 1517 Linden, is in the heart of Mill Creek Valley, one block from Sarah McWilliams's home as of January 1894, eight blocks from the new location of Sumner High School and about five from the colored orphanage. An African-American neighborhood. And in January 1895, four months after John Davis marries Sallie McWilliams, a "John Davis, Washer" is living at that same address on Linden. And in the 1900 U.S. Census report, John Davis is the husband of Sarah, stepfather of Lelia McWilliams, his profession "Steam Laundry" and his skin color "Black."

About the missing "c," I take the archivist's point. As for other Breedloves, the city directory has James living—the January after John and Sallie's marriage—at "rear 1517 Lucas." How can it be that both John Davis and James Breedlove are at an address coincidentally numbered 1517? It takes a magnifying glass and a good map to see that in 1895 Linden twists, jags and then, between Fifteenth and Sixteenth Streets, actually *becomes* Lucas Avenue, continuing on toward Grand.

Unlike the census, city directories are commercial operations. The people who compile the information are hired freelance by private companies, so their main priority might be just getting the job done quickly. James Breedlove either lived with John Davis and Sarah Breedlove Davis and the enumerator confused the spot where Linden becomes Lucas, or else he lived virtually at their back door in a building that faced in the other direction. Odds are the Davises, Lelia and James are all together, as they will be in 1898.

Tote up these facts and figures and the smart bet is that Miss Sallie McWilliams has been our own Sarah all along. And if we go back to 1890 to locate her at 1316 Wash Street, she's exactly one block away from Solomon and Alexander Breedlove, and another half-block from James. And in 1919, when Sarah's friends sign the affidavit confirming John Davis's loutish behavior toward her, they call her Sallie. Perhaps that's her nickname. Or maybe Sarah McWilliams is hiding out from a creditor, or trying out another name—a rather lighthearted and fanciful one, unbiblical and saucy—dropping both the "Mrs." and the "Sarah" to mark the start of a new life. If so, what does this name switch tell us about her? That she is a fluid individual who can adapt to changing circumstances and call herself whatever she likes in order to transcend the probability of doom laid on her head at birth by biology and culture both. That however granite-like her persona became in later years, in these difficult, pre-Madame times she did what she had to. That she's a woman who has been called Winnie, Sarah, Sallie, then Sarah again. And she isn't done yet.

In 1895, Frederick Douglass dies of a heart attack at his home, attended by his white wife, at the age of seventy-eight. Ida B. Wells—after publishing a pamphlet, *Red Record,* that lists all known lynchings in 1893-94—gets married in Chicago. She will again make waves the following year by taking her four-month-old son to the first meeting of the National Association of Colored Women, breast-feeding him between lectures and meetings.

And in September, Booker T. Washington gives the keynote speech at the Cotton States Exposition in Atlanta. In a move destined to catapult him into the chair of leadership vacated by Douglass, he preaches accommodation, patience, industry and racial solidarity. He assures his large and mostly white audience that the black man does not wish to socialize interracially; he wants only the chance to improve himself by learning a trade, and to become a civilized human being. For his race, Washington suggests, it is far better to earn a dollar working in a factory than to spend it on grand opera. This message is received with applause and cheers. Black people pay less attention to the thrust of his speech than to the fact that a man born a slave is addressing rich, important white men; and so they cheer as well, and many of them weep with pride.

In an instant, Booker T. Washington becomes the most famous black man in America. And his speech—known afterwards as the Atlanta Compromise—is one of those rare events that can be exactly pointed to as a moment when perceptions of things changed and history shifted slightly. Grover Cleveland himself visits the Negro Building at the Atlanta exposition. White philanthropists desirous of supporting "safe" Negro progress shower Washington with money. In the near future he will receive an honorary degree from Harvard and be the guest of Queen Victoria at Windsor Castle.

Some black people object to his accommodationist stance, and W. E. B. DuBois says that Booker T. Washington is leading the way backward. But with racial discrimination and violence daily on the increase, many people have lost hope and have come to believe that following Washington's advice may make them invisible, or at the very least, shield them from white men's notice.

The last five years of the nineteenth century are filled with extraordinary events and puzzling paradoxes. Scott Joplin's music is published, and his "Maple Leaf Rag" is a huge hit. People all over the country are listening to ragtime, and Negro musicals are introduced on Broadway. DuBois earns the first Ph.D. given by Harvard to an African-American.

Yet in May 1896, after a light-skinned black man named Homer Plessy is forced from a "white" railway coach in Louisiana, by a vote of seven to one the U.S. Supreme Court upholds the constitutionality of state laws providing separate but equal accommodations for the Negro. In his dissent, Justice John Marshall Harlan writes, "There is in this country no superior, dominant, ruling class of citizens. . . . The thin disguise of equal accommodations for passengers in railroad coaches will not mislead anyone nor atone for the wrong this day done."

In those same five years, an estimated 490 African-Americans are lynched, including Sam Hose, who is mutilated and burned to death in Newman, Georgia, while two thousand white citizens watch, some having come on a special excursion train from Atlanta.

Enumeration

On Lelia McWilliams's fifteenth birthday, June 6, 1900, a white man named Charles S. Lively traipses around Mill Creek Valley carrying a ledger sheet and a pen, going in and out of houses. One tenement he will visit, at 2113 Walnut, includes four separate apartments, a configuration prevalent in this neighborhood. Though not luxurious, the buildings are sturdy and serviceable. "Apartment houses" are defined as having indoor plumbing—more common since about 1890—whereas "tenements" offer facilities on a communal basis or not at all.

Living in one of the apartments at 2113 Walnut is the family of John Davis. In the 1900 directory he is called John L. Davis; Madam Walker's business manager, Freeman Ransom, in his letter to the *Recorder,* refers to him as John H.; and in the Charles Lively census report, he is listed simply as John, born in Missouri in 1872. The birthplace of his parents is unknown. His occupation is steam laundry. He can read and write and is designated head of the family.

His wife, Sarah, has shaved a year off her age—giving her birthdate as December 1868, perhaps because her husband is younger—or maybe somebody else provided this information and got it wrong. Or maybe she simply didn't know for sure. No occupation is given but she, too, can read and write. Her parents were born in Louisiana. John and Sarah Davis have been married for six years. To the question "Mother of how many children?" the answer is "Three." And to "Number of those children living?" the response is "One." The surviving child is listed as Lelia McWilliams, stepchild—all kinship being defined in relation to the head of household—and her age is stated erroneously as fourteen (on this, her fifteenth birthday), and she is further said to have attended school for nine months the previous year, and can read and write. Her place of birth is given as Louisiana.

So there they are: John, Sarah and Lelia, in the 12th U.S. Report, St. Louis, ED 215, page 36, line 5. And while it's thrilling to locate them officially curled up together in one of the National Archives' hundreds of thousands of microfilm spools, caveat emptor. There are surprises and discrepancies; but again, caveat emptor. African-Americans have no particular reason to set much store by a survey conducted by a government that refuses to protect their lives, rights or livelihoods. Some census takers doubled as tax collectors, and so people are wary. They can switch "facts" if it suits their purposes, or get them wrong if they're uninformed or simply uninterested.

And while it's important to know that somebody told Charles Lively that Lelia was born in Louisiana, there's no telling who did— possibly John Davis, at home drinking while his wife worked and he'd just assumed his stepdaughter was born in Louisiana or never bothered to ask. Another possibility is that the young Sarah McWilliams did in fact cross the river in 1885 when her time came, so that the women who had helped raise her could assist at the birth of her child. Maybe Lelia was born, like her mother, in Delta. The 1910 census has Lelia born in Louisiana; the 1920, Missouri.

As to the deceased children, it seems utterly implausible that a family member would make up such a sad statistic, so I think we have to accept it as factual. And such a lonely piece of information as well. Two dead babies. How long did they live, how did they die, where were they buried? Odds are they were born in St. Louis and John Davis was their father. If the births had occurred in Vicksburg, some thirteen to fifteen years prior to this census, I can't imagine why Sarah Davis would mention them now at all, and I doubt she would've told John Davis or, possibly, even Lelia. At the turn of the century, 20 percent of African-American newborns die before they are a year old, from birthing complications, disease and infection. This is double the infant mortality rate for all other Americans. Birthing complications include the health and strength of the mother. The life of a washwoman—the long hours of hard physical labor, the constant worrying, the poor diet—can only increase the possibility of miscarriage or a stillborn or frail child. Hospitals are segregated, and there won't be one for Negroes in St. Louis until 1899, which is probably too late for Sarah's babies. Besides, how could she pay for medical care?

But Charles Lively is not finished. He counts another resident at 2113 Walnut, a forty-two-year-old widow named Ester Smith. Listed as "Sister-in-law" to John Davis, she was born in 1858 in Louisiana, where her parents also were born. She is a servant, unemployed for six months.

This returns us to the Madison Parish courthouse, whose files record a marriage in June 1881 between Amos Smith and "Easter" Breedlove. The rites were performed by Rev. Curtis Pollard, who had married Louvenia Breedlove and Jesse Powell in 1872, and on whose church steps little Winnie Breedlove had played. If Ester and "Easter" Breedlove are one and the same—as surely they are—then she was twenty-three or -four when she married Amos Smith in 1881. She might be Sarah's older sister or her sister-in-law, since by that age she might well have had a previous marriage by which she became a Breedlove.

Whatever the precise relation, she is certainly kin to Sarah. Her St. Louis paper trail begins in the 1897 city directory, when an Amos Smith, Driver, shows up at 1228 Aubert. The following year, Esther (Widow of Amos) is living at 2142 Walnut, with John H. Davis, Washer, and the barber James Breedlove. (Though Sarah Davis is not mentioned, she and Lelia are certainly there as well.) Two years later, those six people are still living together on Walnut Street, just across the street and down the block. James is now married to Hettie Martin, but by the time Mr. Lively comes calling, he and his wife have moved out.

With the Breedlove clan, Delta, Louisiana, has come to St. Louis. They arrive seeking one another out, and no family member is not taken in.

The century turns on a Monday, but the newspapers are more concerned with the Philippines, Cuba and Puerto Rico: small island countries America is considering snatching. Rudyard Kipling's poem defining imperialism as the White Man's Burden has been reprinted so often it has become hackneyed within a year of publication. In the *Louisville Courier-Journal*, the editor offers a cruder version of the same notion: "But the riff-raff," he writes of these potential new citizens, "Lord, the riff-raff: injun, nigger, beggar-man, thief." And then he quotes a popular verse: " 'Both mongrel, puppy, whelp and hound, / And cur of low degree.' "

All African-American newspapers are weeklies, and most come out on Saturday. On December 30, they don't make much of the crossover into the 1900s. The *Indianapolis Freeman* runs its usual front-page photograph of a "Representative Colored Man." An editorial by a minister predicts better things ahead for the black man, but that's it.

A washwoman might not have time to think millennial thoughts or to consider the racist implications of imperialism. She might take closer note of the leading fashion, the shirtwaist, which, although once considered a fad, all the magazines and newspapers announce is here to stay. Women, says the *Ladies' Home Journal*, like the comfort and the mannishness. Tucked firmly into a cinch-waisted skirt, a shirtwaist provides an immediately neat appearance and exchanges the formerly popular look of flutter and frippery for one that is more practical and serious. The washwoman's point of view is more down to earth: a "waist" is far easier to wash, starch and iron than a long, complicated wrapper or dress.

By January of 1901, Sarah is listed in the city directory on her own, as Sarah M. Davis, and she is living much farther to the west, on Locust Street. In his petition to the court after Madam Walker's death, John Davis will claim that his wife deserted him in 1903, but the greater probability is, she has already moved out; the marriage is over and once again the woman born Sarah Breedlove is alone.

She will stay at 3141 Locust for another three years, move one last time, then leave St. Louis altogether. Within a year of her departure she will live with Charles J. Walker, whose name Sarah Breedlove will take and keep for good, and on it found an empire.

Lelia

Between 1894 and 1900, Lelia attends at least two other elementary schools: L'Ouverture and probably Dumas. Despite the constant uproar and trouble at home, her attendance during the 1898–99 school year is admirable, with only six days missed the entire year. But between November 1899 and June 1900 she shows up for only twenty-three days of classes, a stunningly poor record which requires her to be readmitted six times. And while she does manage to graduate from L'Ouverture, Lelia doesn't do well enough on her entrance exam to be admitted to Sumner High, and so her time's her own, and with no supervision or a schedule, she's free to roam the streets while her mother works.

But Sarah's not having this option and so she seeks out a church-minded boarding school instead, far from the ragtime beat and other temptations of Market Street and the Chestnut Valley. And in 1902, after her mother pays $7.85 for one month's advance room and board, Lelia McWilliams is shipped off to Tennessee. Seventeen, over-indulged and feisty, she would not want to attend a school run by white Presbyterians who allow only religious music to be played and have condemned dancing and card playing as immoral and who frown upon even casual conversation with members of the opposite sex. But her mother has saved the money and her mind's made up and so Lelia goes.

Led, run and taught by white people, Knoxville College (or KC) was established in 1875 by the missionary board of the United Presbyterian Church as a normal—teaching—school for Negro children and young adults. Beyond religion, Knoxville has departments in medicine and the classics but also, following the Tuskegee model, offers classes in baking, farming, brickmaking, sewing and—strange irony—laundering. In photographs, students sit tall and stiff-necked as if to assure Presbyterians of their low tolerance for fun and high inclination toward moral rigor.

In the late 1890s and early 1900s, Knoxville College's weekly advertisement in the *St. Louis Palladium* features a drawing of the school and a description of its advantages, boasting of "self help offered through industrial departments," as well as steam-heated, electrified buildings, a location that is "healthful, convenient of access and beautiful" and an enrollment of 477 students from twenty-two states and Central America. KC has a reputation for teaching young men and women how to work, pray and become polished, a school to which an uneducated Negro laundress would feel justifiably proud to send her daughter. How Sarah Davis was able to save up the $7.85 per month, however, remains a mystery, and I have to believe she received help from one of the organizations she's involved with or possibly a family member—especially if Lelia's becoming unmanageable and a little wild. It is also odd how rarely Madam Walker mentioned Lelia's education and that she left nothing to the college in her will. I can only surmise that something happened to tick her off, permanently—possibly a matter involving money, her inability to pay. But then, maybe not.

Tennessee's a long state, west to east, and Knoxville, in a valley between the Cumberlands and the Appalachians, is closer in culture and geography to West Virginia than more sophisticated cities like Memphis and Nashville. When Tennessee seceded, this part of the state considered splitting off and forming its own state, as West Virginia did, not because of slavery or race but because of class. But geography won't explain why the newly arrived seventeen-year-old seventh grader stays at Knoxville College only a year, if that.

Within ten years of the day Lelia boards a train for East Tennessee, her mother will have died a wealthy woman and she herself will soon be known as A'Lelia Walker Joy Goddess of Harlem, famous for wild parties, wearing expensive clothes and jewelry, staying up all night with cross-dressers and beautiful light-skinned women, playing cards and drinking bathtub gin. And within twenty years, at forty-six, she will die from apoplexy, as Robert Burney had, but under very different circumstances, having keeled over in her fancy party clothes after eating a lobster washed down with a bottle of champagne. Her invitation-only funeral will be gate-crashed by hundreds of curiosity seekers, who crowd around her silver casket while a female nightclub quartet, the Four Bon Bons, sing "I Ain't Got Long to Stay, for My Lord Calls Me by the Thunder" and, later, Noël Coward's "I'll See You Again."

No, the future A'Lelia Walker might, under duress, go to the school known as KC, but she will neither like it there nor stay.

Annie Turnbo

In 1896 the Republicans are voted back in and on Valentine's Day in 1901, barely into his second term, President William H. McKinley boldly hosts a dance at the White House at which ragtime is played by an unnamed pianist of undetermined race. More than likely, Scott Joplin's "Maple Leaf Rag" is one of the night's most popular tunes, because it's been a hit for two years, and on the following day the *St. Louis Globe Democrat* takes its city to task for failing to recognize his talents.

In September of that same year, McKinley is shot by an assassin, and eight days later, he dies. Within weeks of taking office, Theodore Roosevelt invites *Dr.* Booker T. Washington (now that he's been awarded an honorary degree) to dine, and the two men sit down at table together. This is a groundbreaking occasion, for African-Americans a triumph and for many white people, an outrage. Then, two months later, at a Christmas party in the East Room, Roosevelt leads off the cakewalk a back-bending, high-stepping, strictly African-American dance dating back to slavery—and also executes a lively buck-and-wing while his guests clap "Juba," an African rhythm.

What does all this racial bonding signify? Anything at all?

No question, the Negro is becoming an acknowledged force in the performing arts, especially in New York City, where the African-American musical play is becoming a box-office mainstay, and in the fast, hot, midtown neighborhood called the Tenderloin there are hotels where black composers and actors, dancers and musicians gather to eat, drink, talk shop and celebrate. In his autobiography, *Along This Way,* James Weldon Johnson called the Marshall Hotel on West Fifty-third Street between Sixth and Seventh Avenues "the radiant point of the forces that cleared the way for the Negro on the New York stage."

However heartening, these enlivened sources of opportunity and visibility don't do much for the families of the 211 black Americans reported lynched in 1900–01.

By 1902, St. Louis is gearing up for its own World's Fair—designed to outshine Chicago's in every possible way—and anticipates that its salutary economic effect will reach as far into the future as anybody can imagine. Drawn by these shiny prognostications, a thirty-two-year-old African-American woman from Illinois steps into our story and into St. Louis from a ferryboat docked on the Mississippi. Wide-faced and bespectacled, stern of demeanor, she has medium-brown skin and the proud carriage of a proper church lady. Loaded down with suitcases and boxes, Annie Minerva Turnbo has a product she believes in and the drummer's instinct for what sells. By moving across the river, she intends to make her fortune as a self-employed beauty doctor, manufacturing and selling her own hair products. To introduce her preparations, she will go door-to-door giving demonstrations and talking up her products to women of her race.

Born in Metropolis, Illinois, in 1869, the tenth of eleven children, Turnbo was orphaned early and raised by an older sister in Peoria. And while she didn't lead a life of luxury, she enjoyed a number of advantages Sarah Breedlove missed out on. School, for one. A library. Parents whose lives had not been diminished by slavery. She even attended high school for a year, where, she says, she especially liked chemistry and applying the knowledge she gained gathering herbs with an "old woman relative of mine . . . an herb doctor [whose] mixtures fascinated me."

Her family is unhappy with her decision to go to St. Louis, not only because she's still unmarried, and by the vision of the time therefore adrift and incomplete, but also because hairdressing is considered indelicate, un-Christian and—if straightening's involved—a slam against the race. But Turnbo's been reading African-American newspaper reports that St. Louis's black community is vibrant and alive, in addition to which thousands more are already buying tickets for special excursion trains to the World's Fair, even though it won't open for another two years. By then she means to be fully established.

In St. Louis, she makes her way up the levee then west down Washington Street toward Mill Creek Valley, the neighborhood she will live in and sell to. And if we place a finger on Annie Turnbo's destination, we only have to inch down slightly to find where Sarah Davis lives.

All women spend a lot of time talking and thinking about hair, but for African-Americans styling is also political— leave it natural, curl it, straighten it, tie it up, wrap it, shape it in flat waves like a white person's?—and in Turnbo's time its care and grooming were mostly left to home remedies and casual practitioners. Every African-American neighborhood had its official hair wrapper, and in Annie Turnbo's she was it. By 1900, when she moved from Peoria to nearby Lovejoy—an all-Negro town named for the abolitionist newspaperman Elijah Lovejoy—Turnbo figured out that the harsh soaps, goose fat and meat drippings used to oil and straighten hair were doing long-term damage. Dandruff—seborrhea—and a form of psoriasis then called "tetter" caused severe itching and inflammation. Women were also burning their skin with straight lye and sulfur, causing the scalp to peel and flake and—as pores became clogged and hair follicles destroyed—their hair to fall out, sometimes permanently. After experimenting on herself, Turnbo "decided to set up a beauty parlor in Lovejoy, and use a liquid shampoo I had invented."

She rented the backroom of a tiny frame house for five dollars a month, taught Sunday school and worked in the temperance movement. Since personal appearances were the only form of advertisement she could come by, like a street pitchman selling wizard oil she went around town making speeches from a buggy and demonstrating her shampoo on herself: seeing is believing. Borrowing from Dr. Washington's lectures on the broom and the toothbrush as civilizing tools, she talked common sense to the women about cleanliness and hygiene. Clean scalps, she told them, encouraged clean bodies, and a better appearance meant greater business opportunities, higher social standing, more beautiful homes, and before you knew it, your male children were voting, your girl children reading. And she used herself as an example and invited women to come feel the softness of her hair, and even the skeptics, in time, "realized I was right."

By 1902, Turnbo had developed Wonderful Hair Grower, a sage-and-egg rinse meant to revitalize damaged follicles and allow new hair to grow back in. In all likelihood, the healing had as much to do with more frequent washing and what the women *weren't* putting on their heads as with this treatment. As word of mouth spread about Wonderful Hair Grower, Turnbo solicited testimonials and cooked up other products, many of which were for straightening hair, but Turnbo described them in terms of health and never used the word "kink." At night, with the help of her older sister, she stirred up pots of her concoctions. There was no inventory. She took orders, got the cash, brought the money home, bought the ingredients, made the product, delivered the goods as if off the shelf. For someone with neither cash nor backing, this system was her only choice, and once she perfected it she worked it day and night.

By the time Turnbo takes her herbs and magic fingers to St. Louis, it's busy building, paving and sanding. The newly elected mayor's idea of reform is to put a good face on for the fair. Sarah Davis's neighborhood, too, is wild with activity. When she walks over to Lindell to catch the streetcar, she finds it's blocked off and being paved; it's the most direct route to the park, and the planners are anxious that visitors should ride bumpless and clean. And a twelve-story hotel is under construction on the end of Locust closer to the river, very near to Alexander Breedlove's old barbershop, and fancy white people supposedly will stay there once it's finished.

World's Fairs almost by definition mark some historical event, and St. Louis's will commemorate Jefferson's 1803 Louisiana Purchase, which opened the West for settlement, starting here. To open and operate the fair, organizers have raised $15 million—the same amount Jefferson paid the French—in equal thirds from popular subscription, the city and the federal government. Missouri kicked in an extra million for a state building, and the U.S. Congress half again as much for a government exhibit.

By 1902, African-American newspapers weekly run drawings of buildings under construction. To make certain his race receives fair representation and participation, St. Louis educator and politician James Milton Turner has proposed a "Distinct Negro Exhibit and Negro Bureau" similar to that at the Cotton States Exposition in Atlanta in 1895, but organizers insist there is no need, because no racial discrimination will exist at the Louisiana Purchase Exposition. "Negroes," they announce officially, "will be considered American citizens." Despite the profound skepticism registered by Turner and other black leaders, the African-American *St. Louis Palladium* supports the decision, expecting the race to be "commendably represented."

In *McClure's* magazine, Lincoln Steffens calls St. Louis one of the country's worst-governed cities, due chiefly to the influence of the "Big Clinch," an elite corps of bankers, lawyers, merchants and manufacturers that now mounts its high horse and goes on a rampage—superficial to one extent or another—against corruption, filth, bad air and poor streetcar service. The mayor has also signed an ordinance declaring the emission of dense smoke to be a public nuisance, with fines assessed to businesses failing to comply with the new regulations. A chief inspector is appointed, and the larger factories install smoke-consuming devices. Within the year, inspectors report a 70 percent decline in smoke. Some days the sky makes an appearance, and at night, once the fair is open, its lights turn the western horizon pale silver.

After work, Sarah comes home to find pamphlets on her doorstep, one of which is called "Keep Our City Clean," asking citizens to tidy up vacant lots and testify against criminals. The Civic Improvement League declares a New St. Louis as its goal; and the Ladies' Sanitary Committee, a moral awakening inspired by freshly painted houses and unlittered door stoops. Women traipse around poor neighborhoods urging people to take pride and fix things up. While African-Americans are not consulted on slum cleanups, the organizers have appointed a pretty, proper and light-skinned teacher named Arsania Williams to help organize Negro Day—August 1—alongside the German, Irish and Italian Days.

As a result of the construction and preparations, there are more jobs for everybody, but black men are still given the work no one else will do at the same low wages, twenty to twenty-five cents an hour, while white laborers make three to four times more. Of the female African-American population, a full 90 percent works in personal and domestic service.

For the most part, black people aren't fretting about any of this. Like every other American, they're excited about the fair, curious to find out what new inventions and foods will be exhibited and which exotic foreigners will attend and perform. So when the ceremonial dedication of the grounds takes place in April of 1903, and twelve thousand uniformed troops march down rocky, unfinished Lindell Street, among the three hundred thousand to four hundred thousand cheering along the street are a great many African-Americans. After all, President Roosevelt—who lately won their favor by praising the bravery of black soldiers at San Juan Hill—is one of the speakers, and his theme this day is that expansion is a mark of American courage, tenacity, honesty and virility.

Annie Turnbo rents a four-room flat at 2223 Market Street on the block where James Breedlove lived the year before. Market, which leads straight to the new Union Station, has become a main thoroughfare. Directly across the street from Turnbo's apartment is Tom Turpin's famous Rosebud Café, and just down the street, the Pink Coat Bar, the Gem and the Newport Café, all offering twenty-four-hour pool, dice, drink, female companionship and ragtime piano. It's a loud, racy neighborhood, with trouble all night long, and you have to hand it to Annie Minerva Turnbo for sheer nerve. She's small-town and naive, and she's made up a product and a marketing strategy all on her own, and she's step-by-step figuring out what to do with what she has, as she goes along. No training in business, no husband to demonstrate her stability and moral correctness, no merchant tradition in her background and no connections she can tap for information, favors or guidance. For a woman to go into business for herself is shocking enough. A woman living in a dicey neighborhood, hawking hair oil door-to-door, puts both virtue and life at risk, especially when, according to conventional wisdom, the only women who knowingly use paints and fake beautifiers are the ones who as W. C. Handy said wear diamonds in their ears while "waiting for company in little plush parlors under gaslights."

No question, Annie Turnbo's on the leading edge. In 1902, there are twenty-plus African-American barbershops in St. Louis but only one hairdresser. To counteract the widespread disapproval, cosmetics companies have categorized all forms of beautification as a science, part of a general system of health and pride. And hairdressers—hoping to acquire an aura of responsible professionalism—are calling themselves "beauty culturists" or "hair culturists," while black practitioners stretch the point even farther and declare beautification an obligation essential to the uplift package.

A nd Sarah? She's on her own again, up on Locust Street trying to make more than $1.50 a day so that she can dress her daughter in a fashionable waist and skirt and nice shoes that actually fit her large feet. By now, the thirty-five-year-old single mother must have arrived at the moment she will describe to the reporter from the *New York Times* only fifteen years from now: "I was at my tubs one morning with a heavy wash before me. As I bent over the washboard and looked at my arms buried in soapsuds, I said to myself: 'What are you going to do when you grow old and your back gets stiff? Who is going to take care of your little girl? This set me to thinking, but with all my thinking I couldn't see how I, a poor washerwoman, was going to better my condition."

A ds for skin and hair products are beginning to appear with more frequency in African-American newspapers, cash in advance, by mail, no samples. Crane and Company claims that its wonderful face bleach will "turn the skin of a black or brown person four or five shades lighter" and that its straightening product will make hair grow long and straight and keep it from falling out. After selling to white customers for years, both Chicago Hair Pomade and Ozonized Ox Marrow realize they've been missing out on a large market and now advertise their hair-straightening products to black women. And Hartona adopts a hectoring tone: "The Negro need not complain any longer of black skin." All these products are manufactured and sold by white people.

At this time, only one mass-market cosmetics company in the country is run by a black person. Born to former slaves in Monroe, Louisiana, only sixty miles from Delta, Anthony Overton founded the Overton Hygienic Company in 1898 with the intention of selling spices and baking powder. But going door-to-door and listening to what women said, he quickly concluded they were far more interested in makeup than in cakes and cookies. And so he introduced the High-Brown Face Powder, which will "harmonize with the color and skin texture of the women of our race." That signifying "our" instantly assures his customers that they're not doing business with a man who would rather stand on a streetcar the whole way home than sit by them for five seconds. And since drugstores don't carry products designed for the Negro market, Overton hires agents—men—to sell his products door-to-door.

America is changing fast. Nothing is strictly local anymore; railroads unify the country, and everything connects. It is as if the country is starting all over again, revising its notion of the dreams and satisfactions of its citizens. Streetcars give people access to a world once available only to those who had money enough for a carriage and horses. Anybody with a nickel can ride. People can shop around instead of accepting whatever's available at the corner store, or they can order from the big catalogues, for whom sewing machines are the biggest seller. Even a domestic worker can stitch up the latest fashion and go out looking as sharp as the woman she works for.

A white woman drawn to business will feel cheered by this, but a black woman's focus is different. In a 1903 American Statistics Association study called "The Negroes of St. Louis," sociologist Lillian Brandt suggests that African-American entrepreneurs are drawing in, closing off, and targeting people of their own race. And with literacy rising, people aren't satisfied with clever pictures. They want testimonials and information, to know what they're getting before dragging out their money, so there's a new advertising philosophy in the air called "reason why" selling, a weaving together of logic, conviction and persuasion.

Annie Turnbo reads the papers and magazines. As does Sarah Davis, when she's not standing over her tubs in a white lady's backyard wondering if this is all she will ever do. In less than ten years, white and black people alike will acknowledge the sharpness of her intelligence, the acuity of her judgments, her skill at gauging what the market will bear and for how long. In another two, she will be called the first self-made black female millionaire in the country. But she can't see into the future from this backyard; all she can do is ponder the past—the days and weeks and years piling up with nothing gained except the one big thing, sending Lelia off to Knoxville, and even that didn't pan out.

Time away from home can change a girl into a person her mother doesn't quite recognize. By 1903, Lelia's back in St. Louis, and at eighteen, might be about to finish high school, but since no Lelia McWilliams appears in the records of Sumner High, it's more likely she didn't—and maybe even couldn't, since when she took the entrance exam in 1901, she didn't pass. Probably her brief enrollment at Knoxville College was her final stab at education. She might have a job, possibly assisting her mother, or doing nothing much at all. Whatever's going on with Lelia, Sarah can't be happy about it.

Meantime, Jim Crow's kicking up his heels. Nothing happens which does not seem to contribute to black people's economic, political and social immobility. Victory in the Philippines inspires Senator Samuel Douglas McEnery of Louisiana to remind his colleagues that the admixture of races ignores a basic law of nature and furthermore that "the Anglo-Saxon blood and brain will always be the superior and cannot be subordinated to the negro." And when Representative G. H. White, a black congressman from North Carolina, proposes to make lynching a federal crime, the bill dies in committee and never comes to a vote. (Curiously, his daughter, Mayme, will become A'Lelia Walker's close companion and will be alone with her in a guest bedroom the night she dies.)

Still, African-Americans have some things to celebrate. Booker T. Washington's autobiography *Up from Slavery* is serialized and then published in book form, with white people all over the country reading it. In Chicago, Robert S. Abbott—told by other Negroes that he won't succeed as a lawyer because his skin is too dark—begins publishing the *Chicago Defender,* which in two years will have the widest circulation of any African-American newspaper in the country. Charles Chesnutt's first novel is published. And at the first meeting of the Pan-African Conference, W. E. B. DuBois makes a statement that reverberates even now: "The problem of the Twentieth Century is the problem of the color line"; *The Souls of Black Folk,* published in 1902, opens with that same sentence.

The Frederick Douglass Center opens in Chicago, where black and white women can meet to discuss issues. St. Louis establishes a branch of the National Association of Colored Women, hoping the organization will hold its 1904 convention there, and, remembering the humiliation suffered by the Harper Union in 1887, founds its own Frederick Douglass Hall for the staging of lectures, dramatic presentations and musical performances. Elocutionist Hallie Q. Brown stars in the opening-night ceremonies; when W. E. B. DuBois comes to St. Louis, he will speak there.

Meantime, more lynchings. Louisiana and Alabama have signed a "grandfather clause" into law, declaring that a man can vote only if his grandfather did, which disqualifies virtually every black resident of the state. Teddy Roosevelt even waffles about his dinner with Dr. Washington—a spokesman declaring that in fact they only *lunched*—and in time will erase the event from his official memory.

A nnie Turnbo hits the streets, modestly dressed, well groomed, polite. "A white woman has only one handicap to overcome," Mary Church Terrell, president of the National Association of Colored Women, has said at a convention devoted to female suffrage, "a great one, true, her sex; a colored woman faces two—her sex and her race. A colored man has only one—that of race." She omits white men from this lineup for obvious reasons.

I am the same as you. So Lydia Pinkham has said, and beauty specialists Madame Paris and Madame Yale. And so hair specialist Annie Turnbo now says, standing in doorways making her introductions, *I know you.* The message is comforting, invites trust. *I understand your problems and your needs because I have had them myself.*

The door opens wider, and she begins her pitch.

The Fair

Door-to-door has taken the country by storm. Newspaper and magazine ads solicit women to become selling agents, with promises of guaranteed weekly salaries. What once was the California Perfume Company has become Avon Products, which now employs some ten thousand agents selling perfume and cosmetics door-to-door; and by hiring women, Avon turns customers into agents while holding on to them as customers, a sensible strategy that will be widely copied.

Within a year of her arrival in St. Louis, Annie Turnbo's doing so well that she hires agents and expands her territory throughout Missouri. At some point she marries "a Mr. Pope" (other accounts simply report that she "became Mrs. Pope"). But this husband vanishes from the story as thoroughly as did Moses McWilliams when, according to his wife, he interferes in her business, at which point the marriage ends, leaving the burgeoning entrepreneur a valuable "Mrs." to place before "Annie," the name "Pope" to use when and as she pleases and no meddling husband to tangle her thinking. Then Annie Turnbo-Pope takes another big step and goes on tour in the South, where some 90 percent of her potential customers still live. Her intention is to introduce Wonderful Hair Grower on a national basis, and without cash reserves her only option is to go on the road, talk it up and demonstrate what it's done for her own hair. But she won't leave until after the fair opens, and in preparation for her absence she has trained three new agents, taking them through their paces, showing them how to do their hair and dress so as to get people to open their doors, what to say once they're inside. More than likely one of them is Sarah Davis. For her, the dress requirement is not a problem. Davis goes to the fanciest church in town and works in rich white people's homes, so she has at least one presentable outfit. As for her hair, in her official rags-to-riches story Madam Walker says it started falling out in patches in the late 1890s, and it couldn't have improved overnight. One possibility is Turnbo's suggested regime of more frequent washing and her own Wonderful Hair Grower. It may be that after Davis used the shampoo, the rinse and the hair oil, her scalp condition improved, and her hair relaxed and then grew back enough that she could make it look nice. This would give her testimonials an even more immediate ring of truth.

Another possibility is that Sarah figured out her own formula and improved her hair herself, then went to work as a Turnbo agent to gain business experience with a view toward running her own. Some accounts claim that she and Lelia stirred up vats of hair remedies at night in their kitchen, then tried out the various formulas on themselves and their friends, until one finally worked; in other versions, Madame claimed to have received the recipe through divine intervention, a dream in which a big black man told her which herbs and oils she needed.

Most people thought the secret ingredient was sulfur, and not until almost a hundred years later will descendants of Madam Walker affirm that, indeed, precipitated sulfur was a major ingredient in the recipe, along with thick petrolatum, beeswax, copper sulfate and a perfume made from violet extract to hide the sulfur smell. She also used carbolic acid and coconut oil. But the formula didn't appear in a flash—or a dream—and there had to have been a great many failed trial runs. In her Harlem days, A'Lelia Walker will almost never be seen without her jeweled turban, which some friends claimed she wore because she had so little hair; one man said flat out that she was bald. Could this be the result of steady chemical experiments she and her mother performed during her youth?

In Stanley Nelson's video account of Madam Walker's life, the ebullient Zenobia (Peg) Fisher, who worked at the Walker Company for some fifteen years, says that when Sarah Davis moved to Denver, she worked as a cook for a druggist named E. L. Scholtz and moonlighted selling Turnbo's product. According to her, the druggist "told her if you can get a can of that I can analyze it, and you can make your own formula. . . . And that's how she got started."

And maybe it is.

Just after Douglass Hall opens, Tom Turpin sponsors a combination piano contest and grand ball that the *Palladium* afterwards calls "one of the largest, finest and best conducted affairs of [its] kind ever held in St. Louis." When the judging is finished, Turpin presents the gold medal to Louis Chauvin, a brilliant early ragtimer who made a career playing in bawdy houses and never wrote down a note of his compositions; then a dance band—"the matchless World's Fair band"—sets up and the ballroom is thrown open and the dancing runs well into the morning hours when factories have begun pumping and the sky is light. Before long, Douglass Hall presents a new musical comedy, *Every Darkey Is a King,* with a grand ball and cakewalk following the show.

These events take place not in direct connection with the World's Fair but certainly because of it. Since African-Americans are not welcome in St. Louis hotels—though no ordinance forbids their presence—an organization called the Information Bureau for Our Colored Visitors places notices in the *Indianapolis Freeman* and other black newspapers advertising rooms in good homes for World's Fair visitors, at seventy-five cents a day. The bureau's address is on Market Street, three blocks from the apartment where Annie Turnbo is operating her business.

The Louisiana Purchase Exposition officially opens on April 30, 1904, when William Howard Taft makes a speech and in D.C. Teddy Roosevelt presses a telegraph lever in the East Room to switch on the lights. In June, Booker T. Washington comes to town and speaks at Festival Hall to a racially mixed audience for the National Education Association, hundreds of "well-dressed colored people" paying two dollars to hear him. He is scheduled to return on August 1 as the keynote speaker at Negro Day.

Do Sarah and Lelia take a streetcar out to the fair to have a look around? Black people, it turns out, are refused service at food concessions, and as Booker T. Washington's personal secretary, Emmett Scott, reports in the *Voice of the Negro,* "Every nation, every government on the face of the earth is cordially invited. . . . But the people who constitute 10.4% of the population of the country . . . have no place there; have absolutely no representation of any kind, character, or degree. . . ." Yet, in the end, he declines to recommend a boycott, concluding that "the Exposition is the crowning glory of the Nineteenth Century, the glorious promise of the Twentieth."

The National Association of Colored Women—the most important organization of its kind in the country—shows no such ambivalence. Their fourth biennial convention is set to run July 11–15, with some of the meetings at the fairgrounds; but in the opening session, Margaret Murray Washington cites instances of general racism and introduces a resolution to abandon those plans. The embarrassed St. Louis delegates try to refute her position, but the resolution is overwhelmingly adopted and the meetings are moved to St. Paul's AME Church. And while Margaret Washington is rarely referred to except as Mrs. Booker T., by taking this stand she flies right past her husband in conviction and courage.

The women congregate at Sarah's own church, in her own neighborhood, and I long to find her there, sitting in the back of the church memorizing each woman's every gesture, listening hard. And she might well be. Local women she knows would attend and would have encouraged her to come, and so let's say she sets aside the time and that she's there when Hallie Q. Brown explains how to organize clubs, and hears Mrs. Ida Joyce Jackson from Colorado denounce ragtime and cakewalks as "disgraceful, vulgar and destructive of good taste and self-respect in all Colored people." She might be disappointed not to get a glimpse of Mary Church Terrell, current president of NACW and one of the great ladies of the race, but Terrell's in Berlin attending the International Council of Women. "Lifting as We Climb" is the NACW motto, and indeed Sarah's spirits would rise up as she sat in the back of the church, convinced that here was an organization she would someday, somehow be a part of.

Ten years hence, a resplendent Madam Walker will arrive at the 1914 NACW convention in Wilberforce, Ohio, in her chauffeur-driven seven-seater touring car. No one there does not know who she is. On the next day, the convention will endorse her business and her efforts in behalf of uplift and cultural beauty, providing a kind of seal of approval of the Walker Company—all this in the presence of Hallie Q. Brown, Margaret Murray Washington and Mary Church Terrell. Afterwards, Madame will issue an invitation to all delegates to visit in Indianapolis to view her factory and offices. And the next week, she is introduced by Booker T. Washington at the annual meeting of the National Negro Business League.

Less than three days before Dr. Washington is scheduled to speak, the Committee on Negro Day withdraws the invitation and cancels the entire celebration for fear of violence. Later that month, and in conjunction with the fair, the third Olympic Games—the last to adhere to the ancient plan whereby athletes compete as individuals, not as members of a national team—are held at St. Louis's Washington University, and George Poage becomes the first African-American Olympic medalist when he takes the bronze in the 400-meter hurdles.

By the close of the fair, the *Palladium* cheerfully reports, the Frisco Railroad system will have carried one hundred thousand black Americans to see it. That same month, two Negroes are burned alive in Statesboro, Georgia, and the governor of Arkansas announces that every time "you educate a nigger, you spoil a good field hand," vowing that efforts toward social equality will result only in "a lot of dead niggers."

By then, Booker T. Washington has chaired the fifth annual National Negro Business League convention in Indianapolis, with Madam Walker's future sponsor the newspaper publisher George Knox in charge of arrangements. From there he travels to St. Louis and attends the National Afro-American Council—along with cohorts and sponsors T. Thomas Fortune, Emmett Scott and, again, George Knox—and then on to New York, with meetings in Brooklyn and at the Waldorf-Astoria Hotel, after which he takes the Archbishop of Canterbury on a tour of tenement housing, politely advising him on sanitation and morals in America.

Two steps forward, one and a half back.

Heat

Politics within the race have turned nasty. The split between accommodationists and militants only widens when in *The Souls of Black Folk* DuBois describes Washington's program as submissive and accuses the Wizard of Tuskegee of being an apologist for injustice; he subsequently establishes the Niagara Movement, which demands immediate abolition of all distinctions based on race. In his autobiography, James Weldon Johnson says that those unfamiliar with Negro life over the next decade cannot imagine the bitterness of the antagonism between the followers of Washington and those who had come to believe in DuBois's activism.

In this edgy atmosphere, it is not surprising when hair becomes an issue. Educators Anna Julia Cooper and Nannie Burroughs excoriate those who advise black women to straighten their hair or sell such products, whom Burroughs calls "Negrophobes." But these are educated light-skinned women whose experience would seem to have little in common with that of a hardworking brown-skinned woman. Sarah Davis will eventually take on these philosophical disputations, but not yet. The women she's talking and selling to don't care. They just want their hair to look nice, and not one of them doesn't know the pain of hair wrapping or the perils of chemical treatments. So when she knocks on a door with her hair up in a fluffed pile and greets the woman of the house by asking if she, too, would like to have soft, full hair, more often than not she's swiftly welcomed, and as soon as she's inside she offers the lure of a demonstration.

But setting up takes time, and while she's at it, Sarah asks her hostess to gather a number of other women together for the lengthy, meticulous process. Today, for the same reasons, most direct-sales organizations stage parties, an idea that hasn't changed much from the days when a hair wrapper worked under the trees or washwomen gathered around their tubs. If she's willing, Lelia might act as a model, but Sarah usually asks for a volunteer. Before she begins washing the woman's hair and treating it with pressing oil—so called because of the procedure's similarity to ironing clothes—she places a specially designed steel comb into or over a flame, from either a stove in the house or a small kerosene heater she carries in a black bag; she has to be careful not to burn the wooden handle or overheat the curved heavy-duty metal teeth, which have to be sizzling yet not hot enough to burn. The Wonderful Hair Grower, the pressing oil and the sage-and-egg rinse can only do so much.

Serious changes in hair texture and shape—whether curling, straightening, lifting, fluffing or flattening—require heat, which can be applied directly through metal instruments or, for those with electric power, by means of fans or coils. In slave days, women heated a piece of flannel before an open fire, oiled their hair with lard or chicken fat, then pulled strands of hair through the hot flannel. In the future, permanent wave and straightening solutions will provide chemical heat, but women used to insert into their hair bone-shaped permanent-wave rods connected by wires to an electrical outlet, then sit for hours while the acrid lotion became activated through the warmed rods. My grandmother used an electric curling iron to create thin, thready ringlets in her baby-thin white hair. It had a green wooden handle, and she used to tilt her head toward her shoulder when she applied it. I can still smell the singeing heat, the warmed hair, and can see her delicate, chubby hands twisting the handle just so.

Heat and oil are the secrets. While methods change, the basic idea remains. Back then, oil didn't come bottled, so women used grease to soften their hair and give it some elasticity. Then came heat, applied evenly and with pressure, starting at the scalp and moving out, to unwind the frizz and create a flat pliant ribbon or to shape and softly curl.

With no running water in most tenements, Sarah would request help toting buckets into the kitchen. After dunking the customer's head and washing her hair with herb shampoo, she rinses and oils it, talking the whole time, explaining what she's doing and how the herbs work. Some of this she believes and the rest she's guessing at. Nothing matters except the end results. And to women who *want* to believe, who look at Sarah's soft healthy hair and *choose* to believe, every word sounds like gospel, so desperate are they to change their lives and their appearance.

Once the oil has done its softening, Sarah divides the hair into even squares and then lifts the hot comb from the stove and spits, as she once did onto a sadiron, and if it sizzles, the comb is at the proper temperature. For a final test she lays the comb on a piece of paper, which should curl from the heat but not scorch. She takes her time and keeps up the talk and the selling, answering questions, giving instructions on nutrition and hygiene, explaining the cause of scalp disease. The procedure is tedious, risky, and can't be rushed.

She lays the teeth of the comb so close to the scalp that her client can feel the heat on her skin and then smell her cooking hair. Holding the woman's head steady, Sarah pulls the comb through a narrow width of clean, oiled hair—one hairdresser says only one-eighth inch wide—turning and pulling as she goes. She has to work carefully but quickly, keeping the hot comb at the right temperature, pulling as hard as she can without causing pain, doing strip after strip and reheating the comb when it cools. When the procedure is finished—after an hour, sometimes two—and the hair is smooth and relatively flat, she rolls or curls it as per request.

She's on her feet the entire time. The strength she's built up at the scrub board comes in handy, but door-to-door doesn't wear her out the same way washing did. At the end of the day she is exhausted, certainly, but each day is different now, every door she knocks on a new adventure for her to explore and manipulate. She must have a hard time sleeping, with planning, inventing and gathering data now part of her everyday life.

The story of the hot comb designed particularly for use on a black woman's hair is complicated. Many lay claim to its design and one of them is Madam Walker, who is mostly credited not with *inventing* the hot comb but with improving it. She is supposed to have done this by substituting a French design for the American one; the former was curvier and had teeth that were farther apart, features which worked better on black women's hair. Some people think Sarah might have seen a French comb used in Louisiana, and though she didn't live in the French part of the state, it might easily have been ordered from New Orleans. Young Sarah Breedlove might have helped out when one of the black women on the farm used the French hot comb to curl Minnie Burney's hair, watching closely and listening to discussions, pestering the women with questions after they finished with the Burney girl.

She knows, at any rate, how to use it, and so at the end of a workday she returns to 2223 Market with money for Annie Turnbo and orders to fill.

IV · Denver, 1905–1907

Climbing

Some versions of what happens next:

"In July, 1905, with $1.50 in savings, the thirty-seven year old [McWilliams] moved to Denver where she joined her deceased brother's wife and four daughters. In January 1906 she married a newspaper sales agent, Charles Joseph Walker." *Black Women in History,* 1993

"Encouraged by the St. Louis success of her products and method, she moved by 1906 to Denver, where her brother had already gone; there she was married to Charles J. Walker, newspaperman." *Notable American Women,* 1971

"After the death of her brother, Walker moved to Denver, Colorado, to reside with her sister-in-law and her four nieces. With one dollar and fifty cents, she began a hair preparations company." *Notable Black American Women,* 1992

"July 19, 1905, [Madam Walker] left St. Louis, Mo. for Denver, Colo., to engage in the hair growing business. After many discouragements and obstacles, she finally was able to convince the people . . . that she could really grow hair. . . . January 3, 1906, she was married to C. J. Walker. After her marriage, she moved from an attic room, which she had been occupying, to more comfortable furnished rooms where she continued her business." *Indianapolis Freeman,* 1911

"Her success was immediate. In less than a year she was doing a business of $25 to $35 a week." *Indianapolis Freeman,* 1912

"I went to Denver, Colorado, and began my business career on a capital of $1.25. I began, of course, in a most modest way. I made house-to-house canvasses among people of my race, and after a while I got going pretty well, though I naturally encountered many obstacles and discouragements before I finally met with real success." *New York Times Magazine,* 1917

July 19, 1905, our traveler exits the grandly appointed waiting room of the St. Louis Union Station and heads for the Missouri Pacific line to Kansas City. The depot is fraught with haste, but experience and focus give her the edge. Having given herself extra time, she can take command of the situation and move at her own purposeful speed.

In those days, people thought that how you looked upon arriving at a new place reflected where you came from and how your people carried themselves. Once again, as on the *Belle Memphis,* Sarah Davis certainly wears her smartest outfit, perhaps a dark day-wear suit with a high-necked sateen shirtwaist. She's corseted, bosoms lifted, waist cinched; her hair's up, and she's wearing a dark straw hat pitched forward at a slight tilt. At thirty-seven, she's no longer young by contemporary standards, but success has made her feel alive and hopeful. She's written to her sister-in-law in Denver, and with the agreement of Mrs. Turnbo-Pope, will represent her in that city, and introduce her product to the West.

Once on board, she stows her suitcase and sample bag, takes a seat by the window and sits tall, clutching her handbag in her lap. She's off again, her life of constant movement now gaining speed and direction, and this time with no child in her lap, no Lelia for distraction or company.

There's a studio photograph of Madam Walker I particularly like, which will be taken only two years from now. She's standing before what looks like a fancy gilt-framed mirror in a three-quarters pose, hands clasped behind her back, perhaps holding a flower. Hair up in a bouffant pouf, she's wearing pearls and a girlish lacy white dress. Her head's cocked to the side, chin tucked, eyes cast demurely down with a withdrawn, even shy look. A coy pose—or maybe she's only standing as fashion and corsets dictate, with chest forward and hips poked out behind. Nearing forty, she's nonetheless wearing a girlish dress with wide sleeves that extend only to her elbow, leaving more arm uncovered than most ladies dare.

Such a complex woman: reticent, determined, passionate, sometimes crass. In later pictures she shelves the shyness and is merely grand, posing as if for history itself, peering down on generations to come like a famous statue.

L ife's supposed to be different in the West—no night riders, less hatefulness—and the atmosphere on the train confirms the rumor even before they leave Union Station. As long as they're heading in that direction instead of back across the Mississippi, black people who can afford the fare are free to sit in reclining parlor chairs same as the whites and can even spring for a Pullman berth and sleep lying down. But Sarah Davis has spent practically all her money on preparations and gear, so she sits in the cheap car with cinders flying and soot swirling about her face, surrounded by white immigrants and gold bugs going west for the big score. For the most part the races sit apart, but by choice and not as a matter of course and the law.

Mrs. Turnbo-Pope is cutting a wide swath, hiring more agents and developing her mail-order business, and so she doubtless considered Sarah's Denver proposal a fine idea. An agent has to buy enough product to get started and, once the demand grows, will have to keep ordering more, always on a cash basis, and so Sarah's employer must have figured she had nothing to lose.

The distance between the two cities is a thousand miles, three days and two nights by train, first on the Missouri Pacific between St. Louis and Kansas City, then on the Colorado Flyer to Denver. Beyond the river, the distance between houses widens and the green of eastern Missouri turns to pale gold and the plains stretch out to the sky as flat as the delta Sarah grew up in. But here the grass and the earth are straw-colored and sandy, and the wind sends the tall blades in easy drifts of watery rolls—nothing like the still wetness of Louisiana, the dark wet blacks and greens there, of mud, swamps and low grasses. With no vines or moss, the trees grow close, thin and whispery with pale peeling bark.

Moving to a new place calls up the past and, making a new home, we reminisce, taking stock of what's behind us—places we lived, what happened in each one—while imagining what lies ahead. Sarah's bound to spend some of the trip thinking of Lelia, who might have refused to go to Denver. Or maybe she's staying behind to take care of her mother's local accounts. Whatever the reasons, Sarah's been a mother almost half her life, spending the majority of her waking hours trying to figure out a way to make life better for her daughter. But Lelia's twenty now, no longer a child, and life has changed for both of them.

Sometime during the months before she left, she met the man who will become her third husband, Charles Joseph Walker. One story holds that she met him in Denver when she called on a newspaper to discuss advertising and there he sat. But since there's no Charles or C. J. Walker listed in Denver until after Sarah gets there, and we do find a "Charles Walker, Reporter," living in the Mill Creek area of St. Louis in the early 1900s, we'll assume she met him before she left.

If she was ever in the thrall of romance, that's over now. Sarah has buried two babies and suffered through a terrible marriage, her health is no longer sound, her daughter is grown and, at this late date, opportunity is staring her in the face. Remember, too, that however soft and demure Madam C. J. Walker looks in that studio shot, she is no sentimentalist but a confirmed businesswoman and capitalist who relishes the moment at which a deal is closed, when the agent must DRIVE THE NAIL HOME! At thirty-seven, Sarah Davis cannot possibly be looking for a husband for any reason other than social convenience and commercial advantage. Besides which, like all driven people, she is a loner who—married or single—prefers solitude. When she becomes Madam Walker and relates her success stories, they are always hers alone: *I* got my start by . . . *I* have always believed . . . *I* began my business. . . .

So how did she meet C. J. Walker? Mill Creek's a tight community, and maybe he heard about Sarah's splendid selling personality and went looking for her. Or maybe she happened to knock on his door, looking for the lady of the house. Or perhaps she'd heard about his experience in advertising. No matter, they somehow crossed paths.

One account suggests that Walker was a man of some education, whether formal or otherwise. Another claims he helped establish the Western Negro Press Association, and while he might well have participated in the conventions, since WNPA membership extended no farther east than Kansas City and C. J.'s home turf was basically the upper South, it's unlikely he was a founder. What matters is that he's a man who can supply Sarah with advice on marketing, a field she has learned something about simply by watching and reading but in which she has no firsthand experience. In those days, a newspaper agent— what today we would call an advertising rep—worked for the paper itself, filling up columns with ads and taking his cut of the fees paid by the advertiser, who had little say in the matter. Walker knows the ropes, and all Sarah needs is a start.

Ahead, she can see the Rockies—the only mountains she's ever seen—looming over the plains ahead, blue and snow-capped, beautiful as calendar art. Snow in July's a wonder, a sight which for a Southerner just won't figure.

C. J. probably thinks they should marry, but more than likely Sarah doesn't immediately agree. For one thing, she already has a husband, and no telling where John Davis is by now. And then there's Walker himself, who, though flashy and hot with ideas, plays a conservative game. He might well have expressed doubts about moving farther west, cautioning her to stay put in St. Louis, get established, then see. And why Denver? How many black people live there?

Sarah turns a deaf ear.

There's a photograph of C. J. Walker in a 1911 *Indianapolis Freeman*. It's a summer day and he's in a light-colored suit, standing with his wife on the sidewalk in front of the substantial brick house they've just bought. The article, titled "House-Warming of Mr. and Madam C. J. Walker," describes a party they've just given for more than 150 people, some from Los Angeles and New York; likely written in advance by Walker, it pronounces the party "brilliant," one that will be long remembered. The couple are standing several feet apart, not touching. The picture is dark and blurry, their faces impossible to make out; all we have is their posture, their clothes and a sense of their demeanor. She's in a dressy white suit and hat, the jacket fitted at the waist and long enough to cover her hips, the skirt hemmed about three or four inches from the ground, her saucerish hat dipped saucily down over her right eye, a purse dangling somewhat awkwardly from her right hand. Madam Walker's a fashion plate, but she stands heavy and staunch, dead-on to the camera, a stolid country girl despite the fancy duds. Her husband's about her height. His hips are pushed slightly forward, his shoulders back, and his left leg is slightly in front of the other in an on-the-move pose, like a man looking for a dancing partner to dip and twirl. He's wearing a suit but has left his jacket open, so between the lapels is a wide expanse of starched white interrupted by a dark tie. His hands are in his pockets and his light-colored hat is pushed forward on his head at a tilt, like a Targee Street dandy.

C. J. and Madame, Indianapolis, 1911. He's at ease when the camera comes out; she goes stiff and formal. He's aslant, she's dead on. C. J. lives light on the earth. Madame might move constantly but is planted wherever she goes.

Perhaps Sarah Davis chats with the porter and he tells her about getting around Denver and how to find the house she's headed for and even which neighborhoods to canvass. He might warn her that while it's certainly a better place for Negroes than any city in the South, white people are always advising Negroes to form colonies out in the Colorado countryside, where they can be with their own people and do the work they love and are meant for, which is farming: this notion, to Sarah and the porter, is laughable. She knows farm life and so, probably, does he, and both of them would rather be struck down on the spot than live a hundred years muling a plow down a field.

Denver's nestled in the Cherry Creek Valley. The train climbs higher and higher until the passengers' ears pop and children cry and first-time travelers chatter nervously; then suddenly they're at the top and she can see the city, down in the valley.

Denver's Union Station is solidly built and plain, with no artwork or geegaws like St. Louis's. The wood is golden and the walls light; the waiting-room ceiling is three stories high, with a skylight set in the center. Not much interested in architecture, Sarah walks brusquely past the long pewlike line of oak benches.

Summer in the West is pleasant, dry and warm. The light bounces like reflections from a crystal inside the eye. But the thin air grabs her chest and the Mile High City—touted as clean and fresh as the plains of Kansas—is cloudy with a gray murk, though nothing like as thick as in St. Louis. Streets are unpaved, and people bundled up in heavy clothes despite the warm sunshine, as if expecting a cold wind at any moment. All of this is new.

A cable car rumbles toward her down Seventeenth Street. The trolley turnaround is just below Union Station, and waiting for it, she takes a nickel from her remaining dollar and change. There's no discernible attitude from the conductor, and they roll on back up the slightly inclined street, the trolley straining slightly, past the Oxford Hotel. The buildings are six or seven stories and made of golden Colorado limestone, grainy and rocklike. The streets are so wide that the trolley could travel sideways. To a newcomer, this openness feels like widespread arms, a welcome.

She finds the right house, and her nieces invite her in. There are four, ages five to fifteen. Her sister-in-law Lucy Breedlove may be out doing wash. The girls must marvel at the very sight of their elegant aunt in her city clothes, especially Anjetta, the oldest and most ambitious. Polite, a little overwhelmed by her presence, they show Sarah to her room, bed, corner, wherever she will sleep.

Thirty-four, Lucy Breedlove has been a widow for at least five years. She's living in the business district in a noisy neighborhood of frame dwellings divided up and rented as furnished and unfurnished rooms. She came here from Albuquerque some four years ago, and finds that Denver has its advantages. Women can vote and there's less racial antagonism toward black people—fewer than five thousand in a population of two hundred thousand—since most of that is directed at the Chinese, who are arriving in increasing numbers and are vehemently disliked.

Lucy Crockett Breedlove and her four daughters will be a part of Madam C. J. Walker's life until the day she dies, and two of the nieces will play important roles in her company. But in chronicling this particular branch of the Breedlove family, we should begin with Sarah's deceased brother Owen. On January 23, 1890—as reported on the front page of the *Albuquerque Daily Citizen*—a man named Frank Harmon sells his Albuquerque blacksmith shop to one O. W. Breedlove (sometimes spelled Breidlove), who announces that from now on, George Hutchison, the champion horseshoer of the Rio Grande Valley, will hold forth in his shop. No skin color is given for Mr. Breedlove, but a year and a half later the same paper describes Owen Breedlove as "colored" and reports that after traveling to Seattle with his wife, possibly to relocate, he has returned to Albuquerque and intends to stay.

Though blacksmithing is a family tradition, once he returns, Breedlove goes into a different business and, in early 1892, opens the Bramlette and Breedlove Saloon on North First Street. J. H. Bramlette lives near the saloon and also is "colored." No neighborhoods in Albuquerque are strictly white or black, and since Western saloons serve a mixed clientele—some of whom might nonetheless call African-American bartenders "Nigger John" or "Nigger Willie"—these two men and their families live a relatively mixed-race life.

A couple of months later, O. W. Breedlove is elected chairman pro tem of the Colored Republican Club. And a few months after that, he swears out a warrant for the arrest of "L. K. T. Irwin, a colored tough," who'd made a grab for the money on the monte table and assaulted him with a knife. A civic-minded man, O. W. Breedlove's a good citizen who doesn't flinch from confrontation and won't stand for lawlessness.

After 1892, though, he disappears and Lucy Breedlove (or, again, Breidlove) officially enters the picture. In 1896–97 she's listed in the Albuquerque city directory under her own name, her profession as domestic and cook. In '96, she's living on Seventh Street and West Tijeras Avenue at the same address as O. W.'s business partner, J. H. Bramlette, and her husband is dead.

This fact is confirmed in 1900 when, a couple of weeks after Charles Lively visits the John and Sarah Davis family in St. Louis, U.S. Census enumerator William H. H. Allison does the count in Albuquerque. At 310 Sixth Street, in a block otherwise inhabited by white people, he finds as head of household a twenty-nine-year-old widow, Lucy Breedlove. Born in Virginia, she is a black laundress and the mother of three daughters, all born in New Mexico: Anjetta, ten; Thirsapen, seven; and Mattie, three. There will be a fourth daughter, Gladys (sometimes Gladis), whom the 1900 census report does not mention, even though her Social Security death record gives her birth date as April 21, 1900. This would make her two months old at the time of the enumeration, which otherwise is so straightforward that chances are the Social Security record is wrong and that on June 21, Lucy is pregnant with her fourth child.

Now, we don't know how old Lucy's husband was when he died or how he got to Albuquerque in the first place or how Lucy got there from Virginia or when and where they married. We don't know what happened to Samara, the St. Louis "widow of Owen," or her daughter Onee Breedlove; what we do know is, her husband didn't die; he left. Maybe after hard times in St. Louis, he went on to Kansas as the Exodusters originally planned, then kept going west until he came to a place where he could find a job and settle. People in New Mexico and Colorado, sympathetic toward the migrants, sent wagons to bring them to the Western territories and maybe he jumped on. Perhaps in St. Louis or Kansas he was recruited to become a Buffalo Soldier and was posted south of Albuquerque at Fort Bayard or up at Fort Mercy, on the Rio Grande near Santa Fe. And conceivably he was drawn to New Mexico by the establishment of two all-colored towns there, Blackdom and Vado.

Or maybe Lucy Crockett came through St. Louis on her way west from Virginia and they left together and wound up in New Mexico.

However they got there, Albuquerque's poor, and after her husband dies, Lucy's bound to be struggling. Her only consolation is that at least she isn't Mexican, or an Indian. Not that the city's without prejudice toward African-Americans, since when the first black students are about to graduate from high school in 1907, white parents will raise such a loud protest that the girls have to collect their diplomas from the university. In Albuquerque, Anjetta and Thirsapen attend a mostly white school while three-year-old Mattie stays home. Lucy rents her home and she has a lodger, a thirty-three-year-old African-American man named Eliazaret Reynolds. Born in New York State, Reynolds is single and works as a porter, perhaps in town or maybe for one of the railroads. Thus, in the matter of Gladys's mysterious birthdate, we now find two other candidates for fatherhood: the lodger, Reynolds, and the business partner, Bramlette. But about this we just don't know.

At any rate, not long after Gladys is born, Lucy heads for Denver, where there are better schools, a more prosperous African-American community, an easier life. Lucy's not exactly ambitious. She never stops being a washwoman, even after her sister-in-law radically alters the Breedlove fortune. Still, she has pluck and nerve enough to gather up her daughters and take them more than four hundred tedious, climbing miles into the Rockies. We find her in Denver in 1901, with no Eliazaret Reynolds in evidence and only one other African-American Breedlove in the city, a forty-four-year-old widow, Mary, who works as a live-in housemaid for the family of John L. Routt, former governor of Colorado. And twenty years later, Lucy and her girls will still be living together in Los Angeles. Lucy, nearly fifty, is still doing laundry. Her daughters will work for Madam C. J. Walker, who owns their house. None of them having married, they all still go by the name Breedlove.

Imagine the effect Sarah Davis has on Lucy's daughters. She dresses well, speaks well, pounds the pavement like a man, runs her own show, imagines herself a success.

Published in 1937, journalist Napoleon Hill's book *Think and Grow Rich* will have a particular appeal for black people (for whom a special edition will eventually be prepared). Hill interviewed some of the wealthiest men of his time, including Andrew Carnegie, and his philosophy holds that to get what you want, first you imagine having it, then you prepare for it, then you go out and get it. Simple, uncomplicated and not dependent on family, wealth or connections. The later edition of this book declares that Madam Walker's success derived from her unlimited imagination, which enabled her to dream big dreams.

Nervy Anjetta clamps eyes on her aunt, makes her mind up to attach herself from now on, to be her shadow, her imitator, her double.

In the late summer of 1905, ensconced in Lucy's place, Sarah's selling on commission—always a dicey proposition—as well as washing clothes and cooking in a boardinghouse for thirty dollars a week. According to some reports, one of her employers is the druggist E. L. Scholtz. But her focus is on canvassing neighborhoods, doing Turnbo demonstrations, establishing her name and her expertise. And nights she makes lists, charts streets, totes up orders, writes for refills and perfects her pitch.

Her second marriage having proved useless, she again becomes the widow Mrs. McWilliams. Perhaps Scholtz does do an analysis of the Turnbo hair grower so she can make it herself and sell it under her own name. This is the West, after all, where starting over is a way of life.

As Christmas approaches, Sarah turns thirty-eight. She's styling hair, making women beautiful for the season, and on Christmas Day she attends services at her new church, the Shorter AME, where the most respected people in Denver worship. Women who go there can afford treatments, and a saleswoman is never not selling. All is well.

By the end of the year, C. J. Walker has arrived.

Big Year

In the late spring or early summer of 1906, Madame will later claim, lightning struck and her life changed overnight. But by that time her name was known, her stories calculated for public consumption. Nonetheless, it is true that after 1906, nothing will be the same for her. Though there will be surprises both up and down, the tune is basically set, the tempo knocked out, the dance steps choreographed. The only thing left to do is keep twirling.

"One night I had a dream," she explained, "and in that dream a big black man appeared to me and told me what to mix up for my hair. Some of the remedy was grown in Africa, but I sent for it, mixed it, put it on my scalp, and in a few weeks my hair was coming in faster than it had ever fallen out. I tried it on my friends; it helped them. I made up my mind to sell it."

This is—in plain words—hogwash. The transformation of a washwoman to a selling agent to an entrepreneur known by the name Madame is a product of work, research, probably stealth and unflagging attention to the task at hand—a process that began before she even knew it was possible and continued until it actually came through. In time, Madame herself will shelve the dream story in favor of a self-help recipe of dedication, hard work and perseverance, but for a while it worked, yielding a sense of divine appointment to a commercial enterprise, lifting it above the fray and out of the accelerating rat race of beauty-product competition.

C. J. Walker had clearly decided to latch on to Sarah and on January 3, 1906, when she's been in Denver less than six months, they marry. At least that's the date she will provide five years later in a Walker Company manual; and when, in 1918, she's contradicted by a friend who swears that the wedding took place in her living room on January

4, Sarah makes no comment. In any case, no Arapahoe County record attests to their marriage in Denver between 1904 and 1908, nor is there a marriage certificate in the St. Louis archives, despite the fact that in 1912 Sarah will file for divorce from Walker. So what did she do—commit bigamy or divorce a man she hadn't married?

Sarah and C. J. will do a lot of traveling, so maybe they stopped off somewhere along the road and tied the knot, moving the date back to January. After all, she can't live with a man she hasn't married; her character has to be flawless in the view of both church and business circles, especially given how much they overlap, and John Davis seems to have vanished for good. As for the wedding's time and place, there's no need to be overly fussy. In 1910 she and C. J. will tell the U.S. Census they've been married for fifteen years, not four.

Sarah may already have moved out of Lucy's house, but certainly, once wed, the Walkers find more spacious quarters, taking rooms in a brick house a half-mile or so out from downtown, in a neighborhood called Five Points. Black people who could afford it were already here when Sarah first got to Denver, since the houses are more substantial, the air cleaner, the streets less jammed. The name derives from the five-street intersection that marks its boundary, and most of Sarah's customers live around it, many of them doing pretty well. Denver's mayor, Robert Speer, is something of a political boss, but he believes that government should be "progressive along conservative lines" and has instituted a number of programs to help people who are struggling. And if African-Americans aren't his top priority, they are inching along.

Relative to others in the neighborhood, the house the Walkers move into, at 2410 Champa, is large and dignified, with the unusual asset of three porches: the one at the front large enough to sit out on, with square brick pillars, a pointed roof, and four concrete steps; the other, smaller two facing the alleys on either side of the house. There's a Church of God around one corner, a large synagogue around another, a stable close by. A relatively quiet street, with homes built to last.

Shortly after Sarah and C. J. move in, Margaret Murray Washington comes to town as part of Woman's Week, her visit sponsored by two of the city's many important "colored women's clubs," the Women's League and the Book Lovers' Club. When she lectures at the Shorter AME Church, over five hundred people attend. The Wizard's wife concentrates, as usual, on uplift, self-help, the importance of home.

She congratulates the Denver women on their voting record, which outshines the men's, and afterwards there's a dinner in her honor at the Rhine Café, where she is served by former Tuskegee students.

Because Mrs. Washington's become something of a queen bee, it's hard to say whether or not she and Madame will meet now or become true friends later. The wife of Booker T. Washington isn't likely to cozy up to a former washwoman. But certainly they will come to know each other and will share the same stage at NACW meetings, and when Dr. Washington dies, Madame will send the widow her warm condolences in a tone of close personal acquaintance.

But Sarah Walker would almost certainly attend Mrs. Washington's lecture, her own interest more than seconded by C. J., who would insist that his wife not just show up—whether at Shorter or at lectures, concerts and socials—but make an *entrance,* whenever the doors open, so that club women and representative ladies could clamp eyes on her and whisper her name when she swans by. She will be selling by her very presence. And since at this point her husband knows more about marketing than she does, she listens.

There are two African-American newspapers in Denver, the *Statesman* and the *Colorado Statesman.* The latter and older of the two runs a column listing businesses and professionals, male and female, who serve the black community. In February 1906, one of the four women listed under Hair Dressers is "Mrs. McWilliams" at 2410 Champa St. Strange, hanging on to McWilliams, though there's a reason for most everything. Maybe she uses Moses's surname because it's already established locally and she's loath to scorn that recognition. Or perhaps her employer still has the say-so on this decision.

A month later, in the same newspaper, she—or C. J.—runs an item in the local chitchat column:

WHY NEED WEAR FALSE HAIR ANY LONGER . . .

when Mrs. McWilliams Walker, the wonderful hair grower, will produce the "real" hair, long, soft and glossy, cure the scalp of all kinds of diseases, and positively grows the hair no matter how thin or short, or refund your money? One treatment positively stops the hair from falling out. She is a God send to Colorado. She is subject to calls in any Colorado town. She also teaches the art of Hair Growing. Home address 2410 Champa St., Denver. Phone, White 592.

Imagine, prepare, go out and get it. The full-out push begins. Seven months ago, Sarah McWilliams Davis was living in a St. Louis tenement, and now she's set up in a big brick house with three porches and a telephone, something a lot of other businesses here don't have. Her closest competitor—Mrs. T. D. Perkins, who features her own cherubically pretty face in ads for her Scalp Salve—won't have a phone for another three months, when she'll give Madame a sideways whack by announcing hers is a private line, unlike the general number at 2410 Champa.

"Mrs. McWilliams Walker" is an odd arrangement of names. Still, Sarah's choice is practical: people recognize the "McWilliams," but now that she's a proper wife, she's Mrs. Walker. "Davis" having already been dropped, her soon-to-be-famous name is almost complete.

E stablished in 1882, the *Statesman,* "the Organ of the Colored People in Colorado, Wyoming, Montana, Utah, and New Mexico," differs from most other weeklies, which run canned, anodyne front-page stories with photographs or drawings of such great and famous men as Frederick Douglass, Booker T. Washington and T. Thomas Fortune. Instead, the *Statesman* often features unusually bold articles of current interest. In the summer of 1905, barely a month after W. E. B. DuBois makes his final philosophical and political break with the Wizard by founding the Niagara Movement, the paper risks its very existence by coming out in his favor. By this time, Booker T. Washington controls many of the race's newspapers, and his posse of supporters is widely known as the Tuskegee Machine. But in the *Statesman*'s front-page article, Bruce Grit (a pseudonym of John Edward Bruce, a journalist and publisher known for his courageous reporting) declares: "Let the Niagara Movement have the right of way."

The *Colorado Statesman,* around since 1895, is more locally focused. Its editor, J. D. D. Rivers, is the city light inspector, past president of the Western Negro Press Association, owner of real estate and a booster of the Five Points area. His paper, which has more advertising and photographs, comes out on Saturday, while the *Statesman,* edited and published by E. H. Hackley, comes out on Friday. Both continue publishing into the 1960s.

In his new career as a promoter of concerts and events, C. J. gets excellent placement in both papers, with tickets available for purchase in their offices. Undoubtedly, he sells ads for both, and might even be in charge of the local-interest columns, thereby making certain of top billing.

In mid-March, an item in the *Statesman* announces that C. J. Walker and B. W. Fields will open a business on April 1 at 212 Fifteenth Street: the Fields and Walker Industrial Employment Bureau, Real Estate, Loan and Rental Co. "It is to be hoped that every race loving Negro in Denver will give them their hearty support. It will be their purpose to place every Negro man and woman applying to them for positions in the very best places to be obtained in Denver, and will do their best to secure for you respectable homes, and thus do away with the embarrassment of being refused by white agents."

And on March 23, both Walkers appear: Fields and Walker announcing it has houses that rent from $6 to $30 and for sale from $875 to $3,000, and just beneath it is the WHY NEED WEAR FALSE HAIR ANY LONGER ad, same as before except the phone number, given incorrectly before and now given as Pink 592. This same column also reports that two men were employed at the fountain at Scholtz's drugstore, suggests French perfume for Easter, gives births, deaths, travel and illnesses and promotes an upcoming dance, the "Fisherman's Horn Pipe," by twenty children at Manitou Hall. Race isn't specified in African-American papers any more than it is in white ones, especially since each notes when it's "the other race."

On Easter Sunday Mr. and Mrs. Walker certainly attend Frederick Douglass Day at Shorter AME. In addition to a long program on Douglass there's an address on "Lifting as We Climb" by Ida de Priest, a founder of the Women's League and member of the Book Lovers' Club.

C. J.'s flacking for the United Order of the True Reformers, one of the fraternal banking and insurance organizations formed in the 1880s to lend money, provide insurance and encourage business development in the black community, and the Denver branch is holding a May Festival and popularity contest on May 10. It costs ten cents a vote, and the young woman receiving the most will receive a gold watch, the runner-up a gold ring. C. J.'s the organizer and he's selling tickets at his home, his real estate and employment office, at the True Reformers headquarters and the offices of the *Statesman.* The festivities will take place in Manitou Springs, a popular resort town south of Denver at the foot of Pikes Peak.

An article announcing the UOTR contest takes the lead position in the "Denver Locals" column on April 20, noting that a "parlor social" on its behalf will be held at 2410 Champa the following Saturday night. Supper at fifteen cents (and up) includes the first strawberries of the season.

Longtime Walker employee Violet Davis Reynolds says Madame was an excellent cook who could feed a household from one stewpot. And when C. J. gives a parlor social, his wife's demonstrating not only her culinary skill but also her hairdo and attire. And surely she's displayed boxes of Mrs. Turnbo-Pope's Wonderful Hair Grower around the room, so her female guests can put two and two together, and she can do her pitch.

Sarah's been in Denver nine months, C. J. less than four. But in that same issue of the *Statesman* is this surprising notice: "We regret to say that Mrs. McWilliams Walker, who has done so much for the ladies of Denver and so truthfully demonstrated her ability to grow the hair, will be with us no more after May 18th, as she expects to tour the West and teach her wonderful method to the hundreds whom she could not reach in Denver. Mrs. Walker has done what others have failed to do, and will leave many witnesses in Denver to testify to same."

This is a ploy she'll come to rely on: teasing her customers by announcing her immediate departure, then not going—yet. First she has to build up cash reserves and then inventory. But under what name?

That same spring, the most damaging earthquake in United States history hits San Francisco in the early morning hours, killing hundreds and injuring thousands even before fires from broken gas mains and exposed electrical wires rage through the city and wipe out entire neighborhoods, leaving some two hundred thousand people homeless. In New York, Harry Thaw shoots famed architect Stanford White at a performance of *Mamzelle Champagne* on the roof of Madison Square Garden. When the Pekin Theatre opens in Chicago, calling itself a temple of music, African-American performers leave St. Louis in droves. Upton Sinclair's novel *The Jungle,* an exposé of Chicago stockyards, becomes a best-seller, and President Roosevelt appoints an investigative committee that affirms Sinclair's findings, eventually resulting in the passage of the Pure Food and Drug Act. African-American poet and lyricist Paul Laurence Dunbar dies of tuberculosis at thirty-three.

Skirts come up a couple of inches to reveal pretty high-buttoned shoes. High stiff collars, the Eton jacket suit and the sailor-boy look are in style. Tiny waists are still a must, and with the Gibson Girl setting the standard, corsets make or break a woman's appearance; the new models are longer below the waist and straighter down the front, with a length of whalebone or metal inserted down the middle, making for a flatter look below the breasts. Since women wish to pile their hair in various ornate shapes, prices for wigs and hairpieces have tripled, and women from China and parts of Europe are clipping their tresses for money. Mail-order catalogues offer fake braids, cluster puffs, crescent hair rolls and pompadours. Unscrupulous goat herders shear their stock, passing off the silky switches as genuine human hair.

When Mrs. McWilliams Walker appears in public, she never looks anything but fashionable. Laced-up bosoms forward, bottom back, the inevitable waddle: perfection, and what every woman wants to look like.

In the West that year, spring's a trickster. Sometimes it blows in for a day or two, and spirits rise as the clouds part and an immaculate sheath of sunlight bathes the landscape in gold. Then it's blown back out again by snow and blizzards. By April, to convince themselves, Westerners lounge on their porches and give garden parties, even though the sky's winter-gray and they have to cover their nice spring clothes with something warmer. By the end of the month, black Denverites and white aficionados of theater and music are hoping that two men heading their way will bring real spring weather with them—a feat those who have seen them perform would not rule out.

Bert Williams and George Walker are probably the most famous comedy act in America. They met in San Francisco at the Mid-Winter Exposition of 1893, standing in for late-arriving Africans in a popular sideshow. Playing Dahomeyans from "darkest Africa," Walker (from Kansas) and Williams (from Los Angeles by way of Antigua) wore animal skins and sang and danced in a jungle of potted palms. After the real Africans arrived, they went to Chicago and developed an act called *Two Real Coons,* Walker telling jokes and playing a well-heeled dandy, Williams as straight man in oversized clothes and burnt-cork blackface. In 1896, they toured the country in a musical farce called *The Gold Bug,* featuring such a memorable, high-stepping cakewalk that many white people thought they made the dance up themselves. Then, in 1902, they produced and starred in *In Dahomey,* a hit Broadway musical, written by the *Clorindy* team of composer Will Marion Cook and poet Paul Laurence Dunbar. And at that moment, as Cook said, "Negroes at last were on Broadway and there to stay. . . . Nothing could stop us, and nothing did for a decade." At the end of the New York run, Williams and Walker took *In Dahomey* to London, where at Edward VII's request they staged a command performance at Buckingham Palace for the birthday of the Prince of Wales.

They've lost no luster by May of 1906, when they are set to perform at Manitou Hall. Afterwards, there'll be a ball in their honor, and women are fluffing up their spring party frocks.

O n April 27, between the announcement of Mrs. McWilliams Walker's imminent departure and the arrival of Williams and Walker, the *Statesman*'s "Denver Doings" touts MRS. WALKER'S OFFER. Beneath this headline is a very nice head-and-shoulders studio photograph, cut beguilingly into a cameo shape.

And so, at age thirty-nine, she finally makes the papers. The photographer has positioned her body straight-on to the camera but has had her turn her head to the right and tuck her chin slightly. She's wearing a satiny, yoked blouse with gathers about the bustline, puffy sleeves and a lacy collar almost to her chin. Her hair's in a soft pile, her eyes slightly downcast in the manner she often favors for pictures, her face relaxed and with an expression of quiet confidence, her gaze steady, her mouth softly closed.

And her offer? That "all persons who will take one treatment before May 15th can secure a letter of instruction teaching them how to grow their own hair, at very reasonable terms." A new idea, treatments coupled with a letter of instruction—and then the ad takes a turn. Instead of providing a critical assessment that praises the hairdresser for being a "God send" who has "done what others have failed to do," Sarah gives a first-person statement of purpose: "I do this so that the very poorest may be benefited and that those who have already been benefited will not suffer in my absence." Of course C. J.'s an old hand at promoting, and might be writing copy in her name, but the point here is the change in strategy.

No "I am like you" assurance, not anymore. Instead, she issues a warning: "Should you fail to take advantage of this opportunity you will always regret it." She then extends her invitation beyond those who have lost hair to others who have it and wish to safeguard it, and makes a final promise: "One treatment will positively stop the hair from falling out." 2410 Champa. Phone Pink 592.

No mention of Mrs. Turnbo-Pope, Wonderful Hair Grower or any other product. The spotlight's on Mrs. Sarah Walker: *her* expertise, *her* generosity, *her* willingness to encourage self-help. And while the ad doesn't repeat the news of her departure, the offer's deadline surely reinforces it.

Suddenly the spring is bustling. Sarah's surely doing hair for the Williams and Walker Ball, the Diamond Ball on the twenty-fourth and the Decoration Day Ball on the thirtieth. C. J.'s hustling tickets for the UOTR May Festival on the tenth and arranging for a one-day excursion to Colorado Springs and the Garden of the Gods on Decoration Day; tickets are $1.50, including round-trip train fare. All this on top of the weekly parlor socials.

Meantime, C. J. and his partner have dropped the employment aspect of their company and extended their real-estate interests to choice lots and homestead land for farming and grazing. "Mrs. Walker's Offer" and C. J.'s revised ad run in the same issue of the paper. Clearly, they're not leaving Denver May 18, just milking the threat.

O n May 4, the day after the Williams and Walker Ball, when people are still in a kind of postdance reverie, C. J. runs plugs for his UOTR festival, the Decoration Day excursion and the parlor social. Madame takes this week's issue off, but the cameo picture appears the next day in the *Colorado Statesman* with an additional paragraph of copy:

> For the benefit of the sceptics I wish to say after once taking treatments of me your hair never falls out. Any one whose hair I treat if only for once will begin growing immediately and if you get my letter of instructions, your hair will never stop growing. As I have a natural gift from childhood for growing hair, give me one trial

and be convinced. Use only Roberts and Popes wonderful grower and beware of imitations. Mrs. C. J. Walker, Address 2410 Champa St., Phone Pink 592.

(The "Roberts" is Mrs. L. L. Roberts, Annie Turnbo's sister.)

So Sarah Walker's not only still working for Mrs. Turnbo-Pope but also bragging about it, warning people of cheesy imitations. This is nervy, to say the least, considering that she herself is in the kitchen right now, stirring up tubs of her own knockoff.

On May 10 at Manitou Hall, C. J. announces a tie in the popularity contest; Mrs. Effie Brown and Miss Owdrie Brown share first prize and both receive a watch. The next day, the shorter version of "Mrs. Walker's Offer" is back in the *Statesman,* but without the photograph. Directly below, the Walkers' landlady, Mrs. Callie Fugitt, offers furnished rooms for rent in a modern house at 2410 Champa Street, Phone Pink 592—possibly their rooms, and maybe they've given notice. Following that is a testimonial letter from St. Louis dated May 5, 1906:

> *Dear Mrs. Walker:*
> *Your letter written me was addressed to 2223 Walnut Street, therefore I was late in receiving it. Now in regard to the oil that woman has, it is just the same stuff these women here have. It is nothing but vaseline with sulphur, quinine and ox marrow. Now if you do not believe this, you just make her an offer for her recipe, and see if she does not tell you the same thing. As I told you, all the people's hair here has come out, so just let that woman do the same for the people there as these fakes are doing here. You know that if I could not do the work and had not a fine preparation I could not have anything at all to do with all the hundreds of people here who are trying to do the same thing. New shops are failing every day from the fact that vaseline is too strong for the hair, and no one has my preparation.*

The letter is signed by—who else?—Mrs. A. M. Pope.

Next day—Saturday the twelfth—the Walkers run an ad in the *Colorado Statesman* featuring the cameo photograph and the longer version of Mrs. Walker's Offer, including Mrs. A. M. Pope's letter and this:

I have been informed that Mrs. Stevenson, better known as Dora Scott, is circulating the story that I am using a preparation made by herself which is absolutely false. I wish to say to my customers to not be led into buying of [sic] her and think you are buying the grower that I represent, Roberts & Pope.

This letter is signed by Mrs. C. J. Walker.

Clearly, the hair-treatment war has begun, and Sarah's in the middle of it. But on whose side? And who is Mrs. Stevenson and why is she known as Dora Scott?

A week later, on the eighteenth, the Walkers run an early version of the ad that will remain a signature for years and years, through the incorporation of the business in 1910 and even after Madame's death.

There are two new head shots of Sarah Walker, side by side. On the left she's directly facing the camera, no tucked chin or lowered eyes. She looks wary and somewhat fearful, as people often do on passports or jail photos. Rather than the fancy satin blouse she wore in the cameo shot, here she's wearing pale linen or perhaps cotton, with lines of white piping down the front. Her hair, parted in the center, falls straight, thick and unstyled, to her shoulders, as if she's washed, toweled and oiled it and is letting it hang before getting out the hot comb. But style isn't the point, only length. In the right-hand photo, she has her back to the camera and her hair's so solidly black that there's nothing much to see except its length and fullness.

Beneath the photographs, the text extends her now-you-see-me-now-you-don't tease:

Mrs. C. J. Walker, the hair grower, through the urgent request of many friends and patrons, has postponed her western tour indefinitely and will remain for a while to convince every person in need of her services of her wonderful power of growing hair. One treatment will positively stop the hair from falling out or money refunded. Her treatments have given perfect satisfaction to every person in Denver who has given her a trial. She also sells letters of instruction to persons whom she can not treat personally, teaching them how to grow their own hair at very reasonable prices. With her treatments your hair begins growing at once. A trial treatment will convince you. Two years ago her hair was less than a finger's length. This is the result of only two years' treatment. Persons out of town wishing letters of instruction, with her wonderful grower, can address her at 2410 Champa, Phone Pink 592.

There's a lot new here: the money-back guarantee; the two-years-ago scenario; mail-order instruction. But mostly a new possessiveness: *her* wonderful powers, *her* treatments, *her* wonderful hair grower. Mrs. Turnbo-Pope's become as useless as a second husband.

The diptych will run through June and off and on until the end of July. Meantime, C. J.'s working on the Decoration Day excursion, and ticket sales are picking up now that he's announced the engagement of the Harris Famous Orchestra, the best-known band in Denver. But the weather's still iffy, and people won't commit to buying a ticket until it lifts. A promoter never rests, but C. J. can only watch the sky and see more dark clouds rolling in.

His wife's stiffest local competition, Mrs. T. D. Perkins, maker of Scalp Salve, has returned from Colorado Springs, announcing that she was kept busy from the moment she arrived until just before her train pulled out. Moreover, she warns her customers about fakers who claim to be her agents, since she doesn't have any. She is, however, flattered by their deception, since "nothing indifferently good is ever counterfeited."

The Decoration Day spectacular has only a so-so turnout, and as May turns to June, Mrs. Walker has to reduce her price to three dollars a month for four treatments, but only for this one month.

Also that June, John Hope is appointed the president of Atlanta's Morehouse College, the first time an African-American has been chosen for such a position. Dr. Hope flies in the face of conventional wisdom by emphasizing academics instead of the farm-and-industrial education offered by Tuskegee and advocated by its founder. Score a point for W. E. B. DuBois.

In late June, Sarah Walker sets out on an eight-week road trip and misses the third annual session of the State Federation of Colored Women's Clubs at Shorter. Madame's busy in Colorado Springs at the time, doing a week's worth of "rushing business in the hair growing line." After which she comes home for a week and then she's off again, a hundred miles south to the prosperous steel town of Pueblo, where she remains for two weeks, then returns home only to find an urgent appeal from the ladies of Trinidad, imploring her to keep her scheduled engagement.

And so on Sunday, July 29, after a week of stirring up hair grower and pressing oil and attending to the hair needs of her local customers, she heads farther south, almost to New Mexico, for a week in Trinidad, a town of coal dust, muddy streets and falling-down houses. Still, the women there want to look attractive. Then follows another week in Colorado Springs, and the realization that she has such hearty support in Pueblo that from now on she'll make monthly trips.

Does she travel alone? Perhaps her niece Anjetta accompanies her, acting as her assistant and model, learning the ropes. And now that Sarah has announced her departure from Denver and is making plans for a long trip to the South, she's been in touch with Lelia, telling her to come at once, sending her money for clothes and a ticket west.

In August, C. J. moves on from real estate and starts a monthly publication, the *Progressive Afro-American*. He's the editor and manager, with a local doctor as his associate and, likely, his backer. And perhaps this is where the false claim that he'd founded the Western Negro Press Association originates. But in the marriage and partnership, he's losing his place and might feel edgy enough to encourage his wife to cut back on travel and accept her local fame and prosperity; after all, Denver's been good to her in a short time, barely more than a year, and maybe she should stay.

But Madame's on a roll, and she will never say no to business. And because of these basic disagreements, after only seven months they are probably feuding, and with this kind of trouble in the works and his wife on the road so much, the demands on C. J.'s faithfulness can only increase. Nor would Madame necessarily expect this from him. Besides, as her business heats up, she needs him less and less, in every respect. Her life is with women, as is her business. She sells to women, hires women, listens to women. A husband can be useful. He lends a woman respectability, makes her seem steady and trustworthy. Just so long as he doesn't, like Mr. Pope, get in his wife's way.

In mid-August, racial politics erupt onto front pages in both the black and white press. When a few Negro soldiers stationed in Brownsville, Texas, respond to racial slurs by getting rowdy, President Roosevelt dishonorably discharges the entire battalion. A huge protest ensues, and Booker T. Washington tries to change his mind, but TR stands firm.

A few days later, DuBois commences the second meeting of the Niagara Movement at Harper's Ferry, West Virginia, where delegates pay tribute to John Brown and march till dawn to "The Battle Hymn of the Republic." DuBois demands that the full rights of citizenship be given to all African-American men. Soon afterwards, Washington's National Negro Business League meets in Atlanta, and the Wizard claims his meeting has helped to improve racial attitudes in the very city where his rival DuBois teaches, at Atlanta University. Less than a month later, all hell breaks loose. Shortly after the opening of Thomas Dixon's white supremacist play *The Clansman* (on which the film *The Birth of a Nation* will be based), thousands of white Atlantans go wild—inflamed by reports of alleged assaults on white women—and use clubs and sticks to beat every black man they find. "In some portions of the street," the *Atlanta Constitution* will report, "the sidewalks ran red with the blood of dead and dying negroes." Even the stodgy, racist Memphis *Commercial Appeal* is shocked, declaring that Atlanta has brought shame to the South.

President Roosevelt has no comment.

By August 17, Sarah's made up her mind and is finally leaving Denver. In the *Statesman,* she runs the cameo shot, and this ad begins, "Mme. Walker, the hair grower . . ."

Madame? Of course, this was a term many women used at this time, especially in the realms of beautification, health and domestic arts, of elocution and palmistry, bestowing a European distinction and hauteur. Still, for Sarah Breedlove it's a new spin entirely.

The ad lists towns Mme. Walker has been to, and states that she'll return to Colorado Springs until the twentieth, then come back to Denver and spend two weeks, "to straighten up her business affairs, after which she will positively leave on her southern tour . . . to put *her* wonderful hair grower on the market throughout the country" (emphasis added).

Annie Turnbo-Pope hears the news and, citing "fraudulent imitations," copyrights a new trade name. From now on she will call her products and her merchandising system by the name Poro, a West African philosophy dedicated to disciplining and enhancing the body both physically and spiritually, as well as a convenient merger of "POpe" and "ROberts." "Beware of imitations!" her new ads warn. "The proof of the value of our work is that we are being imitated and largely by persons whose own hair we have actually grown and the further fact that they have very frequently mentioned us when trying to sell their goods."

Mrs. Pope further insists that Poro Hair Grower is the oldest and best of its kind and refers to herself as the original hair grower. People should make sure the name Poro is on the box, as well as "Prepared only by MRS. A. M. Pope." (Eventually, Annie Pope will marry again and become Annie Malone, and after that she too will often be called Madame, but only as a title of respect, not as a brand name. Her trade name will soon become "Poro," and some people will speak of "Poro-ing" their hair and will refer to her as Madam Poro.) In reply, eight satisfied Pueblo customers write a letter to the *Colorado Statesman* arguing that Madam Walker never claimed that her preparation was as good as or better than Mrs. Pope's, but only said hers was the best on the market. They also vow never to use Poro products as long as Madame's are available, because "until Mme. Walker came here we never heard of any hair grower" and with Mrs. Pope way off in St. Louis, they might have all been bald-headed for all she knew or cared. And they finish off their attack by calling her most recent letter "purely spite work."

On August 23, Madam Walker returns home after three weeks in Trinidad, Pueblo and Colorado Springs, to welcome Lelia to Denver and to "arrange her business affairs before leaving for the South." That same day, the Walkers run a new ad alongside the cameo shot in the *Statesman,* reiterating that "Mme. Walker will only be here for two weeks," after which . . . "Miss Lelia McWilliams, Mme. Walker's daughter, who has taken a course in hair growing in St. Louis . . . [will] take charge of her mother's business at 2410 Champa."

"Taken a course in hair growing" may refer to Lelia's participation in Sarah's kitchen experiments, or even lessons she took from Annie Turnbo; in any case the ad's reference seems only a backhanded compliment, with no mention of expertise or, for that matter, praise for a trustworthy heir.

Next week's ad notes that after September 1, Mme. Walker the hair grower will be located at 2317 Lawrence Street, and after relocating will open for business at 7 a.m. and "positively receive no customers after

4:30 p.m." This new address—a frame duplex on a street filled with houses and businesses, including a cigar-box factory—is certainly less tony than Champa, but presumably they have the whole house this time.

The following week, the diptych is accompanied by the announcement that "Mr. and Mme C. J. Walker" will be leaving Denver on September 15 to place their goods on the market throughout the Southern and Eastern states. They will take the Santa Fe south, making stops at Colorado Springs, Pueblo, Walsenburg, Trinidad and Grand Junction, taking their meals in the dining car and staying in the homes of her customers and agents. Moreover, "Miss Lelia McWilliams, her daughter, will be in charge of her business at 2317 Lawrence St. Agents wanted everywhere. Address all communications to Mrs. Walker" at that address.

On September 4, a Mrs. Laura Carson entertains "Mr. and Mrs. C. J. Walker and their daughter, Miss Lelia McWilliams of St. Louis," with a five-course farewell dinner. And on the fifteenth, Madam C. J. Walker leaves Denver. After her Colorado stops she will head for Oklahoma, Texas and the Deep South.

Except for the new clothes and comfortable living quarters, Lelia can't be wildly enthusiastic about any of this. She has lived in the heart of ragtime St. Louis, experiencing the freedom and anonymity of city life, and she has no head for business. Denver's in the middle of Rocky Mountain nowhere; and so, considering all of this, she is bound to sulk, and yearn to go back where life is livelier, women more stylish and the trends made, not copied. Her cousin Anjetta works for—or with—her, and I can't help thinking that these two young women are destined to be enemies. Anjetta's efficiency gives her a lock on Madame's approval. Lelia's been wildly overindulged, and at twenty-one, has no idea how responsibilities correspond with achievement and material possessions. But she's Madame's baby, for life.

The week after the Walkers leave, a much smaller ad appears in the *Statesman,* without a photograph. "If you want long and beautiful hair, if you want your hair to stop falling at once, if you want your hair to look natural and fluffy, if you want your scalp cured of all diseases, go to Mme Walker's Parlors, 2317 Lawrence St., Mrs. Lelia McWilliams, Successor."

After the hard sell of money-back guarantees, this is a much softer touch, with a far more straightforward message, and the ad runs every week. And now that she's officially part of the business, Lelia's been renamed as well, from "Miss" to "Mrs."—and "Successor."

In his annual end-of-the-year speech to Congress, Roosevelt excuses lynching by declaring Negro men at fault for assaults on white women. After the president's Brownsville decision, Booker T. Washington's practically the last black American of any standing to stick by him. Yet the Tuskegee machine is increasingly criticized, and DuBois essentially accuses the Wizard of paying the press for favorable coverage. Washington makes no comment, realizing he's still popular with the people and will soon gain financial control of the influential *New York Age.*

Because they are planning to make stops throughout the South, Sarah and C. J. have to reach ahead as they go, make arrangements from Louisiana for Mississippi, in Mississippi for Alabama, sending letters ahead to Tennessee and Kentucky, all the way up to Pennsylvania. Train porters are a big help—they constitute a kind of grapevine telegraph that carries migrational news about which city people of the race are moving to, what churches they're joining and, judging by the accommodations they take en route, how prosperous they are, how high their expectations.

Years from now, C. J. will take credit for Sarah's decision to strike out with her own line of products. "It is somewhat trying to me," he will write Walker Company manager Freeman Ransom in 1922, "when I look back to the beginning of the first establishment of this business, and the hard struggles that the Mme. & I had in those days. I alone am responsible for the successful beginning of this business. Otherwise the Mme. would have taken the road for the Poro people." C. J.'s boast flies in the face of Madame's statement that her husband eventually "decided to join heart and hand with her to make her work a success, notwithstanding he could see nothing ahead but failure," having predicted that she would not make expenses from one town to the next.

The Jim Crow laws, commencing in Oklahoma, would be demoralizing to a man like C. J. Walker, while his wife always finds a way to negotiate coolly with reality, even if that means wearing black clothes so that if locomotive soot settles into the weave of her dress it doesn't spoil the impression of her arrival.

Believing that refinement pays, the woman now called Madame sits tall.

Back in Denver, Lelia's presumably keeping watch on Lawrence Street, stirring hair grower and filling orders. Or does she? Whatever's in the secret formula—it's bound to stink. The mixing's sticky, the pouring tedious. Nothing in her character as we know it inclines Lelia McWilliams toward solitude, single-mindedness, an active interior life or the toleration of any kind of unpleasantness. *She always had to be doing something,* her Harlem circle will comment after Lelia's death: gambling at poker or bridge, going to jazz clubs, taking endless shopping trips. Sometimes, her girl-friends report, they'd be driving around Harlem and Lelia would decide they had to go to Atlantic City, so they'd turn the car toward New Jersey, figuring they'd buy clothes or whatever else they needed once they got there.

But twenty-one years old, glum in the high Rockies? Isolation and sameness can drive a person pinball crazy; anyway, who ever said she wanted to live in Colorado when, elsewhere, times are changing fast, people having wilder kinds of fun? In New York, women are smoking cigarettes right out on the sidewalks. Surely Lelia wishes her mother would hurry up and make more money so that they could all head east again, where people know how to kick out the jams and *live.*

On August 9, 1907, an ad in the *Statesman* announces that Madam C. J. Walker is in Louisville, Kentucky, where—after spending eleven months in the Southern states, including Old Mexico—she has been the guest of honor at three receptions. Since they left Denver, Sarah and C. J. have been to Oklahoma, Arkansas, Mississippi, Alabama, Georgia and all over the South, and because C. J.'s sister, Agnes Prosser, lives in Louisville, that's become a kind of home base for them, where they can rest from the road and gather strength before moving on again. After this visit, they will head east into West Virginia, Pennsylvania and New York State.

A grand reception isn't a social affair but an opportunity to sell product, hire agents and spread the word. This is spelled out in Madame's 1917 manifesto "Hints to Agents": "All you have to do is get around among the people, in other words be a mixer, properly distributing your literature, and you will be able to place orders faster than we can possibly supply them."

Madam Walker dresses impeccably on all such occasions, styles her hair flawlessly, and when invited by the host or hostess to say a few words she knows how to waft silkily to the front of the room and explain that two years ago her hair wouldn't grow at all, that she had bald spots she couldn't cover, and now look.

Further hints to agents: "Acquaint yourself with the history and life of Madam C. J. Walker, get on the very tip of your tongue the strong points that you will find in the story of her personal experience, tell your prospective customer about her, do so in an intelligent and emphatic way, watch his or her face, note what statement or statements impress most AND THEN DRIVE THE NAIL HOME."

After speaking, Madame mingles. Since protocol has it that women do not shake hands, when introduced she nods, responds soft and low, makes each woman think that for one quick piece of time she is the only person in the room, then moves on. Meanwhile, the selling never stops, and she is never merely having a conversation; she is always working the room and waiting for the moment when she can turn social pleasantries into a sale. All salesmen know this.

Hint: "Keep in mind that you have something that the person standing before you really needs, imagine yourself a missionary and convert him. Be tactful, if you find that one line of talk won't work try another, ALWAYS REMEMBERING THAT, *YOU ARE THERE TO SELL.*"

Using personal ties and the ingrained habits of community and bonding, women have always gathered—at church and in missionary societies, in the kitchen or out under the trees fixing one another's hair, on the front porch quilting, cooking meals for wedding parties and funerals. Women collaborate, discuss their children and the Bible, drink coffee or tea together, listen to a lecture or a reading given by an elocutionist, search for new ways to uplift themselves and educate their children. While men place more value on individualism, womanhood joins community to entrepreneurship.

"We are anxious to help all humanity, the poor as well as the rich, especially those of our race. There are thousands who would buy and use the goods who are not able to pay the extra cost of having it done for them. The hair may not grow as rapidly nor look as beautiful, but they will get results, as long as they are satisfied and you have made your profit from the sale, all is well."

She speaks of keeping the business in the race, and says that the factory she is planning to build will provide for the "employment of many of our boys and girls." The factory idea is new, but the women nod and believe, astounded and, bound by togetherness, perhaps even happy.

Once again, the beauty business is changing. When Max Factor opens a cosmetics shop in Hollywood to serve the movie industry, he is inundated with mail orders from women from the general public, so he expands his enterprise to meet the demand. At age forty-three, a white woman named Florence Nightingale Graham moves from a poverty-strapped life in Canada to Manhattan, where she wins a job with a pharmaceutical company and studies the behavior and dress of society women. Two years later she takes the name Mrs. Elizabeth Arden—"Elizabeth" for a former colleague, "Arden" for the Tennyson poem *Enoch Arden,* the "Mrs." not because of an actual marriage but because of the dignity the institution bestows—and opens her own shop on Fifth Avenue. In no time, Elizabeth Arden is running a business empire, speaking in an elegant whisper and seen everywhere, swishing in and out of theater boxes snooty as a born blueblood.

Florence Graham doesn't think she has become a new person. She believes that Elizabeth Arden was her genuine self, from the beginning.

The August 9 ad is what the newspaper trade of the times calls a "high-class advertisement," pricey and illustrated—in this case "the latest photograph of Madam C. J. Walker," the one in the short-sleeved white lace dress taken beside the gilt-framed mirror. She is then described as "the wonderful hair grower and scalp specialist of Denver" who, despite opposition and obstacles, has "achieved a greater success than has any other woman in her line. . . ."

Now, Sarah Walker knows she's never going back to Denver, but the ad aims to assure her Rocky Mountain customers she is still one of them and a neighbor. (In a couple of years, in the *Pennsylvania Business Directory,* she omits Denver entirely.) Still, there's nothing of the West in that photograph—neither how she's dressed or standing, nor the dreamy, almost kittenish look in her eyes—and few in the Mile High City would be fooled.

The phrase "greater success than . . . any other woman in her line" is bound to irk Sarah's former employer. And "scalp specialist" would certainly annoy Mrs. T. D. Perkins, Denver's resident hairdresser, who was using the term in 1906 when Sarah was merely an agent for Mrs. Turnbo-Pope.

The ad provides a rosy account of the Walkers' eleven-month trip. In Dallas, Madam Walker was royally entertained at a party given by Mrs. Ella Noble and Miss Julia L. Caldwell, who invited only the city's most exclusive set; the same was true in Knoxville, C. J. Walker's "old home and birth place," and throughout the tour. Meanwhile, demand for her own Wonderful Hair Grower has shot up to thirty gallons a day, and so Madame once again mentions the possibility of quitting the road to build a factory and offices, though no clue is given as to possible locations.

The advertisement concludes with the bold prediction that within a few years Mr. and Madam Walker might be numbered among "the most wealthy Negroes in this country." And though the Lawrence address is given, Lelia's name is not mentioned. Communications are to be addressed to Madam C. J. Walker. And the Walkers sign off with a hearty toast to themselves: "To them luck, health and wealth."

How in the world can Madame and C. J. come by thirty gallons of Wonderful Hair Grower a day? Say thirty's an exaggeration and it's only ten. Only the women in Denver could be producing it. Once the Walker Company is incorporated and her factory's up and running, Madame will set her sister-in-law and four nieces up in Los Angeles, buying and furnishing a house for them, giving them jobs and publicizing her magnanimity. ("Tell them I bought my sister-in-law a house in California free and clear," she will instruct her business manager to write in a press release.) Madame never forgets a favor—or a slight—and Lucy and her two older daughters may be earning their future upkeep now, stirring the pots and shipping the boxes, oiling the wheels of business.

The hale closing toast in the *Statesman* ad is exactly that: farewell to the city in which Sarah McWilliams Walker replicated Wonderful Hair Grower, appropriated Annie Turnbo-Pope's brand name and became, for life, Madam C. J. Walker. Many questions remain as to the origins of Wonderful Hair Grower; many tales have been told slanting the evidence one way or the other. But odds run strongly against Sarah Walker as its creator, and in the matter of the brand name there is no mystery: it belongs to Annie Minerva Turnbo.

The following May, Turnbo-Pope announces that scalp specialist Mrs. M. A. Holley from St. Louis will soon set up shop at 2118 Arapahoe, only two blocks from Madame's Lawrence Street office, as Denver's "sole agent for the famed preparation, 'Poro.'" That same month, according to a column in the *Statesman*, "Madam C. J. Walker and Miss McWilliams, her successor, wish to announce to their customers, old and new, that they have decided to open up business elsewhere and close up their business in Denver."

Time to move on.

V · Pittsburgh, 1907–1910

The Fame of Her Goods

Denver, she concluded, was too far west. . . . The fame of her goods was established. . . . She settled at Pittsburgh, where she remained for two and a half years.

INDIANAPOLIS FREEMAN, JANUARY 11, 1911

Within two months, the national economy goes bonkers. First, Manhattan's Knickerbocker Bank is rumored to be running out of cash; overnight, people line up in queues stretching for blocks, to cash out their accounts the minute the bank opens. Within days, this is repeated at other banks, and not surprisingly the dominoes fall. The Knickerbocker closes, then other banks. Business blames the government, President Roosevelt blames business and foreign markets. By the end of the year, the Panic of 1907 is in full swing nationwide and the Walkers are still on the road, probably in the South.

Industrial cities take the hardest hit, and mills respond in Andrew Carnegie fashion, by laying off workers, cutting wages or even closing. For over two decades, a steady stream of European immigrants has moved into Pittsburgh, drawn to a city where most of the country's glass and more than half its open-hearth steel is manufactured. By 1907, in a population of about half a million, some 150,000 people are working in over a hundred firms along the Allegheny and Mononga-hela Rivers, making glass and steel and machine parts, processing iron and coke. Fiery mills and factories ribbon the riverbanks, including the Carnegie, Clark and Moorhead mills, the Westinghouse electrical machinery manufacturers, Gulf Oil, Armstrong Cork, the Black Diamond Mill, the Diamond Coke and Coal Company. Their owners enjoy unprecedented wealth, but now even they join the panic. By early 1908, layoffs and wage reductions have reversed the immigration flow, with more people leaving than coming.

Nonetheless, for the Walkers western Pennsylvania makes good business sense. Madame's primary markets are the East and the South, with Pennsylvania in the middle. Philadelphia has a bigger African-American population, but Pittsburgh's more receptive to new ideas and its black population—already twenty-five thousand—is growing even during the Panic, mostly people fleeing from the rural South. And since Pittsburgh has no weekly race paper, C. J. has it in mind to publish a local edition of his Denver monthly, the *Progressive Afro-American*. He can kick the paper off fast enough; it's only four pages, and he can pack the inside two with syndicated ads, then fill page 1 with canned, illustrated stories of representative men like Teddy Roosevelt and Booker T. Washington. Page 4 will be devoted to local news: church and club announcements, weddings and sports.

As a springboard for the paper and to let people know he's in town, C. J. is planning a conference, a big one, with the best-known names in the race—Washington, Trotter, DuBois, Fortune, Terrell—talking about the issues of the day. All he needs is one yes, then the rest will follow. And afterwards, he'll be set.

Lelia might have contributed to the Pittsburgh idea. She later proves adept at zeroing in on the next hot city or going fad, and during her stint at Knoxville College, she wasn't all that far away; moreover, as we'll eventually see, she has other connections to the Pittsburgh area. She may in fact already be there when her mother arrives.

By the time the Walkers have made the decision to go—at least by December 23, 1907, when Sarah turns forty—the Pittsburgh Stock Exchange has shut down for three months due to the recession; and in 1908, when they board the train east out of Louisville, the economic news remains bleak. In Pittsburgh the Carnegie Steel Company has followed its owner's philosophy by reducing workers' wages at his Homestead plant by as much as a third, without reducing their hours. Muckraking reporter Lincoln Steffens says that during these years, Pittsburgh "looked like hell, literally. Arriving of an evening I walked out aimlessly into the smoky gloom of its deep-dug streets and somehow got across a bridge up on a hill that overlooked the city with its fiery furnaces and the two rivers that pinched it in. The blast furnaces opened periodically and threw their volcanic light upon the cloud of mist and smoke above the town and gilded the silver rivers. . . ." And he categorizes the city in two ways: politically as "Hell with the lid on," physically as "Hell with the lid off."

But C. J. and Madame don't pay much mind to all this bad news. According to the annual report of the National Negro Business League, Sarah's 1907 income is $3,652, triple that of the previous year. And anyway, because African-Americans live outside of the news of the day, the Panic is strictly white people's business. Even in a few years' time, when unions gain some power to improve workers' lives, black men and women will remain different and apart. Statistics about industrial workers refer only to white people; African-Americans are placed in their own category and still do not, in any meaningful way, *count*.

And so, despite the Panic and the layoffs, the Walkers soldier on into the Steel City.

While St. Louis was pasty-gray and Denver grimy, in Pittsburgh the smoke and soot collaborate to turn daytime to night. A black man who migrated there from Richmond said that he found Pittsburgh a "smokey hole," where "until almost 3 p.m. in the day, you couldn't see nothing." Mills pour out their dark effluvia at all hours. No city filtration system is yet in operation, so any steelworker who tries to quench his great thirst by guzzling from a communal jug increases his risk of typhoid. When the English writer Anthony Trollope came to visit in 1862, he reported that he made black footprints when stepping from his bath onto a pale green rug. And philosopher Herbert Spencer reckoned a month in Pittsburgh justification for suicide.

The Walkers might arrive sometime during the winter or early spring months of 1908, when oil-powered streetlamps create flickering yellow balls in the miasma. Since black men are thought to have an inborn affinity for horses, they drive the cabs and buses and do the teamstering. Seeing such a prosperous-looking couple, the driver of a horse-drawn bus would make a beeline—not because of race but because they're obviously good for the tab.

Their destination—2518 Wylie Avenue—comes as no surprise. Though well-to-do African-Americans have been moving toward the East End for a year or so, Wylie's still known as the prime Negro street. Running east-west along a ridge in the upper Hill District, Wylie was once overwhelmingly Jewish, then Italian, and then some parts went Irish or German, but by now everyone's gone except the blacks.

When I drove up Wylie Avenue in a steady drizzle, many buildings had been torn down, and the Civic Auditorium sits where the lower part of the avenue used to be. The steel mills are closed, the air clear. But the Walkers' house still stands: brick, two-story, narrow and, at ninety-plus years old, obviously somewhat sturdy. That day, two single mattresses were piled up on the sidewalk, the wrought-iron railing by the front steps was leaning and from the second floor, a long wire dangled down the front of the house, hanging from a cracked, taped upstairs window. There was no telling if anyone lived there.

Bourgeois and rough-edged, Pittsburgh began as a wilderness fort and became—a century later and due to its confluence of rivers and great mineral resources—the grazing land for the hungry bankers and industrialists of the Gilded Age, especially after the Pennsylvania Railroad hit town. "The apotheosis of American civilization," a local booster calls the Steel City. And if civilization means the pursuit and rewards of money pure and simple, that's correct. The Mellons, Heinzes, Carnegies, Fricks, Westinghouses have all built lavish mansions here, though they often decamp for Florida, Newport and New York City, leaving the millworkers to their shacks on the city's steep hillsides.

Sarah Walker is forty, which in 1908 is not young, and since childhood she has worked so hard that her health is sometimes fragile. In her time, diabetes plagues the African-American population, though most don't realize it; in middle age they simply begin to feel odd, and then other symptoms hit. But poor health isn't something she has time for, and so she waves it away. Nor can she waste time second-guessing the decision to move east, especially since she's the one who probably made it. Up to now, C. J. might've been the facilitator and promoter, the expert in sales and marketing, but by now Sarah's figuring things out for herself; and while her husband may still think he's in charge, when it comes to her business she never submits to an idea she does not believe in.

There are things about the East which neither of the Walkers can properly have assessed: for instance, an ingrained snobbery that spans all racial and ethnic categories. There are clubs no black man or woman can get into without being OP, Old Pittsburgh, which derives from the free-born, light-skinned families that settled here before the Civil War. Of course the Walkers have known social prejudice within the race before now, but when Madam Walker says in her advertisement that in Dallas only the most exclusive set was invited to her party, she cannot have had any notion how easy it is to breach exclusivity in Texas as compared to Pennsylvania.

For starters, Pittsburgh already has its star hairdresser, Mrs. Virginia Proctor, the daughter of Lewis Goodson: barber, minister, civic leader, scion of a family whose roots in Pittsburgh go back to 1830. Proctor's "Hair Shop," where her husband, Jacob, barbers the likes of the Carnegies and Westinghouses, is one of the city's most successful businesses. Though there won't be a black public-school teacher in Pittsburgh for another twenty-five years, Mrs. Proctor's first cousin, Lemuel Googins, sits on the City Council, the first black man elected to city office.

No question, Mrs. Proctor is seriously OP. And the question is, can a community of twenty-five thousand make room for *another* hair diva?

Immigration from Europe has flooded the job market. While the best hotels once hired only black waiters, now they prefer Italians and Germans. Same with barbers. But at the upper levels, educated and skilled people of the race are holding their own. OP's are doctors, lawyers, ministers, barbers, postal employees and elocutionists, none of whom wish to mingle with darker-hued refugees from the South, who then are denied entry to the all-important clubs. Women belong to the Married Women's Culture Club or the Young Married Ladies' Social Club, while men join the Masons, the Knights of Tabor and, most importantly, the Loendi Club, where "the latch string ever hangs upon the outside to strangers," but once admitted within its portals, a man will find himself "within the charming circle of the best people in the city."

Denver was easier, friendlier, but maybe the Walkers don't know that yet. Climbing Twenty-eighth going crosstown, the bus passes alleys piled with trash and running with sewage, then comes to Wylie, where the driver reins his horse west, toward downtown. They pass the Little Gem Café, the Warren Gymnasium (a private establishment where in warm weather refined young people of the race indulge themselves in the newest hot sport, lawn tennis), the Industrial Home for Boys, a rowhouse whose window sign reads MARY DAWSON, HAIRDRESSER, a grocery store with produce displayed under an overhang. In the 2600 block there is a combination doctor's office and pharmacy.

The Hill District begins where the Civic Auditorium now sits, on the edge of downtown at Fifth Avenue, from which Wylie gradually ascends. The Lower Hill, built up first, was once the choicer area, but it has suffered years of poverty and civic neglect, so while houses on the higher-numbered blocks are smaller, narrower and more closely jammed together, they are newer and therefore—thus far—nicer.

Pittsburgh is not an easy city to get around in, and its hills and rivers and sharp valleys make for naturally defined ethnic neighborhoods: Poles in the South Side and Polish Hill, Italians in Bloomfield and East Liberty, the so-called Scotch-Irish hither and yon. From high on Wylie, the Walkers might occasionally catch a flash of light from across the Monongahela when one of the Homestead furnaces opens for a moment.

The dampness of a river city is especially chilling. Standing on a dirt sidewalk either glazed over with ice or deep in black mud, everything she owns jammed into bags and boxes, Sarah Walker, as always, must feel—is—alone, even as her husband carries their luggage toward the front steps of 2518 Wylie Avenue. Down the street, unemployed men stand on the corner smoking cigarettes, nothing else to do but wonder what might happen next. In the alleys she saw men down on their luck, drinking and playing cards or dice. Hard winter, hard times, another dark street. And in fact, this will be C. J.'s business address, not hers. From Wylie Sarah cannot fairly compete with Virginia Proctor just down the hill, and one way or another she *will* compete, because this diva and OP is behind the times. Mrs. Proctor does no mail order, hasn't established agencies or redesigned the hot comb; she can't make hair grow, and hasn't heard the news that using wigs to cover bald spots is passé. Sarah Walker will drive a wedge right into her business by creating a desire that the women of Pittsburgh don't even know they have, and which only she can satisfy. The very thought of this kind of competition emboldens the natural seller, warms the drummer's blood and gives the entrepreneur a great rush.

Built between 1905 and the Panic, 2518 Wylie has a flat roof and is crowded on either side by similar row houses. The front door is to the left, with four concrete steps leading up to it, and there are two windows on the ground floor, three on the second. The Walkers lug boxes and trunks into the dark hall. Presumably, since they have not yet established permanent residence, they are still renting furnished rooms and bring with them nothing they can't themselves haul.

In no time, Sarah will be running her business from 139 South Highland Avenue in the fashionable East End, where nobody ever expected to see Negroes. This is the general neighborhood where the Carnegies and the Fricks built their mansions; but in the northern blocks, closer to Pennsylvania and the railroad tracks, there is a section open to smaller homes and businesses. And this is where refined African-Americans are moving, proudly stamping it on their cards and stationery: E. EMORY PAYNE OF RENFREW STREET, EAST END. Sarah has to work where the money is. Lelia will set up housekeeping three blocks away. And they will not only be many blocks from Virginia Proctor's Hair Shop, but also in a better location.

As for C. J.'s big conference, anything is possible. He's certainly nervy enough to dream up a national gathering, and he knows about staging shows, but the best-known black men in America are in great demand and, unless they believe there is some benefit in it, would not dream of sitting down together at a conference organized by a man nobody knows. Nor have they heard of his publication. But C. J. will invite the Wizard and DuBois and announce their acceptance without receiving it. And he believes it will all end well, because he can't afford to think otherwise.

I imagine Madame falling exhausted into bed, restoring herself for the next day's business as C. J. makes his way back down to Wylie Avenue to have a drink at the Little Gem and talk up his plan to anybody who'll listen. Talk can turn hope into a certainty, even before anything's actually happened. He and his wife both have big dreams, but hers depend on a formula she believes in and knows how to sell, while C. J.'s spin, toplike, on their own.

"Afro-American Notes"

Since 1843, when abolitionist Martin Delany published the *Mystery,* Pittsburgh's black community has seen a dozen newspapers come and go. Some of the most recent were the brainchildren of Rev. T. J. "Broad Axe" Smith, who published three failed papers in a row, the last of which, the *Broad Axe,* lasted from 1896 until 1901 and left its founder only a nickname. Subsequently, another paper, the *Independent,* drifted in and quickly out.

This gives C. J. an empty market to fill, and his timing is auspicious. This is the year of the sesquicentennial of Pittsburgh, 1908, and like St. Louis in 1904, the city is going all out. C. J.'s banking on this both for his convention and, ultimately, his *Progressive Afro-American.* And Madame certainly envisions similar benefits for her enterprise.

For the moment, black people turn to a column that runs once a week in the *Pittsburgh Press,* a white newspaper. "Afro-American Notes," a kind of community bulletin board, is edited by Dr. John W. Browning, a light-skinned local pharmacist with degrees from Tuskegee and Howard who serves as a kind of social arbiter, deciding what's news and what's trash, so his column is widely read and quoted. And on July 12, 1908, C. J. Walker gets a mention: "Plans are being made for a big eastern interstate negro press convention to be held here on September 1, 2, and 3. This meeting is principally for the purpose of uniting representatives of the press and discussing the political situation as it touches upon the negro race. C. J. Walker, editor of the *Progressive Afro-American,* N. S. Boone, C. H. Harris, the Rev. C. M. Moses and the Rev. A. J. Duval compose the local committee on arrangements."

For C. J., this is uncharacteristically modest—as if the event were developing on its own. As for the committee, Boone (or Buhne) owns a printing company, and while there is a Reverend *Henry* J. Duval listed in the directory, he is not affiliated with any particular church. I can find no trace of Moses; Harris, who lives on the lower end of Wylie, is an agent, like C. J.

Another item in that day's "Notes" describes the rousing sermons given by AME Bishop W. B. Derrick of Flushing, New York, on the occasion of the reopening of the St. James AME Church after a fire. A man of renown, the bishop visits Pittsburgh often, and in the coming years will make regular treks to Indianapolis. In 1917, his home in Queens will figure hugely in Madame's plans. And since St. James is in the East End, not far from Madame's shop, perhaps she hears Bishop Derrick's sermons and, like many other African-Americans, counts him from this time forward as someone to honor and emulate, not so much on religious grounds as an example to the race.

After listing the ubiquitous club meetings, the "Notes" gives big play to the sesquicentennial. The official celebration kicks off on the Fourth of July with a parade and the unveiling of an Augustus Saint-Gaudens monument in memory of the millionaire political boss Chris Magee. But the main events will run from September 27 to October 1, and Dr. Browning suggests that the city's Afro-Americans start making their plans now.

Two weeks later, he runs a press release:

C. J. Walker, editor of the *Progressive Afro-American,* of this city, has issued a call for a mass convention of the negro newspapers of the country, to be held in this city, September 1–5 in the John Wesley A.M.E. Zion Church. He has elaborated quite an imposing program in which appears the names of many of the prominent men of the race in the country. The condition of national politics, the Brownsville incident and many things objectionable to the colored race will be discussed and measures to best serve the interests of the colored people will be determined. The gathering is to be non-partisan. The committee in charge of arrangements has sent out 5,000 invitations to colored citizens who are not connected with the newspapers, requesting them to attend the convention. . . .

The list of luminaries invited includes Washington, DuBois, Monroe Trotter, Mary Church Terrell, and George Knox.

The committee has expanded, Walker adding Dr. John W. Brown, a physician; Mrs. Maggie Wilson, who will become Madame's top Pittsburgh agent and a lifelong friend; and Mrs. Sarah Walker herself. The list of honorary vice-presidents includes lawyers, ministers, another printer, a caterer and a porter, Grant White, who lives at 2518 Wylie and is a friend of Lelia's (underscoring the gathering likelihood of her presence in Pittsburgh)—all in all, an impressive bunch.

Conferences and annual conventions have become customary occasions all over the country, and in staging this one, C. J.'s following in the illustrious footsteps of Booker T. Washington (the National Negro Business League) and W. E. B. DuBois (Niagara Movement). But his main goal is not to discuss national politics but to publicize his little newspaper, and to ensure his success he's using a familiar ploy, implying that everybody who counts will be there and invitees had better act fast or risk being left out.

By summer, the city directory has C. J. Walker living at 2518 Wylie Avenue, but since neither Madam Walker nor her hairdressing establishment is listed, there or any place else, we have to assume that although she's certainly open for business, she's still pulling things together, getting herself established. Also listed on Wylie Avenue is the *Progressive Afro-American,* which moreover appears in the Newspapers and Periodicals category in the directory's business section.

As the summer moves into its hottest, meanest months, six men in Houston are lynched on suspicion of plotting a murder. In Springfield, Illinois, a white woman accuses a Negro man of raping her and in response the governor calls out the militia. Racial tensions are already running high, since black men are being used as strikebreakers in the coal mines; and when the woman makes this charge, whites go on a frenzy of beating, burning and lynching. By the time the white woman recants and confesses that the rapist was white, eight African-Americans have been killed and many hundreds hurt. In the aftermath, some two thousand black people flee the city that claims Abraham Lincoln, and whites try to drive out those who remain, even issuing anonymous death threats to businessmen who refuse to fire black employees.

The only positive result of the Springfield outrages comes when Mary Ovington White, a wealthy white citizen, attempts to form the nation's first biracial organization to oppose racial terrorism and discrimination.

The first week of September passes without word of the "eastern interstate negro press convention" meant to occur from the first through the fifth. On the sixth, "Notes" announces that it will be held at the John Wesley AME Zion Church on October 14–16 and will address the "general condition of the race in this country and to devise some methods for their amelioration." But Dr. Browning has downgraded its importance by coupling it in the same paragraph with another meeting, possibly due to the postponement and the lack of hard information. Then, on September 27, he reprints a press release that declares the National Conference of Negro Newspapermen will open as planned, and adds that "just who will attend and what will be transacted is not even guessed at. Many men of national prominence have been invited." Fewer names are given for the local committee, but Mrs. Sarah Walker remains. The statement is a model of vagueness, grandeur and the passive voice.

The sesquicentennial commences with a huge pageant on the Monongahela, and top-hatted participants include Vice President Charles Fairbanks, representing Roosevelt, and the big man who will become the next president, William H. Taft. Roosevelt's daughter christens a boat, the flag is raised by a doll-faced young woman and some three hundred thousand curious observers line the river from east of downtown to where it joins the Allegheny and the Ohio.

On Tuesday, October 14, when C. J.'s conference is meant to open, there is instead a scalding notice in "Notes":

> The Colored Interstate Press Council, which was heralded to be held in this city during the past week, by a man named Walker, who conducts a little 2 × 4 patent inside and outside weekly paper, failed to materialize. Most of the colored editors are just now too busy politically to waste valuable time talking generalities, especially when it is all a boon for the other fellow, and he is a newspaper stranger and not much of a newspaper man. . . . The project has been sent along because of the good of the city and not because there was any tangible good could come out of it. Quite a number of fellows who could not tell a composing stick from a "hell-box" were going around wearing blue delegate

badges and one or more real editors did actually put in an appearance, but the thing was a frost from start to finish, as it deserved to be.

With this, both C. J. and Madame disappear from Dr. Browning's "Notes" for good.

Two weeks later, Republican William H. Taft defeats Democrat William Jennings Bryan in his third and final run at the office, with Socialist Eugene V. Debs taking a surprising 424,000 votes. Despite Bryan's longstanding support of the working man, Taft has the backing of most African-American newspapers. As a sop to the race, he features two black men in his inaugural parade and in his speech that day announces that Negro rights have been secured. Of this year's eighty-nine lynchings, and of Jim Crow restrictions, and of rigged polls in the South, Big Will follows presidential tradition and says not a word.

A Lucrative Business

Talking to the *New York Times* in 1917, Sarah Walker confesses to having a few interests beyond her obsession with business: the advancement of her race, music, cars and sports. Following the flop of her husband's convention, three of her enthusiasms make splashy headlines across the country, while the fourth more quietly makes its mark. Given her curious nature, Madame would have noted them all.

On Boxing Day, December 26, 1908, in Sydney, Australia, ex-stevedore John Arthur "Jack" Johnson knocks out Canadian Tommy Burns in fourteen rounds and places the world heavyweight crown firmly upon his African-American head. The next morning, the Wizard of Tuskegee finds he has relinquished his title as the most famous black man in America.

For African-Americans, this is bigger news than the Doctor's dinner at the White House: there's no denying it happened, for one thing, and for another, it's not a social occasion but a *victory* pure and simple. So they celebrate like crazy while sports-minded whites desperately scout for a candidate to bring the title back to their side of the color line. The most vocal among them settle on former champ Jim Jeffries, but he refuses, despite the stream of urgent visits to his California farm, during which he is plied with favors and reminded of his patriotic duty. Still, black people couldn't care less about any of that, and at Hill District saloons like the Little Gem the celebrating doesn't subside for weeks. Jack Johnson will not relinquish his title for seven years, and during that time, his photograph will appear every week in some race newspaper, along with stories about everything from his shoe size to his wife's suicide and the cost of the monument ($3,500) he placed at her grave.

That same season, Henry Ford changes the face of the nation by getting what he calls his universal car out of the factory and onto the streets. The Model T sells cheap and sweeps the country, with more than eighteen thousand cars sold in the first two years. The idea of an affordable automobile titillates America's imagination, and in no time everybody wants to own one. African-Americans see cars as a key to privacy, dignity and the freedom to choose both a destination and the route while bypassing racist laws like *Plessy v. Ferguson.*

Certainly cars will prove of greater fascination to Madame than boxing, and in time she will amass quite a collection. But her interest might have begun long before she made her first purchase—perhaps in Pittsburgh when, riding down Wylie on the trolley, she looked out the window and saw ordinary people behind the wheels of these Model T's. But could she envision the occasion, only a few years hence, when someone will snap a photo of her at the wheel of a handsome Cole Palace Touring Car, with Anjetta Breedlove beside her and two employees in the backseat, all four of them in fine hats and fur-collared coats, looking straight at the camera with an impression of entitlement and hauteur, as if to say, "*So?*"?

As for her greatest passion, a momentous meeting is held in New York City in February of 1909 on the anniversary of Abraham Lincoln's birth. The efforts of Mary Ovington White have led forty-eight white liberals and six black men to establish the National Association for the Advancement of Colored People. Booker T. Washington is not among them, and when the organization appoints W. E. B. DuBois the editor of its magazine, *Crisis,* the Wizard is given clear notice that his power and his accommodationist theories will be challenged without letup.

Within a week of the first NAACP conference, Washington stages his annual Tuskegee Negro Conference; and lest anyone think he'll give up without a fight, by the end of the month he hits an emotional bull's-eye by appealing to the general public for funds to liquidate the mortgage on Frederick Douglass's home.

At this point, Madame's a dyed-in-the-wool Bookerite, but the NAACP will come to play a significant part in her life—as will Frederick Douglass's mortgage.

Meantime, she reports her 1908 income as $6,672, nearly double that of the year before, and by the middle of 1909 she's listed as a resident at 2518 Wylie Avenue, as is C. J.'s *Progressive Afro-American,* now classified as a publishing company. She's also conducting business at 139 South Highland Avenue in the East End and may be living there, at least part-time. After less than two years in Pittsburgh, she's seen her star climb fast, perhaps higher than Mrs. Proctor's. But her business can't continue to grow and prosper at this pace until she builds a factory, and Pittsburgh's the wrong place. Eastern real estate is too pricey, and the African-American business community isn't progressive enough to suit her.

She's edgy all right and making plans to move on, but she hasn't left yet, so when the publishers of the *Pennsylvania Negro Business Directory* offer the Walkers space in its current edition, they take out a full page, most of it devoted to an oval photograph of Madame in the white lace dress, beneath which is a short bio:

> Mrs. Walker, formerly of St. Louis, Mo., but for the past two years a resident of Pittsburgh, is one of the most successful business women of the race in this community. Madam Walker has established a reputation for her hair grower and pressing oil that extends throughout the country. Having made the treatment of the scalp a thorough study, she has successfully established a lucrative business. She treats persons by mail or at her well equipped parlors, 2518 Wylie Ave., Pittsburgh, Pa.

The only Pittsburgh resident who occupies more space in the directory is Cumberland Posey, master of transportation of the Diamond Coal and Coke Company and certainly the wealthiest black man in the city. We see Cum Posey, as he is called, in an oval cutout similar to Madame's. A light-skinned man, he has a moustache and the usual no-nonsense look of the times. On the next page is a photo of his even lighter-skinned wife, with soft hair and a narrow nose, a prominent figure in the "Ladies' Federation of Clubs," who also hand-paints china, does silk handiwork and works in oils and watercolor. Many of her pieces are said to adorn the homes of the city's wealthiest people. A photograph of the Poseys' large house occupies the entire page opposite Sarah Walker's picture and bio, and given the cock of her head and her expression, she seems to be looking wistfully right at it.

The time is not far off, if her business keeps growing, when she'll have a home every bit as swell as Cum and Anna Posey's, and all the hand-painted china and watercolors she wants. On South Highland near her home there is a very fancy house called Rowanlea, huge if not particularly attractive. Unlikely Sarah would have been inside, but she might have heard things, such as the fact that there are four gold-plated pianos in the mansion—gold everywhere but the keys! Since nobody in the white family plays, the pianos sit there.

Music is Madame's fourth passion. Wherever she lives, she will install a phonograph, an organ, a harpsichord or a harp, often both. In Indianapolis, Harlem and Westchester County, all of these will be gold. And when people come to Villa Lewaro, the first thing they want to see is the gold Estey pipe organ.

In the summer of 1909 Sarah travels to Wilberforce, Ohio, where she speaks about hair care and personally treats fifty-one women and girls. That December she turns forty-two, and later that same month, Edwin Nathaniel Harleston, a former security guard at the H. J. Heinz food-packing plant, presents himself at the offices of African-American attorney Robert Lee Vann and asks him to edit the weekly newspaper he has run single-handedly since 1907—serving as "editor, reporter, treasurer, business manager and a complete newspaper company all in one." Thus far, the paper has functioned mostly as an outlet for Harleston's own poetry, but now he wants it to become more businesslike. While interested, Vann has no professional newspaper experience himself or any real confidence in this former security guard.

Harleston manages to pull together an issue himself, and on the snow-blown Saturday of January 15, 1910, he and his business partners hit the streets and hawk their paper—mostly borrowed from syndicated material printed in other papers, probably without permission—door-to-door, in barbershops, stores and saloons throughout the Hill District. They sell most of their first run, and thus is born one of the best-known and longest-running African-American newspapers in the country, the *Pittsburgh Courier.* And Robert Vann, who will serve as its editor for thirty years and who later refers to the early version of the paper as "a two-page sheet initiated by a Negro in a pickle factory," will one day allow his name to be used in Lelia McWilliams's first divorce suit.

That same month, ignoring the snow, Madame and C. J. pack up and head for Louisville, where with the help of C. J.'s sister Agnes Prosser (called Peggie) they have set up appointments. Then they're going to Indianapolis, where they will stay with Dr. Joseph H. Ward, Indianapolis's best-known black physician. They have already arranged for advertisements in the *Indianapolis Recorder* announcing that at Dr. Ward's residence, "the Noted Hair Culturist" will demonstrate the art of growing hair. But, the ad warns, interested women and girls should sign up right away, since Madam Walker will be in Indianapolis only for a few days. More than likely the Walkers have already decided to become permanent residents of the city Booker T. Washington has praised as a place where black people give a good accounting of themselves. But the will-she-stay-or-will-she-go dance step is one the Walkers have come to rely on, to keep people on their toes and wondering.

At Pittsburgh's Union Station, the Walkers board their train and settle in for the overnight, four-hundred-mile trip through Cincinnati, on what used to be the L&N but by now has been made part of the Illinois Central.

Sixty-nine black people are reported lynched in 1909. The advent and popularity of photography has added a new element to the hangings and burnings and mutilation: easy documentation and an I-was-there immediacy, as photographers set up temporary developing sheds on the spot and create instant postcards from their snapshots to send home as souvenirs. When Will "Froggie" James is hanged on Commercial Avenue in Cairo, Illinois, one spectator sends a postcard of the scene home, the front marked with an X. The message on the back reads: "Where they lynched the coon."

Lelia Robinson

S ometimes it's hard to know what to believe. One report has Lelia living in Pittsburgh since 1906; others insist she stayed in Denver until after her mother had settled in. An additional issue of some thorniness is Lelia College, a beauty school Madame and her daughter are supposed to have established in Pittsburgh. This story often has been reported as cold fact, and though Lelia College will eventually become a reality in New York, there is no hard evidence that it existed at this time. About Lelia's movements we can only make an educated guess, and mine is that she's been in the vicinity at least since the sesquicentennial, possibly teaching hairdressing and training agents in Bluefield, West Virginia, where a coal boom in the late nineteenth century attracted a significant black population. It may well have been Lelia who advised her mother to set up her business in the East End.

My hunch is Lelia did, in fact, conceive of and push the idea of a beauty college, but while generally approving, Madame refused to see it through until after she built her factory. So Lelia has to wait, and when the Walkers set out for Louisville, they leave her in charge. No word from Madame how she rates her daughter's management skills— or, for that matter, her new marital status.

Not much is known about John B. Robinson beyond the certainty that in October 1909 in the Washington County, Pennsylvania, court-house, he and Lelia McWilliams marry. In the late 1920s, Edgar Rouzeau, a reporter for a Harlem society sheet called the *Interstate Tattler,* will declare that Robinson was a hotel telephone operator who "had a nice figure and looked like somebody in his uniform," while her friends say he was a hotel porter, about five-nine and handsome, with dark brown skin, a trim figure and a bossy manner. Yet in the city directory, he's listed as a laborer. And when Rouzeau has A'Lelia Walker calling her first husband the only man she ever loved, we have to wonder, because once again it's hard to know what to believe, the facts being further obscured by Lelia herself, who states on the Washington County marriage-license application that this is her second marriage, her first having been dissolved by death. And so, reading Rouzeau's report, we have to wonder, *which* first husband? And if she's been married before, when did it happen, and to whom? And why was it important to keep all of this information under wraps? Keeping secrets is a time-honored method of taking charge of one's own life, especially among women, and maybe by sneaking off like a teenager, the woman known as "the Successor" is doing just that, and as a side benefit, getting her mother's goat.

Whatever the reasons, the marriage takes place in Washington, Pennsylvania, which lies about halfway between Pittsburgh and Wheeling, within thirty miles of either city. Cozied up to the foothills of the mineral-rich Alleghenies, these are hardscrabble, working-class mining and industrial towns. Wheeling is also Lelia's residence, if the marriage license is to be believed. Her husband, the license states, was born in 1885 in Columbus, Ohio. In census reports, Lelia's birthplace varies from Louisiana to Mississippi to Missouri, and on this particular wedding day she claims she was born in St. Louis.

The mother of the bride does not attend the ceremony, and afterwards, the newlyweds move into Lelia's new East End digs at 5707 Mignonette.

Letter to Dr. Washington

A couple weeks into the new decade, the Walkers once again lift their bags and boxes off the train, this time in Louisville, the hub for a number of railroad lines carting coal and other minerals to the north and west. Having been here many times, by now they take little notice of the waiting room's special features: the three-story barrel-vaulted ceiling, the art-glass rose-colored windows, the very fancy decorations. And they probably need a little time to recover from the Cincinnati-to-Louisville leg, since the minute the B&O line crossed the Ohio, all black passengers were instructed to file through a wooden partition into the "colored" compartment; the constitutionality of Kentucky's segregation has been tested by several lawsuits, but so far the Supreme Court has upheld those laws, with only Justice John Harlan, a native Kentuckian, dissenting.

Louisville's at once Southern and somehow not. Along with Charlotte, North Carolina, it ranks high in the black press as a place to live, and it does have its advantages. Located in craggy bluffs lining the Ohio, Louisville has always looked toward the industrial-minded North—Indianapolis, Chicago, Cincinnati—for its customs and culture. Forty thousand or so African-Americans live there, many of them having escaped the poverty of the rural South for better jobs, and some twelve thousand or so vote regularly. There are no black banks or hotels, but there's a Carnegie-funded Negro library and a Negro YMCA. The former, the first public library in the country with an exclusively African-American staff, sits on the corner of Chestnut and Tenth in the heart of the African-American neighborhood and a block away from the Y, which serves as both hotel and general meeting place for the race.

C. J.'s sister Agnes Prosser lives two blocks from the library. And since her husband is a driver, it's possible he picks up the Walkers at the depot. A reception for Madame will have been scheduled, perhaps a parlor social at Mrs. Prosser's, probably another one or two at a church. In Louisville, even though Madame's staunchly AME, the Walkers' strongest connection is to the Baptist church, which makes business sense; the majority of black Americans are Baptists, as both Walkers were as children. C. J. especially has kept close ties to his original affiliation.

The community here is still talking about last August when black businessmen from all over the country came to town for Booker T. Washington's ninth annual National Negro Business League convention. The YMCA was filled to capacity, and local residents opened their homes to the overflow. As always at NNBL conventions, there were presentations on such practical topics as running a dry-goods store and sewer contracting, but according to the *Freeman* and the *Louisville Courier-Journal*, until the end of the week, "The Servant Girl Question" was the week's hottest draw.

But what people really wanted to hear was Washington's keynote address, so on Friday some three thousand African-Americans—and a fair number of whites—crowded into Liederkranz Hall, standing in the aisles, sitting on the steps, packed double into chairs. The gist of his speech was that the secret to success lies within, and that a successful businessman does not dwell on wrongs done him or rights withheld. Injustice, by implication, must be ignored, to allow for full concentration on self-improvement, including—of course—hygiene and personal cleanliness. The Wizard rounded out this thought by declaring that his people should be particularly grateful to the Southern white man, because without the support and loyalty of those "who have believed in us and stood by us and stimulated and encouraged us," no advancement of the race could have taken place.

There's no record of how the audience responded, but the *Indianapolis Recorder*, which ordinarily championed Dr. Washington unreservedly, ran this uncharacteristically ironic headline: "WASHINGTON LAUDS SOUTH. Race Progress Due to Loyalty of Southern White Men." And while many at the meeting were reassured by the familiarity of his counsel—assimilate, accommodate, be patient, don't make trouble—others would feel he hadn't properly acknowledged the loud protestations of the Niagara Movement and the NAACP. And his praise of President Taft was said to have fallen on deaf ears.

What Dr. Washington does not mention, of course, are the compromising deals he has made with some of the richest white men in the country. Tuskegee is heavily funded by Carnegie and Rockefeller, and Teddy Roosevelt sits on its board. After reading *Up from Slavery,* Sears bigwig Julius Rosenwald visited the institute, whose elementary school he now pays for, along with the twenty-five black YMCAs he has established nationwide. He and Rockefeller are locked in a kind of good-works contest, and in the Negro-philanthropy stakes they look to Dr. Washington for advice. Moreover, all these magnates have a financial stake in the reclamation of the South, a process that—as Washington also knows—depends on cheap labor. So it is the "responsibility" of the black man to play along.

The Walkers know important people in Louisville, including C. H. Parrish, of Calvary Baptist Church, who led the opening prayer at the NNBL meeting. He, of course, knows the Wizard and has told the Walkers they can use his name if they wish.

To start a business, you need either a bank loan or a well-off relative or friend to put the touch on. Since neither of those strategies is available to the Walkers, they sit down and write a fund-raising letter—dated 1/19/1910—to Dr. Booker T. Washington, making a case for themselves and the practicality, race-worthiness and God-fearingness of their endeavor. It is, I'm convinced, C. J.'s work. The letter's typed, for one thing, and as a newspaper agent he would have a machine and know how to type. But his wife would certainly serve as editor, wouldn't she? After all, it's her name on the stationery.

The letterhead lends a professional touch and employs three different typefaces: at the top, "Madame C. J. Walker" done as a perfectly wrought signature; below that, in no-nonsense block lettering, her profession and street address, "Hair Grower and Scalp Specialist, 5707 Mignonette Street"; and just above the body of the letter, "East End, Pittsburgh, Pa.," in heavy Old English Gothic, formal, fancy, official, like a diploma. Just above the logo, in very small print, is a promise: *Positive guarantee to grow hair or money refunded.*

Honorable Booker T. Washington
Tuskegee Alabama

Dear Sir;
While in this city, in the interest of my goods I was advised by Dr.

Paris and Miss Kelly to write you and explain my proposition to you, they believed you would help me.

This would be C. H. Parrish and Alice P. Kelly, who works and teaches at Eckstein Norton, a nearby business school, and who also spoke at the NNBL meeting. Soon she will follow Madame to Indianapolis and work as her forelady, traveling companion and private tutor.

I have a Remedy, that will grow any kind of hair. It has been tested and proven to be the only thing that does not record a failure white and black alike. it my [may] seem strange to say it is the product of a dream. now what I would like to do, is to astablish [sic] a factory and advertise it properly, to do this, I tho't if I could interest one hundred men and women to the extent of five hundred dollars, we could form a stock company at a capital of five thousand dollars then we could sell shares and make this one of the largest factories of its kind in the United States, and would give employment to many of our boys and girls. I know I can not do any thing alone so I have decided to make an appeal to the leaders of the race, I have been made some good offers from different white firms, but they want me to sell out my right to them which I refuse to do as I prefer to keep it in the race if possible. I feel no hesitancy in presenting my case to you, as I know you know what it is to strougle alone with ability to do but no money to back it, but God raised up friends to you and I believe he will do the same for me, hoping an early reply, and beliving [sic] you will do what is in your power for me I am Sinc.

Yours

P.S. Please answer to Pittsburgh Pa. address above.

The signature—a grand "(Mme) C.J. Walker," penned with a bold, quick flourish—is certainly not hers. In the first place "Mme" is not only abbreviated but parenthesized, which she never does. Also, when in a year's time she signs promissory notes to the Fletcher National Bank in Indianapolis, "Sarah" is misspelled ("Sarrah") and her signature is uncertain and shaky. C. J., on the other hand, signs quickly, boldly. The other possibility is her mentor Alice Kelly, who has attended and taught at schools where penmanship is valued. In any case, it's an imitation of the logo and not a genuine signature.

As to the contents, suggesting that white firms had offered to buy her out could be a ploy, but not necessarily. The cosmetics industry in general is on a roll—manufacturers have given up trade cards and posters and are conducting heavy advertising campaigns in newspapers and magazines—and the demand for African-American products is running high, especially for hair care. Even pharmacists, patent-medicine makers and barbers are piling into the trade. Besides, the fame of Madam Walker's goods is established, her business steadily growing more lucrative. But she's holding out.

The letter then turns Washington's techniques back on himself, using a sentimental reference to the race as a way of tweaking his conscience. As to the "dream," while it will soon become a standard advertising strategy, Sarah might not be quite committed to using it yet, and so she throws it briefly into the mix, then skitters away. "White and black alike" is a puzzle. If Madam Walker has white customers, did she find them in Pittsburgh? Unlikely, but possible. Both races live in the East End, and there are white businesses on Highland. But she could be stretching this point to appeal to his assimilationism. Concerning the backers and the dollar figures, the Walkers' arithmetic is obviously off, which must have embarrassed them if they noticed it later (not likely, since they probably didn't make a copy). The statement "I know I can not do any thing alone" flies in the face of her most famous mantra, "I got my start by giving myself a start." But when you're asking for a favor, modesty plays better than bravado.

This is hardly the first time the Wizard has received such a request. He's heard it all and doesn't yield easily. Moreover, he would have no interest in a business whose purpose, as he sees it, is to make black women look white. Nannie Burroughs, who is secretary of the National Baptist Convention and a prominent speaker in her own right, is dead set against all forms of hair finagling, and her sponsorship means a lot more to him than helping some hair-oil peddler.

In a week's time, on January 26, the Wizard responds to "My dear Madam" on Tuskegee stationery. "I have your kind favor of some days ago." He appreciates most cordially her bringing this matter to his attention, but "it will not be possible for me to go into the matter as you so kindly suggest." Because his time and attention are almost wholly occupied with the work of Tuskegee, he does not feel he can possibly undertake other responsibilities but hopes very much that she will be successful in organizing her stock company and in putting her preparation on the market. "Yours very truly."

The letter travels first to Mignonette Street, where Lelia is handling mail orders while her husband works as either a porter or a waiter. Lelia sends the letter to her mother, who takes the Wizard's rejection in stride. She is far, far from finished with Dr. Washington. He will be hearing from her again, often and soon. An alliance with Booker T. Washington—his respect and approval, and membership in his circle—is in her plans, and like that gold piano, she will, by God, have it.

The Walkers plan ahead, and by telephone and post arrange for demonstrations at the Indianapolis home and sanitarium of their illustrious sponsor, the loyal Dr. J. H. Ward.

VI · *Indianapolis, 1910–1916*

The Walker Co.

O n February 10 at the Louisville Union Station, the
Walkers buy two $1.50 tickets to Indianapolis.
Rail traffic between the cities is constant and so they have choices, but
more than likely take the Pennsylvania Flyer, on the Pittsburgh,
Cincinnati, Chicago and St. Louis line. When they board, state law
directs them into the "colored" compartment until the train crosses
the Kentucky-Indiana bridge over the Ohio, when they are free to sit
where they like.

Rivers are a constant in Sarah's life. The one she knows best is, of
course, the Mississippi, but she has heard about the Ohio since girl-
hood and, as a young woman heading north from Vicksburg, saw the
tail of it at Cairo, where it meets the Mississippi and disappears. In
Pittsburgh, she lived at its source, and now, like many others before
her, she is crossing it into another new life. Her husband would certainly sit beside her, but the distance between them has grown, and in
all likelihood they no longer carry on casual conversations. In
Louisville, Agnes Prosser warned Sarah about C. J.'s inconstancy,
which she experienced firsthand when he abandoned her after their
mother died, leaving her alone. Agnes lived with relatives, she said,
and her brother didn't return until sixteen years later, when she
tracked him down and asked him to come visit, and even then he
showed no remorse for his behavior but only asked for return fare to
St. Louis. "My heart went out to [Madame]," Prosser will say, years
from now. "I knew she was a good woman struggling to make a name
for herself. And I knew what a hard fight she had." Even worse,
Prosser suspected her brother of tapping into the company till by
"meeting the postman, getting the mail, not filling orders." And so as

the train moves north across the Ohio, Madame has to be considering this new information and wondering how much longer her third husband will be an asset to her and her business and when and how she will make that determination.

They move to better seats.

Some four hours and a hundred miles later the Flyer crosses over the newly constructed elevated tracks into the Inland Queen City—which also calls itself the Railroad City—where the Walkers are likely greeted either by their host or by his emissary. Soon afterwards, Dr. Ward announces to the community that he is happy to have Madam Walker in his home and predicts that she will bring a new prosperity to the black community of Indianapolis, should she decide to stay. Though he cannot provide what Madame asked of Booker T. Washington, Ward is well respected and can help her make contact with a bank, and with the realty companies that cater especially to black people, the Afro-American Realty Company of Indiana and the American Home Buying Company. Three years from now, when she has her picture made at the dedication ceremonies of the colored YMCA, Ward will be one of the six other prominent Indianapolis citizens in the photograph. And in May 1919, when she is dying, he will be at her bedside until the end.

In the 1911 *Indianapolis Freeman* interview, Madam Walker declares that she was "so impressed with [the city] and the cordial welcome extended to her" that she decided to make it her home. But odds are, she has visited the city at least once before now—probably in 1909—and that many other factors play into her decision as well, starting with Indianapolis's large black middle class—twenty-one thousand and on the increase—which is settled in a central neighborhood and not riven, as in Pittsburgh, by class and station. Indianapolis is also the country's largest inland manufacturing center, and this means excellent train service and banks willing to finance start-up companies. Considered a Western city, it's nonetheless accessible to both Chicago and Cincinnati and Madame's large Eastern markets. Meanwhile, there are only four African-American hairdressers in town, none of them with anything like her renown.

After Ward sets them up in ample accommodations, the Walkers unpack. Again.

On February 12, 1910, only two days after their arrival, Madame announces her presence in the *Indianapolis Recorder,* one of the city's two black newspapers. Accompanied by the photograph of her standing dreamily beside the mirror, a news item reads: "The above cut is the latest photo of Mme Walker. Mr. and Madame C.J. Walker heads of the Walker Manufacturing co., of Pittsburgh, Pa, Manufacturers of Mme Walkers Wonderful Hair Grower, [are] in the city at the residence of Dr. Ward and are very much impressed with Indianapolis."

Above this is an advertisement for the white-owned Nelson Manufacturing Co., touting the "finest hair pomade on the face of the earth for colored people . . . for turning stubborn, kinky and tangled hair soft and supple as silk." Below, a column called "Y.M.C.A. Notes" announces several upcoming events, including a program on February 20 to commemorate the death of Frederick Douglass.

Two pages later the Walkers run an advertisement two columns wide and about eight inches in length, announcing in bold letters of varying typeface and size that "Mme C.J. Walker, of Pittsburg, Pa., THE NOTED HAIR CULTURIST is in this city at the residence of Dr. J. H. Ward, 722 Indiana Avenue," where "she will demonstrate the art of growing hair." Below this is the Walker triptych, which will be their trademark and signature for years: three photographs of Madame lined up side-by-side in a mock hinged frame, like family pictures. The middle shot, "Before Using," has been cut into a rectangle, while the flanking "After"s are oval. The "Before" shot is the same as the one she used in Denver: a young Madame in a dark, high-necked frock, a frizzy topknot of hair bunched in the center of her forehead, the rest short or pulled back over her ears. In the other two, her hair is unstyled but very long. The photograph on the left is new, a near-profile shot in which her hair is completely flat to her head and falls board-straight down her back, ending well below her shoulders. Her chin is lifted and she's looking off into the distance, and because of the pose and the angle, her features seem more delicate, her face thinner. Beneath the triptych is the reminder: "Every woman of pride should see her during her stay in this city which is for a few days only." And while the notion of "pride" is a new one, the word defines her work as Madame wishes it to be perceived, not just as a service but as a mission. The urgency of "a few days only" has, of course, become the Walkers' standard ploy.

Then come the testimonials. A group letter from Pittsburgh swears to the worth and value of her work beyond even her own claims and says that in her two and a half years' residency, the undersigned found Madam Walker to be an honest businesswoman and a hair grower "without equal." The letter is signed by several ministers as well as prominent women: the president of the Woman's State Convention of Pennsylvania, a national delegate to the convention of the women's division of the Knights of Pythias, the well-known journalist and speaker Lavinia Sneed. Following the letter is a list of "others who know and recommend her," including ministers from Nashville and Knoxville and women from St. Louis, New York City and Muskogee, Oklahoma.

The ad closes with one last nudge (Don't fail to call and see Mme Walker), a promise (no charge for a consultation) and a final request (kindly bring a comb, a brush and two towels). On this same page, Dr. Ward has his own ad, for his combination sanitarium, nursing school and hospital, also located at 722 Indiana Avenue.

The Walkers' decision to place their first ad in the *Recorder* instead of the *Indianapolis Freeman* is curious, given their history with the older and better-known newspaper and its editor, George Knox. Sarah Walker has had a connection with the *Freeman* since St. Louis, when James Breedlove sold it at his barbershop. And when C. J. announced the lineup of participants in his ill-fated newspaper conference, he listed Knox as a distinguished attendee. Knox spoke at the Louisville NNBL meeting and his paper does not waver from the Tuskegee line.

George Stewart, editor-publisher of the *Recorder* and a native Indianian, co-founded that paper in 1897 and keeps a tighter focus. He's affable, smart and highly regarded locally. He has something of an avuncular role in the Indianapolis black community, people often writing letters to him when they're in trouble or are looking for help and advice. Stewart began his professional life editing a church publication and still attends to religious announcements and stories, although by now he's moving more into news reports. The *Recorder*'s offices are in the Knights of Pythias Building, and Stewart—politically active, a staunch Republican—will be elected permanent chairman of the local chapter in 1911. Focused more on local news, he isn't as close as Knox to Dr. Washington, though he is on good terms with him and maintains an active membership in the NNBL. His newspaper is "devoted to the best interests of the Negroes of Indiana" and claims to be the "leading and best newspaper of the Race in Indiana."

The Walkers have certainly taken all of this into account and have probably received advice from Ward, Rev. Parrish and others. While they know the ropes regarding the power of the Wizard, they may have decided that a local pitch makes better sense. And maybe Knox is still smarting over the convention fiasco and is steering clear of C. J. Perhaps Stewart offered better rates, or a package deal for Madame and Dr. Ward. In time, however, Madame will restructure her priorities and send her advertising dollars more frequently to the *Freeman.*

At any rate, the triptych, they decide, is a keeper, and on February 26 she runs it again, along with an announcement that she has extended her stay until May. The sales pitch is somewhat more aggressive this time, offering a $25 refund to anyone whose hair doesn't grow by May and a three-month free treatment to the first customer who sends Madame new business. She can make these offers with fullest confidence in her preparation and her treatments because, unlike others, her formula and methods are a "Divine Gift, having come to her in a dream." The religious theme is continued when the ad concludes, "If there is a Doubting Thomas here, now is your time to make her prove or pay." She runs the same notice the next week, along with a classified ad stating prices—treatment $1, hair grower 50 cents—and an oddly undecipherable fortune-cookie aphorism: "Nothing beats a trial but a failure."

That week's *Recorder* reports that the Sumner League Minstrel Show will perform at Tomlinson Hall on May 31 and "eclipse all former entertainments in grandeur, talent and size," with the latest in "Noveltry and Modern Minstrelsy . . . Nothing old but the name." Roscoe Conkling Bruce—son of the Mississippi Reconstruction senator and former Tuskegee administrator, current assistant supervisor of public schools in D.C. and a very big name to African-Americans—has been in town speaking at the National Educational Association. A meeting of the Men of Broadway will consider a fascinating question pertaining to the depth of Christian charity: "Should the Negro Christian Pray for the Recovery of Senator Benjamin [a.k.a Pitchfork] Tillman?"

Madam Walker may or may not have noted these, but she certainly would have zeroed in on another little item: the announcement that her former employer—who is now calling herself Annie Pope-Turnbo—has moved her company from the house on Market Street into a fine big brick building on a corner lot on Pine Street, west of Jefferson Avenue, which, as Madame well knows, is a residential area of St. Louis previously not open to Negroes. The ad boasts that Poro "Blazes the Trail and it Still Leads." Mrs. Pope-Turnbo now travels with a secretary (possibly her sister) and is making her way throughout Pennsylvania, New York, Ohio and even Indiana, warning her customers not to be fooled by latecomers and imitators.

So the two women who began their professional lives walking the same streets selling the same product, teaching the same lessons, are rising together—buying houses, hiring office help, conducting national campaigns—in hot competition, much as in the political world, the camps of Booker T. Washington and W. E. B. DuBois are squaring off.

At the end of March, Madame announces her permanent residence at 638 North West Street in a five-room flat she and C. J. have rented, not far from Dr. Ward's sanitarium. She solicits the "patronage of every woman of pride who is in need of her services" and issues a call for new agents. She also includes a testimonial from a customer who declares that since receiving Madam Walker's treatment seven months earlier she has grown an entire new head of hair, seven inches in front and six in back, and sends her love and best wishes for continued success.

Within a week after Madame's announcement of her new address, Charles Walker makes his first solo foray into the hair-culture business. Calling himself a scalp specialist, he travels to Muncie to conduct demonstrations and consultations at the home of their Muncie agent. In April, the Walker Company runs an ad in the *Recorder*, Madame again promising $25 to any woman whose hair doesn't grow and again advising, "Nothing beats a trial but a failure."

All of this activity is significant, but the Walkers' biggest campaign yet is still in the works, one which will catapult Madame into the national advertising market and eventually allow her to create a national system of agents, hairdressers and teachers. They launch it on April 6, a kind of statement of purpose that takes up nearly all of page 2 of the *Indianapolis Freeman*.

Under the triptych, in place of the usual "Is Your Hair Short?" is a bare-bones declaration: "It Makes Short Hair Long and Cures Dandruff." There's no need for Madame's name any longer, since the triptych—in only three months—has become, like the white-haired

Quaker on the oatmeal box, a signifier. When people open the paper and see the familiar rectangle in the middle with ovals on either side, they don't wonder who the woman is with all the hair; they know.

The ad copy's different this time, from its straightforward, unfussy opening right down to "The Walker Mfg. Co., 638 N. West St., Indianapolis, Ind. Agents Wanted Everywhere." And my guess is that Madame is starting to take control. Not that she's terse. Indeed, the text is quite discursive, and begins by calling her Hair Grower "one of the most wonderful discoveries of the age," positively guaranteed to produce hair growth of a half-inch to an inch a month if used as directed. "It matters not what the condition of the scalp. This is Madame Walker's own discovery and has positively grown hair on thousands of heads." After explaining that the photographs are of "Madame" Walker (sometimes without the closing *e,* another experiment), the narrative becomes a first-person testimonial. Madame explains that for eighteen years she used other preparations to improve the condition of her own hair, but without results until "through the divine providence of God, I was permitted in a dream to discover the preparation that I am now placing at the disposal of the thousands who are in the same condition in which I was, just three years ago."

Wonderful Hair Grower, she continues, cures the scalp of all diseases, which stops hair loss and then encourages new growth: pretty much how Annie Turnbo pitched her sage-and-egg rinse in 1902. She concludes this part of the ad by saying she hadn't intended to market this discovery until, after using it for a year in Denver, it became clearly her duty to share this gift from God with "those who appreciate beautiful hair and healthy scalps, which is the glory of woman."

In the second section, under the heading "The Reason Why," she lists eight reasons why her products work, starting with "Because it came to me as an inspiration from God—through a dream." The other seven, including customer satisfaction and the growth in her own hair of sixteen inches over three years, have some merit, but the underlying rationale is circular: it works because it works.

The third section is made up of the usual endorsements—letters from Pittsburgh, several from Oklahoma and Kansas, one from Austin, Texas.

And at the end, a new angle: "Persons desiring one of Madame C.J. Walker's matchless $5.00 steel combs can secure same for $3.00 if order reaches this office before June 15." The offer is limited to the first hundred, so please mention the *Freeman* and include postage. More-over, "Don't fail to send for a bottle of C.J. Walker's Sure Cure Blood and Rheumatic Remedies."

So Madame goes into direct sales, and launches her successful hot-comb business, which will prove to be a huge success. And C. J. bottles home remedies, which more than likely contain a high percentage of alcohol, as do most cure-alls of the day. A smaller version of the triptych ad runs in the *Freeman* for six weeks.

Thus the Walker Manufacturing Company is born and goes national. The copy from this ad will appear word for word in a pamphlet Madame will distribute wherever she goes, even tossing it from train windows in depots she's passing by, knowing that waiting passengers have time on their hands. And in a year or so, she'll send one to Booker T. Washington.

A week or so later, Halley's Comet blazes across the horizon for the first time since 1759. People sit on front porches to watch for it, and some preach Doomsday sermons from the Book of Revelations about the fire next time, but nothing happens. Andrew Carnegie discovers he has so much money he can't give it all away; and when the library he's funding at Washington, D.C.'s black Howard University opens in May, he himself attends, as does President Taft. Jim Jeffries finally agrees to come out of retirement and challenge Jack Johnson in Reno on the Fourth of July, and despite concerns that the Great White Hope is out of boxing condition, his supporters are convinced his superior intelligence will carry the day, while black people trust that their man will once again come through.

Decade's End

For middle-class African-Americans in the early 1900s, late summer and early fall is the peak season—the convention months, when organizations travel en masse to distant cities and gather in Y's and churches and city parks and armories to evaluate their progress and assess the general racial situation, talk politics, exchange ideas, draft resolutions and elect officers. People bring news from home. There are countless speeches, at least one parade and nightly musical performances followed by dancing. The Order of Colored Knights of Pythias and its women's auxiliary, the Court of Calanthe, will hold a joint convocation in Richmond, Virginia; the National Negro Business League and the National Negro Press Association, in New York. The National Political League will travel to Atlantic City; the NAACP, to Boston; the Baptist Sunday School Convention, to Lexington, Virginia. At its second convention, the NAACP creates a permanent national structure, and DuBois quits his job at Atlanta University to devote himself full-time to writing, and to editing the *Crisis*. But Tuskegee's commencement services get a bigger play in the black press. The *Indianapolis Freeman* condemns those who accuse the Wizard of political dictatorship. And when the World's Sunday School Convention bars Negroes from its annual meeting, the resultant protests compel the organization to offer Booker T. Washington a lifetime membership, which he accepts.

Jack Johnson predicts a knockout by the twentieth round and then betters that prediction by five and takes home a purse of $117,000. Jeffries offers no excuses, saying he couldn't have whipped the black man in a thousand years. According to a sociology professor from California, Johnson's victory suggests not only that the Negro derives from a branch of the Caucasian race and is therefore not inferior, but also that within three hundred years the black race will become extinct in America, due to intermarriage and unspecified climatic conditions.

Today, except for a family-owned funeral business, the 600 block of North West Street is a series of empty lots; but when the Walkers moved into 638, it was flanked by two other large brick homes, possibly identical, one of which, at 640, soon comes up for sale. Quite large—twelve rooms—and made of the dark-yellowish brick favored all over Indianapolis, it has big plate-glass windows trimmed in white and wide, white-railed front porches both upstairs and down. Like Cum and Anna Posey's home in Pittsburgh and Annie Turnbo's in St. Louis, 640 North West Street looks solid and immovable, the residence of a person of substance. And since 1910 promises to be yet one more record-breaking sales year for her business, Madame sets the wheels in motion, and in late July officially purchases the $10,000 house when she signs four years of promissory notes, predated and filled out for $20 monthly, to be paid to Henry F. Shoemaker at the Fletcher National Bank in Indianapolis, with 10 percent attorney's fees and interest marked down from 8 percent to 6 percent. The loan is to Sarah Walker—no mention of a husband—and she signs the forms in one sitting, the signatures nearly identical. Throughout, she misspells her name "Sarrah" and has pressed the nib down too hard, allowing clumsy splotches to blur some of the letters. Unlike most people who grow more nervous as the size of a risk becomes more evident, Madame's hand—while nervous and childlike throughout—grows steadier as she goes, and the twentieth signature is far bolder than the first.

She spends the Fourth in Noblesville, Indiana, with some Pittsburgh ladies who are visiting kin. Since she's a sports fan, she doubtless convinces them to tune in to the fight. That same week, she unveils the triptych ad in Denver's *Statesman*. Annie Pope-Turnbo continues to advertise there as well, and occasionally the women's notices run side by side.

A week later, six hundred women gather in Louisville for the week-long biennial convention of the important National Association of Colored Women, which Madame has been aware of at least since the summer of 1904, when she was in St. Louis and Margaret Murray Washington boycotted meetings at the World's Fair. All the leading women belong to the NACW, and this year they're gathering a quick train ride away, in a city Madame knows, and so, without question, she's going. The timing is perfect: she's buying the house, planning to add rooms and build a factory with offices; she's launched her biggest ad campaign; the Walker Company is coming together; now's the time to beat Annie Turnbo to the NACW. Then, once she's a member, she'll work on her next goals: a formal introduction before the membership and, after that, their official seal of approval, which amounts to an endorsement of her products. Not to get ahead of herself, since some of this will take time; but the initial move begins today.

She's accompanied by Mrs. Ora Day, whose hair has responded so well to treatments that it now reaches her waist. With the help of a porter, they board the Flyer. Usually Madame takes her little stove with her, closed up in its black square case, but not today. In Louisville there will be no demonstration. She'll simply stand before the women and first tell them who she is and where she came from and how great a gift God has bestowed upon her and about her plans for a factory that will employ many young women of the race. Then Mrs. Day will come out, and Madame will unpin her hair and stand back to let Wonderful Hair Grower speak for itself.

Her presentations never use white definitions, such as "kink" or "straighten." Instead of talking about hairstyles and standards of beauty, she addresses larger issues, of pride and health, of woman's glory and the obligation of a divine gift. In Louisville, she will demonstrate through her bearing, appearance and sincerity that she is as refined and dignified as the women in the NACW, some of whom disapprove of what she does—for instance, Nannie Burroughs. But Madame won't shy away from criticism; on the contrary, she'll study the arguments used against her, then find a way to turn them in her favor.

The light-skinned, educated women running the NACW have no way to comprehend the secret strengths of Sarah Walker, never having picked cotton, scrubbed clothes or cooked and cleaned for a living; their parents never having been inventoried like fence posts. Women who grew up reading whatever they felt like when and if they felt like it can spurn her at every turn, but they cannot keep her from coming on, because Madame is like the first famous door-to-door salesman, Alfred Fuller, who when doors were slammed in his face said that rebuff was nothing, and that whatever they dished out couldn't touch the rigors of farm life in Nova Scotia.

Many other well-dressed black women from Indianapolis will board the Flyer on this Sunday morning: Ida Bryant of the Women's

Improvement Club; Beulah Porter, physician and school principal; and, most significantly, Lillian Thomas Fox. The daughter of one of the first black teachers in the Indianapolis public school system, a childless widow and an elocutionist of national renown, Mrs. Fox writes a weekly column for the *Indianapolis News,* a white newspaper that covers the activities of the black community. She also handles feature and news articles, and though the *News* doesn't allow her a byline, everybody knows which ones she's written. A major player in the club world, she founded the Women's Improvement Club and helped organize both the local Anti-Lynching League and the Indiana branch of the NACW. Honorary state chairman of the 1910 meeting in Louisville, an extremely attractive woman with deep-set eyes and a strong straight nose, Mrs. Fox is, in short, a woman whose approval and business Madame would certainly crave.

As the Flyer passes through Columbus, Seymour and Scottsburg, the women gather in one car, chatting, laughing, catching up. If white passengers take a look and, either uncomfortable or disapproving, move along to another car, the conferees don't deign to notice, instead welcoming aboard other delegates from towns in southern Indiana. Coming down from the North, they won't be in Kentucky long enough to meet Jim Crow before they disembark in Louisville.

Madame's friend Rev. Parrish will deliver the opening prayer that afternoon at the Fifth Street Baptist Church, and then discuss his trip to the Holy Land. Courtesy of his wife, who is secretary of the NACW, Madame has examined the seriously crowded conference schedule, hoping that with her friends' help some time will be made available to her and Mrs. Day. Either Agnes Prosser or her daughter Lillian greets them at the station and conveys them to the opening session. The sanctuary is alive with color, decorated in the NACW's royal purple and white, and liberally festooned with its flower, the violet. When Madame makes her entrance, she might appear cool and blasé, but inside she must be roaring with happiness, now so well-heeled and stylish and such a *force* that she's worthy of being introduced.

A number of prominent women—including Mary Church Terrell and Margaret Murray Washington—give short speeches about the work of the NACW, but each talk is followed by a musical number, and so the afternoon goes on. Nobody minds the heat or the length of Rev.

Parrish's talk; they are anxious to hear about the Holy Land. And whenever someone intones the NACW motto, "Lifting as We Climb," they can't help applauding and cheering yet one more time. And then they all raise their arms and give one another a communal greeting called the Chautauqua Salute.

The conference receives extensive coverage in the Indianapolis black press, much of it devoted to the local delegation, and since Madam Walker's demonstration isn't mentioned anywhere (including her own advertisements), it probably didn't happen. Overbooked, the gathering quickly falls behind schedule, and many demonstrations and talks are postponed until the 1912 meeting or canceled altogether. Still, Mary Talbert gives a talk on "How Women Should Dress," Mrs. Washington presides over a Tuesday-evening musical performance, Ida B. Wells-Barnett speaks on "The National Negro Conference— What It Has Done for the Negro Race," Azalia Hackley sings, Nannie Burroughs is introduced, there are reports on the work of the national YWCA. But most of the papers involve such domestically focused and family-oriented topics as "The Mother's Responsibility in the Intemperance of Her Boys," "The Mother's Part in the Social Life of Her Children," and "The Domestic Training a Girl Should Receive from Her Mother." Nothing on business or health.

On Thursday night, Booker T. Washington—scheduled to give the keynote address—wires that he "cannot possibly be present," perhaps because after promising racial justice in his inaugural speech, President Taft has begun removing every black appointee in D.C. from office, and as his adviser on "colored affairs," the Wizard is having a hard time helping the chief executive save face. To fill his spot, Azalia Hackley gives another much-admired performance. On the last day of the conference, Ida Bryant of the Indianapolis Women's Improvement Club wins the door prize.

On Saturday afternoon, when Madame reboards the Pennsylvania Flyer with Mrs. Day, it's unlikely her demeanor reveals a trace of her disappointment about the week's events, or that she says anything until she's home again. But once she's at 640 North West, she might kick her shoes off and give in to a brief sulk. Food, and plenty of it, has always cheered her up, so perhaps she pads into the kitchen. Ladies' magazines of the day are now cautioning readers about the dangers of extra weight, and Dr. Ward is constantly after her about her diet and, citing her high blood pressure, nagging her to lay off rich food. She tries, fails, and he rails on. But how can she cut back? When she was growing up, heft was a sign of health and prosperity, and she's known hunger too long not to eat whatever she wants to, now that she can.

A woman named Parthenia Rawlins, whom everybody calls Grandma, also lives at 640. Born during slave times, she entertains other residents with stories about welcoming the Union troops and catching a glimpse of Lincoln, and she will be mentioned in Madame's will. Walker employees will one day praise Rawlins's tender Dixie biscuits, and perhaps Madame can't help indulging in one or two of those.

By the next NACW meeting in 1912, the name Madam C. J. Walker will be one to reckon with, and she will be so famous they will not dare leave her out of anything. She'll be invited to every fancy reception, sitting right up front at many of them, and by the 1914 meeting she'll be asked to give a talk not during the afternoon sessions but in the prime-time evening. And in Louisville, if nothing else, she did make at least one important connection. After the meeting, Lillian Fox consulted with Madame about her hair, and later this year she will lend her name to a testimonial that appears in the pamphlet sent to Booker T. Washington. So this time off was not wasted.

C. J. may or may not be at home. These days he's on the constant move—ostensibly for the company, but rumors say otherwise—and stays away longer than he needs to. Still, she's not lacking for company and in the end is better off without him. Sunday, she attends services at AME Bethel, begins a new business week on Monday, signs the promissory notes on the twenty-second—and by the end of the month gets some not unexpected news from Pittsburgh.

Sometimes a parent stops heritage in its tracks, and the next generation has a chance to regard itself, and to live, differently; when this happens the family, in a sense, begins anew. Minerva Breedlove may well have done that for her youngest child, providing, beyond prayers for education and mobility, an actual shift in self-assessment. Most parents can't pull this off, and some can't help passing on the ills done to them. Many mothers *want* their daughters to have wider options, or want to think they do, but they're too damaged or too limited in imagination themselves to alter patterns which, in the end, turn out to be self-perpetuating and as insidious as an addiction.

As a mother, Sarah Walker's been aiming to open up Lelia's life and horizons, the way Minerva did hers; yet because her nature is to take command, she cannot help wanting to manage the transformation and remain in constant charge. And so in an attempt to claim control of her own life, the daughter rebels, over and over again, and the mother responds as she must, and before long the two are in cahoots, maintaining the status quo by holding change at bay.

Factually, nobody knows much about the marriage of Lelia McWilliams and John Robinson, and a lot of the information we do have is suspect, including a hotel where Robinson is said to have worked, which seems never to have existed. But from the arc of Lelia's life before they tied the knot, and the detailed descriptions we have of her afterwards, we can speculate fairly reasonably. Indulged by her mother, she has never had to contemplate a life filled with demeaning jobs. She's been afforded an education and the ability to think for herself and, one way or another, to get whatever she wants. In another time, she might have waited to marry instead of following in her mother's footsteps, or she might have remained single. But Lelia is nothing if not in tune with the times, and the times demand that she find a husband fast. In addition, in contrast to her mother, her nature inclines her toward lethargy and sullenness, and she needs heat from others, ideally a spicy companion to jazz up her days and fill her life. Her Harlem posse implies, and sometimes declares outright, that she's a woman of blunt sexuality, unforgiving and possessive.

As for John Robinson: Born in post-Reconstruction Virginia in 1887, by his early twenties he has escaped the Deep South, gone west and north to Wheeling, in the other Virginia, where the trees aren't as lush or the manners so refined but a black man can make a decent life for himself. Though Wheeling's industrial, John doesn't work in the mills or the mines; he's described as a sharp-looking young man with a ready wit and easy smile, and so he snags one of the best jobs available to him—he becomes a waiter (porter? telephone operator?) in a snappy tight uniform, a job in which his clothes and his hands stay clean.

Lelia has an instinct for liveliness and a fondness for hijinks; she undoubtedly finds Robinson sexy and energetic, but it's hard to imagine her having the intuitive skills to please a vain, handsome and probably domineering man. It's not so much that she objects to kowtowing, simply that she doesn't know how. And there are other issues. For one, he's said to be five-foot-nine and in heels she'd tower over him. Testifying at her divorce hearing, two of Lelia's Pittsburgh agents and her boarder and friend Grant White will suggest that because she supported herself financially, Robinson had grown to resent her sassy independence. Lelia states the case more simply: "We had a quarrel. He left and said he wasn't coming back." One woman says she saw John Robinson in Chicago, where he declared he intended to stay.

Lelia remains in Pittsburgh, running the business. She can't file for divorce yet, even if she wants to; only after a year or two can she claim abandonment and expect a judge to pay attention.

On the other hand, her new status and the company's prosperity is giving her ideas, and she's clearly feeling antsy. She has friends in Pittsburgh, and a home, but New York's becoming a distraction she wants more of. While not yet on fire, Harlem's warming fast as the new territory for black development, and Lelia Robinson, nothing if not strictly à la mode, would certainly know this. John G. Taylor has gathered fellow whites to form the Harlem Property Owners' Improvement Corporation, whose strategy is designed to send Negroes back "to the slums where they belong," but meantime, the *New York Age* reports, the "colored invasion goes merrily along."

Unattached, semi-independent from her mother's attempts to run her life, Lelia has a new friend, Eva DeVoe. "Miss DeVoe" may or may not move into the house on Mignonette Street as a boarder; in any case, the two women do become traveling companions, and in 1912, the *Recorder* will have the two women returning together to "their" home in Pittsburgh.

M adame takes her son-in-law's departure in stride; in all likelihood she never approved of him to begin with. And while at forty-two she's bound to be hoping for a grandchild before too many more years go by, neither she nor her daughter seems to have inherited Minerva's childbearing ease, and Lelia's not inclined to settle down in one place anyway. As far as marriage goes, Madame can hardly criticize her daughter, having been less than a success at it herself.

She travels to St. Louis, visits old friends, plays whist, gives demonstrations, sells product. She might check out the new Poro digs on Pine Street or have someone else do it for her. By now, Madame acts as if she's never heard of any hair product other than her own.

Returning to Indianapolis, she decides to make a little extra cash by opening her home to a boarder or two. And in an amazing display of synchronicity, on December 10, 1910, three people who are destined to work together for nearly a decade advertise in the same newspaper, the

Recorder, on the same page, only columns apart. In the classified section, Madame advertises rooms to let to the up-to-date traveling public in her "beautifully furnished home," with all modern conveniences offered, including heat and "best board, served family style." To the right is a small notice for a company called Browder and Ransom. "We are doing a Real Estate Business. You will save time and money by placing your business in our hands. Give us a trial. Good homes in select parts of the city for sale." Just above this is a tiny notice for R. L. Brokenburr, lawyer. John Browder and Freeman B. Ransom are lawyers as well but, as newcomers to the state, can't apply for admission to the bar until registered as voters. Not wishing to waste time, they've opened a realty company. Browder, Ransom and Brokenburr will eventually form the nucleus of the Good Citizens League, a legal-aid bureau devoted to questions of public interest, particularly "those relative to the Negroes and their civil rights."

Born in Grenada, Mississippi, Freeman Briley Ransom is twenty-seven, single, a former literature and theology student who has studied law and religion at Walden University in Nashville—named valedictorian of both classes—and read law for two years at Columbia in New York. He will later tell his family that he had met Madame even before this time, during his student days, when he worked as a Pullman porter and dining-car attendant and she was a passenger. He said they struck up a conversation, and Madame told Ransom when he finished school to look her up, and maybe he did; at any rate, in December 1910 he answers her ad and moves into her home as a boarder. Though short-lived as a resident of 640, in every other respect Ransom will never leave Madame's side. He will serve as her great champion and her company's attorney and business manager for the rest of her life, and then her daughter's, until he dies in 1947.

Robert Lee Brokenburr, educated at Hampton and Howard, has worked for the International Liberty Union, an investment and insurance company, and now deems himself a "real high class lawyer," vowing never to divulge any of his clients' affairs, not even to newspapers. He, too, will board temporarily in Madame's home, then work for her as Ransom's assistant, and will go on to become Indiana's first black state senator. These two are the only men on whom Madam C. J. Walker will ever bestow positions of authority.

By late December, when Madame turns forty-three, Ransom may have moved in. Alice Kelly, though still teaching in Louisville, is probably making regular trips to Indianapolis as a part-time tutor, giving

Madame private lessons in grammar, punctuation, penmanship, vocabulary and elocution so that she might move easily among women of culture and education. Parthenia Rawlins is almost certainly still living there, probably paying no rent but set up as resident historian. C. J. has been traveling and in all likelihood is still on the road. And as if testing her stamina, Madame is working night and day: in the backroom manufacturing product for part of the day, then "doing heads in another room for the rest," sometimes cooking for her boarders herself—a meal for everybody from one pot—and doing her own washing at night. "You understand she was struggling then to get a foundation," Ransom will later write, remembering those days when he and Madame began their partnership and he moved in.

Lelia comes for Christmas, and they celebrate together in Madame's new home.

On the national scene, lynching continues apace. By combing newspapers for stories, Monroe Work—editor of the *Negro Year Book* and a Tuskegee employee—has compiled annual figures, but the distinction between lynching and murder or accidental death (due to heart attack, for instance, while running from vicious dogs) comes under so much discussion that in 1911, a meeting will be held at Tuskegee to define the term. For the most part, lynching is thought of as a kind of community-sponsored murder, distinguished from conventional murder, assassination and insurrection by popular justification and public sentiment. If and when communities turn against it, lynching vanishes. Still, does death by hanging qualify as a lynching prior to, or in the absence of, public burning? At any rate, by Monroe Work's definition, fifty-seven blacks are lynched in 1910.

Housewarming

Nineteen-ten was a great business year for Madame, her income well over ten thousand dollars and climbing; nonetheless, there's a publicity lull at the beginning of the new year. No accident, this: Madame's busy turning 640 North West Street into a showplace, meant to serve not only as her home but as her base of operations; and so instead of traveling, she's home studying fabric swatches and tapestries, examining samples of sterling flatware and English bone china, considering photographs of oak settees, a curio cabinet painted in gold leaf, a Tiffany chandelier.

She's also rethinking her marketing strategy yet again, and is contemplating a popular new concept, the *system,* which emphasizes organization, order and the application of a carefully planned methodology over the outdated appeal of "Trust me—I am like you." Now that she has a permanent location, she can centralize, and require all agents to send paperwork and money through Indianapolis, however remote the agent is and whatever the size of her territory. Not that she, personally, will necessarily examine every scrap of paper submitted, but it must seem as if she does. With Ransom's help she will make Indianapolis her headquarters, from which agents will order, products will ship and decisions will be made. The workload will be significant, but with the right system they can stay on top of things—as they must— and find ways of growing even faster.

Anthony Overton has moved his High Brown cosmetics manufacturing plant to Chicago, a hub city for railroads, to facilitate distribution and transportation, and with five full-time traveling salesmen he's placing his line in drug and variety stores and drugstores, which never before stocked African-American products. Overton's coup demonstrates a whole new sales opportunity, but Ransom's afraid Madame's agents won't appreciate having retailers competing for their business. Ransom's young but he's steady and sober, and Madame agrees to put the drugstore idea on hold.

In addition to renovating and furnishing her home, she's building a combination factory and office building behind it. This costs plenty, but the investment is not only within her reach; she's convinced it's necessary. Ransom's become her chief legal adviser, and his duties are quickly spilling over into other areas. He's still in partnership with Browder, selling real estate and lawyering, and she can't pay him enough to quit, but it doesn't take her long to realize that, as C.J.'s usefulness diminishes, Freeman Ransom will become essential to her company. When he tries to hold down expenditures, she pays attention, even if she refuses to go along, because his suggestions aren't from small-mindedness but part of long-range plans that both build the business and keep it grounded and stable. He's more cautious than she, no question. But unlike C.J., whose agenda has always focused first and foremost on himself, he has her interests at heart, and so she listens. Still, on certain issues she refuses to compromise and one of them is her home, which must be not just serviceable but *grand*. Another is real estate, which she starts accumulating as an investment about now, both vacant lots and houses.

In the early spring, C.J. buys a big car, a Stevens-Duryea, and takes it on the road. Gone again, and rumors of his high life and big spending keep drifting back to Indianapolis. But Ransom holds conventional views about marriage and its efficacy; even if people wrongly assume that it's C. J. who runs the show, Madame shouldn't waste time worrying about misperceptions. She needs a husband, and that should be the end of it. But as C. J.'s behavior grows increasingly unacceptable—drink, women, carousing—deferring to him starts to seem plain silly. More and more Madame realizes that her true purposes go beyond hair and even self-esteem; she's stirring up notions of women's independence, from both white expectations and male domination. In time, if she's going to exemplify those ideals, her husband has to go. Ransom certainly cautions her to go slow here, too, but the truth is staring them in the face and soon they're going to have to face up to it.

Meanwhile, she saves time for her studies in grammar, diction and penmanship and now is trying to convince Alice Kelly to leave her teaching job in Louisville and come work full-time for her as forelady. Kelly knows Greek, Latin and the classics; she's single and therefore mobile, and has the instincts of the aunt to whom young people will turn for advice and sanctuary. Ransom's set to manage the company, but Madame wants women in charge of everything else.

S cheduled for August is a week-long encampment of the Knights of Pythias and its female wing, the Court of Calanthe. Some fifty thousand people are supposed to attend, and the *Freeman* is predicting it will be like nothing Indianapolis has ever seen. Booker T. Washington is the featured speaker, with a day named in his honor. There will be receptions and performances, speeches and recitations and discussions, dancing and food. The local Pythians have also arranged to use Wonderland Park, where they will offer bands, dancing and carnival rides.

Madame has to be ready by then. She'll host people in her home, and it will have to be so splendid that women will go home thinking about becoming agents or, at the very least, carrying boxes of Wonderful Hair Grower and the desire to tell their friends about it. People don't want to know about hardship anymore. They don't want to hear sad stories about a tragic past. They need success. And whatever it takes to make her home a testament to her accomplishments, she'll come up with it. C. J. and Ransom may complain but in this, she won't back down. She knows she's right; still, the steady outlay of cash and the pressure of the schedule must keep her on edge.

Before the encampment, she intends to have a housewarming that will attract the best people of Indianapolis and represent her official coming out as a doyenne of the social scene. Printed invitations will be sent to selected guests from all over the country: Chicago, Pittsburgh, St. Louis and Los Angeles. She is already thinking about what to wear and what kind of flowers to decorate with. She has ordered an Italian harp from the Wulschner-Stewart Music Company downtown, and has engaged a harpist for the evening; the harp costs a fortune, and she can only pray that it arrives in time. But since she spent another fortune on the Chickering baby grand piano and a Victor talking machine, both gold-encrusted, it's in Wulschner-Stewart's interest to keep her happy.

The end of June is exactly the right time to unveil 640 North West. Her factory will be finished by August, and she has already invited the Wizard to witness at first hand the employment she's providing for the race, and she will see that her young women are dressed in starched black-and-white dresses and are neat and clean—teeth brushed, hair neat, breath fresh—in accordance with his teachings.

She is thinking of calling the new building a laboratory instead of a factory, so that people will think they are using scientific methods to come up with new products and improve old ones. Though this doesn't jell with the idea of divine gifts, probably no one will notice.

When she's ready, Madame discusses her mail-order ideas with Ransom. She also wants to create a school whose curriculum incorporates not just hairdressing but a whole system of beautification, including manicuring and massage. Moreover, she wants to incorporate her business and invest in more real estate. Ransom's already in this business, so he can get her in on deals before they're listed. From childhood she has had an ingrained belief in the value of land.

If there's a divine gift at this juncture, it's not the formula for Wonderful Hair Grower but Freeman Ransom. Single-minded and loyal, he has the gravity to balance Madame's intensity and restlessness and the wit to manage a business that has no precedent, no structure, no long-term plan beyond what Madame cooks up. He's not a man of ideas; what he can do is stay home and run things, honestly and efficiently, leaving her to travel freely. Ransom's mission is to save the business from becoming so entranced with its own success it loses track of common sense and goes haywire. Moreover, he can channel his own desires into serving another while holding on to his dignity and finding both financial and personal satisfaction in that role. Both lawyerly and in need of a job, he's a real find, his formal rigidity a considerable relief after the other men in her life. And although Madame might not have admitted it at the time, the two of them are, in fact, a perfect team.

The house is finished in time.
She calls the drawing room her Gold Room. Furnished in soft colors of rose and gold, its dark wood floors are partly covered with plush Oriental rugs, set off by settees made of quartered

oak and upholstered in a rose-and-gold pattern. She is particularly proud of a curio cabinet in one corner, painted in gold leaf and filled with carefully chosen bric-a-brac. In the middle of the room, under a Tiffany chandelier, is an enormous onyx table from Mexico, framed in and supported by gold bands.

The Chickering baby grand is in the library, a room of music and literature, some of the walls lined with leather-bound books, others displaying etchings and engravings of Longfellow and other famous American poets; a bust of Shakespeare stands in one corner. Of course she will never have time to read these books, but literature is a sign of the good life, and it comforts her to have beautiful books to look at, and thumb through and wonder about.

But perhaps it's her dining room she loves best, with its grape-cluster wallpaper, massive oak table and the two china cabinets, each displaying a full set in a different pattern. For the housewarming she'll fill her huge coin-silver punch bowl and set out its matching gold-lined mugs, along with her Haviland china and sterling silver tea set and silver trays. Perfect.

The open house is held on June 27, and four days later the *Freeman* runs a photo of 640 North West Street, with the Walkers standing out front, Madame stiffly in that white suit and hat, C. J. in his dancerly pose.

"The Walker home on North West Street," the caption reads,

> is one of the most artistic of those owned by colored people of Indianapolis. It is a twelve-room modern brick structure. On the premises is a laboratory and a garage. The home is excellently appointed. The furnishings are the richest and of the latest design. The value of the home is above $10,000. Mr. and Mrs. Walker are engaged in the hair culture business—manufacturing remedies, etc. in connection with the business. They have made their money within the last six years. Mr. Walker travels extensively, while his wife looks after the business at home.

Clearly submitted by the Walker Company prior to the actual event, this text suggests the influence of Alice Kelly. It's definitely not Ransom's prose style, and nothing like what we've seen previously from the Walkers. But Madame has certainly read and approved the copy, and it's instructive to read it with that in mind. Never shy about listing her material assets—because she believes, like Booker T. Washington, that her people will find the example of her success both inspiring and uplifting—she emphasizes size and cost. By the end of her life, having been made to feel ungenerous toward all those who wrote and asked for money, she changes her mind and is less quick to talk about these things. But here the boast seems appropriate. On the other hand, she's careful to show how cultured she also is, her home "artistic" and "excellently appointed," the furnishings extravagant and up-to-date. And the coda at the end will explain away any questions about the Walkers' domestic particularities.

The accompanying article describes the evening as a "brilliant affair and one that will be long remembered by the good people of Indianapolis, as well as the host and hostess." Of the 200 invitations extended, more than 150 people responded, many of them from out of town, which demonstrates the esteem in which Madame Walker is held by her many friends and patrons. Gifts were beautiful and numerous, among them a set of pearl-handled knives from friends in Chicago, a silver vegetable dish from Agnes Prosser, a set of sterling silver tablespoons and a double set of teaspoons from Lelia and a tall cut-glass vase from friends in Cincinnati. Other gifts listed include Chinese cuspidors, Dresden and Haviland china and a silk quilt. Guests from as far away as Los Angeles, Chicago, New York, and Marshall, Texas, are noted, as well as locals including Lillian Fox, George Knox, Dr. and Mrs. Ward and Thomas E. Taylor, secretary of the YMCA.

The "sweet strains of an Italian harp float[ing] from behind an embankment of palms and ferns" would have provided a balm to Madame's nerves during the evening, as music will throughout her life. When she is living in the Harlem brownstone, she often has a uniformed employee to stand by the talking Victor to turn the crank and play records nonstop. Madame also likes to dance, and in private she appreciates the popular music Lelia goes in for; but she craves to learn about finer things, including art and classical music, not just for show but for her own edification. So much to learn, and her lessons have begun late; sometimes it seems there will never be enough of anything to satisfy her enormous appetite.

The article closes on a note of gratitude, Mr. and Madame Walker extending their thanks to Mrs. Fox, Attorney Ransom and Miss Lillian Prosser from Louisville for their help in receiving and caring for the guests.

This significant social event shows Indianapolis society just how far-reaching Madame's influence is. And though for some reason Lelia isn't able to attend, she will arrive, via Denver, in August, in time for the encampment.

Three weeks later, Madame writes Dr. Washington in Tuskegee on letterhead stationery: "The Walker Manufacturing Company, Manufacturers of C.J. Walker's Blood and Rheumatic Remedy, Mme C.J. Walker's Wonderful Hair Grower."

Dear Sir.
Having learned through our local committee that you will be in our city during the supreme session of the K. of P.'s I thought to again remind you of your promise to visit and inspect our home and factory. Hoping you can make it convenient to do so. I beg to remain

Respectfully yours . . .

The signature—*(Mme) C.J. Walker*—is in the same florid hand as the Louisville letter asking for financial help.

Though the letter is peppered with strike-overs, the grammar is solid and the language without undue frills, which suggests that Miss Kelly lent a hand to its composition.

The Wizard has directed that all letters sent to Tuskegee must be answered the day they are read, and so his reply arrives quickly: he indeed hopes to be able to visit her facilities, but of course he will be "in the hands of Mr. [George] Stewart's committee," and compelled by whatever program has been arranged for him. In any case, he thanks her for the kind invitation.

Things are not going especially well for Washington these days. More people are turning against his assimilationist philosophy, and he may do himself more damage than good when, apologizing for Taft, he reminds his people how much better off they are than, say, Russian serfs. Beyond the NAACP's growing influence, there's the humiliation the Wizard himself suffered that March in New York, when sometime after nine o'clock on a Sunday night, a white man named Ulrich beat him within an inch of his life. He wasn't consciously attacking the famous Booker T. Washington, only some Negro trying to enter an all-white apartment building. And when the police stepped in, they too assumed the bloodied victim was just another black man, and it wasn't until they got to the station that they discovered this was not just any Negro but *the* Negro.

For some, however, the pressing question is what he was doing in that neighborhood in the first place. Near Central Park at 11½ East Sixty-third, the building isn't far from the racy Tenderloin district, and to make matters worse, a number of attractive white women of questionable profession live there. Washington's explanation—that he got lost going to meet his bookkeeper—falls apart when the accountant admits he was in Tuskegee at the time. Nonetheless, Washington sticks to his alibi, trusting in the loyalty of his people, and the tawdry affair drags on, in newspapers and the courts, as suits and countersuits are filed. The black community doesn't know how to respond, since the beating, whatever the circumstances, was clearly unjustified. But the Wizard's been holier-than-thou his entire life, and those who believed in his piety now can't help feeling betrayed, while his critics and declared enemies try not to gloat. The more faithful among his followers stand firm and decide not to believe any of the accusations. Their loyalty receives a boost of support when others make a public show of rallying to the Wizard's cause: President Taft sends a letter of support, and Andrew Carnegie visits Washington in his hotel to wish him well. And eventually his strategy of innocence pays off when, on a subzero night in D.C., only days after the beating, he lectures on Negro business development and the hall is packed with cheering "substantial" people. In the words of newspaper columnist R. W. Thompson, "the Wizard has not gone back" in popularity.

But public humiliation has clearly cost him. He looks tentative, unlike the bold Chief of old, and his health is failing. On the very Sunday of his disgrace, he'd just returned from the J. H. Kellogg sanitarium in Battle Creek, Michigan, where he lived on a diet of vegetables and grains and a regimen of exercise, water treatments and electricity-charged sinusoidal baths. Although he's been advised to slow down, his schedule remains as punishing as ever, and in photographs taken between now and his death in 1915, the frailty is unmistakable.

When Madam Walker's letter crosses his desk in July, Dr. Washington's lawyers are busy trying to cobble together an out-of-court settlement and he's looking for another New York hotel to stay in, since his favorite, the Manhattan, will no longer accommodate him.

The great man might have suffered a setback, but he's far from out of the game, and has no intention of getting in a rush to involve himself and Tuskegee in the politically dicey business of hair straightening, whatever Mrs. Walker wishes to call it.

The Wizard in Indianapolis

The summer social season continues with an open house, on August 2, of Madame's new laboratory and factory. The general public is invited, with a grand-opening offer of a box of Wonderful Hair Grower to anyone who spends one dollar on a treatment. C. J.'s back on the road, presumably driving his big car through Illinois, Missouri, Nebraska, Kansas, Oklahoma and Colorado. Lelia hit town briefly, on her way to Denver, and will be back by Sunday the twentieth, when the encampment begins.

Meanwhile, black Indianapolis is charged with excitement, and as late as the nineteenth Madame's advertising in the *Recorder* for a first-class cook capable of serving large numbers of people. The Pythians and the Calantheans come mostly by train, though some arrive in their automobiles. In all probability, among those attending the encampment are Charles K. (C. K.) and Jessie Batts Robinson, steadfast friends of Madame's from her St. Paul AME days in St. Louis and active members of the Court of Calanthe and the national K of P. In the years to come, Jessie Robinson will often invite Madame to speak in St. Louis, and it will be in her home that Sarah suffers her final illness in 1919.

A parade kicks off the festivities and flags fly, bands play and uniformed troops march down city streets. Wonderland Park boasts enough rides, music, dances and speeches to exhaust anyone. Two days later, the Wizard arrives from Little Rock, having just wrapped up the twelfth annual National Negro Business League convention, and George Knox formally proclaims this Tuesday Booker T. Washington Day and introduces the man whom the Pythians have christened the Sage of Hope and Sound Advice. After his speech on the importance of morals, thrift and energy, the rapt audience applauds robustly and at length, a heartening show of support in his time of troubles.

Afterwards, he would have time to visit the home and factory of Madam C. J. Walker, but may not. From the publisher George Stewart's point of view, she's an economic force and a steady advertiser in both the *Recorder* and the *Freeman,* and he'd like nothing better than to please her, but he isn't likely to press her case if his guest appears reluctant. Does Washington go? In the following year in an extensive interview in the *Freeman,* Madame lists the luminaries she has received in her home, and he is not among them—proof enough, it seems to me, that he'd begged off.

Washington has to consider not only his views of her trade but also the opinions of those who've come out against what her business stands for—not to mention her competition, especially the more respectable Anthony Overton. And if she's angling for an opening into Tuskegee—as indeed she is, ideally setting up hairdressing classes there—this represents an endorsement he simply can't afford to, and won't, give. Besides, he doesn't hand out favors, he sells them, and she doesn't have anything to trade that justifies the risk. Someday maybe; not yet.

Certainly Madame attends his afternoon speech and his follow-up appearance that evening at the Coliseum, where his audience again responds to his traditional sermon with devotion. But perhaps some of them notice the weariness in his face and posture, the halt in his step. The next day, good weather follows him out of town and a steady midwestern drizzle sets in. Outdoor activities are postponed, the main parade is canceled and Madame has missed another shot at engaging the attention of the Wizard.

Now that her house is decorated and her factory up and running, Madame—always on the watch for another diversion—has developed a new passion: driving. She's bought a $1,600 Pope-Waverley Electric runabout, a little black box of a car, manufactured right in Indianapolis, and somebody's taught her to drive. The electric lacks power and range certainly, but while it's less grand than C. J.'s big touring car, she loves to hum around town in it, taking quick trips between plug-ins. In a photograph of Madame behind the wheel of the Waverley, her eyes are bright and she looks mischievous and quite pleased with herself, with a half-secret, girlish smile she's trying, but can't quite manage, to hide.

And so when Lelia gets back from Denver, it's likely she'll find her mother waiting in the Electric at Union Station, but Lelia has other things on her mind, namely real estate, specifically Harlem property. She might even have torn out the recent *New York Age* story headlined NAIL AND PARKER PULL OFF BIG DEAL, concerning the sale of ten deluxe apartment buildings on West 135th Street between Seventh Avenue and the Stanford White Public Library on Lenox. St. Philip's Episcopal, the richest black church in the country, has purchased the buildings in a deal brokered by John E. "Jack" Nail and Henry C. "Phil" Parker, who for years have been trying to open up Harlem to black people looking for nice homes in a safe neighborhood. They've enjoyed some successes, but nothing major until now. And this one—which in their words will provide the best living accommodations that colored tenantry has been invited to rent—is a doozy.

St. Philip's is not only rich, it's snobby, with a congregation that is almost exclusively light-skinned. Catering to "the better element of colored people," it is the only black church in Manhattan with a pew system, in which members outbid one another for the best seats. Its pastor, Hutchens Bishop, who looks white enough to pass, has made a number of Harlem purchases using this subterfuge and then turned the property over to his church. Consequently, a grand new edifice is now under construction in Harlem, designed by Vertner Tandy, the African-American architect who one day will work on Madam Walker's home in Westchester County.

These apartment buildings went to St. Philip's in a swap with the Pennsylvania Railroad, which needed property downtown for a new station; the church owned a large plot on West Thirtieth, which it intended to turn into a cemetery; the railroad company owned the apartment buildings. Nail and Parker matched these desires and brokered a deal by which the church bought Penn's property for $600,000 and the railroad bought St. Philip's prospective cemetery for $450,000. Meanwhile, other black churches are heading north. The uptown branch of the Mother Zion AME Church is currently under construction in Harlem, and although the Abyssinian Baptists won't move there until 1923, their minister, Adam Clayton Powell Sr., will one day assert that he knew as early as 1911 that Harlem would be their new home.

The black community has always followed its churches, and now that the Harlem block covenants have been broken and important churches are headed there, the migration of black New Yorkers from midtown has begun in earnest, and wealthy, stylish people are moving in. Lelia's determined to be on the leading edge of this trend, but to do that, she has to convince her mother to act fast. But the bills from 640 North West haven't been paid, and there are the two new cars and the school, and Madame's not willing to plunge into another speculative deal until she sees how 1911 goes. Lelia, every bit as hot-tempered as her mother, almost certainly protests, but in the end there's nothing for her to do but back off.

Incorporation

The fall of 1911 turns out to be an even more momentous season than the summer. On September 19, Madame files incorporation papers in the name of the Madame C. J. Walker Manufacturing Company of Indiana, the capital stock of which is $10,000—suggesting that she might have put her house up for collateral—to be divided into one thousand shares at $10 each. The company will "sell hairgrowing, beautifying and scalp disease-curing preparations and clean scalps with the same," and its board of directors will consist of Madame, Lelia and C. J., but all stock is assigned to Madame.

Brokenburr sets it up. Madame signs a stock certificate as president; C. J. signs twice, once as secretary, once as treasurer. Madame's signature is still crabbed, splotched and uncertain, while his is a zestful flourish.

A month later, Madame scores a coup that nobody else in her company could have predicted or even, more than likely, would have endorsed, had she asked for their approval. African-Americans have been interested in the YMCA movement since its inception. Leaders approve of its character-and-body-building mission and consider its facilities a safe and proper place for boys to socialize outside the home, to read and study and to "quicken their thoughts" on the moral and religious topics of the day. But the all-white national organization, more attuned to Jim Crow than to Christian charity, has suggested that if colored people want YMCAs, they'll have to build their own.

Indianapolis has a black YMCA organization—George Knox is its board president—but no building. In September, Knox editorializes, "We must get busy. We need the building. Others have done the thing, and what others can do, we can do and must do." And by the next month, Julius Rosenwald, the Sears, Roebuck magnate who is funding schools and Y's for African-Americans all over the country, has pledged $25,000 toward a goal of $100,000 to build a colored Y in Indianapolis, leaving the community—black and white—ten days to raise the rest.

Thomas Taylor, secretary of the colored Y, immediately calls a meeting at the Knights of Pythias Hall on Sunday, October 22, the day before the fund drive officially begins. But before the general meeting, the Central (white) Y sends its chairman and secretary to help organize the drive. Together, the black and white groups devise eighteen African-American teams, each led by a captain and assigned to canvass a particular set of neighborhoods and businesses, and twelve white teams to fund-raise among the majority race. All volunteers must emphasize the urgency imposed by the deadline, as well as the great need for young black men to have a safe place to congregate.

Since the housewarming and the incorporation, Madame has become even more famous locally, and when the music store runs an article in the *Recorder* encouraging Negroes to buy a piano, citing the examples of Indianapolis Negroes who have "wakened to the advantages of good citizenship . . . by purchasing comfortable homes" which *in some cases are furnished palatial*, everyone knows who they mean. She attends the October 22 meeting.

Like any fund-raiser, the gathering begins with rousing speeches interrupted by lengthy bouts of applause accompanied by general foot stomping. Ransom, Brokenburr and Dr. Ward are introduced as volunteer captains, with Knox heading up the Colored Citizens' Committee. Their goal is $75,000—$60,000 from the white community, $15,000 from the colored—by Rosenwald's deadline, November 2.

When the chairman kicks off the campaign by asking for subscriptions from the audience, one white businessman pledges $5,000; another, twice that amount. Knox and Ward come up with $250 apiece, then Madam L. E. McNairdee makes an appearance. African-American clairvoyant, phrenologist, physiognomist, member of the ancient Southern Clairvoyants of New Orleans and owner of a local boardinghouse, she raises the stakes by doubling the offers of the two well-known men. And that's when Madame rises to the challenge.

"The Young Men's Christian Association," she announces, "is one of the greatest institutions there is. I am very much interested in its work. I certainly hope that it gets the new building and I think every colored person ought to contribute to the campaign. If the association can save our boys, our girls will be saved, and that's what I am interested in. Someday," she adds, "I would like to see a colored girls' association started."

There is no response to that suggestion and there will not be for some time, but Madame is not finished. And in a moment of inspired boldness and instinctive marketing know-how, she doubles the clairvoyant's offer. *A thousand dollars.* The hall fairly throbs with cheers and foot stomping, and then she reaches into her purse. Everyone else has made a pledge, but Madame comes up with hard cash: one-fourth of her total contribution, on the spot.

Now, Madam Walker does not have an extra $1,000 to give away. An employee will later say that at that time, Madame couldn't have been worth more than a round $25,000 total, including house and factory. Cash reserves? Close to none. She incorporated her business barely a month before, has just finished fixing up her house and factory, and has hired Alice Kelly as her forelady and Eckstein Norton graduate Lucy Flint as her bookkeeper. A few weeks from now, she will report her current income as $1,000 a month.

But never mind the details; she's a high-stakes player and she's made history. This is a moment to which only one other thus far can compare: the time when she stood before the Sunday-school class at St. Paul's to ask for money. In many ways that was the bolder, even more significant, moment of the two, but this one turns her into a star. And from now on she has her honorific, by which she will be unfailingly introduced: the First Woman in the World to Give $1,000 to a Colored YMCA.

The final YMCA tab is $104,229, of which African-Americans account for over $20,000. And ground is broken at the corner of Michigan and Senate.

Madame's generosity assures her of George Knox's unreserved support, and so it is no accident that in November, the *Freeman* runs a front-page feature story about her, complete with the dreamy picture beside the mirror. She is described as America's best-known hair culturist and the first and only woman in the world to donate $1,000 to a colored YMCA, a statement that will have to be revised when, in St. Louis, Annie Pope-Turnbo also contributes $1,000 to that city's colored Y.

And so on November 11, 1911, the public is given the first version of Madame's full biography, starting with her birth in Delta to parents Owen and Minerva Breedlove, noting that she was orphaned at seven, reared on a farm until ten, lived in Vicksburg with her sister and cruel brother-in-law, married at fourteen. There is no mention of the work she did as a washerwoman; instead she's called a young woman who "endured many hardships and much toil" and in 1905 discovered a hair remedy she perfected on herself and then took to Denver, where she was quickly "successful in building up a fair business."

After her present marriage and a move into better quarters, she "became awakened to the needs of the colored people in this line and her discovery was regarded as one of the wonders of the world." And so she decided to travel, at which point C. J. comes in for some gentle trashing. "Notwithstanding she was discouraged by her husband and many patrons who said she would not be able to make her expenses from one town to another . . . she was determined and felt inspired to [go]." The story then turns wackily religious: just as "Christ converted the world by miracles He wrought before the Jews, by placing her hand in His, she might convert the world by the wonderful good she would do her people."

The article moves along in a more secular vein and has Madame hitting the road with her husband, and though he can see nothing ahead but failure, after a few months he becomes a believer (joining with her "heart and hand"), and they travel for another year and a half. Mail-order sales increase in the meantime and they move to Pittsburgh, establish a business there and then go traveling again, leaving Madame's daughter in charge, and eventually arriving in Indianapolis on February 10, 1910.

The ten-thousand-dollar home is noted, and her factory and laboratory is said to be the most complete of its kind in the U.S. The article reports the details of her incorporation and says she has 951 agents and a turnover of $1,000 a month.

There is an indirect mention of her previous profession ("She has made possible the way for many colored women to abandon the washtub for more pleasant and profitable occupations") toward the end of the piece, and her daughter's name is given as Mrs. Lelia *Walker*

Robinson. This is a practical move, designed to connect Lelia officially to her mother, the better to claim her inheritance and position of authority in the company.

On page 2, there are pictures of the factory, her hair parlors and one of Madame herself, giving a manicure. In the first photograph, seven employees stand in front of the dark frame building; and in the second, a like number are shown fixing hair in curtained booths, everything neat and polished. The picture of Madame is a long shot and doesn't reveal much, not even that she actually did manicures instead of only posing. The captions comment on Madame's "planned system" of advertisements and sales agents nationwide and describes both their local and foreign business as "rushing."

Order and organization are emphasized. "Madam Walker," the story continues, "as president of the corporation, contents herself with acting in a supervisory capacity, the immediate management being under a forewoman, an estimable and competent lady from Springfield, Illinois." And it further notes that several other young women are employed, including a bookkeeper and stenographer.

On this same page is yet another write-up on Madame, this one signed by F. B. Ransom and so astonishingly hyperbolic that I have to think the attorney must have been at least partially responsible for some of the front-page article as well. It begins: "Like a dream from the Orient, or better still, like a legend from some Egyptian city where Ethiopian Queens in royal splendor reigned supreme; or like a mighty effort of the imagination fired by a belief in some unseen power, swayed and urged on and on by an invisible, yet potent, force, is the life story of Madam C.J. Walker—her beginning, her struggles, and her ultimate success." And so it continues in the purplest of prose to chronicle Madame's clash in the night with sophisticated ignorance, defining the dream which brought her the formula for hair grower as "the supreme effort of a mind trained to think," and comparing Madame to Joan of Arc, Ponce de León, and H.J. Heinz.

An invitation to ridicule, the piece is nonetheless touching in what it reveals about Ransom's eagerness to please and his desire to write like the Victorian masters he studied in Nashville at Walden University.

Two weeks later, C. J. travels to Topeka for a meeting of the Western Negro Press Association, which he promoted in Denver, and there manages to push through a resolution congratulating Madam C. J. Walker on her generous contribution to the YMCA in Indianapolis.

And in December, Madame prepares for a trip south. The events and stresses of the past year might well be taking their toll about now, and—as her undiagnosed medical condition quietly settles in—she might feel tired and low much of the time, and during the night experience discomforts, thirst and hunger, pain and pressure. So when Ward prescribes rest and a better diet, she suggests going south, where she can be nourished by the midwinter sun. But her health is only one factor, and of course rest is of no interest to her, and anyway there's no reason not to do a little business while she's down there.

Tuskegee's annual farmers' convention takes place in January, and she'll plan her trip around it. And this time, she means to be in the thick of things, not just sitting in the audience listening.

Undaunted by his no-show in August, she again writes to Dr. Washington asking if she might visit on January 17 to introduce her work and sell her goods at the institute. Unlike her previous letters, this one is grammatically flawless and immaculately typed. To give him an idea of the business in which she's engaged, Madame encloses her new booklet, thanks him in advance for an early reply and signs off "Respectfully" in an exquisitely schooled hand. With C. J. in Kansas, her amanuensis would be Alice Kelly.

As usual, Washington replies promptly, addressing her as "My dear Mme Walker." He then thanks her for her letter but fears that she misunderstands the nature of the conference, a "meeting of poor farmers who come here for instruction and guidance and who have very little or no money." (As if she didn't know firsthand about farming and rural poverty.) Then his tone turns testy. "I am well acquainted with the business in which you are engaged, but somehow I do not feel that a visit to our conference would offer the opportunity which you seem to desire."

And so the Wizard bares his impatience—*if* he's the one who composed this curt letter. His trusted secretary, Emmett Scott—who'll be appointed a special assistant to the secretary of war during World War I—now runs the Tuskegee office. In his boss's absence, Scott often answers Washington's letters and signs them with his name, and that may be what happened this time. In addition to rejecting her request, whoever wrote the letter also didn't bother to mention Madame's jam-packed booklet, whose sixteen pages contain pretty much every ad campaign she's ever conducted. Most of it we've seen before, but there are a few new features. For one, the quiet suggestion on the bottom of the cover: "Ask your Druggist for Madame Walker's Preparations." And on the frontispiece, exhortations that include: "These wonderful preparations were discovered by Madame Walker three times in a dream." There are several photographs, including the triptych, the one of the Walkers in front of 640 at the housewarming, and a new picture of the steel comb. The copy is better edited than in earlier editions, with some Poro-ish warnings about imitators, and a great many more testimonial letters, some from very notable figures. The YMCA donation is twice invoked as evidence of Madame's "great, big, generous, and race-loving heart." A new item compares growing hair to planting grass—in terms remarkably similar to those used in an ad for a rival product called Hair Seed—and there are three new paragraphs about Madame's agents, her factory and her "well-planned system of advertisements."

All the biographical sketches are included—Christ, the Orient and all—with C. J. again playing the Doubting Thomas.

A week later, a small notice in the *Freeman* again suggests that Madam Walker's prospective customers inquire at their druggist's before ordering by mail. Following Overton's lead, Madame certainly understands that distributing products through drugstores will cut into her agents' business, but profit comes first, and her reasoning follows Carnegie's: if she doesn't prosper, how can she be of service to those less privileged?

A few days after that, in a letter to *New York Age* editor Fred Moore, Booker T. Washington once again takes a stand against the hair business when he criticizes that paper for running false claims by such advertisers as clairvoyants and hair-straightening manufacturers. The Wizard hopes that Moore will "consider the matter seriously," and since he subsidizes the *Age* and helped Moore buy it, his warning carries considerable weight.

Undeterred, Madame readies herself for a January trip to Alabama—but first, Christmas. Lelia's coming home and, having looked forward to the visit—according to Ransom—with "joyous expectation," she spends the rest of December with her daughter, enjoying the season.

In politics, with Taft running for re-election and the Democrats backing Woodrow Wilson, the unpredictable Teddy Roosevelt has formed the Progressive Party and may throw his hat into the ring. In a three-way race, the candidates look to woo the Northern black vote. Important African-Americans, such as DuBois, Monroe Trotter and Bishop Alexander Walters come out for Wilson—a Southern intellectual—believing the race will gain power by switching parties and attracted by Wilson's vow to be "President of all the People." The solidly Republican *Recorder* endorses Taft, warning that a vote cast for Roosevelt only benefits Wilson, and a Democratic victory would bring back the soup kitchens and bank failures of the Grover Cleveland administration. Nonetheless, many voters recall TR's dinner with Dr. Washington and his praise of black soldiers' bravery in the Philippines and, despite Brownsville and his other racial failures, stick with the Colonel.

The Wizard's choice remains a mystery, but the majority of the newspapers he controls eventually endorse Taft—who has no response to the sixty lynchings reported in 1911.

Visit to Tuskegee

Having arrived at Tuskegee on opening day of the conference, Madame addresses yet another letter to the Wizard. "Mr. Washington," she rather briskly begins,

> *I would like to ask you the kind favor of introducing me to this conference. I do not want to explain my work, but I do want them to know that I am in the business world not for myself alone, but to do all the good I can for the uplift of my race, which you well know by the great sacrifice I made in the interest of the Y.M.C.A. of Indianapolis. I believe that if others knew of my great struggle from the age of seven years without any parents to assist me up to six years ago when I entered the business arena at that time and having succeeded in building it up to where my income is now more than $1,000 per month, it would be a great inspiration to them to do likewise. Trusting you will not deny me this one opportunity I am:*
> *Obiedently* [sic] *yours,*
> *(Mme) C.J. Walker*

Odd letter, even a little chilly; the point is, in spite of the snub she's still after him. In no other instance does Madame behave in this way, but then nobody else has the Wizard's clout or his ability to grant favors, should he so choose. His endorsement would automatically increase her business and give her some sway with the black newspapers he subsidizes, as well as with the NACW and his wife. So no wonder she panders. But hers may be a more complicated quest. It's as if she wants Washington to *validate* her by acknowledging that even a dark-skinned washwoman born to slaves can *be* somebody. Or maybe she thinks that because of their similar pasts, Washington owes her at least some recognition, as people sometimes feel about celebrities who manage to move beyond the limitations of a similar background. Whatever the underlying or obvious reasons, she's relentless.

Emmett Scott replies to Madame's letter within hours: "I have talked with Mr. Washington and he agrees to arrange for you to speak for 10 minutes tonight in the Chapel. We will have a very full audience there at that time and it will be more proper we think to speak tonight instead of in the regular conference." This time Scott signs the letter personally.

He also adds a postscript explaining that because it was addressed to Dr. Washington, he is not returning the letter of Thomas Taylor but placing it in the Tuskegee files. So it seems that the Wizard gave his begrudging assent at least partly because Taylor, secretary of the Indianapolis Y and a politic, light-skinned Bookerite, wrote on her behalf. But Madame may also have taken matters into her own hands. According to Washington family legend, she simply showed up at the Wizard's home that afternoon, uninvited and unannounced. "She came knocking on his door at his private home," asserts Washington biographer Louis Harlan. When the Wizard tried to discourage her, she insisted, having arrived fully prepared to conduct hairdressing demonstrations. Following the convention, Madame will testify to having done eighty-four treatments in Tuskegee, some of them on members of the Wizard's family. This story may or may not be factual, and Harlan himself describes it as family "folklore." In any case, however it happens, Madame gets what she came for.

The night meeting in the Chapel is set up for less noteworthy speakers and spillover presentations, and is much less desirable than "the regular conference," but she certainly won't turn down the invitation. That afternoon, the farmers are admonished to buy homes and farm machinery, to improve the character and standing of their pastors and to hire better teachers. Good ideas, to be sure, though they have to wonder how to manage all that. Other speeches are the standard Tuskegee boilerplate: cooperate with landlords, stay put and don't move, because "the habit of unnecessary moving costs the South each year millions of dollars." White planters are lauded for awarding prizes to black tenants who both produce the greatest yields and demonstrate moral improvement, prizes that are thought to prevent their regrettable migration toward urban employment.

That night, Washington commences the evening session by introducing Monroe Work, editor of the Tuskegee *Negro Year Book* and compiler of lynching statistics, whose subject is the necessity of saving money. Other brief speeches touch on schools, banks, jobs and land investment. After Madame is introduced, she speaks modestly, seemingly moved, even awed, by the situation. "I feel like that the best way to save money is to invest it in property. That is what I have done. And another thing I believe in is, that in proportion to as God blesses us we should reach and help our fellows."

If she says anything else, the Tuskegee campus paper—which reported at length on the conference—doesn't record it, or make mention of her husband, who allegedly accompanied her that night. But after she leaves, Madame sends a bread-and-butter note to the Washingtons, thanking both of them for the kindnesses shown at the conference to herself and her agents.

Flushed with success, before leaving Tuskegee, Madame sets up a permanent facility nearby and—in a decision she will come to regret—appoints Dora Larrie, an energetic Indianapolis agent whom she trained personally, as her local representative. Larrie's capable and ambitious, and once she's securely ensconced in the new offices, Madame feels free to leave. She and C. J. confer and, after agreeing to divide up the Southern territory, depart separately. From New Orleans, Madame sends word to the Indianapolis press of her decision to extend her trip, and in early March she's still there, staying at the YMCA, selling products, giving lessons and signing up agents. Later that month, she and C. J. reconnoiter briefly in Jackson, Mississippi, after which he heads back toward Alabama while she remains in Jackson, instructing new agents.

The Walkers are almost never together anymore, and with good reason: C. J.'s drinking has become a bigger problem than ever, as has his general profligacy. He's been carrying on with various women, one of whom—a certain "Louise" in Kansas City—has written him letters in which she flatters his bruised ego by calling him a "big, sensible, strong businessman," as if he alone were responsible for Madame's success. None of this is a secret anymore—certainly not to Madame—and while there's no way of knowing exactly what went on during the Walkers' Jackson trip or what kind of ultimatum might have been issued, it's not hard to guess.

Unconvinced, the irrepressible C. J. bounds off to Birmingham to meet up with his next inamorata, who happens to be Madame's new Tuskegee agent, Dora Larrie. She, too, has persuaded her lover that he is the brains behind the Mme. Walker Company, and that with his knowledge of hair products and her ability to do the work, together they can make a fortune. C. J. buys into this notion and the two decide to launch their new enterprise in Atlanta, with C. J. as "master of the situation." (The characterization of this meeting and his life with Larrie comes from C. J. himself, in a letter of confession and apology he will write to the *Freeman* in 1914.)

Wise to these goings-on, Madame returns to Indianapolis to consult with Ransom. One unverified story takes her first to Atlanta to peek through the keyhole of the lovers' hotel door, a loaded pistol in her purse. That she doesn't shoot either her husband or his mistress is, to me, the only believable element of this often-repeated tale. At any rate, the betrayed wife returns home and, after reportedly being arrested in Jackson for selling without a license, C. J. quickly follows, his trip cut short, according to the *Freeman,* by pressing matters which demand his attention at home. After meeting with Ransom, he exits 640 North West Street and, as far as we know, does not return.

In April, W. E. B. DuBois lectures in Indianapolis, but his talk is not well attended and neither newspaper can find much positive to say about a black intellectual who's backing the Democratic presidential candidate. In response, Knox's *Freeman* also sniffs that Harvard and Heidelberg don't necessarily prepare a man for leadership and runs a letter to the editor chiding DuBois for treating Dr. Washington shoddily.

The presidential campaign gathers momentum, with Roosevelt clubs popular among blacks in Indianapolis. But the West is far more concerned with strikes and portents of class war, and some regard the workers' movement as a grave threat to civilization. Jack Johnson's skin color saves his life when, in Liverpool, he's not allowed to board the *Titanic.* But fame and hatred create a toxic mix, and within days his wife, a white woman, commits suicide.

In April Madame gets the acknowledgment she's been longing for, not in a local paper but in the *Cleveland Gazette,* in a column called "Afro-American Cullings." Among the women celebrated as the "clod of earth out of which the rose rises" and the great civilizers of the race, the column lists Nannie Burroughs, Ida B. Wells-Barnett, Mary Church Terrell and "Mme. C. J. Walker, philanthropist." To be included within the ranks of such choice company—including her nemesis, Burroughs—is a great triumph for a former washerwoman, especially since she's not dubbed hair straightener or even beauty culturist, but *philanthropist.*

Later that month, she officially opens her school of head-to-toe beautification, including manicure, massage, hairdressing and the Walker method of growing hair. Hair-growing classes are restricted to eight students and require a supplemental fee. Her triptych returns to the *Recorder* the next month, and Annie Pope-Turnbo simultaneously runs an ad announcing the opening of Poro College, with nine accompanying photographs. Turnbo is referred to as a specialist in scalp treatment and the growing of luxuriant, beautiful hair, and her college is said to offer the most modern electrical equipment and scientific instruction available. And so—with Turnbo advertising in *Madame's* city, in *her* local newspaper, asking potential hairdressers and agents to leave Indianapolis and come to St. Louis—the rivalry between the two women continues. As both companies prosper, it seems, their owners only wish for more.

B y the summer of 1912 Madame's hit the road again, and she spends a number of weeks in the Carolinas, offering discounts to entice people to learn the trade. And as she prepares for another summer of national conferences, she advises *Recorder* readers of her new seriousness of purpose. Now that C. J.'s gone and she's achieved some financial and worldly success, she has the time and energy to focus on political issues and to develop a closer attachment to what she describes as the "moral and social questions affecting her race." Yet her background still nags at her, and she constantly seeks out the advice of educated women.

On this trip she's traveling with Mary Lynch, described as a "scholar and president of the Colored Women's Christian Temperance Union of South Carolina." During these weeks, Madame has time to grill her companion closely, to absorb her thinking and understand her language and theories. It's not that she underrates her own intelligence, only that she needs to know how to express herself fully and to good impression. And being in the company of someone more polished and sure can only help.

From the Carolinas, the two women travel to Hampton, Virginia, for the biennial NACW convention, which Madame has been looking forward to since Louisville. In Hampton, the current NACW president—Elizabeth Carter of New Bedford, Massachusetts—allows her a formal introduction to the four-hundred-strong audience. She speaks briefly, and agrees to lead a fund-raising campaign to benefit Mary McLeod Bethune's Daytona Normal and Industrial Institute for Negro Girls. Over the course of the week-long meeting, the women adopt resolutions which, among other things, denounce the "uncomfortable and inferior" accommodations of Jim Crow cars and deplore lynching. They also declare in favor of full woman suffrage and voice their opposition to the execution of minors by sending a petition to the governor of Virginia, requesting leniency for seventeen-year-old Virginia Christian, a black washerwoman from Richmond who'd been sentenced to die for murdering her white employer. A committee headed by Mary Church Terrell delivers the petition to the governor, who declines to relent, and Christian is electrocuted that afternoon. That night, Madame announces that she will pay all expenses for this trip.

Hallie Q. Brown and Margaret Murray Washington also attend the Hampton meeting, and later even the Wizard shows up. After a leisurely boat ride to Newport News, the delegates go ashore at the Navy Yard and listen to the Hampton brass band and a speech by Dr. Washington. There's no way of knowing if he and Madame exchange pleasantries, but he certainly would've heard from his wife about her introduction and the gifts she's bestowed.

Early in August, Madame returns home for three and a half weeks to confer with Ransom and Alice Kelly, and then, in her chauffeur-driven open touring car, she journeys to Chicago, where she will take her place beside George Knox in the main sanctuary of the Institutional Church on Dearborn Avenue, for the Thirteenth Annual National Negro Business League convention.

Standing Up to the Wizard

Some two thousand NNBL delegates and visitors attend the opening session on Wednesday, August 21, among them Knox and Madame, when Booker T. Washington reiterates his faith in capitalism and economic growth. An unflagging supporter, Knox fully expects to introduce Madame to the conference, but after Washington's speech he and Madame wait out the better part of two days, during which two other hair-care people—Anthony Overton and a female druggist from Washington, D.C.—are officially recognized by their host. After Overton—whose business Washington tags the "largest Colored manufacturing enterprise" in the U.S.—apprises the convention of his current campaigns and successes, Knox seizes an opportunity to rise and ask "this convention for a few minutes of its time to hear a remarkable woman. . . . She is the woman who gave $1,000 to the Young Men's Christian Association of Indianapolis. Madame Walker, the lady I refer to, is the manufacturer of hair goods and preparations."

But Washington dismisses Knox's request, reminding him that the topic at hand is not hair or philanthropy but life memberships, leaving the devoted Hoosier no choice except to sit back down. The Wizard then calls on an Oklahoma man who says nothing about life memberships but instead continues the Overton discussion. Doubtless, Knox is stunned and Madame steaming—at once humiliated and furious—and on Friday, as the conference draws to an end, when Washington again moves past her name to introduce a Birmingham banker, she rises and brazenly interrupts the proceedings.

"Surely," she begins, "you are not going to shut the door in my face. I feel that I am in a business that is a credit to the womanhood of our race. I am a woman who started in business seven years ago with only

$1.50. I went into a business that is despised, that is criticized and talked about by everybody—the business of growing hair. They did not believe such a thing could be done, but I have proven beyond the question of a doubt that I do grow hair!"

Imagine the response: the craning of necks, the turning of heads, the frowns, foot shuffles and clucks of confusion and then disapproval at this disrespect for the Chief—and from a woman, no less. Poor Knox, the polished diplomat, must've sunk through his seat. As for Dr. Washington, he coolly waits her out. Worse than this has failed to ruffle him. Once, during a meeting held to promote racial harmony in the South, a white speaker lost his head and began to berate Negroes in the most derogatory and insulting language. Sitting on the dais awaiting his turn to speak, the Wizard kept smiling during all of this, and when it was over, got up and made his talk as if no unkind word had been spoken. It will take more than a speech by a woman whose business is ironing hair to perturb the Wizard.

A few people snicker when she mentions hair, but when Madame moves on to talk about money, their mood shifts. "The first year I was in business," she begins, "I took in $1,366; the second year I took in $3,652 . . ." and she proceeds, increasing her profits from $6,672 the third year to a staggering $18,000 thus far in 1912. "This makes," she adds up the figures, "a grand total of $63,049 all told, made in my hair business in Indianapolis."

The NNBL report of the proceedings records "prolonged applause" following that statement. But she is far from finished. "I have been trying to get before you business people," she explains, "and tell you what I am doing. I am a woman that came from the cotton fields of the South; I was promoted from there to the wash-tub; then I was promoted to the cook kitchen, and from there I promoted myself into the business of manufacturing hair goods and preparations." Urged to concentrate on uplift and possibilities, the NNBL speakers rarely linger over the difficult past, but Madame fearlessly ignores this trend. "I am not ashamed of my past," she declares. "I am not ashamed of my humble beginning. Don't think because you have to go down in the wash-tub that you are any less a lady! Everybody told me I was making a mistake going into this business, but I know how to grow hair as well as I know how to grow cotton."

And when she says she owns property valued at $10,000, has built a factory on her own ground, employs seven black people and owns automobiles, the membership once again breaks into enthusiastic applause. Washington, of course, simply bides his time and says nothing.

"Please don't applaud," Madam Walker tells her audience, "just let me talk." And to correct the impression that she may be interested only in making money, she assures the membership that her objectives include not simply buying things, but to "use a part of what I make in trying to help others." And she vows that with the help of God and the cooperation of her people, she will build an industrial school in Africa, a second Tuskegee Institute. Since this previously unmentioned notion poaches on his turf, Washington must be seething by now, but before he can take charge of the meeting once again, George Knox stands and confirms Madame's assertions about her accomplishments in Indianapolis and protests that she has left out many more, including her $1,000 gift to the YMCA. And when *he* finally sits back down, the Wizard still makes no comment but calmly returns to his original schedule, moving to the next speaker, Mr. Hadnott, a cashier from Birmingham.

It's not that hairdressers are unwelcome at the NNBL convention. One from Springfield got her chance at the second meeting, in '01, but she didn't talk about divine gifts or solving people's problems; at the Wizard's insistence, she told how to build stock and save money. This is Overton's second appearance in a row, but he's a major businessman who makes a number of products and is a benefactor of Tuskegee—not to mention the obvious fact that Business League members are more comfortable hearing from a man.

And there's Mrs. Julia H. P. Coleman from D.C., who also spoke this year. But she didn't go on about her struggles. And even though her talk is called "Manufacturing Hair Preparations," Washington ameliorates the situation by pointing out that Mrs. Coleman is a graduate *pharmacist* and the first woman of the race to practice that profession in the U.S. Moreover, she lambastes the "caricatures of before and after," then goes after charlatans who make hair concoctions for "kinky, stubborn hair," just as Washington did in his letter to Fred Moore at the *Age*. Her own product, Hair-Vim, is scientifically prepared and compounded and recognized by the Pure Food and Drug Law, a prescription containing no deleterious substances and duly registered in the U.S. Patent Office.

But Madame's pushiness rankles the Wizard, perhaps because having come from the same background, he knows exactly how far she's willing to go to get what she wants.

On Saturday night, the NNBL festivities conclude with a reception and promenade at the Seventh Regiment Armory. Booker T. Washington leads the grand march in high style, a Chicago society dowager on his arm; Margaret Murray Washington is only steps behind him, her hand resting lightly on the arm of the dowager's husband. The armory is alive in color, the fashions brilliant, the music spirited, the optimism high.

Three weeks later, the *Freeman* attributes Madame's success in Chicago to her striking personality and her emphasis on concrete achievements. No mention is made of the circumstances surrounding her address, which the paper says was a big hit. Washington's talk is described as the speech of his career, which establishes him anew as the veritable Moses of his race.

K nox comes out for Taft in the *Freeman*. And the black man who knocked out Jim Jeffries to retain the heavyweight championship can't seem to stay out of the papers. First he has his own brother, Charley, arrested for grand larceny, forgery and assorted other crimes. Then, in choosing a burial plot for his wife, Johnson again makes headlines when he picks a spot near the J. P. Morgans' and has the grave lined with cement, a startling new idea. When he buries her in September, some twenty thousand gawkers show up and press against one another in the muggy afternoon for a better view of the casket, Jack's tortured features, some little piece of the famous boxer.

America's Foremost Colored Woman Takes Charge

Freeman Ransom—a teetotaler and a devout Christian—doubtless believes that marriage is a sacred institution and that a union blessed by God must not be torn asunder. Yet on September 5, 1912, this upstanding lawyer makes his way to the Marion County Superior Court and files a civil suit in the name of Sarah Walker, plaintiff, who is suing her husband, Charles J. Walker, for divorce. Fastidiously dressed in his customary black three-piece suit, Ransom bears as evidence incriminating letters to C. J. from Dora Larrie and the woman named Louise. There is no marriage certificate, but Ransom wants to cover all bases, in case C. J. claims a common-law marriage. After examining the evidence, the judge orders that a summons be sent to the defendant, granting him ten days in which either to appear or to yield all rights to protest or participate. After signing the pertinent papers, F. B. Ransom goes back to his office at the Walker Company.

In his heart, he's bound to be against it. But business is business, and the church gives some leeway in the case of adultery; in this regard Walker has overstepped many times over. Ransom may be the strictest of Christians, but his job as a lawyer is not to make judgments but to follow his clients' instructions and see to their legal and personal needs. Moreover, by now he's become devoted to Madame, and as newly appointed manager of the company, he feels certain that it cannot stand to risk the potential liability posed by Charles Walker, financially and otherwise.

On September 16, the plaintiff arrives in court, accompanied by her attorney. When called, she steps before the bench and answers the judge's questions, after which he orders that the missing husband be called three times, loudly, as the law requires. The name "Charles J. Walker" is vigorously intoned by the bailiff, and when said defendant doesn't respond, he is judged therein wholly in default. Thus does C. J. Walker forfeit all rights and any claim to the company which officially and by the laws of incorporation bears his name.

The prosecuting attorney for the state of Indiana summarily finds no reason to take the case to trial, and the judge rules that Sarah Walker is entitled to be divorced and that no money shall change hands and that Charles Walker shall pay court costs and taxes. The divorce is declared final on October 5, and Madam Walker's third marriage comes to an end.

Life is contrary. A husband, a wife or a marriage is never as easy to shuck as we might hope or think, no matter how acrimonious or businesslike the parting. Hope dies hard while regret and anger linger. Madame's been spending her nights alone for some time now and C. J. has ground whatever feelings she had left for him into pulp. During the past year, she started giving him a generous weekly allowance, and still the unpaid bills rolled in, people on the road knowing full well where to send them and to whom.

Not that Madame's ungrateful; in the early years, her third husband encouraged and taught her. She has said many times, in the beginning his energy and drive were infectious and gave her a push. But she's moved far beyond the boundaries she and C. J. thought impossibly distant, while he's stayed in the same tired spot. To put it simply, Sarah Walker has no further need of C. J. Walker, or for that matter, any other husband. Her life is with her business, her family and her race. In order to keep what she's created within her family—and build not just a business but a *dynasty*—she needs her company to be invulnerable to threats from within or without. She can no longer trust C. J. to work with her on that score, and besides, he shouldn't have humiliated her by going off with other women, especially her own trusted agent.

As for C. J., he quickly regroups and—perhaps using a payoff quietly arranged by Ransom—goes into business. On September 14, two days *before* his name is called in the Marion County Courthouse, he runs a big ad in the *Freeman* for C. J. Walker's Wonderful Hair Preparations. At first glance the notice appears to be

Madame's, since he's carefully copied the signature layout he may even have helped design. At the top, in three ovals, are two little girls dressed in white with big white bows in their hair, two of the shots face-on, the other from the back. "The above are two sisters whose hair did not exceed one inch in length when they began using C. J. Walker's Wonderful Hair Grower. Here are the results of five months using. We can do the same for you. TRY IT." The copy rather directly explains the mail-order policy and then urges prospective agents to sign up, at a certain address on Twelfth Street in Louisville.

Two weeks later, another ad duplicates the original even more closely, with one woman taking the place of the two girls. Though never positively identified, she may be Dora Larrie. The ad runs several times, courtesy of the Walker-Prosser Company, C. J. Walker, manufacturer, 1314 Chestnut, Louisville, Kentucky. This, of course, is the address of Agnes "Peggie" Prosser, his sister, who still works for the original Madam C. J. Walker Company.

Madame makes no public comment, having put Ransom in charge of all business concerning her ex-husband. And the lawyer must figure that with no inventory, no formula, no money and no business sense, C. J. will soon fold his tent and disappear. But for obvious reasons this doesn't happen, since what in the world else will ever provide C. J. with the lifestyle he once enjoyed as Mr. Madame? And less than two years from now, in March 1914, he will fill in some blank spots when he writes the *Freeman,* asking for "space in your valuable paper, to warn men against the use of strong drink and women."

While somewhat weepy and certainly self-serving, in the end the letter is quite touching. He begins by lavishing hyperbolic praise on his ex-wife, calling her the "best, purest and noblest woman Christ ever died for," in contrast to Dora Larrie, the "designing evil woman" who convinced him he was being badly treated because he wasn't allowed to handle the Walker Company money. This, "notwithstanding the fact, I had no responsibility, not even my clothes to buy with $10 a week to spend as I pleased." And so it was that C. J. let Larrie persuade him to leave "the woman I still love better than life."

They met at the Dunbar Hotel in Birmingham where, he writes, they "laid [their] plans." C. J. found a place in Atlanta, Larrie closed the Tuskegee office, and they became business partners. Soon after his divorce, they moved to Louisville. Larrie was still married at that time, and because the couple "did not do so well under the name of the Walker-Larrie Company . . . she planned to get a divorce so that we could marry." Thus would Larrie become the *new* Madam C. J. Walker. But once this happens, instead of making him master of the situation, Dora Larrie Walker has her husband arrested for interfering with "her" business, then ties up "what little mail there was coming in, so [he] could not get a cent," other than ten cents on Sunday for a paper and a shoeshine. Dora Larrie was, C. J. swears, the cause of all his sorrow, and he never wants to see her face again in his life. He thanks his sister in Louisville for taking care of him, because otherwise he'd have been crazy by now instead of merely "broken in health and spirit," if happier than he's been in some time and determined to start anew.

There is no official response from his ex-wife, and when C. J. writes to ask her for money, Ransom sends thirty-five dollars in a letter which chides him for letting drink and a "designing evil woman" ruin his life and suggests that he go somewhere where Madame has few agents— say, Key West or Cuba—and there "keep sober and build up a big business" of his own. But C. J. stays in Louisville and a few months later writes again, asking for one hundred dollars. This time, Peggie Prosser herself warns Madame off by revealing C. J.'s plans for yet another business venture, this time with a woman who C. J.'s sister says is even worse than Dora Larrie. And so once again Madame holds out. But C. J. persists. "My heart is changed," he swears in another letter, which he says he is writing with tears dripping from his eyes. Sometimes he changes tactics. "Say, Mme," he breezily asks a few months later, "how would you like to give me employment as one of your traveling agents?" After all, he reminds her, no one else knows the work better. But no help is forthcoming, and after accusing C. J. of selling the Walker formula to others and teaching it to three or four women, Ransom warns him not to make an "unwarranted" legal action because his former wife would "spend every penny that she ever had in court before she would agree to give you one penny."

Publicly, Madame says little on the subject of any of her marriages, but as late as 1916 she will tell a reporter that this one failed because of business disagreements. And once again, she harks back to their first years together: "When we began to make ten dollars a day, he thought that amount was enough and that I should be satisfied. But I was convinced that my hair preparations would fill a long-felt want, and when he found it impossible to agree, due to his narrowness of vision, I embarked in business for myself."

"Business disagreements" certainly contributed, but they don't begin to tell the whole story.

W ithin a couple of months of her divorce, Madame makes two big changes in her household. She announces the first in the *Recorder:* "Miss Anjetta Breedlove of Denver, Colorado arrived in the city Tuesday [October 8] and will make her future home with her aunt, Madam C. J. Walker." Given the twenty-three-year-old's business skills and Lelia's lack thereof, the implication is that Anjetta will follow in Madame's footsteps and become her successor. Exactly what this move means for Lelia isn't exactly clear, but Madame has a birthday coming up, her forty-fifth, and with a business that's expanding in a number of directions and a doctor who's nagging her about cutting back on her schedule, she probably feels constrained to assess the situation and make whatever changes seem necessary. One possible implication is, Lelia will scout for information and cultural trends and act as her mother's stand-in, while Anjetta does the real work of running the show. That way, Madame can consider delegating some of the workload so that she can concentrate on marketing strategy and personal appearances.

She's been planning to move Lucy Breedlove and her daughters out of Denver anyway, since the African-American market there has peaked, while meantime, according to Lelia, the West Coast is catching fire. If Madame buys Lucy and the girls a house in Los Angeles, they can run the agency and she'll end up with not only a nice investment but a place to stay. San Francisco's Pan-Pacific Exposition is opening in a year or so and she wants to go. And thus it is that Anjetta moves to Indianapolis to work closely with Madame and gain hands-on experience in the business.

And then there's the other, far more complicated household drama. By October—and probably before then—a tiny girl on the verge of her fourteenth birthday is working for Madame as an errand girl. Fairy Mae Bryant is light-skinned, with slightly angular features and large soulful eyes. To emphasize her Cherokee ancestry, she parts her long, lustrous hair in the middle, braiding it in thick plaits that fall in soft columns down her chest. As early as 1910, Madame had advertised for young girl solicitors to work on commission, passing out fliers and delivering merchandise, and Fairy Mae may have been one of the many girls who held this position, but because of her appearance she attracts special attention. One story claims that Lelia noticed her first, perhaps when she was in town for the Knights of Pythias encampment, and thought she'd make a good model for their advertisements. In another story, it's Madame who decides that Fairy Mae's long thick hair would be worth a thousand words on behalf of Wonderful Hair Grower and that her education—through the eighth grade—might enable her someday to take some responsibility in the company. At any rate, the teenager, who lives nearby with her mother and six siblings, is given a job and the chance to improve her life. A nice idea, a simple plan. It's the next step that's perplexing.

It could be that mother and daughter put their heads together to decide how Fairy Mae might best contribute to their lives and, more importantly, the company, or maybe Lelia dreams up the idea or perhaps Madame makes up her mind and informs Lelia what's going to happen. One way or another, they choose to take Fairy Mae Bryant into the family. Desperate for an heir, Madame's ready to give up on Lelia, who at twenty-seven is beyond her healthiest child-bearing years, in addition to which she's not yet divorced from John Robinson. And so, with no marriage prospects on the horizon, time is running out. Possibly Madame's also hoping that this version of "motherhood" will ground her daughter somewhat.

And so they approach Fairy Mae's mother about adoption, an idea that probably made perfect sense to both families at the time. Sarah Etta Hammond Bryant receives the idea, as far as we know, with an open mind. Since the death of her husband, Perry—a factory fireman—she may have had a hard time making ends meet. The Hammonds, her family, are well thought of in the Indianapolis community, having been among the first blacks to settle in the state, and like most parents, Sarah Etta wants the best for her children. So when Lelia and Madame make their offer, she has to consider it seriously.

The Walkers promise to educate Fairy Mae and to make for her a fine, exciting life, filled with travel and the company of the most important figures of the times. There is no way Sarah Etta can provide anything close to this for her daughter, and so while giving up a child cannot be easy, she nonetheless strikes a deal with Madame and Lelia, who, in addition, agree to allow the Bryant family continued contact with Fairy Mae. And so it happens that one family loses a daughter to another one, the Walker Company acquires a model and Lelia Robinson, future Joy Goddess of Harlem, becomes a mother.

Within the context of the bland official version of the Madam C. J. Walker story, this detail—*And then they adopt a fourteen-year-old girl who worked for the company*—comes to seem familiar, not even that surprising. But given any reflection at all, while intellectually sound, considering other grounds, the decision seems fairly shocking. And while black communities define "family" and the roles within it generously, beyond blood and fact, this shy adolescent has her own large, doting family, and furthermore, she knows the women seeking to replace it only as employers, celebrities, rich people. She's bound to be intimidated, and has to have noted that her adoptive mother doesn't actually live in Indianapolis or even come there much. Will she actually see her own family that often? Will she really go to school, and if so, where? Who will be her mother *really*?

But it's easy to imagine the young girl's excitement. After all, she's been told she can basically have it all—the life of a princess along with normal access to her own family—and may well have considered herself the luckiest girl in the world. And perhaps her mother made the decision for her, and Fairy Mae had no choice but to go along.

Whatever the feelings or reasons regarding this decision, in October, with Sarah Etta's consent, a Pittsburgh judge signs off on Lelia's petition to adopt, and with the understanding that the girl's welfare will be promoted by the adoption, Fairy Mae Bryant becomes Mae Walker Robinson, Lelia McWilliams Robinson's legal daughter and heir. The name change adds yet another layer of complication to the situation, since the girl is assigned the surnames of two men who will play no part in her life—or the lives of her adoptive mother or grandmother, for that matter.

What then? Lelia goes back to Pittsburgh and New York, to confer with John Nail and others about Harlem real estate. Madame gives an elegant breakfast party for Madame Anita Patti Brown, a respected coloratura who performed at Dr. Washington's convention in Chicago, then adds another car to her growing collection. In November, Mae Robinson celebrates her fourteenth birthday, but it isn't mentioned the following month, when the *Freeman* interviews Madame at length about her life from Delta onward. Then the "grandmother" blows out of town as well, to celebrate her forty-fifth birthday, Christmas and New Year's with old friends in St. Louis.

Presumably, since it's her first Christmas as a Robinson, Mae stays in Indianapolis for the holidays; certainly she would have lavish presents to open. But with whom? Her natural grandmother lives close by, and Parthenia Rawlins is at 640, certainly, but Ransom has moved out. Once his financial situation improved, he married his college sweetheart and they're living in a house on California Street. Perhaps Anjetta and Alice Kelly are there to keep the girl's new home from seeming too strange and empty. She might have gone to Pittsburgh with Lelia, or maybe she simply goes back home to be with her brothers and sisters, her mother and grandmother.

So many questions have no satisfying answers. Does Mae call Lelia Robinson "Mama"? Does Anjetta miss her little sisters on what may have been her first Christmas away from home? Did anybody think any of this out, or is everybody too busy to even stop and wonder? Important to keep Madame's background in mind: the poverty that stalked her childhood, the oppression she ignored at her peril, the endless hours of adult-sized labor. This kind of life often makes people supremely practical in their attitudes and decisions, and the opportunity she's offering Fairy Mae must seem to her very simply like a dream come true. She would have no way of understanding how anyone else would not agree—even Mae, who of course has not known that kind of hardship.

I
n St. Louis, Madame is entertained splendidly nonstop, with dinner parties, receptions, teas, a breakfast and two whist parties, taking first prize on December 28 and second two nights later. She also takes the opportunity to speak at her old church, St. Paul's AME, and at AME Zion. This is all very gratifying, but sometimes, remembering her grim St. Louis life, she can't help indulging in a display of vengeful triumph. As she tells Freeman Ransom about a different trip to St. Louis: "You should have seen the dictey who did not notice the washerwoman falling on their faces to see her, and everyone wanted to entertain me, but I didn't accept one social call."

D
ivorce, new cars, more real estate. Creating a new generation in one fell swoop. Coincidence can hardly explain this wild rumble. Divorce has to have played a part, and maybe Madame's brooding about age and death, now that she's nearing fifty, and has decided to make a new family of women with whom to nourish her life and maintain her business. Sometimes change brings about a rush of energy that won't tamp down, and Madame seems to be in

that mode. Naturally, the household goes along, because they all know that Madame is impulsive and hotheaded and does *not* like being alone, and that Lelia's *not* moving to Indianapolis. Nobody expects life with Madame to be ordered and calm. Besides, in the end she's the boss and everybody knows it.

That same fall, Madame's other attorney, Robert Brokenburr, becomes the first black state congressman in Indiana on the Progressive ticket. Teddy Roosevelt takes enough of the Republican vote to swing the election to Woodrow Wilson, the first Southerner to win the White House since Zachary Taylor in 1849. And Congressman Seaborn Roddenberry from Georgia, calling Jack Johnson's mixed marriage more revolting than slavery, introduces a constitutional amendment to bar such unions in the future. A black postal worker who writes letters critical of Booker T. Washington soon finds himself unemployed. The newly founded National Urban League advises African-Americans migrating north to imitate the behavior of that exemplary citizen the Pullman porter, whose soul is "as white as snow." Another sixty-one blacks are reported lynched in 1912.

It is during Madame's holiday absence that the *Freeman*'s headline describes her as AMERICA'S FOREMOST COLORED WOMAN. This time, the caption next to the accompanying photograph of her house makes no reference to *Mr.* Walker, and among the other photographs featured is one that will become widely reproduced, of Madame at the wheel of her new open touring car, reared slightly back in her seat, wearing a dark suit with a large white collar and a very broad, plumed cavalier's hat. Alice Kelly and the new bookkeeper, Lucy Flint, are in the backseat, and sitting beside Madame up front is smug, pouty Anjetta, her eyes lit with high expectation. Indeed, parked there on North West Street, they all four look as if they're sitting just about on top of the world, and in some ways they almost are.

The Negro Woman in Business

Madame arrives home from St. Louis a few days after New Year's and by the next month she's launched an entirely new campaign, the first notice of which runs on the front page of the *Recorder*. Entitled "Woman of Rare Business Tact," this clearly self-authored article refashions the Madam C. J. Walker story yet again and offers a revised set of reasons for her success. There are no divine interventions or voices in the night; instead, the new Madame is said to have accomplished great things gradually and purposefully, through education, persistence and making every opportunity count.

Her early life comes in for the usual treatment, but this time in far plainer language: "At an early age she was thrown on her own resources, and with a heart full of inspiration to accomplish something in life, she sought the schoolhouse, books, Sunday school . . . everything that had . . . an elevating influence." Nothing about being orphaned at seven or the cruel brother-in-law, no early marriage (there is no mention of a husband at all), no daughter to raise. Instead, the emphasis is on a young woman's determination to become not famous or even accomplished, but educated: "With a desire for education, she found her way to St. Louis" and there "secured employment doing cooking, washing and ironing and going to night school" (note the switch from the more emotional "endured many hardships and much toil"). And from her example she would like people to know that "a mind, once made up, can accomplish wonderful things." No longer does Madame claim to have made her advancement by fiat or miraculous revelation but "step by step . . . in education, influence and wealth, taking her place among other women of the race who are doing something and who stand for unity and co-operation and for mutual uplift."

Someone very grounded is advising her in the writing of this article, and my choice is the schoolteacher and grammarian Alice Kelly. With C.J. out of the picture, the two women and Ransom are in charge, and together, they have decided to move on from magic and drama to the everyday virtues of patience, tenacity and learning. They describe the beginning of her career: "Having secured a fair education, the next thing was to recognize the fact that there was a place for her in the world and something for her to do. To find it was the next thing." At this point, the dream might have made its appearance, but except in pamphlets and sales manuals that print original material unedited, the dream has vanished. Instead, "Many avenues opened to her, but none seemed to dwell on her mind more than that of hair culture. Right into Denver she went and there established a business. . . ."

The concluding section describes the Walker Company, then proudly declares that since she now gives employment to over a thousand people of her race in various parts of the country, others should consider her life story an example to follow. And she hews to the Tuskegee line when she advises young women that "instead of sitting around and complaining they should get up and do something," but first, "Madam Walker advocates preparation. . . . Be sure you are able to deliver the goods . . . then launch out." This borrows from mailorder magnate Richard Sears, who advised prospective entrepreneurs to "have the goods and then deliver."

She also compliments herself on her push and industry, her honesty and reliability, then lists some concrete assets and achievements: her runabout and bigger new car, her thousand-dollar contribution to the Y, the employment of Lucy Flint and Alice P. Kelly, her contributions to missionary causes in Africa. Comfort, she insists, has not caused her to lose sight of "her people, her struggling race." She is into, she assures her readers, "everything that tends to advance their elevation in life."

This revisionist declaration is targeted as much toward the NNBL, the NACW and other clubs as to potential customers. Madame means to break through their wall of exclusivity this year, to gain, first, inclusion in their membership and, then, endorsement of her business. Clubwomen, she's decided, don't want to hear about divine gifts and sudden success, and they don't want to be told the same old washerwomen stories. They have to believe that *their* path into the inner circle—through hard work and education—is the *right* one, and if Madame wants in, she has to have walked the same steps. And so evangelism takes a backseat. And from now on, her ads will de-emphasize hair growth and money-back guarantees to focus on women's financial independence: "Learn to Grow Hair and Make Money," one of them urges; attend the fledgling Lelia College, another one exhorts, and earn a passport to prosperity. During the coming spring and summer she will make a speech called "The Negro Woman in Business," in which she encourages women to follow the precepts of Booker T. Washington and by the practical application of thrift, industry and mental training acquire a footing in the soil of financial independence by entering the business world. No longer calling herself a hair culturist, she refers to herself as a woman making her mark in the world of "commercial pursuits and high finance," the same as Mrs. Maggie L. Walker of Richmond, Virginia, the first woman in the United States to become president of a local bank.

The day before Woodrow Wilson's inauguration there is a big parade in support of woman suffrage on Pennsylvania Avenue. In his address the next day, the former university president says that the masters of the government of the U.S. are capitalists and manufacturers. Most black people are skeptical about Wilson's "President of All the People" remark, and indeed, he's backed off the statement somewhat by saying he didn't mean what people are thinking. The Wizard gives a newspaper interview in which he claims to have great faith in the new president's sense of fairness, but within two months, at the request of the postmaster general, Wilson gives government departments the right to racially segregate workers in Washington. And by the end of the year there will be separate working areas, bathrooms and lunchrooms in many office buildings, and then Wilson appoints white male ambassadors to Haiti and Liberia for the first time since Reconstruction.

When the NAACP and other African-American organizations protest, Wilson demurs. There is no discrimination along racial lines in Washington, he purrs, but a regrettable social line of "cleavage which unfortunately corresponds with the racial line."

Madame spends the spring of 1913 in the South, training agents and giving demonstrations in Florida, Georgia and Alabama. To keep her informed, Ransom sends regular reports, all upbeat. "Your business is increasing here everyday," he writes in May. And when her receipts exceed $3,000 for three months in a row, he calls her the "money-making wonder of the age," then—always the conservative—cautions her that, having taken in more than $11,000 in the first four months of the year—almost as much as her entire income during the previous year—she should now keep a little mum on the subject, since ratification of the Sixteenth Amendment, imposing a federal tax on all personal earnings greater than $3,000, seems a certainty.

Ransom also writes occasionally to Lelia, who has already left Pittsburgh for New York. "Madam is in a fair way to be the wealthiest colored person in America," he informs her that spring. "I am ambitious that she be just that." And then he asks for Lelia's cooperation—"You will help me, won't you?"—slyly suggesting that she curtail her own expenses. But 1913 will be a year of extraordinary spending by the Walker women, and when Ransom writes again to ask Lelia to join him in urging Madame to bank a sizable portion of her money so that it will accumulate and draw interest "for possible rainy days," his request is ignored, and not just by Lelia.

To make the impression she's looking for at the summer conventions, Madame has decided she needs yet another new car, the splashiest model she can come by, driven by a liveried chauffeur. She already has the touring car and the runabout, but now she wants something fancier, and she decides to buy local. The Cole Motor Company, located only blocks from her factory, assembles cars with a snob appeal. Its owner, native Indianian J. J. Cole, goes in for big advertising campaigns, often targeting women customers with such slogans as "A Man's Car Any Woman Can Drive and Drive It She Does," and "The Choice of American Womanhood." One widely reproduced ad features a pretty young woman at the wheel of a touring car, off for a drive in the country with her three girlfriends, two of whom sit in the backseat—called the tonneau—curled around a lone young man looking quite happy to be thus surrounded and without driving responsibilities.

Then, on May 10, 1913, while she's still in the South, Cole comes up with exactly what Madame's looking for. In a full-page ad in the *Saturday Evening Post,* he announces the advent of his new Series Nine models, among which is a limited-edition, six-cylinder, sixty-horsepower, seven-seater open touring car with—among many special features—an adjustable ventilating windshield, a mahogany dash with an eight-day clock, and eleven-inch-deep black leather upholstery. Priced at $2,600, next to the limousine the seven-seater is the biggest, most powerful car Cole sells, and less than two weeks after the ad runs, Madame has one. And just after her return from the South, on Saturday, May 23, she gathers up four women and takes them for a test drive.

The seven-seater Cole seats two in the front and three in the tonneau, with adjustable, folding seats for two more. Madame at the wheel, the women travel down through Indiana and across the Ohio to spend the weekend in Louisville. Alice Kelly's along for the ride and so is Lucy Flint, Anjetta Breedlove and a Miss Wallace of St. Louis. The five women must have a whale of a time motoring powerfully down the highway in their hats and good traveling clothes, snubbing the gawkers, stopping for a box lunch, taking Sunday drives in Louisville. Madame makes no bones about her reasons for buying the car. The *Recorder* quotes her intentions to put it to much use this year and the next, going from one convention to another with a carful of ladies. Even Ransom can't help being impressed. "Oh," he writes Lelia, "it's the latest thing in autos." And he reminds her of her good fortune: "So you see, you are quite an heiress."

Business rolls on, and midsummer, Madame scores a huge victory when Booker T. Washington accepts her invitation to stay in her home during the formal dedication of the new YMCA building, from July 6 to 8. While there's no way to know exactly why the Wizard finally gave in to her persistent entreaties, in the end the transaction seems to have happened simply. On her own, Madame wrote and issued the invitation. Perhaps finally convinced that her success and increasingly high stature might prove useful to him, the physically ailing Wizard says yes.

Scheduled to make the keynote address on Tuesday the eighth, Washington doesn't arrive until 1:45 a.m. that same day, but, anxious that he be shown "every courtesy," Madame has promised to make the Cole and her chauffeur available during his stay. And so when he arrives at Union Station at that early hour, her chauffeur is there to greet and drive him.

Upon arrival, Washington repairs to Madame's home for a rest, but after only a few hours' sleep he rises to find an "army of newspaper people" from both white and black papers lined up for interviews.

After speaking to the press, he cheerfully takes a ride in the Cole—Madame at the wheel—then returns to give another interview, this time to Will Lewis of the *Freeman,* who finds the Wizard relaxing in "the best of those splendid rooms of the Madame's mansion." When Lewis asks for a special story, Washington shies away from politics. Wilson's election, he explains, is over, and besides, he protests, "I am not in politics. I leave that for the adepts."

Close to eight—the scheduled time for Washington's appearance at the Y—another newspaperman abruptly ends the *Freeman* interview, saying Washington has no more time. And either Madame or her chauffeur drives him downtown to give his speech. The ceremonies actually began two nights earlier with a Sunday open house, followed by Citizens' Night on Monday, George Knox presiding. On those evenings the crowds were respectable, but on Tuesday night, more than a thousand people show up to hear Washington's address. The audience crowds into the new gymnasium, and when a storm blows up, the additional five hundred waiting outside are forced to return home. Introduced by former vice president Charles Fairbanks, Washington doesn't take the stage until after ten, but in his speech he finally gives Madame a little of what she's been after, praising "Mrs. C. J. Walker, of Indianapolis, who was the first colored woman to give $1,000 to the YMCA work." Noting the recent migration of black people from the South into cities such as Indianapolis, the Wizard encourages local residents to persuade what he calls the "floaters" to go back home and "plant themselves in the country and on the soil" where they belong.

Thomas Taylor then reads a telegram from Julius Rosenwald, reminding the "colored people" of Indianapolis of their responsibilities toward one another and assuring them of his belief in the justness of their cause. It's almost midnight by the time the Good Citizens League serves an elaborate meal at the Y Café in the Wizard's honor. Of the one hundred people who attend, certainly Madame is one, especially since Ransom and Brokenburr are officers of the league. And perhaps at some point the table talk turns to Jack Johnson, who has been convicted by the U.S. government of violating the Mann Act, transporting a woman across state lines for "immoral purposes"—namely, commercial sex. The government has had to work hard to concoct this charge, since the first time they tried, the "abducted" woman—white, of course—married Johnson in response. And so they found another woman, whom the boxer transported from Pittsburgh to Chicago in 1910. After receiving a prison sentence of a year and a day, Johnson has packed up and fled to Paris. This is a big topic in the black community, and if the subject arises, the Wizard may well remain quiet, having already commented publicly on the situation that "a man with muscle minus brains is a useless creature." Unfazed, the defiant Johnson responded in kind, saying that at least he "never got beat up because [he] looked in the wrong keyhole."

That night, Booker T. Washington again sleeps at 640 North West Street. And the next day, Madame dresses up in her fine dark dress with the three-quarter sleeves and fixes the spray of white flowers across the soft V-neck of her bodice, preparing to have her picture made with the Wizard and six other men on the steps of the new downtown Y. She arranges a rolled-brim hat with billowing plumes at a slight angle across her forehead, chooses a ladylike white fan (which she may well need, dressed in such dark attire on a hot summer day) and sets off. She, Ransom—in light suit and straw boater—and Washington are driven by her chauffeur, Homer West, to the corner of Senate and Michigan, where they meet up with George Knox, Dr. Joseph H. Ward, Thomas Taylor and two other businessmen on the steps of the Y. The men must be sweltering, dressed this way in humid July, but in the photograph taken that day, no discomfort is in evidence. Knox and Taylor stand on the bottom step, Knox in a light-colored overcoat that seems tight across the middle. Madame's on the next step, the top of her hat about even with Knox's. And Washington's up yet another level, in cutaway, vest, bow tie and boutonniere, standing dead center, the only man holding his hat instead of wearing it. Ransom's behind Madame, looking intense, along with Ward and two unidentified businessmen. The seven men stand square to the camera, but this time Madame has turned herself at a more flattering three-quarters angle, while still managing to confront the camera lens dead-on, like the men. In this picture, she appears a little drawn, if supremely self-possessed.

As for the Wizard, he looks terrible. He's thin and slightly slump-shouldered. His hair's gone gray and his eyes have the caved, dark look of a man in nagging pain; nonetheless, within a month he'll be in St. Louis speaking at the opening of the Booker T. Washington Theater.

After the visit, Washington leaves a book he's written as a gift for

Madame and writes to thank her for the courtesies she showed him in her home.

Omitted from all speeches and press coverage during the ceremonies that week is the disappointing news that less than half of the $20,000 pledged by Indianapolis's black community has so far been submitted.

So That Other Women of My Race May Take Hold of Similar Work and Make It Good

A week after Washington's visit, Mrs. William James of Columbus, Ohio, writes, "Dear Madam, I take great pleasure to inform you what your wonderful Hair Grower has done for me." And she describes the dry, damaged condition of her scalp prior to 1910, when she had her first Walker treatment. At that time, writes Mrs. James, her hair was only one and a half inches long, but in the three and a half years since, her scalp has become healthy and her hair grown more than eight inches. Having also worked as a Walker agent for three years, she declares Madame's "discovery . . . a Godsend to unfortunate women who are walking in the rank and file that I had walked." Before hiring on with the Walker Company, Mrs. James made a "working woman's wages," but now she has purchased a home and can meet her financial obligations. She averages $23 a week, made $944 in the past ten months—as compared to $793.65 for her entire first year and $882 for the second. Mrs. James includes a partial rundown of her week's wages during the past three years, and closes by sending blessings of the Lord upon Madam Walker and her company and adding, "My husband joins me in love to you all."

This is the kind of letter agents regularly write Madam Walker, and in 1988 Freeman Ransom's daughter, A'Lelia Nelson, will attest to the love and gratitude agents felt for her, and not just because of healthier, more manageable hair. Once becoming franchised agents—running their own shops, filing their own reports, ordering products when the supply ran low—women who had previously felt doomed to "walk the rank and file" their entire lives found themselves in a position to enjoy more productive, interesting lives than they'd ever thought possible, to give their children new opportunities and to be independent—from men and from white people. Women who had made as little as a few dollars a week working as domestic help reported making as much as ten times that *in one day*.

What Madam Walker did seems simple now only because it worked: using herself as an example, understanding that appearance in fact *did* matter, she defined women's needs and then, using her own experience as a model, offered concrete options for change, which worked for many women and profited her handsomely—a business-woman's dream.

In early August, she runs a page 1 article in the *Recorder* called "Progress Among Women," which focuses on the successful entrance of women into specific enterprises of "the larger sort," which only a few years earlier were conducted exclusively by men. These include work in education, domestic science, medicine and business, and women's achievements in those fields will be celebrated at many of the upcoming expositions marking the fiftieth anniversary of emancipation.

When it summarizes her past, the article relies on boilerplate Walker language ("She was thrown upon her own resources early in life, worked on the farm in her native state, Louisiana, attended the country school, did washing and ironing . . . and . . . by thrift and economy saved enough of her hard earnings to start a business concern of her own") and may well be a forerunner of a speech she'll present regularly this summer and fall, called "The Negro Woman in Business."

The article ends with the announcement that "Mme. C. J. Walker has recently purchased the four-story brownstone house at 108 West One Hundred Thirty-Sixth Street, New York . . . [a] magnificent dwelling," the first floor of which will be given over to Lelia College, "devoted to the training of young women in hair culture and . . . in charge of Mme. Robinson, an accomplished young woman of pleasing address." It is the last sentence, however, that contains the real surprise: "Mme. Walker will in the future divide her time between her business in Indianapolis and New York."

The fact is, within a year or so Madame will have purchased two adjacent town houses, one block north of the luxury apartment buildings owned by St. Philip's Episcopal Church and two doors west of

Lenox Avenue, the main street of Harlem. The four-story brown-stones are large, graceful Adams-style buildings, pale gray stone with long arched windows on the second floor and French doors for ground-level entry. To aesthetically join the houses, Lelia will eventually install leaded-glass windows between the French doors and add a newly minted "Walker Crest" in the center of the third-floor exterior wall. The first two floors of 108 will comprise Lelia College and the beauty parlor, which the *Chicago Defender* will describe as "the most completely equipped and beautiful hair parlor that members of our Race have ever had access to." The top floors will hold Lelia's lavish living and entertaining quarters and Madame's bedroom. After her mother's death, Lelia will move out of the town house, and during the Harlem Renaissance the third floor will become a meeting place for poets and artists, called the Dark Tower.

Mortgage payments for the first purchased town house—108—begin, significantly enough, on June 6, 1913, Lelia's twenty-eighth birthday. Like Lucy Breedlove's house in L.A., the houses are purchased in Madame's name, and it's she who will foot the bills for the many renovations and furnishings Lelia will order. And since Madame deals only in cash, contractors and workers often find themselves waiting for Ransom to track her down to get permission from her to write a check. This frequently puts Ransom in a tight spot, especially when Lelia's purchases make for bills that quickly exceed the original $7,000 budget Madame has approved. Terrified of her mother's wrath, Lelia then exacerbates Ransom's difficulties by asking him to act as her mediator. In one letter she implores him to do her a friendly turn. "Am dodging behind you," she admits, "to keep the bullets from hitting me." And she encloses a contractor's bill for $15,000, along with the suggestion that instead of an outright gift, he consider the money a "loan from Mother in a businesslike way," which she will repay with the same interest a bank would charge, even doubled. "I'll pay it, my word of honor as a woman, Mr. Ransom," she swears, without any indication of how she intends to fulfill that promise. Acknowledging the imposition, she nonetheless begs Ransom not to let her mother "get sore at me and ball me out, for I certainly am one nervous child."

These are difficult matters for a mother and daughter to sort out, particularly when they are as inextricably entangled as wire mesh, yet as different as fire and ice. And so they struggle and often cause one another deep pain. With so much on Madame's mind, it's not hard to imagine her response to Lelia's profligacy when Ransom passes the information on; the only question is to *whom* she voices her outrage— Ransom? Alice Kelly? Anjetta? In response, though disapproving of Lelia's extravagance, Ransom still does what he can to ameliorate the tension between the women, praising Lelia's letterhead stationery ("perfectly beautiful") to her mother and predicting an even "more powerful business firm" for the mother-and-daughter team in the future.

But Madame can find it in her heart to do nothing except fulfill her daughter's every wish. Under ordinary circumstances, she's a very tough negotiator, but when Lelia asks she cannot say no, partly because she's the one who spoiled her in the first place and also because she so desperately wants her daughter to be successful and *right* and a part of the company. And so while steadily complaining and criticizing, she nonetheless yields to her baby's wishes, and the work continues, exactly as ordered.

Within a couple weeks of the "Progress Among Women" piece, Madame and Alice Kelly pack some suitcases and climb in the Cole, and with Homer West at the wheel, head north to inspect the town house and examine Lelia's plans. After a few days, they will take off again, driving to Philadelphia for the National Negro Business League, then to Atlantic City to see the ocean, and to Baltimore for this year's Knights of Pythias encampment. In D.C., they'll go to the theater and attend whist parties and be lavishly entertained, and Madame will make her "Negro Woman in Business" speech ten times at ten different churches. On the way back to Indianapolis they'll stop in Nashville to attend the National Baptist Convention, which runs September 17–22. This year, in addition to the standard church meeting, there will be an exposition celebrating the progress of the race and the anniversary of the Emancipation Proclamation, which some ten thousand to twenty-five thousand are expected to attend. After Nashville, Madame, West and Miss Kelly will come home.

These are important events, each requiring an extensive wardrobe, and so the women would have packed heavily. They'd wear traveling hats, veils tied loosely across the face for protection, a dark suit, the usual foundation garments, stockings and high-top shoes. The distance between Indianapolis and New York is about nine hundred miles, and while the Cole's about the most powerful car on the road, about thirty-five miles per hour is its top speed. Considering unlighted, unpaved roads and unfriendly driving conditions, about a hundred miles a day is all they can expect to make.

Long driving trips are a new phenomenon, and more than likely nobody else in the Walker Company has been on one, and so wouldn't they all stand on the porch and wave goodbye, and stand there waving until the car was out of sight? Can't we imagine that happening, because this is what people do when watching loved ones leave, especially on a dangerous trip, in a time when the very fact of a cross-country automobile trip seemed a miracle in itself?

Many advance preparations would have been necessary. At this time, hotels don't mix the races and many cities have no Negro hotels, and so accommodations were secured in advance. Madame stays with agents on the road. And she may request that West take the Southern route, stopping the first night in Louisville, where she knows people, before turning northeast toward Cincinnati, Columbus, Wheeling and Pittsburgh, 370 miles away. Pittsburgh to New York is another 400 miles, which would require another overnight stop, perhaps in Harrisburg, where Madame might have at least one agent, who would be thrilled to accommodate Madam Walker's entourage and fix them up with food and water for the road.

A week after leaving Indianapolis they arrive in Harlem and undoubtedly cause quite a stir, especially now that J. J. Cole has run an extraordinary six-page ad in the popular *Saturday Evening Post,* featuring the seven-seater. Entitled "The Story of Cole, the Standardized Car," the ad illustrates stages of progress in transportation, from a covered wagon pulled by a couple of desultory mules to a steam engine puffing cross-country, followed by an ocean liner heading east and, in the star corner, Madame's car.

Tracking Madam Walker's life and marketing strategies, I find the copy for this ad particularly intriguing. Beneath the stages-of-progress illustration, a column called "Yesterday" begins, "Across the plains, into the vague obscurity of nothingness, the prairie schooner and the savage have melted." And "Today"? "Standardization is an empty word to those who have not sensed its meaning," which Cole describes as a kind of benchmark for excellence: the standard by which all other models are measured. And he elaborates: "Standardization took the experiment of Bell and gave us the telephone; perfected Watt's engine and gave us the Transcontinental Limited; took the old galleys of Rome and built the Olympic. It was Standardization that took the first Atlantic cable and bred out of it a spawn of nerves over which the sensations of the continents vibrate . . ." and so on.

And now listen to Madame in her 1918 interview with the *New York Times:* "Perseverance is my motto. It laid the Atlantic cable, it gave us the telegraph, telephone and wireless. It gave to the world an Abraham Lincoln and to the race freedom . . ." and so on.

The lyrics are new but Madame covers the tune in fine style.

S he examines the town house and studies Lelia's bills. If she does in fact bawl her daughter out, neither she nor Lelia says so, and odds are she doesn't. The houses are perfectly located and quite beautiful, and now that she's been there, Madame's become convinced that Lelia was right about moving into Harlem and that once she's finished with the overhaul and redecoration process the Walker Company will have established itself on the leading edge of the high life of trends and taste. So thoroughly impressed is she with Lelia's perspicacity that when her daughter requests that *her* house and offices exclude a factory, with its smells and mess, Madame relents, assigning the unpleasant part of the business to Indianapolis.

New York's the place to be. And Lelia is making important friend-ships with world-class celebrities like Enrico Caruso and the com-poser and conductor James Reese Europe, whose all-black Clef Club orchestra stunned a Carnegie Hall audience with its proficiency and skill, playing classical music with no formal white training. Everything is happening in New York, and since Lelia will live nowhere else, Madame seals her plans to go there as well.

O n Tuesday, August 19, Homer West drives Madame, Miss Kelly and perhaps Lelia the ninety-nine miles south to the NNBL meeting in Philadelphia, where Madame is to be an invited speaker. The convention begins on Wednesday morning. On the first day, the women sit through speeches by delegates on such subjects as "Potato Growing" and "Making Farming Pay." After lunch, the dele-gates are driven to the John Wanamaker department store, where Wanamaker himself greets his guests in the store's famed Egyptian Hall, to show them the plaster mummies, then give them a tour of the store—a move that secures Madame's very healthy clothes-shopping business for Wanamaker's from this moment on.

That night, Booker T. Washington delivers the keynote address, and the *Recorder* says, "The Doctor drove home to the hearts of his great audience his arguments in favor of the necessity of character building, industrial and commercial development within the race and the cultivating of the respect of the best white citizens." In the Carnegie tradition, he also defines present handicaps as incentive to forward motion. Afterwards, a number of delegates speak on topics Washington has assigned, such as "Making Bootblacking Pay."

Thursday, there are more talks, including a tribute to Annie Pope-Turnbo by, of all people, Madame's old friend C. K. Robinson from St. Louis, who praises the owner of Poro as a "progressive business-woman who has built up . . . a large and magnificently appointed establishment devoted exclusively to hair culture." This cannot have pleased Madame, though she says nothing publicly; after all, in this sit-uation she has the upper hand. Somewhere along in here Madame manages to have a word with Emmett Scott about her plan to build an industrial school in Africa similar to Tuskegee. She had mentioned the possibility in her impromptu speech in Chicago, but briefly. Noncom-mittal, the secretary of Tuskegee tells Madame she should write Dr. Washington for information along that line. And the conversation comes to an end.

Thursday evening is Madame's night to speak. She, Lelia and Alice Kelly sit through "Catering," "Negro Occupations in Philadelphia" and other talks, until the very end of the evening, when Washing-ton gives her a gracious introduction: "I now take pleasure in intro-ducing to the convention one of the most progressive and successful businesswomen of our race—Madam C. J. Walker, of Indianapolis, Indiana, who will talk to us on the subject of 'Manufacturing Hair Preparations.' "

And she rises and after a quick nod of acknowledgment in the Wiz-ard's direction, turns to the membership and says she's decided to talk about something else; that instead of dwelling upon the details of her business, she thinks that in the limited time allotted, it would be more interesting and profitable to tell how she has succeeded in the business world, "in order that other women of my race may take hold of similar work and make good."

She begins by citing figures: the $1.50 capital she started out with, the income of the one thousand women she says are now working for her, and her own income, which now amounts to $34,000 annually. She gives the born-in-Delta, orphaned-at-seven talk, the hardships and much toil in St. Louis; says in 1905 she left St. Louis for Denver to engage in the hair-growing business, then stumbles a little in her figures by saying it was in 1908 that she discovered a remedy for growing hair. She then whizzes through her travels, her life in Pittsburgh, the move to Indianapolis with the cordial welcome extended, the $10,000 home, the incorporated business, $10,000 capital stock. . . .

Because its primary focus is on commerce, the NNBL is less interested in refinement than is the NACW, and so Madame now makes a statement she would never have used in the ladies' presence: "I have made it possible for many colored women to abandon the washtub for a more pleasant and profitable occupation."

The membership—overwhelmingly male—applaud heartily.

And then she boldly refers to a promise she made in Chicago the year before, to double her income of $1,500 a month by this year's meeting. (She, in fact, made no such promise, but never mind.) Beginning in September 1912 and running through August 1913, her income comes to a grand total of $32,496.43.

"You can readily see," she proudly pronounces, "that I have been able to make good my promise to you last year."

Prolonged applause gives her extra time to consider how to wind up.

Once again, she demonstrates her willingness to storm purposefully into a thorny patch. "Now I realize," she says, "that in the so-called higher walks of life, many were prone to look down upon 'hair dressers,' as they called us; they didn't have a very high opinion of our calling, so I had to go down and dignify this work, so much so that many of the best women of our race are now engaged in this line of business, and many of them are now in my employ."

She concludes by attributing her success to honesty of purpose, determined effort, the real merit of her preparations and the fact that she is not and has never been "close-fisted" but, as those who know her will attest, is a liberal-hearted woman, who started with $1.50 and now owns a well-established business and pays taxes on $43,000 worth of property, all accumulated within the past eight years.

Prolonged applause, and Madame sits down. Washington tells about the $1,000 to the Y, thanks Madame for her excellent address and all she has done for the race, laughs and says if the men don't watch out the women are going to excel them in a business way. The entire audience then sings "Blest Be the Tie That Binds," and the evening ends with no further comment about people in the "higher walks of life" who once looked down on hairdressers.

Friday night, Madame and Miss Kelly attend a banquet at the Horticultural Hall, and the next morning they join an excursion up the Delaware as far as League Island, where they are shown aboard naval battleships at anchor. And then to Atlantic City for a few days' rest. Knox happens to be in town at the same time, making a speech, and perhaps he visits Madame and they take in the sea air together. He may even ride in the Cole to Baltimore and the Knights of Pythias encampment, where Madame will once again work the crowd, taking people for car rides and letting them know what she's after. At the meeting of the Court of Calanthe, her campaigning pays off when a "sponsor" (possibly Jessie Robinson, her St. Louis confidante and now the Calanthean supreme inspector of Missouri) moves that the convention endorse Madam Walker's products as the best on the market and further proclaim her "the foremost business woman of the race." The motion passes without opposition.

I keep wondering what, or how much, she's after and what might satisfy her. Her objective seems to be to effectively take command of the entire hair-care industry and proclaim it hers. The rampant increase of cosmetics and hair businesses all over the country might have made her nervous. The black newspapers are filled with ads run by itinerant companies. But it's hard to believe she considers them a real threat and impossible to know how she feels when C. J. runs another triptych, followed by a similar one advertising the products of another Indianapolis resident, Madam Wm. H. Brice, manufacturer of Afro-American Scalp Food and Always Young Face Cream. Mme. C. West, also of Indianapolis, weighs in with her Hair Seed, meant for thin, short, kinky, or breaking-off hair, while Madam Baum's Hair Emporium of New York, advertising wigs, plaits, puffs, straightening combs and pomades, calls itself the largest Creole hair manufacturer in the country. Gloss-o claims it can grow straight hair in three months. And in what may be the first convention of professional black women in the country, Annie Pope-Turnbo gathers her agents together in St. Louis. Only six weeks prior to the sitting of the Calantheans in Baltimore, Mrs. Turnbo stages a company outing at her expense, described in the *Freeman* as a "day of joy for working people." Accompanying the article, a picture of her workers sitting in her six-seater, six-cylinder, sixty-horsepower Speedwell—deemed one of the most beautiful automobiles in St. Louis—must particularly gall Madam Walker.

The question is who's copying whom, if that's the case. Money and current fads may be making for duplications which appear to be the pirating of good ideas instead of simple, if powerful, coincidence. In any case, there is no doubt but that the success of Annie Turnbo sticks in Madame's craw, or that her summer offensive doesn't mean to wedge the other woman out of competition by obtaining sanction by the country's leading organizations.

In D.C., she and Miss Kelly attend theater parties, dinner parties, whist parties, breakfasts, and motor parties to Alexandria, Baltimore and the suburbs. Tireless, Madame makes her speech ten times in ten days. And Ransom once again gets to write copy. "The nation's capital has myriads of sojourners," a front-page sentence in the *Freeman* intones, winding its serpentine way to a point, "within its borders in the course of a year, but no woman has ever come to Washington and made a more profound impression in a short time than has this wonderful business genius from the Hoosier metropolis." And he goes on to compare her to Caesar, who also came, saw and conquered, and describes her visit as a "veritable march of triumph." And gives her Cole a big plus for efficiency, as shown by its ability to travel on all kinds of roads in all kinds of weather, and Madame one for generosity for having "invited all classes and conditions of humanity" to ride in it with her.

They hit the road again, headed for the National Baptist Convention in Nashville, another seven hundred miles away. There, Madame reprises the "Negro Woman in Business" speech, exhorting women to rise above the laundry and kitchen and aspire to a place in the world of commerce and trade, as "the Jew and Italian women are doing." She meets with the women's auxiliary, makes comments on emancipation and listens to her former antagonist Nannie Burroughs speak on the progress of women. After she and Alice Kelly tour the exposition grounds, they all go home.

Later, Madame will figure that while the 2,500-plus-mile trip was the most expensive she has ever taken, the cost was worth the compensation it will bring.

Three days after arriving home, she writes "My Dear Mr. Washington" to speak with him of Africa and her plan to build a Tuskegee there. She tells him of her conversation with Emmett Scott and his suggestion that she write the Wizard. "Now of course," she protests, "I haven't a large sum of money to start a school, but I have thought I might start at the bottom as you did Tuskegee and build up." This statement seems more than slightly outrageous, especially addressed to a man who has only two months before spent time in her opulent home partaking of meals on her fine china, listening to a musician strum her Italian harp, taking rides in her mammoth automobile. Yet she continues:

"I know absolutely nothing about building a school, but am willing to furnish the means as far as I am able. I am writing to ask your advice along this line, as to how I shall begin, or what steps to take in order to start the work. Any suggestions you might be willing to make . . ." Humbly yours.

Dr. Washington replies to "My dear Madam Walker," wishing he could offer some suggestion and stating his own desire to build such a school, pointing out, however, that Africa is a long way away, and the biggest problem is to find people to go there who would be both modest and determined to succeed and who would know how to get the job done. Yours very truly.

The Chief comes off friendly enough, if cool, but then he's not disposed to go for any idea that isn't his, especially one having to do with a school, even in Africa.

Later that same month, Madame throws a Sunday-night dinner party in honor of her former St. Louis pastor, D. P. Roberts, then takes out her bags once again, this time for her first foray out of the country, a combination business and vacation trip with Anjetta, to Jamaica, Haiti, Costa Rica, Cuba and the Panama Canal Zone. Following a farewell reception at home, her new chauffeur, Otho Patton, drives the two women to Louisville for more parties and then turns east across Kentucky and Ohio, through the late-fall chill of the Alleghenies, probably into damp, dark Pittsburgh and north to New York. Their Harlem stay is brief; on November 8, only two weeks after leaving Indianapolis, aunt and niece meet up with Madame Anita Patti

Brown, the coloratura soprano Madam Walker feted at a fancy breakfast gathering a year before, and—along with the singer's musicians, instruments and costumes and the hair culturist's products, promotional material and car—sail on the steamer *Oruba* for Kingston, Jamaica.

Upon arrival at Kingston on the thirteenth, they are greeted by numerous businessmen and government officials reportedly vying for their attention, and then Madame drives through the narrow streets in the Cole, and the predominantly dark-skinned Jamaicans surely gawk and wonder at the soft-haired American woman, who had her car shipped so that she could drive around whenever she wanted to.

A week later, Pittsburgh lawyer and publisher Robert Vann files an Order for Alias Subpoena against John Robinson in Lelia's name, the first step toward divorce. On December 5, the subpoena will be formally issued, and during January, the court will make a "diligent search and inquiry" as to the whereabouts of Robinson, accused by his wife of "willful and malicious desertion and absence from the habitation . . . without reasonable cause, for and during the space of two years." If Robinson doesn't turn up, in February "legal notice of same" will run once a week for four weeks in the *Pittsburgh Dispatch* and in the *Pittsburgh Legal Journal.*

Madame and Anjetta stay in Jamaica through November, travel to Haiti and Cuba in December, then return to Jamaica to celebrate Christmas and Madame's forty-sixth birthday. Madame describes the trip as a felicitous mix of moonlight sails and motoring through the lush countryside, side by side with business—signing up countless agents (one of whom has assured her that since African hair presents the same problems all over the world, she will soon realize her dream and become an international celebrity) and taking more orders for goods than she can supply.

While she's away, another page 1 Walker Company story runs in the *Indianapolis Ledger.* Written in first-person plural by an anonymous "Observer," the piece is called "Mme Walker Cheers 50 Homes: Bighearted Woman Sets Good Example," its florid writing style distinctly that of Freeman Ransom.

It begins with a meandering lead about the Wise Men and the manger, then goes on at length about the true meaning of Christmas and finally, about two-thirds of the way through, arrives its subject matter. Last year, it seems, Madame announced practically on her way out of town that from that year on, she would supply fifty homes with Christmas dinners. And so the "Observer" decided to take in the basket dispersal this year, to see firsthand how it was faring. He describes men and women of up to ninety years of age hobbling into the office to gather up a basket, rejoicing when Miss Kelly and Miss Flint send them off with their bounty. The process takes a long time, and even though it was supposed to be over by midnight, "the ladies were kept busy until nearly noon of the morning of the 25th, making up extra baskets for the late comers." A "Miss Roberts" is one of the volunteers delivering baskets, but there is little way of knowing exactly who this is, or whether Mae is spending her second Christmas as a Robinson with Lelia in Harlem or in Indianapolis distributing meals and visiting her brothers and sisters.

By New Year's, Madame and Anjetta have gone traveling again—to Cuba, Costa Rica and Panama. There's no record of how things are going between aunt and niece at this point, but since they are within two years of a falling out that will never heal it's reasonable to wonder how the relationship might be faring about now. I keep remembering that pouty look on Anjetta's face in the picture with the other women in the open car. Madame doesn't exactly go for sulkiness, especially from family. And so, given the oft-described hot-headedness of Breedloves and the ordinary rigors of travel, mightn't the two women be feeling some strain down there in the Caribbean? In about three months, Anjetta will disappear from official Walker newspaper stories, and a year or so after that she will leave 640 North West Street for good. When Madame makes the final changes in her will, she will omit Anjetta's name from her list of beneficiaries.

A lasting breakup doesn't happen overnight; however sudden it seems, if we look back we inevitably discover a buildup of slights and aggravations. The long trip together may well have sown the seeds of discord between aunt and niece, which will eventually result in Madame telling Ransom that Anjetta's attitude has made her "tired of fooling with these ungrateful Negroes."

Letter from Haiti

From Port-au-Prince, Madame sends home a travel report. "Haiti," she begins, "the land of L. Ouverture [*sic*], is in many ways an interesting and remarkable country . . . a Negro republic, governed and controlled by Negroes." And in this vein she goes on to suggest that the Southern Negro with money might well consider moving to this island nation, "as there are thousands of acres of rich, uncultivated land here that may be bought or leased for almost nothing compared to what we have to pay," with a climate hospitable to crops familiar to an American Southerner. All the country needs, she asserts, is new blood and money "in the hands of men who know how to use it" and who will replace island slackness with "wideawake hustling and progressive American customs and habits." (She doesn't specify which Southern Negroes with money she's talking about, but if "in the hands of men who know how to use it" sounds familiar, it's because Booker Washington made a near-identical remark about finding the right people to run a school in Africa.)

Our traveler could, it seems, find nothing to complain about in Haiti until, on the advice of a friend, she visited a local prison, which she describes as degrading and crude, with men and young boys lying on dirt floors without a mattress, many of them having been tossed into a cell on the slightest pretext, to be beaten and often forgotten. Political prisoners, she writes, come in for even worse treatment, chained hand and foot to the wall in perpetual solitary confinement, a situation she deems all the more pathetic "because these prisoners are men who occupied high positions and places of influence in the life of this people." Horrified, she orders holiday baskets sent to the inmates—eighteen chickens, a turkey, and regular Christmas dinners—but wonders whether in truth even one prisoner had so much as a taste of turkey. But—she waves the bad news to the winds—"away from these prison walls, away from the theater of political activities . . . one will find Haiti like other well-governed countries and in many respects the most beautiful country it has been my pleasure to visit." And she sends warm wishes to her friends for a happy new year.

If taking a tour of a prison on one's first trip to a foreign country seems a strange thing to do, we might consider reasons why she did. For one thing, while certainly materialistic and a confirmed capitalist, Sarah Walker doesn't seem to feel automatically *entitled* to her affluence; instead, privilege has instilled in her a sense of obligation—unswerving, if sometimes patronizing—especially to her race. Maybe she took the prison tour because her "friend" made the arrangements, and she didn't think she had the right not to go.

As for Haiti itself, it has been of interest to African-Americans since the late 1700s, when the slave Toussaint L'Ouverture organized an army that saw the defeat of Napoleon and installed itself in power. And so when Madame refers to this same country as "well-governed," she's sending a message of hope to her people, assuring them that, contrary to the opinion of most white Americans, black people are perfectly capable of running a government efficiently. As composer-singer Noble Sissle will say in another context: "When such things are noticed it parts the shadowy haze of doubt which stands between the Negro race and success and gives a hopeful ray of light for the future."

In late January, Madame and Anjetta sail back to New York, where they presumably stay a few days before heading to Indianapolis. For weeks afterwards, large boxes arrive at the Walker house, marked with strange postmarks, packed with straw and filled with bric-a-brac, furniture, dishes and swirly, unstructured clothes imported from all over the world. And maybe it happened and maybe not, but I like to imagine the resplendent Madame sitting in her parlor surrounded by her admiring staff as she holds colorful glass pieces to the light and lifts pale exotic dresses by the shoulder seam and remembers out loud where she bought each item, as a way of recreating the trip for those who in all likelihood will never go.

"She was not beautiful in features," hair stylist and longtime Walker employee Margaret Joyner will say of her, "but in ways."

At about this same time, a Leland, Mississippi, mob of three hundred men and boys capture a black man named Sam Petty, who has been accused of shooting a deputy sheriff, and chain him inside a dry-goods box. As Petty prays and begs for his life, the men stuff oil-soaked cotton around his manacled body and then apply a match. In his adrenaline-stoked fear, Petty breaks his chains and, clothes ablaze, runs for his life, but there is nowhere to hide in the flat Mississippi Delta landscape, and so he is quickly shot and killed. Feeling cheated by their captive's quick death, the men toss his bullet-riddled body back into the flaming box and watch as it burns to ashes. Might this not be considered an even cruder system of justice than allowing a young man to lie bound and starving on a dirt floor? These are ugly quibbles, one version of brutality compared to another.

Within weeks of rolling into Indianapolis from New York, Madame rolls back out again, to speak at the Tuskegee Farmers' Conference, but this year in the assembly room, a better venue. Once there, she gives a speech about how to hit the mark despite the handicap of color, then describes the rewards that grow out of thrift, industry and Christian faith. After her appearance, she pushes on back toward home, but not without doing business as she goes, including the hiring of a slim and very pretty seventeen-year-old native of Birmingham who will come to work in Indianapolis as a stenographer and assistant bookkeeper, marry the letter carrier who delivers Madame's mail and remain a Walker Company employee for sixty-seven years.

In a 1980 television interview, Violet Davis Reynolds says she was living at home in Mobile with her mother—a friend of Alice Kelly's—and had enrolled at Talledega College when Madame stopped by and, after a quick conversation, offered her a job on the spot. In a newspaper interview, however, Reynolds says she was attending Eckstein Normal when Madame came looking for a bookkeeper's assistant and stenographer. And since she had been recommended by Alice Kelly for her "responsible upbringing, her interest in scholarship and her ambition to be proficient in business," Madame offered the bright young girl a job. "Madame wanted me to begin work as soon as possible," and so Violet Davis headed straight for Indianapolis. "I couldn't believe I was being singled out for a position in a big city I had never visited," Reynolds exclaims, still lively and beautiful in her early eighties.

On the train to Indiana, Davis met a Louisville woman and NACW officer, Georgia Nugent, who was en route to an elegant musicale and ball being given that very night by Madam C. J. Walker in honor of her daughter, visiting from New York with friends from the music and the-ater worlds. So the two women took a taxi to Madame's home and there Violet learned that she too was invited to the festivities, and on that very night she met her future husband, David Reynolds.

The spring musicale will be the first of several elaborate events Madame will stage in the next two years, to signify her gratitude to the people of Indianapolis and assure them that she does not leave them easily. Invitations to the April event are sent to 200 to 300 people—including a carful of aging ladies from the Alpha Home—too many for a house party, and so Madame makes use of the Pythian Temple and engages the highly touted Kiota Barbers Orchestra. "The Madame," reports the *Freeman*, "is noted for her lavish hand in affairs of [this] kind, but this time she eclipsed all of her former efforts." The color scheme is gold and white, with twelve white pedestals arranged around the hall, garlanded with yellow and white flowers. "Sweet strains of music . . . poured from behind a group of palms, giving that entrancing oriental effect [desired] by the fin-de-siecle hostess," while above the partygoers' heads, brilliant lights festooned with green and yellow decorations shimmer in the darkness.

Matching the color scheme, Madame wears an "East Indian cre-ation . . . brought . . . from Panama . . . of silk Maltese lace, draped over cream charmeuse," accented with diamond jewelry, a gold band in her hair and gold buckles on her white slippers. Lelia's Empire-style Parisian gown is of white crepe embroidered with gold threads; in her hair, a diamond-studded gold headdress shaped like a bird of paradise; around her face, more diamonds. Anjetta wears yellow chif-fon and a matching corsage, while Mae's in "a beautiful gown of blue messaline."

The evening's entertainment features a star-studded cast of per-formers, with singing by Noble Sissle, the reading of a Paul Dunbar poem, soprano solos by Marie Peek Merrill from New York and a jazzy performance by Frank Fowler Brown, "the well-known tenor," who entertains "à la cabaret." After the program, the floor is thrown open for dancing. Her card filled, Madame swings out on the first tune with the painter William Scott, then dances the night away. The *Freeman* calls the occasion "the most elaborate affair ever seen in Indianapolis."

During the postparty weekend, Madame takes her out-of-town guests for a joy ride, perhaps in the Cole, or maybe they take Madame's brand-new Waverly, another sixty-horsepower seven-seater, which she bought only a week or so before, for $3,000 cash. At any rate, everybody has a fine time, and before leaving on Sunday, some of the guests are said to have declared the weekend the best of their lives.

By this time, F. B. Ransom has been officially named general manager of the Walker Company, and while he still maintains a law practice on Pennsylvania Street, he spends most of his time handling Madame's business. He and his wife and new son, Frank, still live in the California Street house, and Violet Davis takes a room with them, paying $3.50 weekly from a $6 salary, with another $2.00 going to her sister for school tuition. But Davis is content. "I had 50 cents for myself," which she says was more than enough, since she didn't need clothes and could see a western movie or buy an ice-cream cone for five cents. And often, she says, she ate her noon meal with Madame, who then might ask the young girl to play cards with her— preferably a game called Flinch—for relaxation and company. Reynolds says that office equipment at the Walker Company was minimal: a typewriter, a telephone, a filing cabinet, paper, pencils, pen and ink, nothing more. But, she shrugs, that was all they needed to "build a world-known business—that and a leader like Madam Walker, ingenuity and hard work." It must have been exhilarating for a seventeen-year-old girl from Birmingham to work for a company that in the early days was often referred to as "the house that revolutionized the Negro personality," because of Madame's concern with how people, especially women, felt about themselves based on how they looked, and how that concern brought them new self-respect and possibilities for stature and even some power in the world.

The Foremost Businesswoman of Our Race

That same spring, Madame approaches the Wizard once again, offering to fund five fifty-dollar scholarships to be given to students already enrolled at Tuskegee, so that they can attend day classes instead of holding down regular jobs. But because of the size of her fortune, Washington apparently considers her offer mingy and, in addition, questions her motives for giving the money directly to the students instead of the school. When he (or Emmett Scott, who now handles almost all the Tuskegee correspondence) tells her this in a letter, Madame gets testy.

"My Dear Dr. Washington . . ." she writes. "It was thoroughly explained to me that there were two kinds of scholarships of which I [chose] the one to help the student," being under the impression that in giving scholarships she "was not only helping the student but the school as well." And if that wasn't the case, well, then, she has missed her mark.

The letter is messy with type-overs, blackouts and handwritten insertions. My guess is, Madame typed it herself, in a heat. She uses stationery with C. J.'s Blood and Rheumatic Remedy still on the logo, perhaps her subtle way of demonstrating frugality. Or maybe it was just the first sheet of paper she ran across.

"While I am deeply interested in Tuskegee . . . ," she assures him, "I do not feel able to assume the entire responsibility [for] five students at this time." Why? Because "while it is true I have a large business, yet with the increase in business comes the increase in expenses." And besides, "I am unlike your white friends who have waited until they were rich and then help, but have in proportion to my success . . . reached out . . . which may have been a mistake because I have been mistaken for a rich woman, which has caused scores of demands for help. Many of whom are so pathetic that it has been impossible for me to turn them down."

Some of these sentiments are shamelessly self-serving, but in the end I expect she has no regrets about expressing them; after all, he struck the first low blow.

Backing off a little, she attempts to negotiate a deal, reminding the Doctor of the proposition she made some time ago, asking him to include her in the Tuskegee curriculum, since by now she has surely demonstrated the legitimacy and profitability of her business. With the givens in place, she names her terms: "Should you see your way clear to reconsider and establish this work in your school, if successful it would mean thousands of dollars to both Tuskegee and myself. You would not only help me, but would help thousands of others who are needy and deserving."

Now, since in all probability she knows he will not give in to this, she's ready with a backup offer. "If you cannot see your way clear to adopt the work, I do hope you will be willing to give me your [e]ndorsement in a public way." She ends by trusting he is well and wishing him unbounded success in his work and is sincerely his.

This letter signals yet another change in Madame's attitude toward the Wizard. Now that she no longer feels the need to pander, she can operate from a position of strength and—writing as colleague and worthy adversary—feel free to let him know that from time to time he's going to have to play by her rules.

She writes the letter on May 5, but the usually punctilious Wizard doesn't respond until May 22. "Dear Madam Walker: I have your letter of May 5th. So that there may be no misunderstanding about the matter, I am proceeding once more to try to state the proposition with reference to the students whom you wish to help here."

And in that patronizing tone he re-explains the situation she has already described, then doubles back on himself and says that they at Tuskegee will be glad, when it is convenient for her, to place money in their treasury for the five students she selects, who will be able then to enter day school, as she suggested. As for the course of study, the answer is the same. "I have already written you frankly and fully with reference to placing your work in our course of study; our Trustees and Executive Council do not see their way clear to follow your suggestion."

Further complicating the situation, in July, Tuskegee announces that Mme C. J. Walker, the noted businesswoman of Indianapolis, is to provide a number of scholarships to Tuskegee for the training of workers in the African field. Thus the wily antagonists move toward a mutually beneficial deal.

By the middle of 1914, people are starting to jack up the good times and play harder, as if to have fun fast before it's too late. For U.S. citizens, war seems a remote possibility, but the news from Europe is dark, and it's hard to know what Wilson will or should do, so the partying becomes a little desperate, and Madame's no exception. Every week, one of the papers reports at least one reception, whist contest or dinner party at her home. This nonstop schedule of entertainment continues until midsummer, when it's time to start gearing up for the conventions. In July, with Lucy Flint and Nettie (Mrs. Freeman) Ransom, she takes a two-week trip to Chicago. Mrs. Ransom brings along her young son, Frank, who reserves a special place in Madame's heart, even though, as she lightheartedly admits to Ransom, she greatly prefers girls.

While Madame's in Chicago, Lelia attends her final divorce hearing in Pittsburgh, at the offices of Robert Vann. Divorce is not always easy to obtain, especially in a Catholic city, so Vann rounds up friends and neighbors to testify that Lelia was a good and proper wife who kept a decent home, which her husband left for no good reason. On July 16, they meet with a master of the court, who swears in the witnesses and receives from the stenographer a report showing that John Robinson has not responded to the subpoena and has not been located, even after a diligent search and inquiry. The judge rules that a decree of divorce is in order. And with that Lelia becomes single again, as free to marry as if she and John Robinson had never wed.

As usual, August is a big month for Madame. On the fourth she goes to the NACW meeting in one of her touring cars. This year, the women are meeting in Xenia, Ohio, at Wilberforce University, only a hundred miles from Indianapolis, an easy afternoon's ride. After making her initial flashy appearance, she sits quietly and mainly listens, biding her time. W. S. Scarborough, president of the college, speaks; Margaret Murray Washington presides; there are recitals and musical performances, and the women pass resolutions in favor of national prohibition, woman suffrage, and a modest style of dress for women as a way of promoting health and proper sanitation. They make their annual protests against segregation and lynching.

On Friday, the last day of the conference, after the decision to meet in Baltimore in 1916 is announced, Madame is introduced from the floor. She rises to acknowledge the notice and, further, to invite all of the women present to her home for a postconvention get-together. Since seven hundred women are reportedly in attendance, the invitation must have caused quite a stir. Not that everyone will show up. But even to offer is a bold move, signifying her generosity as well as a belief in unity, camaraderie and—never one to forget the possibility of gain— the lasting effect of the great gesture.

That night, after final reports and prizes for attendance are presented, Mrs. Victoria Clay Haley, one of Madame's old St. Louis friends, rises to propose that the NACW endorse the work of Madam C.J. Walker, "who is doing so much for the elevation of the race." The motion carries unanimously, and with that, the prestigious National Association of Colored Women grants its seal of approval to this proprietor of a hair-treatment business.

When Mrs. Washington is presented with a hand-painted jardinière by the membership, she comments that "no woman is ever so happy as when she is loved by another woman." And as if in agreement with that, the conventioneers stand and join together singing "God Be with You Till We Meet Again," and the Ninth Biennial of the National Association of Colored Women is adjourned.

The NACW minutes say simply "Carried," nothing more. Why so easy this time? Because she figured out the story that *worked* and told it in a way that suited the ladies. Because Victoria Clay Haley wouldn't have made the motion if she hadn't been certain it was going to pass. Because Madame's been busy laying groundwork since the meeting in Louisville. But mostly because she's finally become important enough to make the perceived benefits equal to or greater than whatever compromises the women feel they might have made. And when the NACW sends news of her endorsement to the press, it emphasizes Madame's dedication to the education of Negro boys and girls, not her business, and even mentions a school she has "established" in Africa.

On Saturday she returns in triumph to Indianapolis in a packed touring car. Her passengers include Oberlin graduate and NACW vice president Mary Talbert and her daughter, singer Sarah May Talbert; Victoria Clay Haley; and Arsania Williams, the St. Louis schoolteacher who tried to negotiate a way for Booker T. Washington to appear on Negro Day at the Louisiana Purchase Exposition in St. Louis in 1904. Including Madame, six women ride together from Xenia to Indianapolis. Her guests remain through the weekend and enjoy a reception in their honor on Sunday. On Tuesday, the women participate in an "Echo Meeting," in which they re-create the conference for several hundred local women, who then ask questions and discuss the proceedings.

But August has only begun, and once everybody's gone, Madame packs up once again, headed west with Alice Kelly for Muskogee, Oklahoma, and the National Negro Business League meeting. Madame isn't officially listed on the program this year, since she had her say in Philadelphia, preceded by that impromptu speech in Chicago, but she's going nonetheless, and Lelia has made arrangements to come as well, despite her aversion to crowds, speeches and provincial towns like Muskogee. The trip from New York to Oklahoma is long, hot and unpleasant, but Lelia manages to get there in time.

On the second night of the conference, after introducing an Oklahoma homesteader who made his way through hard times by living on a diet of roasted acorns, the Wizard interrupts the schedule of events to acknowledge the presence of Madam C. J. Walker in the audience. "It is always encouraging to know," he remarks, "that people are successful in business but it is always more satisfactory to see them willing to distribute some their profits among all good causes. We are therefore pleased to have with us this evening Madam C. J. Walker, who not only makes money in business but gives liberally to many worthy enterprises."

Presumably, she stands. And then Washington makes a surprise announcement: "We are going to give her five minutes' time in which she can talk to us about anything she chooses, and she always says something we are glad to listen to." Do we buy this? Washington's not exactly a fan of spontaneity, and he knows full well what Madame's after and what she's likely to ask for, and since—as we shall see—Madame has come fully prepared for this moment, I don't think so. My guess is, they worked out a private deal ahead of time, which included an "impromptu" introduction by the Chief.

When the applause dies, Madame launches into her five-minute allotment by fluttering on about what an unexpected pleasure it is being called to the platform on this evening, especially since she had her say last year at Philadelphia and two years ago in Chicago. And so she actually doesn't believe she even has the right to speak tonight. *But*—she quick-steps around her reservations—*nevertheless,* "I have been asked by our worthy president . . . to present my own cause and in coming before you I simply want to ask a favor of you in order that I, in turn, may be able to do more favors for our race"—not, she assures the league membership, because she needs help herself.

As a point of information, Washington didn't actually ask her to present her own cause; he said she could talk about anything she wished. As for her logic, it still seems to come down to a matter of personal expediency: help me make more money so that I can help the race.

She speaks briefly about her business, which she calls "manufacturing hair and toilet preparations." But she doesn't want the businessmen to get the wrong idea. "I am not merely satisfied in making money myself, for I am endeavoring to provide employment for hundreds of the women of my race." And for the benefit of those who haven't heard it, she recaps the orphaned-at-seven story, which drives home an important point: "I had to make my own living and my own opportunity. But I made it." And that's why she wants to advise every Negro woman in the audience not to "sit down and wait for the opportunities to come, but . . . get up and make them."

Since this is the uplift message in a nutshell, applause rocks the room. To extend the moment, Madame furnishes her audience with the information everyone's waiting for, her current worth. As she will tell Ransom, "It is my accumulations that have brought me into the limelight and this side interests most." In the nine years she's been in business, she informs the NNBL membership, she has amassed more than $53,000 worth of real estate, all of it paid in full, except for $1,000 owing on some New York and California property. In Indiana she owns twenty lots in Gary and five houses elsewhere, plus the $10,000 business establishment in Indianapolis and $20,000 "out on interest." The energetic applause comes as no surprise to this very canny speaker; she's milked it.

And then she says an extraordinary thing. "I am preparing myself so that *when this hair business falls to the ground* [italics in NNBL minutes] I will have an income and I won't have to come down. You know there are so many hair preparations on the market now, that I am preparing for the future should my business in the face of so much competition, not continue to yield as handsomely in the future as it has in the past."

Not *if* it falls to the ground but *when?* Does she believe this? In terms of relative growth, the business is at its peak, and profits will continue to escalate for another seven or eight years, past the end of her life. But the industry is changing, and she can see ads for black beauty products everywhere she looks. Drugstores are taking the place of agents; in Memphis, white businessman and healing-oil peddler Abe Plough has bought a drugstore on Beale Street, the heart of the black business district, where he sells his own brand of cosmetics and hair products, Black and White, below Walker and Poro prices. Soon he'll advertise in black newspapers, and once he's become their largest advertiser, he'll use his position to obtain reduced rates and special favors. So far, Madame's business instincts have never missed, and maybe she's simply leapt ahead of others, envisioning a future in which change will be not only beneficial but a necessity.

"Now . . ."—she returns to her original request—"I have come before you this evening to ask you to endorse my work. Some of you who have come to this convention may ask why I should desire this endorsement. I ask it because it will help me in the struggle I am making to build up Negro womanhood."

In fact nobody wonders why she's asking; what African-American businessperson would not? The question is why they should give it. Again, to back her argument she offers the trickle-down theory of personal wealth: help me to make more money because the richer I am, the better off we'll all be. To confirm her premise, she gives examples of women she has inspired to make a decent living, lists some of the causes she has supported, and tells of being the first Negro woman in America to give $1,000 to the YMCA. Winding up, she speaks of educating three boys and two girls at Tuskegee, so that when she establishes a Negro industrial school in West Africa, she will be able to send qualified teachers and administrators.

Surely this takes longer than five minutes? Appearing to conclude, she pays fulsome tribute to the Wizard and his work and says she stands shoulder to shoulder with him in everything he is trying to do, and on a lighter note, "If the truth were known there are many women who are responsible for the success of *you men.*"

But back to the favor. She happens to have on her a resolution, "drafted by some of my friends," which she would like to read aloud. The proposal simply says, "We, the undersigned delegates, appreciating her good work, do respectfully ask the Business League to endorse Madame C. J. Walker as the foremost business woman of our race."

The resolution is signed by a number of NNBL members, including Mary Talbert, Arsania Williams, Victoria Clay Haley, Margaret Murray Washington, J. C. Napier and Fred Moore, the Wizard's handpicked *New York Age* editor.

Napier, the former registrar of the U.S. Treasury and current president of the NNBL—one of the black appointees in Washington whom Wilson dismissed—moves that the league "endorse the sentiment contained in the address of Madame C. J. Walker and commend her work to the general public in this country."

Hearing no objection, Washington declares the resolution to be "the sense of this convention" and therefore "considered passed."

Passed unanimously, at last and after all—and at $250, a steal. Still, the Wizard said only that the resolution was "considered" passed, without giving his own personal amen to it, and his "sense of this convention" carries little conviction. Still, a deal's a deal, and he's come through.

But when an article on the convention appears in the October issue of the magazine *Outlook,* a photo of Madam Walker that was supposed to accompany the article does not run. When an NNBL official questions the deletion, the Chief replies that the magazine made the cut for reasons of space, and he regrets it very much.

When Madame, Lelia and Alice Kelly arrive in Indianapolis, Ransom recounts a successful trip he's made to Jackson, Mississippi, to request a pardon for a young black man accused of a white man's murder, reportedly the first time in that state's history that such a case has been granted clemency. A week or so later, Madame entertains houseguests from Jackson, Chicago and Louisville and takes them to Dayton, Ohio, on an overnight touring party. Days later, there are more reports of German atrocities in Europe, and while some of them are exaggerated or untrue, Walter Lippmann darkly comments, "Nothing can stop the awful disintegration now."

Success extracts its price, especially when the achieved goal has been this hotly pursued. The sleep of a woman endorsed as the foremost businesswoman of her race has to be jagged, iffy. Political questions loom. There are so many complicated domestic issues to consider already, and now she has to keep up with international news. As an exemplar and leader, she'll have to figure out what patriotism means to a woman whose parents were slaves and whose people continue being mercilessly lynched. When she does that, she'll take a public stand. But for now, the more immediate concern is sleep. To pass the long dark morning hours, she might get up and put on some music or wake up her daughter to come play a game of Flinch.

The Mistake

Only a day or so after returning from Dayton, she and Lelia head east to New York for a few days; then Madame continues alone, making a lecture tour to cities in Massachusetts and Rhode Island, and then back to Long Island, Brooklyn and New York City—in all, twenty-five lectures in forty-two days. Once she has arrived in Harlem, Lelia throws a dinner party in her honor, with a guest list that includes *New York Age* editor Fred Moore, conductor James Reese Europe and Philip Payton, the realtor some people call "the Father of Colored Harlem."

Like most speculators, Payton's had his financial ups and downs, and at the time of the dinner party he's had to shut down his Afro-American Realty Company altogether, but he keeps his hand in. Maybe he's even waiting for the moment when, during dinner, Madame voices a desire to buy her own house in New York, a big place, maybe not in the middle of Manhattan, where she can hold meetings and even grow things—vegetables, berries. The accommodating realtor then comes through with the perfect property: Bishop's Court, located on Prince and State Streets in Flushing, Queens—a veritable estate and the home of the late, distinguished AME bishop William B. Derrick.

Convinced that all Madame has to do is clap eyes on the twenty-room mansion with its spiral staircases and lush grounds—including one tree said to be worth $5,000—Payton quickly arranges for a tour. Within days of Lelia's party, a number of the dinner guests take a ride to Flushing: Madame, Payton, Moore, Europe and the Shakespearean actor Richard B. Harrison. Instantly taken with the four-story house with its marble fireplaces, frescoed ceilings and potential public-relations value, Madame puts down a deposit and—more significantly—signs a contract with Clara Derrick, the bishop's widow. Later, she will admit that she'd been impressed not so much by the house itself, grand as it was, as by its association with the revered Derrick, who often visited Pittsburgh when she lived there and both were cited in the *Press*'s "Afro-American Notes," as well as by the publicity she would derive from the purchase.

A few days afterwards, she goes to the studios of the society photographer Addison Scurlock to sit for what will become her official portrait from now on, used in ads, labels, news stories, posters and obits and, in 1998, on a commemorative postage stamp. Like many other African-Americans, Scurlock is a new resident of Harlem, having moved there from Washington, where he was considered *the* portrait photographer of the D.C. black upper class. Unlike previous pictures, Scurlock's shuns wistful girlish modesty in favor of a magisterial, glamorous head shot.

She's wearing a pale, soft dress—either cream or white—that dips at the neckline in a wide, deep V, with intricate smocking around the shoulders and bustline and knotted tassels of shiny thread hanging from the hand stitching. The gown has a gauzy, unstarched look, unusual for the era, and may be the one she bought in Central America and wore to the April musicale. Small teardrop stones dangle from her earlobes. Her necklace is a delicate gold chain, strung with what seem to be diamonds and pearls, a pendant lying easy and casual on her brown chest.

The camera's to her right and Scurlock's positioned her at a three-quarters angle, looking off in the distance, but this time with expert lighting, cast obliquely to show off her strong profile and high cheekbones, her flat nose and those dark, burning eyes. Her eyebrows are surprisingly long, extending well beyond the outside corners of her eyes and with very little space between them and her eyelids, giving her a look of perpetual seriousness. Her mouth is relaxed, not tense and purposeful as in other photos. As for her hairstyle, she's adopted a simple version of a currently popular cut called the Diana, in which the hair falls unlifted from a center part to slightly below the ears, where it is cupped under and pulled back to resemble a short pageboy, leaving the back of her neck brazenly bare, foreshadowing the short bobs of the era to come. No more Gibson Girl pompadour, no curls, no fuss; she is simply *grand.*

On October 24, she makes a speech in Philadelphia, possibly does a little shopping at Wanamaker's, then sets off on the six hundred miles home. Once there, she announces details of her latest acquisition in the *Recorder,* which entitles its page-one story "Madam C. J. Walker Buys Splendid Eastern Home," quoting the selling price at $40,000 and expressing regret that Indianapolis is soon to lose "our own Madame Walker." The next week, the *Age* runs a similar story, reporting that in a deal negotiated by Phil Payton, Madame has made a $10,000 deposit on an approximately $40,000 purchase price, the remaining amount to be paid in cash, once she gets a satisfactory report from the title company. It is said, the *Age* continues, that Mrs. Walker will spend $10–20,000 on remodeling and that while in New York, she went on a shopping spree and bought a $2,850 dining room suite, a $2,200 bedroom suite and another for $625, and that she will engage, at a liberal salary, a "prominent young New York society matron" to be her social secretary. The story is accompanied by the Scurlock photo in what may be its very first appearance.

In fact, Madame has made a deposit of $1,000—not $10,000—on a promised $8,000 down payment toward a purchase price of about $25,000, but even then, the sale doesn't go well. Fearing Madame may have been snookered, the skeptical Ransom writes S. A. Singerman, the Nassau Street attorney who helped with the Harlem purchase, for an assessment of Bishop's Court. On November 5, *before* "Wealthy Woman Buys New York Property" appears in the *Age,* Ransom receives the following response:

> *Dear Mr. Ransom:*
> *Further answering your communication of the 29th ultimo I wish to say that I have investigated thoroughly the property of the late Bishop Derrick of Flushing, New York, known as "Bishop's court" and herewith hand you my report: I find that the property is situated on a plot 206' × 259', being 206' on State Street and 259' on Prince Street. The property is located in the poorest part of Flushing and is only good for the erection of cheap tenements. The house is worth nothing, as it is an old building of no consequence; and the property as it stands altogether is worth no more than $17,000. In fact no one would purchase the property for $17,000 in the market and I doubt whether anyone, at a public sale, would pay over $13,000 to $15,000 therefore. A full market value would seem to be about $1,000 a lot or from $40 to $50 a square foot. These figures are the result of a minute investigation, as well as the opinion of experts in that locality.*

Apparently your client has been fearfully imposed upon and I would by all means suggest that an endeavor be made to obtain a return of the deposit.

Doubtless Ransom delivers this information to Madame, but to little effect. Clara Derrick is now threatening to sue for the remaining $7,000 promised on the nonnegotiable contract. Besides, Madame's become intractable about the house: she wants it. Given the situation, Singerman explores other possibilities, and on November 28 informs Ransom that he has succeeded in getting the widow's attorney to lower the price to $20,500, which is, he declares, "absolutely the best settlement that could be made, aside from litigating the matter." And he goes on at length to explain the details of the sale, including a closing date sometime around December 1. Once the $7,000 has been paid, he feels, "objections to the title can be fully disposed of."

In a final note, Singerman advises Ransom that Mrs. Robinson, who has been discharged with receiving and distributing payments for the Flushing deal, has inexplicably hit the road for Richmond, Virginia, to stay at the Miller Hotel for some ten or so days. Perhaps, Singerman suggests, since the transaction must be concluded with some dispatch, Ransom might want to get in touch with the vanished daughter to find out when she plans to return. Ransom dutifully writes Lelia that day and confides, as an aside to the business at hand: "As you know, Madam had gone into this before consulting me. . . . And even had she consulted me she would not have taken my advice for her heart was and is set on this property and on moving to New York." He had hoped, he says, to convince her to wait for at least eighteen months to make a purchase, after she had settled her debts and "piled up a snug sum for rainy days," during which time he might find a way to deter her from making the move at all. But, he rather poignantly muses, there is little he can do. "There are those who say live while you are living . . . but I can imagine no greater disgrace than to be known as your mother is known, and in the end give your enemies a chance to rejoice in the fact that you died poor."

Ransom's cautionary point is well taken, but by overstating the doomsday possibilities he sabotages his own purposes, leaving Lelia and her mother free to dismiss his hyperbolic exhortations. And so— since Madame is dead set on having Bishop's Court—her business manager has no choice except to fork over the $7,000 cash down payment. But even after the mortgage is signed, he can't stop harping, and a year later she sets her foot down. "As regards my coming back to Indianapolis, Mr. Ransom, that is clear out of the question. Even if I don't build in New York, I will never come back to Indianapolis." Admittedly, she regrets leaving her friends, but she cannot resist relocating to a place where there is so much joy and "not so many narrow, mean people," a possible reference to an incident at a local movie theater, the Isis, when Madame put down the usual dime for a ticket only to be told that tickets for "colored people" now cost twenty-five cents.

Thus far, Lelia and Madame have reason to feel optimistic about money, since their business is, indeed, keeping up with the extravagant outlay of cash, despite the growing competition within the beauty industry that Madame correctly foresaw at the last NNBL meeting. The *New York Age* story, "Wealthy Woman Buys New York Property," floats in the middle of a sea of advertisements for hair products and services. Two columns over—just beyond a notice for Mme Gonzales Hair and Scalp Tonic and one for Kink-no-more, "the greatest hair straightening preparation on earth"—are an ad for Greenberg's Hair Dressing Parlors and another for Mme Baum's wigs and straightening combs. Companies pop up overnight, go broke, disappear, reappear under different ownership or a new name. Included in the jumble of ads on that one page is a notice for Walker's Hair Parlor and Lelia College in Harlem, with Indianapolis listed as company headquarters but without a street address. Customers are advised, instead, to send mail to Lelia Walker Robinson on 136th Street. (Note the name change, by the way. She has no legal claim to Charles Walker's surname, but to make her connection to Madame and the company obvious, she takes it on, holding on to "Robinson" for now.)

The next week, a different ad appears, listing Madam C. J. Walker as president of the company and suggesting that customers call Lelia College only if in New York, otherwise to address all communications to 640 North West Street, Indianapolis. While mother-daughter difficulties often have to do with issues of autonomy, this struggle reaches beyond that and will continue throughout Madame's life, especially regarding the Harlem facilities, which Lelia would like to run independently. But Madame refuses to relinquish control, and by way of emphasis her ad includes the Scurlock portrait.

As the year ends, Ransom is still working out details of the Derrick contract while Madame cultivates new ideas and waits to move in. She's bought other property as well—more lots in Indianapolis and Savannah, some Oklahoma mine stock, a plot in the Father Moses Dickson Cemetery in St. Louis. A worker in the Underground Railroad during slavery and later an AME minister, Dickson set the land aside as a place where middle-class blacks could be buried. Madame may have bought the plot to support the enterprise, never intending to be buried there, but the site, hard by the front gate, to this day is marked with a modest obelisk engraved MADAM WALKER.

Nineteen-fourteen began hopefully, with progressivism still so noble and thriving a notion that one newspaper writer predicted a new world ahead, in which dissent is encouraged and there is "a genuine and sincere awakening to the social and economic and political ills that [have] so long afflicted the country." Another writer summarized the time preceding World War I as one in which "it was easy for a young man to believe in the perfectability of man and of society, and in the sublimation of evil." These words were written in nostalgic reflection, after the onset of war.

By August, much of Europe is engaged in a battle that current thinking predicts will be brought to a swift conclusion by new weapons of destruction. Woodrow Wilson's wife dies in the White House. Monroe Trotter, the iconoclastic black editor of the *Boston Guardian,* obtains an audience with the president—whom he, along with W. E. B. DuBois, supported in his race against Taft and Roosevelt, yet who quickly orders him out of his office for using insulting language with a "background of passion." After passage of the Federal Reserve Act, the Clayton Antitrust law and the bill creating the Federal Trade Commission, Wilson announces that the reign of privilege is undone, and calls a halt to further movements of reform.

Madame turns forty-seven, anticipating her move from the Midwest, to live closer to her daughter and to make a new, almost royal life for herself in surroundings that might well be called palatial. Perhaps she's already thinking ahead to the invitations she'll issue to members of organizations like the NACW and NNBL, the parties she'll give, the political and intellectual discussions she'll sponsor, the advertisements she'll run featuring stories of her rise from croppers' daughter to a refined woman of influence who holds court in a bishop's estate.

Never before has she made so clear a blunder. There have been previous missteps (the marriage to John Davis, which she so cleverly expunged) and possible errors in judgment (the breakup with Anjetta, her boundless indulgence of Lelia), but given her stark childhood, her temperament and the exigencies of the times, these are understandable lapses and, furthermore, fit comfortably into a general sense of her psychological makeup. But this one's troubling. Making a mistake on a car or a fur coat is one thing; but signing a binding contract on a pricey piece of real estate without consulting local zoning laws or seeking what Singerman calls "the opinion of experts in that locality" is a serious error, and we have to wonder how that happened, why she allowed herself to be taken in, what dulled her keen business instinct.

When he came into the business, Ransom declared it his mission to keep the Walker Company from drowning in its own success, and that seems to be what's happening—if not yet to the entire firm, then to Madame herself. Not that she doesn't have reason to feel smug. Everything's going so well: the multiple endorsements and rising income, Lelia's ongoing success in Harlem, the respect and veritable *love* she feels wherever she goes. She's been right so many times—about moving to Indianapolis, making the contribution to the Y, building the factory, divorcing C. J., buying the Cole, changing her advertising strategy—that it's a wonder she doesn't feel practically invincible by now, if not almost infallible. Thus, she's buying more cars than she can ride in, throwing one lavish party after the next, shopping, buying, traveling, riding the wave as if challenging it to go flat on her. And for a long time, it doesn't.

Pen in hand, sitting with the bishop's widow and the Father of Colored Harlem, she's operating in a kind of fog of buoyant conviction, just as Burney had when he took on all those debts some fifty years prior to this moment. What can go wrong? Who would dupe her now, or even want to? *Nothing. Nobody.* And so, uncharacteristically vulnerable to the setup, she signs. And while there's no proof that Philip Payton and Clara Derrick worked together—or separately—to create the "fearful imposition" on Madame's willingness to believe, there's no question that somebody knew what was what in Flushing at this time, including the planned rezoning ordinance that will soon transform the entire neighborhood into a business district.

In addition, there's her health. Within two years, Madame's blood pressure will spike so alarmingly that doctors will recommend she cancel all business appointments and take a minimum of six weeks' rest; friends and colleagues will write Ransom to express shock at her obvious fragility and the startling decline in her health. A year after that, when her kidneys start to fail, she will be diagnosed as having interstitial nephritis, which in another year will result in her death, less than four and a half years from the day she signs the contract on Bishop's Court.

These symptoms point to another possibility: she may also be suffering from diabetes. This is speculation, based on the times and the state of medicine then as compared to what we now know. In 1914, there are no sophisticated tests for the disease, and so even if she consulted Ward, it's highly unlikely he'd have diagnosed it. But at that time, diabetes was particularly prevalent among African-Americans, and her other maladies point to the likelihood that she has it now. If this is the case, the snowballing effect is simple; its final outcome, if unchecked, all but inevitable. She's already been diagnosed as hypertensive; this makes the heart work harder, and the consequent stress irritates the lining of the arteries. Fatty tissue forms, restricting blood flow. Waste products collect, damaging delicate filters in the kidneys. With late-onset diabetes, percentages become probabilities. Diabetics are twenty times more likely than others to suffer kidney failure. Odds are, Madame's experiencing early symptoms, including frequent urination, constant thirst, poor circulation—especially in her lower legs and feet, causing pain, cramps, sores and swelling.

The most common complaint among diabetics is "I don't feel like myself anymore." And because moderation is not in her, Madame responds to this unease not by practicing caution but by throwing it to the wind. Where, after all, would she be if she'd listened to conventional wisdom and lowered her expectations? Still in St. Louis? Or even Vicksburg? She signs the papers thinking it will all work out because it has to.

To extract her from this unfortunate contract will take Singerman and Ransom almost two years.

In the meantime, extravagant parties pave her exit from Indianapolis. In February, she stages a fund-raiser for a struggling sixteen-year-old music student, Frances Spencer, said to be the only black harpist in Indianapolis. A number of local businesses donate goods and services, but the *Recorder* gives Madame all the credit: "The seemingly unlimited generosity of this woman was expressed by this great turn-out," which earned Spencer a $300 check—enough for a down payment on her own harp—even though her performance is described as a "trying event." The next week, she writes Madam Walker in care of the *Recorder.* "You have done more for me," the young girl declares, "than anyone, including my mother, and I a stranger." But relations grow quickly poisonous between the harpist and her patron when, hard on the heels of the concert, Spencer asks for more money. Then, according to Madame, she "came to my house and begged me for a home. . . . I told her that I had been so badly deceived in girls that I did not want to take her in." But when Spencer persists, she yields, only to find that after being treated as family and receiving a $6 weekly stipend for two months, the harpist "stole out everything which she had, including the harp."

Infuriated, embarrassed and hurt, Madame extracts her revenge publicly. "Now I want to say, and this," she declares to the *Chicago Defender,* "is final, that I am through helping so-called people. . . . There isn't a day that I am not besieged by people for help . . . and near as I could, I have tried to help them." But, she swears, "in the future all appeals will be turned down and consigned to the waste basket." This pronouncement, of course, doesn't last, but her experience with Anjetta and the harpist may have hardened her heart somewhat—enough, at any rate, that she is moved to categorize those two young women, and possibly others, as "so-called people." To help sustain her resolve, she places Ransom in charge of all "begging letters," even ones from her sister, Louvenia, whose son, Willie Powell, has been in a good bit of trouble with the law. Through Ransom's impressive efforts, Powell has been released on a manslaughter charge from Mississippi's infamous Parchman Prison, but when his mother asks that Willie be allowed to move to Indianapolis, Madame refuses to give her consent. "People know that he has been in prison," she sniffs, "and every step he makes will be watched. . . . The least thing he does will cast reflection on me." And after receiving yet another "sassy letter" from her sister, Madame blows up. "I do not care to have any more communication with her," she informs Ransom, because "it seems the more I do for my people they are harder to please and I am going to quit trying to please them." But two days later she's asking if Ransom knows anybody in New Jersey from whom she could buy one or two acres for Louvenia and Willie, so they could raise chickens and pigs and have a garden. (Since Louvenia's now well into her fifties and Willie his thirties, we might well wonder if they truly want to live together, much less raise pigs and a garden in New Jersey—a question that cannot be answered.)

Later that spring, when Monroe Trotter comes to town, Madame heralds a new, more politically engaged—and certainly more independent—period in her life by inviting the controversial editor to dine and, afterwards, to spend the night in her home. Trotter is conducting a lecture tour, advocating immediate manhood suffrage for African-Americans and lambasting the racial policies of Woodrow Wilson. As editor and publisher of the *Boston Guardian,* Trotter has relentlessly attacked Booker T. Washington, accusing him of promoting disfranchisement, peonage, submission, even lynching. His question "Is the rope and the torch all the race is to get under your leadership?" leaves little doubt as to his feelings.

Madame, on the other hand, has publicly avowed her solidarity with Washington—shoulder to shoulder in every way—and so we have to wonder why she would offer his sworn enemy such hospitality, perhaps even the same bed once occupied by the Wizard himself. Certainly her decision transcends commercial expedience, since it's more likely to hurt than help the Walker Company. My guess is that she's testing the powers of her own authority and convictions, which up to now have been secondary to strictly financial considerations. Now that she's received endorsements from the country's leading black organizations, she has some leeway and can start exploring various political options as a way of finding out what she herself believes. And so she takes the first steps toward engagement in the most serious campaign of her life and one which Trotter has been involved in for years: the anti-lynching crusade. Not that she switches allegiances. That same month, she stages an even more elaborate party in honor of Robert Russa Moton, who teaches at Washington's alma mater, Hampton Institute, and is destined soon to be named his successor at Tuskegee.

Within weeks of Trotter and Moton, two important women visit Indianapolis as well, one of whom—Mary McLeod Bethune, longtime NACW official and founder of the Daytona Normal and Industrial Institute for Negro Girls—receives Madame's warm welcome, in the form of a contribution to the school. But when her longtime rival shows up, Madame turns her back. Annie Turnbo, now married to former

Bible salesman E. Aaron Malone, comes in for front-page treatment and a great deal of praise in George Stewart's *Recorder,* which refers pointedly to her as someone who "gives and says nothing of it" and, unlike others, is "never heard to boast of what she has done." Modesty aside, Mrs. Malone does not hesitate to boast of her seven-passenger Packard, "one of the best cars made"—a photograph of which, closely resembling Madame's, is featured prominently—or in making the claim that she has "dignified the hairdressing business and influenced the establishment of all the noted hairdressing parlors for Negroes throughout the country." And perhaps Madame's temper rises to the boiling point when Malone asserts that most hairdressing-company proprietors received their first training from her and her sister.

More than likely, this article was written by Poro staffers; nonetheless, Madame takes its publication by a hometown paper as a personal insult and is still fuming some five months from now when she tells Ransom, "Now in regards to George Stewart and the Popes etc., I don't care a rap of my finger. I am no copy cat. They copy from me. I have naturally got the lead and there is nothing Stewart's paper can do for me. I bet they haven't 500 subscribers in the city of Indpls."

A few weeks later, she throws her second spring musicale, this one featuring shades of pink. Once again, Lelia attends, and afterwards they take the Cole on a motoring tour to Xenia, Wilberforce, Dayton, and Springfield. It's early June by the time they head to New York, arriving in time for Lelia's thirtieth birthday. That summer, Madame splurges on a Cadillac for Lelia, goes north again to speak at the New England Baptist Missionary convention, then makes the seven-hundred-mile trip back home.

She doesn't stay long. One trip demands another, and the next will be her biggest adventure yet: a five-month trip over the Rockies and across the Continental Divide, to Denver, Salt Lake City, Los Angeles, San Francisco, Seattle, Portland and Butte. In San Francisco she'll visit the Panama-Pacific Exposition, which celebrates the completion of the Panama Canal and the reconstruction of San Francisco after the earthquake. It was opened in February, when Woodrow Wilson signaled an aerial tower in New Jersey which relayed a wireless radio message across the country, to an antenna atop the 435-foot Tower of Jewels. Located at the entrance to the exposition, the tower is made up of fifty thousand pieces of glass, each one backed with a mirrored surface so that by day the light dazzles in the sun and by night sparkles in the glow of searchlights. There'll be Japanese and Samoan houses, pineapple juice, a battery-operated rocking chair, movies and the new synthetics Bakelite and cellophane.

In late June, the *Recorder* makes the announcement "Business Woman to Make Lengthy Far West Tour" and subheads it "Activities of Mme. C. J. Walker Noted Along Many Useful Lines." Alice Kelly will accompany her, to help conduct business as they go, but Madame likes to be up-to-date and this time she's giving illustrated lectures, accompanied by the showing of hand-tinted slides flashed onto a screen by means of a stereopticon projector. The photographs—of herself, her factory, her employees and products and some of the famous people she has met—will provide "ocular proof" of her accomplishments, as well as give other women hope that if she's come so far, so can they.

Meantime, the nation faces trouble from a number of directions. A month or so before Madame's set to take off, the pleasure ship *Lusitania* is torpedoed by a German submarine, and 124 Americans are among the 1,200 who drown. When war starts to seem inevitable, William Jennings Bryan resigns as secretary of state, feeling little a part of what he sees as the country's mood. And bored, party-less Teddy Roosevelt abandons his Progressive ideals, re-ups with the Republicans, and—remembering his own days on the front—rails at Wilson about the country's lack of preparedness. Henry Ford disagrees. Preparing for war, he says, is "like a man carrying a gun. Men and nations who carry guns get into trouble." And he sends a peace ship to Europe to get the boys out of the trenches by Christmas, with Bryan serving as his ambassador and seeing the ship off.

Taking advantage of local strikes and political unrest, the U.S. Marines land in Haiti once again, where they remain for nine years, turning the Negro republic run by Negroes into a U.S. protectorate. Some people think federal troops should concentrate instead on the domestic front. In Atlanta, after Jewish factory manager Leo Frank is railroaded into a rape and murder charge, found guilty and sentenced to die, the *New York Times* accuses a black witness of withholding evidence to save his own skin. When Frank's death sentence is overturned, a lynch mob drags him from the jail, hangs him and mutilates his body. A month later, D. W. Griffith's *Birth of a Nation* opens in that same city, after premiering in Los Angeles and Boston. Since word of the film's white-supremacist message precedes the Atlanta premiere, by opening night circuit-riding preacher William Simmons has appointed himself Imperial Wizard of the revived Knights of the Ku Klux Klan and, promising to further white supremacy, patriotism and Liberty bonds, orders the new Klan to come out in full bedsheet regalia, to ride horses up and down Peachtree Street while firing rifle salutes. Afterwards, some Klansmen scale Stone Mountain, an eighteen-hundred-foot escarpment east of Atlanta, to burn a cross that can be seen from any place in the city.

Having spent two years in Paris, reportedly having romances with the likes of Mata Hari and Moulin Rouge star Mistinguett, Jack Johnson comes back to take on Jess Willard, a six-foot-six white Kansas farm boy, in a forty-five-round championship fight. Because of his Mann Act conviction, he can't enter the U.S., and so the fight takes place outdoors in 103-degree heat in Havana, Cuba. The out-of-shape Johnson nonetheless dominates the first twenty rounds of the fight, but in the twenty-sixth, Willard finally knocks him out. Five years from now, he'll return home to serve out his prison sentence at Leavenworth for a crime he didn't commit, and he will later claim he threw the fight—and perhaps he did. There won't be another black heavyweight champion until Joe Louis, in 1937.

Having sent a representative to Waco, Texas, to investigate the burning alive of a Negro, the NAACP, under DuBois's direction, prepares to publish its detailed findings—including gruesome photographs of the charred body—in the *Crisis*. And in Indianapolis, Ransom files a suit in Madame's name against the Central Amusement Company for raising the price of a movie ticket from a dime to a quarter because of her race.

In July, she writes Booker T. Washington asking for letters of introduction to people of influence in California, Oregon and Washington. Apparently the Wizard comes through, since soon afterwards she sends a check to Tuskegee for $250. And then she and Alice Kelly set off, making their first stop in St. Louis. By August they will have reached the country's far edge and there lay eyes on the ocean of America's imagination, the great Pacific, which the man who owned her parents hoped to get to, traveling on the railroad line that crossed the Mississippi at Delta within walking distance of his plantation. Burney didn't make it to the Pacific, but the daughter of two of his slaves will, and in very grand style indeed.

Her World Opens Up Yet Again

For many of us, travel invigorates the imagination, and this seems to be the case for Madame, who—from someplace out west—informs Ransom of a plan to appoint a few capable women as special agents, who will travel on her behalf to promote her products, not as commissioned saleswomen or franchised agents but as salaried employees, hired at $100 a month, with an additional 10 or 20 percent bonus for all business over $100. Their job will be to "introduce, advertise and create new markets for the Madam C. J. Walker Hair Preparations; to travel . . . from place to place, teaching the art of hair culture and . . . to advertise and represent the business and goods of Madame C. J. Walker." And while she's considering allowing them some say in the territory they'll cover, they should concentrate on the important South and Midwest, where they, too, will present illustrated lectures using a stereopticon projector, provided by the company. This is a new concept for a woman who resists delegating the least shred of authority or autonomy.

Somewhere en route, she also decides to rework her pamphlets to emphasize women's potential for independence and underline her position as America's foremost businesswoman of the race. From late summer of that year until her death, between ten thousand and twenty thousand of these will be published and distributed every month. Most impressively, in early November, she wires home a deposit of $10,000, presumably from sales made during the trip. When Ransom congratulates her on this noteworthy achievement, Madame agrees that indeed, the increase in her bank account is almost as remarkable as her expenditures—which she's hoping will prove justified once the returns are in.

While she's in Montana—possibly in Butte, where there is a sizable middle-class black population—Booker T. Washington is hospitalized in New York, after a serious illness. For three weeks the family has managed to keep the news private, but on November 10 word gets out that the Wizard has suffered a nervous breakdown and is confined to bed. Obviously there's more to his condition than nerves, but no concrete information is offered until a Dr. Walter Bastedo breaks the customary doctor-patient rule of confidentiality and reports that "racial characteristics" may be in part responsible for Dr. Washington's decline—a phrase often used among medical professionals to indicate a "syphilitic history." Nothing is proven and no facts are offered, but by the time Bastedo retreats from his statement, the news has spread across the country like a grass fire.

On November 12, when Washington is given only a few days to live, he insists on being taken to Tuskegee, even though doctors doubt he will survive the journey. "I was born in the South," he explains. "I have lived and labored in the South, and I expect to die and be buried in the South." And he pulls himself up from his deathbed and manages to get to Penn Station, spurning a wheelchair, boarding the train while leaning on the arms of his wife and two doctors. He reportedly survives the train trip to Tuskegee, but dies at about five the next morning, in his own bed.

On November 15, at 9:45 a.m., Madame goes to the Garrison, Montana, railroad station and wires Margaret Murray Washington her most sincere regrets of the untimely passing of "the greatest man America ever knew," concluding that "we as a race feel that in him we have lost the truest friend the race ever had. I mourn with you your great loss. Yours in deepest sorrow. Madam C. J. Walker." She also wires Ransom to send a large floral arrangement "of exquisite . . . design," made in the shape of a cross, beneath which should be a wreath encircling a photograph of Washington, and under that the inscription "Thou who so bravely bore our cross, Thy place can ne'er be filled." And she requests that he go to the funeral as her representative.

On the day Booker T. Washington is buried, school flags in D.C. fly at half-mast by order of the board of education, Teddy Roosevelt mourns the loss of this "useful citizen," the Montana *Missoulian* headlines its front-page story, "Noted Negro Succumbs to Illness." For black people of that time, the effect of his death can only be compared to the passing of royalty. As Madame will later say, he was one of those people nobody thinks will ever die.

Sometime during the trip, Alice Kelly seems to have been replaced by Mae Robinson, who feeds the lantern slides into the stereopticon projector and, according to Walker stories, helps Madame train agents, even though she's still only sixteen years old. Madame sends home reports of huge audiences, thunderous applause, grand receptions and the red-carpet treatment wherever she goes. After postponing her return several times, she finally arrives back in Indianapolis some four months, eight thousand miles and fifteen states after her departure.

In no time, she's at her desk dictating a letter to Emmett Scott at Tuskegee, inquiring after Margaret Washington's health and wondering why the widow has not replied to her letter of condolence. On December 17, Scott writes back, perhaps a little tartly, that Mrs. Washington appreciates Mrs. Walker's kind inquiry, is bearing up under her sorrow, and will try to write soon, but that thus far so much has demanded her attention that it's been impossible for her. And he ends the letter by testily reminding her that "of course I have already told you how much we appreciate the beautiful floral design."

On January 17, 1916, Madame presents a travelogue at Tomlinson Hall to benefit the Alpha House, a residential home for aged women, and show her Indianapolis friends where she's been. "Travelogue! Travelogue!" the *Freeman* reports. "Everybody's talking travelogue." The evening begins with a recitation of Paul Laurence Dunbar poems by his aging mother, followed by songs from the baritone Louis Depp and an elocutionist's recitation of "Hagar's Farewell." Lastly, after an introduction by Dr. Ward, Madame gives a "splendid speech," then moves into the meat of the evening's entertainment and shows slides of "Pike's Peak, Palmer's Lake, Colorado Springs, the geysers, the Royal Gorge, Collegiate Range, Mount of the Holy Cross, canyons, Ananas Cave, Minerva Terrace, Jupiter Terrace, Paint Pots, Morning Glory Geyser, palm drives, giant cactus, pepper trees, Old Mission bells, Tent City at Coronado, Old Cave, La Jolla, San Diego, U.S. Grant Jr.'s home, glass bottom boat, seals, flying fish, divers, a Japanese bungalow, high school and stadium, Tacoma, Washington, Mt. Rainier, Chimes University, Seattle, the Devil's Teapot, Butte, Montana . . . and many more places. . . ."

Afterwards, Madame hosts a dinner party for her out-of-town guests, including her old friend from Louisville Dr. Parrish (now moderator of the Kentucky Baptist Convention), Louisville journalist and educator Lavinia Sneed and, according to the *Freeman,* "E. K. Jones of New York, representing the society for the advancement of the colored people." (Presumably, this is Eugene Kinckle Jones, who actually works for the National Urban League and who will serve as an honorary pallbearer at Madame's funeral.) Conversation centers around Jones, "fresh from the vicinity of DuBois," with the occasional nod of respect and praise in the direction of the late Dr. Washington. Madame no doubt oversees this discussion and from time to time steadies its direction, but the inclusion of a DuBois supporter is worth noting. The next week, Will Lewis of the *Freeman* reports that all in attendance agreed that they had benefited from the informal "conference." After dinner, coffee is served in the drawing room, the young baritone sings again and short talks are made by a few of the guests, mostly in tribute to Madame, who then responds with "that grace and dignity, yet modesty, that have characterized her since known in this city." And perhaps Jones discusses the NAACP investigation of the Waco lynching, while others speak of the war in Europe. Whatever the conversation, by 10:45 everyone has left except the three out-of-town guests. And at 640 North West Street, E. K. Jones retires to one guest bedroom, Lavinia Sneed to another, Reverend Parrish to the third. And Madame closes the door to the master bedroom of her private, rose-colored world, which no longer is her real home.

A week later, Lelia invites a reported ten thousand people of "fashion, wealth and the elect" to the grand opening of her opulent beauty parlor and the "monster establishment," Lelia College. In an article marked "Special to the *Chicago Defender,*" the occasion is described as one that has "set the city agog." This is, of course, company propaganda, but editor Robert Abbott runs it without cuts or comment. Entitled "Mme Robinson Follows Famous Mother: Reared and Educated in St. Louis—Showed Aptitude for Business Ability in Early Youth—Now a Distinguished Woman of the Race, Superior Training," the article declares the joined town houses at 108–110 West 136th Street to be owned by Madam Robinson. As we know, Lelia McWilliams Robinson never showed any aptitude for either school or business and owns neither the town houses nor any other real estate, but since nobody's checking facts, the hype rolls on to describe the opening as an event "signalized" in a blaze of glory and the beauty parlor as one of the most completely furnished anywhere in the East, an establishment where Madam Robinson can "teach young race women the finer points of the lucrative business in which her mother has been so long engaged and from which she has accumulated more wealth than any other race woman in America."

While Lelia's sending out invitations and setting the city agog, New York builder Gust Ericsson's preparing a past-due bill for $4,520.68, verified by architect Vertner Tandy, for work on the town houses. While Ericsson doesn't want to cause any unpleasantness—the work was finished in time for the opening—even though the party's in progress, he and several subcontractors have yet to be paid, a situation that hardly seems fair. The fact is, in his words, "the building has cost more than she [Lelia] estimated for" and now that the grand opening's scheduled and the invitations sent, "she, of course, is looking to her mother to help her out." And when, some time ago, Ericsson proposed that Lelia raise the money by notes, he discovered she couldn't do that on her own, since all the property's in her mother's name. Six weeks from now, when Madame herself arrives, none of these bills will yet have been paid.

But no cloud darkens the sky over 108–110 West 136th Street. Lelia herself, resplendent in a Paris frock which matches the soft gray-and-blue interior of the parlor, conducts a tour of the premises, and the article reports what a joy it is to be led so entertainingly by the woman "whose business genius is responsible for this immense venture," this "monument to a great woman's achievement by the great woman herself . . . the greatest achievement of the race for the employment of women and girls. . . ." The conclusion, however, pays tribute to the founder of the company, describing her as a female prodigy and the foremost businesswoman of the race. And though the article focuses on Lelia, it is Madame's new photo that accompanies it.

An alumnus of Tuskegee and the first black graduate of the architecture school at Cornell, Vertner Tandy oversaw the transformation of the two town houses into one, and while some have criticized the proportions, from the outside they appear as if never having been anything else. Between the two entrances leading to the ground and basement floors, he's installed five French windows in the curved, marble-trimmed facade, with the one in the middle as a kind of hinge. The Walker crest embedded in the brick between the third-floor windows further integrates the two buildings. Potted boxwoods flank the double doors at 110, and the carriage-type lamp hanging over them indicates this is a business address, open to the public. The glass-doored private entrance at 108 is less adorned and opens directly to stairs leading to Lelia's home—and Madame's bedroom—on the third floor.

After all the bickering about the cost, when Madame finally inspects the town house in late February, her description borders on the ecstatic. "It is just impossible for me to describe it to you," she writes Ransom. The salon "beats anything I have seen anywhere, even in the best hair parlors of the whites." And she quotes the decorators who worked on it as declaring that "of all the work they had done here in that line there is nothing equal to it, not even on Fifth Avenue," where Helena Rubinstein and Elizabeth Arden conduct their salons.

Since the San Francisco fair, wicker's become fashionable, and Lelia's installed a lot of it, giving the parlor a curvy lightness nowhere to be seen in the dark, squared-away furnishings of the Indianapolis facility. There are delicate gray French wicker chairs, wicker tables and floor lamps, along with curtained booths, electric driers, foot rests, long windows looking out on the backyard, pale silk swag shades to lower over the five windows across the front. In the waiting room, tea is served from a silver urn to customers lolling on a Hollywood banquette. Some may wish instead to retire to the tea room, where there is a wicker table at which to sit and leaf through the latest magazines and scandal sheets. Lelia Robinson—said to have received telegrams and letters of congratulation from all over the country—is described as being of such pleasant temperament as to be considered the "most affable and courteous among race women anywhere."

The article closes by noting that Madam Walker will be giving lectures in Chicago during February on "The Negro Woman in Business" and that the lectures will be accompanied by stereopticon views showing the wonderful progress she has made in ten years' time, then issues a reminder that Madame is in demand as a speaker nationwide and that every ambitious man, woman and child in Chicago ought to avail themselves of the opportunity to see her. After all, as the *Colored American Review* (a publication she will soon own) will assert later this year, "To honor Madam Walker is to honor one's self."

Two weeks later, to reassure the people of Indianapolis that she has not forgotten the cordial welcome they extended to her in 1911, Madame announces her plans to visit them once or twice a year. A number of photographs accompany an article the company runs in the February 12 *Freeman:* the Scurlock; an oval cut of Alice Kelly, high-minded but not unpleasant in a stern high-necked blouse; a shot of perky Violet Davis in profile and another of the very formidable book-keeper Lucy Flint, whose chin looks permanently raised from wearing stiff high collars, her large eyes magnified by a lorgnette pinched fiercely on the bridge of her nose. The item rhapsodizes about the beneficence and sweet impulses of this "big-hearted, race-loving woman," her charitable nature, her willingness to give paroled con-victs a start in life, the resplendence of her entertainments, her amiable disposition and rare business tact, the lofty status of her business as "not only a credit to her and her race, but a monument to Negro thrift and industry throughout America . . . the largest of its kind in the world. . . ."

In all, this story reprises much of the travelogue and dinner party, but with one surprise. Having already banished wine and strong drink from her home, henceforth for fear of being "misunderstood" Madame has decided to use her influence directly or indirectly against "dancing and other questionable amusements." The statement is vague enough to protect her from future reproach, and I wonder if it didn't emerge from the description of her as a dancing fool at last year's musicale. Maybe she received letters of protest from her large Baptist clientele; on the other hand, these avowals quickly vanish from her repertoire and presumably don't apply in Harlem, where dancing and questionable amusements all but define the nightlife.

And as for the paroled convict given a new start in life, surely this is her nephew, Willie Powell, whose plight first provoked more annoy-ance than charity.

Now, obviously the Walker Company is not the only African-American (or white) business turning out press releases they expect newspapers to run as news. Many others do the same thing, in exchange for advertisements, which gives Madame not only a particu-larly wide selection of venues, but also a good bit of leverage over smaller cosmetics companies, since she runs ads in most big papers around the country. Ransom regularly receives letters confirming the papers' compliance, saying they are "pleased to run the notice of the Mme C. J. Walker meeting . . . free of charge as you have asked, inasmuch as she is an advertiser in our paper" and that they "expect to run the complimentary write-up of the Madam Walker villa in our Christmas number. . . ." And if some editors complain about "created news," in the end Ransom gets what Madame wants by reminding them how much the company spent last year on advertising and how much it has presently budgeted for this year.

In the very next issue, when Madame's hardly unpacked her suitcases in New York, "Mr. and Mrs. E. Aaron (Poro) Malone" appear in the *Freeman*'s front-page story about the recently completed YMCA fund-raising campaign in St. Louis, to which Julius Rosenwald pledged his usual $25,000 and the board of directors of the (white) St. Louis Y, $75,000. Exceeding their $50,000 goal, the African-American community contributed $69,060, and the biggest donors were Annie and Aaron Malone, who "established a world record among Negroes" by giving a whopping $5,000. In gratitude, the Malones—who are always pictured together, as exemplars of marriage and family life—have been presented with a loving cup and a note congratulating them for setting a new high mark of giving on the part of colored people.

The rivalry continues.

Margaret Joyner and "Our Hair"

To get an impression of Madame's training sessions, we turn to the many magazine and newspaper interviews conducted with Margaret Stewart Joyner, an energetic and affable Chicagoan and fifty-seven-year Walker employee. In 1916, the recently married Joyner decided that since her husband, Robert, was busily engaged in his podiatry textbooks, she should learn a trade as well. After she enrolled in the A. B. Molar Beauty School and became its first black graduate, she opened a beauty shop on South State Street in a mixed neighborhood. Because she was particularly adept at using a French iron to create a marcel wave—the broad, flat, ribbony crimp that originated in France and later was made famous in the 1920s by Josephine Baker—she attracted a large clientele, all of them white.

Liking the marcel, one day her mother-in-law asked for the same hairstyle. Joyner describes the results: "She looked like an accident going somewhere to happen. She said, 'You can't do anything with my hair [but] there is a woman coming to town. . . . I am going to give you money to go down to her class; she is teaching how to do black hair.' " (Nettie Johnson, who ran her own beauty shop in Indianapolis from 1906 until 1946, faced the same situation: "I had a white shop. Everybody who was anybody came to my shop." But she couldn't take care of her own hair until Madam Walker came to town and "taught us how.")

And so Margaret Joyner paid $17.50 to take a class Madame herself was teaching—"a workshop on how to wash and straighten hair with a hot comb"—while she trained women to be agents. "You know, how to sell her hair products. She had her own shampoo, soap, and a hair preparation that helped hair grow."

Joyner says Madame was a fantastic teacher and could show you "inside a couple of days how to straighten hair. She showed me the proper way to wash black hair and then how to straighten it." Once she had the knack of pressing hair, Joyner showed the class how to put in a marcel. And when Madame saw how well she did it, she asked Joyner to join the organization and travel with her, but Joyner—because she'd just gotten married—declined. Madame kept after her, and after working for a while as a Walker agent in Chicago, she eventually gave up and went on the road, holding seminars in different cities. When asked what it was like to travel with Madame, she answers succinctly: "a lot of hard work." Then she becomes more reflective. "It just looked like she and I dovetailed things together so well. I guess it was fate that I happened to meet her at all. She was a great lady, she was." Eventually Margaret Joyner invented a number of hair products, became the national supervisor of Walker schools and was made a vice president of the company.

While in Chicago, Madame checks on her branch offices and conducts the setup classes Joyner describes, advising hopeful women how to conquer their doubts and be more than they ever dreamed of while reiterating the Tuskegee philosophy of hygienic necessity. If her agents expect to be successful, they'll need to wear freshly starched clothes and be sure their own hair is fixed and clean, their teeth brushed. And if they can't afford to open a real beauty shop and have to do hair in their kitchens, they need to come down fully *dressed,* not in night clothes and a wrap-around. They have to smell nice, look nice, present themselves *as if* they had expertise and confidence, and after a while they will.

The setup course lasts anywhere from one to three days, depending on how long a student can afford to stay. Graduates leave with a certificate, a hot comb and a bag of preparations, after signing a contract saying they will use Walker products exclusively and will purchase supplies only from the main office in Indianapolis.

Although there is no mechanism in place to check out applicants' claims, the Walker Company requires agents to have an eighth-grade education, so they can understand the instruction manual well enough to explain hair structure to customers and why pullers flatten the hair unnaturally while the curved hot comb conforms to its natural shape and straightens hair without doing damage. The company also hopes that if agents represent the Walker Company with dignity, they will then convince other women to enroll and, by receiving a commission of a little more than 10 percent of the $17.50 setup fee, rise to the third level of the multilayered market strategy.

For the women who sign up, these figures seem almost magical, since in 1916 the great majority of African-American women still do domestic work for around $1.50 a day, maybe $2. Washing a tubful of clothes pays fifty cents. As one grateful agent writes Madame, "You have opened up a trade for hundreds of colored women to make an honest and profitable living where they make as much in one week as a month's salary would bring from any other position that a colored woman can secure."

And to her critics, Margaret Joyner explains, "Her method was to beautify, not make somebody look white."

By 1917, a year from now, Madame will have achieved one of her chief goals by forming a national organization of her agents. They'll hold their first convention in Philadelphia, and by then she'll have incorporated her setup instructions into a formal, oft-quoted and very forceful policy statement:

HINTS TO AGENTS

Madam Walker is very desirous for all of her agents to make good, hence these hints to agents.

1. Keep yourself clean as well as your parlor or room in which you do your work. The room should be cleaned thoroughly before beginning your work every morning. Open your windows—Air it well—When the room is not in use even in winter, throw up the windows, it will drive out germs.

2. Keep a waste basket in your parlor and after each customer clean up the hair and matches from the floor. [Sometimes the ends of hair were burned to seal them off and prevent splitting.]

3. Cleanse and sterilize comb and sponge after each customer. It would be well to keep such things on hand that each customer might purchase his own.

4. Ten cents worth of Oxide of zinc in a little bag will keep away odors from the body if applied lightly to the parts affected or

dust with it once a day. It would be well to make several little bags of it and keep it on hand to sell to customers.

5. Keep your teeth clean in order that the breath might be sweet. Five cents of mints will last a week. Put one in the mouth before beginning a customer. If her breath is offensive, offer her one.

6. See that your fingernails are kept clean, as that is a mark of refinement.

7. See that your hair always looks well in order to interest others you must first make the impression by keeping your hair in first class condition.

8. Do not use two combs as there is danger in getting them too hot. Combs should not be used hot enough to do a deal of smoking.

9. Do not use pullers, the hair is round, they pull and flatten it out which closes the glands which prevents nourishment and will finally cause it to become very thin.

10. Do not be narrow and selfish to the extent that you would not sell goods to anybody because they do not take the treatment from you. We are anxious to help all humanity, the poor as well as the rich, especially those of our race. There are thousands who would buy and use the goods who are not able to pay the extra cost of having it done for them. The hair may not grow as rapidly nor look as beautiful, but they will get results, as long as they are satisfied and you have made your profit from the sale, all is well.

11. Always keep a full supply of Walker Preparations on hand and individuals will have no need to go to the drug store or write this office. We will be compelled to fill out all orders unless you are prepared to supply them.

Then comes an announcement: "Because of so much adulteration, after August 1917 all boxes will be sealed with a specially designed Walker Seal or Trade Mark. Accept no goods without the seal, or if the seal is broken. After August we will give 50¢ per hundred for all boxes returned from agents or customers."

Sometime during the next year she will tack on another addendum:

We are pleased to know that you have decided to become one of our agents. Under a separate cover we are sending you literature and facts with reference to the MADAM C. J. WALKER'S WON-DERFUL PREPARATION, and while you will distribute these among your prospective customers, we cannot too strongly urge that you make yourself familiar and master of the facts therein contained, keeping ever in mind THAT YOU CAN NOT HOPE TO IMPRESS OTHERS, WHEN YOU YOURSELF ARE UNFAMILIAR WITH THE ESSENTIAL FACTS ABOUT THIS WONDERFUL PREPARATION.

Acquaint yourself with the history and life of Madam C. J. Walker, get on the very tip of your tongue the strong points that you will find in the story of her personal experience, tell your prospective customer about her, do so in an intelligent and emphatic way, watch his or her face, note what statement or state-ments impress most, AND THEN DRIVE THE NAIL HOME. You will do well to learn to place the proper estimate upon the value of your time. Make Every Moment count; when you make a call remember that you are there to MAKE A SALE, and ALSO A CUSTOMER FOR THE COMPANY; for every customer you send in will bring you that much nearer to a permanent salary over and above your commission. Keep in mind that you have something that the person standing before you really needs, imagine yourself a missionary and convert him. Be tactful, if you find that one line of talk won't work, try another, ALWAYS REMEMBERING THAT, *YOU ARE THERE TO SELL.*

The above is intended as a guide to you, only in districts where the people have not heard of Madam C. J. Walker's wonderful Preparation, for as a general rule you will find every one anxious to buy, this is, and has been the experience of all of our agents. All you have to do is get around among the people, in other words be a mixer, properly distributing your literature, and you will be able to place orders faster than we can possibly supply them. From what we have learned of you we take it that you are a HUSTLER. If, however, you are asleep, or a dreamer, in all kindness we advise that you not take the agency; on the other hand you have a for-tune in your grasp if you only wake up and WORK.

And finally, don't doubt your own ability, remember that scores of others are doing this same work and are making big money out of it. Don't fail to act fairly with the company, keep in mind that you are working for a corporation that TAKES A KINDLY, YES, PERSONAL interest in its agents. We stand ever ready to help you, don't hesitate about asking advice. Make all remittance promptly, never grow careless with the company's money. We can deal harshly if called upon to do so, and while you can, and no doubt will, easily make from three to five dollars a day, remember that the company stands ready and will pay you a salary in addition to your commission as soon as you prove worthy of such salary. KEEP EVER IN TOUCH WITH THE COMPANY, send weekly reports of goods sold, territory covered, etc. These REPORTS MUST BE IN AND RECEIVE THE COMPANY'S OK before any attention will be given new orders. Hoping to receive your order within a few days.

We are, Yours for Success,
THE WALKER MANUFACTURING COMPANY.
Dictated by Madam C. J. Walker.

Madame will stay in Chicago for two weeks before traveling to Pittsburgh and then New York, where she will remain until April, when she sets off on a tour that takes her from Harlem to Salisbury, North Carolina, and from there to Tuskegee, Montgomery, Atlanta, Nashville, Pittsburgh, Philadelphia and back to Harlem. After a brief rest, she'll motor up to New Haven and Boston, then come back to New York before heading South again. Among the cities she'll visit on this trip are Lexington, Kentucky; Atlanta, Macon, Savannah, Washington and Augusta, Georgia; Birmingham, Alabama; Greenwood, Clarksdale, Jackson, Meridian and Vicksburg, Mississippi; Memphis, Tennessee; and most importantly, her birthplace, Delta, Louisiana.

This punishing schedule—coming on top of the four-month western trip—will land her, unsurprisingly, in a Hot Springs, Arkansas, hospital and health spa, where she'll take heat treatments and then defy doctors' orders by checking out early in order to hit the road once again. From there, she continues her last Southern tour, making Louisiana stops in New Orleans, Baton Rouge and Bogalusa before crossing into Texas to call on Temple, Austin, San Marcos, Seguin, San Antonio, Houston, Beaumont and Orange, then circling back to towns in Tennessee, Kentucky, Indiana, North and South Carolina . . . the list goes on and on. Why can't she stop? Or even slow down?

She doesn't because she can't. Either she feels an icy presence dogging her footsteps and is trying to outrun it or else she has willed herself to ignore the obvious. During her last days, a minister will testify to her long-standing premonition of an early death. Haunted by that, maybe she's afraid that if she stops, she'll die. In any case, instead of slowing down, she goes harder and faster than before. As a result, 1916 will take a healthy chunk out of her stamina, her health and her life.

VII · *Harlem, 1916–1918*

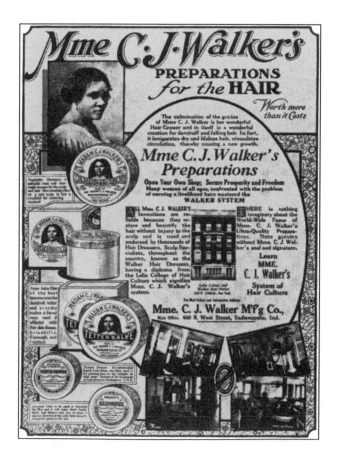

From Delta to the Dream

She's there. Harlem's not home, but the Hudson's her last river and it flows nearby, on the other side of Broadway, the very street that will soon provide her final address. This is not to suggest that she is preparing for her last days, only that a natural readiness seems to have settled in. In Lelia's home, she receives guests, gives interviews, plays music on the phonograph, rests in her mahogany bed. Maybe she reflects on all the times she's moved and how much easier it was to sit on that steamboat going up the Mississippi, with only a baby and some boxes to transport. Or to ride the *Geisse* from Delta to Vicksburg with practically nothing. Now, she has books, precious china, silver, furniture she loves . . . *stuff.* When a writer for the *Kansas City Star* comes for an interview, she describes Madame entering the 136th Street drawing room, carrying her "generous weight" gracefully on high French heels as she floats into the room in "an expensive pink-flowered lavender silk dressing-gown." It's a weekday morning, and Madame shows up for the talk late because she's been resting, but she greets the journalist with a "lack of self-consciousness few of us know when we get on our Sunday clothes." When the *Literary Digest* reprints this article, it depicts Madame as the "Queen of Gotham's Colored Four Hundred."

There's time for only the briefest break in her schedule before she receives a personal, undoubtedly embarrassing visit from Gust Ericsson about Lelia's overdue remodeling bills, which Madame requests that he send to Ransom, who will expedite the matter. Ransom, of course, will vent his displeasure, then send the check. For him, this is nothing new. During 1915, Madame often wrote from the road, asking him either to send money to Lelia—as much as three or four thousand dollars at a clip—or to make sure her balance was sufficient to cover a check she'd already written.

Indianapolis is behind her. The *New York News* runs an editorial entitled "Welcome to Madame Walker," a woman who "has risen to command the respect of tens of thousands of both races." And when a reporter from the *Age* comes for an interview, Madame reports that she now has ten thousand agents in the field—two hundred in New York alone—some making as much as five hundred dollars a month. And while others admittedly might not do that well, "all of them are earning a good living." But when asked about her own financial worth, she hesitates. "Well," she finally replies, "until recently it gave me great pleasure to tell in my lectures the amount of money I made yearly, thinking it would inspire my hearers. But I found that for so doing some looked upon me as a boastful person who wanted to 'blow my own horn.' And then again, I received so many requests for money. . . ." Then she backslides, disclosing the fact that her annual income last year ran into six figures, a record she'll do her dead level best to eclipse in 1916, leading readers to assume she's looking toward the magic seven.

Finally, when asked to supply the secret of her success, Madame smiles significantly. "I first want to say that I did not succeed by traversing a path strewn with roses. I made great sacrifices, met with rebuff after rebuff, and had to fight hard to put my ideas into effect." C. J. comes in for a rebuke, with no credit this time for the "push" he'd given her. "Why, when I started in business a little over ten years ago with my husband I had business disagreements with him, for when we began to make $10 a day he thought that amount was enough and I should be satisfied." When the two of them "found it impossible to agree," she asserts, "due to his narrowness of vision, I embarked in business for myself."

This story—as she has reminded us from her first public appearance—is hers alone.

By late March or early April, when preparing to depart, Madame begins addressing the likelihood she foresaw that her business, as it is currently structured and focused, might someday fail due to the level of competition. She schedules part of her upcoming Southern tour around a new idea: to install her system within the curriculum of African-American colleges, especially schools concentrating on industrial and vocational education. The company will provide the instructor—a trained, licensed agent to live on campus and teach the system free of charge. Students will learn the trade by giving treatments to local women, who pay a reduced rate, with profits split fifty-fifty between the instructor and the college. If, however, the agent opens her own franchised shop in town—which she is free to do—she can charge full price and keep the entire amount for herself. To sweeten the pot, Madame offers a $100 donation toward construction of a classroom, with an additional scholarship fund of $500 for a deserving student chosen by the college. The final stipulation is that all preparations be purchased directly from the Walker Company *at full price.* Everybody gains: the college, the students, the agent and—with a minimal outlay of cash up front—the Walker Company.

In time, many schools will latch on to this idea, but the only one she really wants, Tuskegee, will hew to the Wizard's line and decline the opportunity. Undaunted, later in the year she'll take an even bolder step and ask Ransom to write the new president, Robert Russa Moton, to suggest that she be appointed to the school's all-male board of trustees, replacing Seth Low—former Columbia University president and mayor of New York—whose death has created the vacancy. But despite the lavish dinner party she threw in his honor and her $300 contribution to the school, Moton regrets that the custom of Tuskegee is to maintain the board's balance: in other words, to fill the place of one powerful, wealthy white man with another.

Another of her new ideas comes from Louis George, a friend of Lelia's and a C. J.-like figure who works freelance in advertising and marketing. George thinks Madame should buy a women's magazine and use it to push her products. Courtesy of S. A. Singerman, he even knows of one that's for sale. This transaction doesn't pan out, but Madame is attracted to the idea of having a magazine as a mouthpiece, and "as you know," she writes Ransom, "the way with most Negro magazines is you are never able to depend on them for they haven't sufficient capital behind them to keep it before the public until it begins making money. I thought should I take it on I would set up a printing establishment which would not only be able to get out the magazine but would do a great deal of job printing and all of my own literature which amounts to several thousand dollars per year." Ransom, naturally, is skeptical—especially about Louis George—and she's too busy to research the possibility on her own, and so for the moment it fades.

Before leaving New York, she kicks off yet one more initiative by calling a meeting of local agents to form the Mme. C. J. Walker Agents'

Benevolent Association, which she hopes will grow into a national organization made up of local chapters from any town with five agents or more. Her plan is to conduct contests among the agents and give prizes for state organizations with the most new members, the highest sales figures and the biggest charitable donations. By encouraging cooperative action, she hopes women will teach one another new hairdressing methods, work together to increase sales and learn the practical value of philanthropy. She has been involved in such collective activities at least since St. Louis, possibly even Vicksburg, and she'd like to put that experience to work on as many levels as possible. More than a hundred women attend the inaugural session and, in their first act, pledge $100 to the Booker T. Washington Memorial Fund, of which $28 is raised that evening. For Madame, the benevolent association represents a kind of amalgamation of the two national organizations she regards most highly: the NNBL, with its emphasis on business and profit, and the NACW, which focuses more on social and political issues. Within the framework of the association, she also returns to the idea of hiring a few special agents as salaried employees to travel in her stead, giving illustrated lectures and recruiting others, and now she's upped the pay scale to a generous $125 per month.

Then off she goes, to Montgomery, Birmingham and Normal, Alabama; to Atlanta; to Nashville's Roger Williams University, where she receives a standing ovation; to Louisville, where she speaks at the general conference of the AME Zion Church; then to Pittsburgh and Philadelphia, before returning to Louisville to help the AME church with fund-raising for its Bureau on Temperance.

From Philadelphia, her new driver, young Lewis Tyler—whose name she consistently spells "Louis," even though he signs it the other way—drives her into New England. Her first stop is in New Haven, where the "elite of Afro-American society exert[s] itself" to honor her. Mae's along, operating the projector, and will travel with her through Connecticut and into the South. The two are royally entertained with dinner parties and luncheons, a musicale and several driving tours into the surrounding countryside. Madame visits Yale and meets the mayor, goes to the theater and attends many church services and another tea. After a short trip to Bridgeport, the trio motor west into the Housatonic River Valley, and Madame makes quick stops in Ansonia, Shelton, Derby and Waterbury, making regular appeals for contributions to the Washington Memorial Fund. Subsequent stops include Boston, New London and Springfield.

While Madame's on the road, Ransom's at home dealing with real estate. Vertner Tandy—whom Madame has hired to design her new home—reports that "Bishop's Court is not as desirable a site as it might be for the home that Madame wants to have," since he has learned that a tenement building will be erected in front of the house and, further, that once the city divides the various boroughs into manufacturing, business and residential zones, Bishop's Court will be on a borderline between business and residential. John Nail—one of the realtors who pulled off the St. Philip's Episcopal–Pennsylvania Station deal in Harlem—has been engaged to replace Philip Payton, and he agrees with Tandy, adding a few more discouraging details: to the west of Madame's property are tenements occupied by "the most ordinary Irish people," and to the east an empty lot where the police store motorcycles, and a railyard. The neighborhood has been in its present condition for twenty years, Nail concludes, and probably will only get worse.

Living in Bishop's Court is, in other words, unthinkable, and both men strongly suggest that an effort be made to work out a property exchange that would prove beneficial to all. It's up to Ransom to convince Madame to do this—because when Tandy last spoke to her, she refused to budge—which, somehow, he manages. Then, with Nail and Singerman, he works out a private deal with the sellers, probably involving property and money, and unloads the Flushing house. And by August 31, only three months later, John Nail's come up with an alternative piece of property straight up Broadway: four and a half glorious, sloping acres in Irvington-on-Hudson, overlooking the river, only nineteen miles from Manhattan. Instead of tenements and parking lots there are palatial homes and formal gardens, lawn tennis and croquet, evenings spent looking across the river at sunsets over the magnificent Palisades. Her home will be built in a world of wealth, among the richest men in the country.

Irvington's practically on Madame's route from New Haven, and perhaps she, Mae and Lewis Tyler make a quiet stop there. If they do, it's without fanfare, since there's no need to alert the Tiffanys and Rockefellers about who's planning to sink roots in their rich man's paradise. No one sees her, no one knows.

It's almost too perfect to take in, that a girl chopping cotton on the banks of the Mississippi might one day build a mansion with a dining room, patio and pergola from which she can view another river, the mighty Hudson, at her leisure. Moreover, she's buying into a neighborhood so expensive that nobody thinks there's a need to ban African-American residents. Because Bishop Derrick had stature and prestige among the race, to purchase his home would be to reach a pinnacle within it. But she's making a bolder leap now, beyond racial definition, even challenging its measurements. For her the gamble is not how white people will regard this move—no mystery there—but what her own people might say and think.

Midsummer, war draws closer when the British lose 670,000 men in the first eleven minutes of the Battle of the Somme. Only days afterwards, DuBois meets with NAACP leaders in Amenia, New York, to discuss racial and political issues, including what policy to support if the U.S. sends troops to Europe. Having contributed money to the organization, Madame is one of only two hundred people who are invited, but because of her travels she cannot attend.

Egged on by Robert Abbott, editor of the *Chicago Defender,* the great Southern migration of Southern black people has moved into high gear. Some twenty thousand African-Americans have been lured to East St. Louis, Illinois, to work at factory jobs for which white men are demanding higher pay. More than twice that many will move to Chicago in the next three years.

In early August, Madame motors down to Baltimore to attend the biennial NACW conference, the emphasis of which is on temperance, suffrage, railroad conditions, lynching and women's responsibilities within the domestic sphere. She shows slides of her business and the Harlem house during a short talk, and takes particular interest in the NACW's decision to assume the $5,000 mortgage on Frederick Douglass's home in Anacostia, Cedar Hill.

Meanwhile, Ransom's in New York to oversee the initial building contracts, and while there he receives a letter from Robert Brokenburr, who's taking bids from builders. Trying to keep costs down, Brokenburr favors a builder named Pierson, who turns in an estimate of $47,000 if they build the front-porch columns of stucco, as Tandy has designed them, or $46,000 if they use stone. Tandy will eventually scotch these efforts at economizing by challenging Madame's willingness to build the kind of home she really wants. And on the last day of August, her commitment to the Irvington property is sealed when a series of complex property transferences are conducted at the Westchester County Courthouse in Greenburgh, New York, about fifteen miles from Irvington, in which a $20,000 mortgage on 4$^{297}_{1000}$ acres along the westerly side of Broadway (formerly known as the Highland Turnpike or the Old Albany Post Road) is eventually transferred to Sarah Walker of 640 North West Street in Indianapolis, for the same $100. Madame does not attend the closing, and neither does any other black person.

L ate that summer, during her tour through Virginia, Georgia, Alabama, and Kentucky, Madame makes a special stop at Atlanta's Spelman Seminary, an all-girl school founded in 1881 to provide training for teachers, missionaries and church workers, where Mae will be enrolled. She'll turn eighteen in a couple of weeks and hasn't attended school since she was adopted exactly four years ago—when, in the legal agreement, Madame and Lelia promised to educate her—a fact that clearly causes some consternation among the Spelman administrators. And so Lelia and Madame secure recommendations for Mae from various people, including Margaret Murray Washington, who vouches for the girl's adoptive family and health. When asked why her daughter hasn't been to school for four years, Lelia claims that she has been "managing our business."

Oddness abounds, but Mae registers and Madame moves on—accompanied by a newly hired traveling companion, Louise "Lulu" Thompson—heading to Birmingham, Montgomery, Meridian and Greenwood. Toward the end of October, she crosses the Mississippi at Vicksburg, making her first return trip to her birthplace.

A report of this visit has been written by Minnie Murphy, the former newspaperwoman who, after her husband's death, wrote stories about Madison Parish. In researching Madam Walker's story, we should recall, she interviewed Celeste Hawkins, her chatty black employee, about her childhood friend Winnie Breedlove, who wore her hair up in strings while picking cotton and catching crawfish. We should also remember that Mrs. Murphy's report was written some twenty-five years after the fact, and composed with an undying nostalgia for a vanished way of life.

At any rate, on a "soft summer day" in 1917, according to Mrs. Murphy, Madam C. J. Walker came to Delta for a reunion with Anna Burney, which took place on the front porch of the original Burney place. Married to George Long, who restored the property to its original status as a working farm, Anna Long—apparently now called Lida—is, according to Mrs. Murphy, standing on the porch when a "middle-aged colored woman" comes drifting up the walk. (Murphy has the year wrong—it's 1916—and in Delta, there are precious few summer days that might be described as "soft"; but let us go on.)

At first, the former Anna Burney is confused. Having lived in Delta her entire life, she's pretty sure she knows "every hand on Grandview Plantation," but the black woman is a stranger. There is no mention of the stranger's finery and carriage, which must have confused her even further. Imagine her looking up on an ordinary day to find an unrecognizable African-American woman dressed fancier than the most stylish resident of Vicksburg come walking up her front walk, when all the black people she knows are "hands."

But when the stranger gets to the front porch, she says (in a voice the story claims has not lost its gentle drawl), "Why, Miss Lida. I don't believe you know me!"

And there she is, daughter of Owen and Minerva Breedlove, conversing with the daughter of her parents' owners. I'm sure she didn't say "Miss Lida," or introduce herself as "Winnie Breedlove, born and raised on this very plantation," but the meeting doubtless occurred, and Murphy has recorded one detail correctly when she reports that "Winnie Breedlove Walker" earnestly urges her Delta friends to visit her in New York, because apparently Lida Long's daughter will, in two years, take her up on that offer. Also, in Madame's archives, there's a newspaper account of the visit of the "richest Negro woman in the world, C. J. Walker, proprietress of a hair straightener remedy" to the place of her nativity. The story reports that Madame was born Winnie Breedlove, "daughter of Owen Breedlove, a slave owned by Mr. Robert Burney," and that she came to call on Mrs. George M. Long, "the only daughter of Mr. Burney living here," and that Mrs. Long has a childhood recollection of Madame's father as one of her father's "lead hands." Madame herself, it is reported, was quiet and unassuming, a "fine example to her race."

The name of the obviously white newspaper making this patronizing report (especially noteworthy is the absence of any form of address before black people's names, resulting in Madame being identified as "C. J. Walker") has been clipped off, probably by accident, and in the only mention Madame herself makes of the visit—to Ransom—she says nothing more than that she went there.

Hot Springs

Sometimes Madame's politics—fueled by her own experience—speak directly from the heart. While she's on the road, her bookkeeper, Lucy Flint, discovers that women engaged in manual labor at the Indianapolis factory are making a bigger salary than those who do the book work, and she complains to Ransom, raising a slight commotion among other women doing white-collar work. Ransom reports the dissension to Madame, who in early December writes him that her policy has always been "a bone of contention between Lucy and me." Apparently Lucy contends that Alice Kelly—who supervises the factory work, including mixing and boxing preparations—should not be paid more than she is merely because her own job primarily involves "brain work." But Madame maintains that "I take the stand that laborious work such as done in my factory is worth more than office work. You would find many persons who have been trained for the office and could fill any one of their places much easier than you could Miss Kelly's, for everybody is looking for an easy job."

Her stand is made even more interesting by her publicly stated belief in the importance of education and her conviction that the race will progress only when black people have gained independence from low-level manual labor and can move into jobs set aside for the trained and educated. Yet she can't help standing up for the unskilled workers in her own plant, presumably because she knows their lives and how they think. When Ransom questions the wisdom of this decision, Madame grows more than slightly testy, and there is no indication she ever changes her mind.

A week or so later, she announces the first convention of Walker agents, to be held the next year in August, in preparation for which she's staging a contest, with prizes ranging from $50 to $100, based on sales and recruiting efforts. She also warns that as of the first of the year, goods will be shipped only to registered agents, and that as a further protection against fraud, she intends to organize them into a national body with strict rules and regulations. To sweeten the message, she then promises more prizes, with the proviso that the Walker Company "will not regard any agent as loyal . . . who refuses to become a member of the Union" and that "if you expect the company's protection you must attend the Union."

This brings up another political matter. As management, Madam Walker has preempted her labor force by forming a workers' union based on her perception of their needs, *before* they have the power or cohesion to organize for themselves or proclaim their own basic rights. More than likely she regards herself conveniently not as management but as the same as her employees. This allows her to ignore the agents' biggest beef: her decision to sell products through drugstores, bypassing the individual saleswomen altogether. At any rate, there's no question who's in charge, and in her agitated state of exhaustion and illness, she's probably asserting her authority even more energetically now. This becomes particularly clear when she proposes that all New York mail-order business be forwarded to Indianapolis, a step that would lower Lelia's income considerably and almost certainly make it more difficult for her to meet her mortgage payments. Indeed, Lelia writes Ransom to complain. "I know mother is the best hearted person on earth," she writes. "All the same my feelings should be considered." And she swears that if she is to be threatened with the loss of her house every time it pleases her mother to do so, she'd rather move west—to Oakland, say—and open her own hair parlor, where she could "buy my preparations from mother and have peace of mind and freedom." Citing the differences between them, she describes her mother as an "impulsive baby" and proclaims, "I am no Breedlove. I am a McWilliams and that impulsiveness does not run in my blood."

These strong words are issued in a rage, and their importance can easily be exaggerated. Nonetheless, by defining herself as belonging to her father's line, Lelia reveals a strategy she uses to claim her independence and lets us know how strongly both these women believe in heredity, right down to tics and temperament. She further feeds her threat to move to Oakland with a self-dramatizing, if revealing, "Contentment in a two room flat beats being pulled by the nape of my neck, whether it be [by] sister, brother, husband or mother."

Ransom receives this letter in early November, and there's no telling whether he shared it with his employer. These difficulties lose their immediacy anyway when, just before Thanksgiving, Madame, Lewis Tyler and Lulu Thompson are nearly killed at a railroad intersection near Clarksdale, Mississippi, when—just as their car moves onto the tracks—a freight train starts backing up without signaling. Someone yells for them to get out of the way, and Tyler luckily shoots the car forward, but the train "all but grazed the back of the car in which we were riding." Madame ends her letter to Ransom with a prophetic "I haven't been myself since."

In Memphis the next night, a doctor gives her something to help her get through her lecture, but because of the spike in her blood pressure and her weakened physical state, he recommends that she cancel her remaining commitments and take at least a six-week rest. Exhausted, Madame tells Ransom she has agreed to do so but instead of going home will check into the Pythian Hotel and Bath House in Hot Springs, which is owned by the black K. of P. At the end of Madame's note, Lulu Thompson adds a personal message, confirming the doctor's diagnosis and confiding in Ransom that "the doctor told me she was on the verge of a nervous breakdown." Thompson reveals her own fears for her employer, saying simply, "She was so very ill."

Like all the health spas in Hot Springs, the Pythian offers heated baths in smelly natural waters, promising miracle cures for every known condition, from gout to weakened manhood. As we now know, this is a poor treatment for hypertension, but for Madame, any respite from traveling would have a salutary effect, even though she cannot resist conducting business from her room. Convinced that the business can't get along without her, she's simply doing what she thinks she has to, carrying on alone.

And so, from the spa, she communicates with various schools about her plan to install her system of hair care within their curriculum, and Alice Kelly comes to Hot Springs for a visit. Madame turns forty-nine and spends Christmas with her doctor and his family. And around New Year's, Lelia arrives at the spa—according to Madame, on the advice of *her* doctor. During her stay, mother and daughter work out their differences, and Madame allows Lelia to hang on to her agents' business for the New York office, at least until she returns home. But once she's alone again she starts to rethink that concession, and within two months she's reneged and Lelia's asking Ransom to help Madame see things the right way, which is that her work in Harlem is separate and therefore should be hers alone—the chief bone of contention.

In December 1916, Patent #114,597, for the Mme Walker Hair Preparation Beneficial for the Growth, Gloss and Shampoo of the Hair, comes through, and by the end of the year her income is reportedly up to $119,000, triple what it was three years previously. Add to this the value of her real-estate holdings and her total worth moves into quarter-million-dollar territory. By this time, the Walker Company has begun beating the drums about her purchase of the Irvington property. "Independent and fearless in her investments," an article in the *Freeman* begins, from time to time Madame has "surprised and electrified the reading public by some great gift or big investment," and because her business is the greatest of its kind in the country and her financial resources "almost unlimited," it would seem that nothing she did anymore would startle or surprise. But she's blasted that notion to smithereens, exclaims the newspaper—and more than likely, Ransom—by purchasing land in Irvington, New York, for $75,000 and designing a $100,000 home. Indeed, "this latest investment, the location of the property, the vast amount involved," is so out of the ordinary that people must be "impelled to say 'Three cheers for Madam Walker!' and hail her as not only the great Negro business woman but as one of the world's great and successful citizens and a credit to any race." Her many accomplishments are again paraded, along with her contributions to Indianapolis and the current health of her business. Never lacking in gall, the company machine then takes this occasion to anoint its boss "the Female Wizard of the Business World."

When a white paper—the *St. Louis Post-Dispatch*—covers the same story, the headline is NEGRO WOMAN GETS IN SOCIETY ADDITION, subtitled, "Will Build Herself $100,000 Home Next to America's Oil King: Hair Grower on Negro's Heads and Oil Magnate Will Be Neighbors If Plan Goes Through As Arranged." Skepticism reigns in this article, which notes that this "wealthy negress of New York" has made the claim she will build a home near the estate of John D. Rockefeller after paying a New York bank $10,000 more than the mortgage called for. But when the newspaper asks for exact figures, Madame declines to comment. Instead, she says, "I intend to erect on that property a home that will cost me no less than $100,000. And it is going to be very swell."

In the presidential election, Wilson defeats Charles Hughes, embarrassing the many Eastern newspapers announcing HUGHES ELECTED! before votes in the Western states are counted. Relations with Germany have deteriorated, and Englishmen are dying like flies, but the U.S. is still hoping for a negotiated end to the war. Meantime, New York governor Charles Whitman authorizes the formation of the all-black Fifteenth Regiment within the state's National Guard, and Vertner Tandy, Madame's architect, is made an officer. Fifty black men are reported lynched in 1916, and black migration north continues. The *Defender*—which now has ten thousand subscribers in Memphis alone—sends out chain letters exhorting people to "come North where there is more humanity."

Early in 1917, Madame leaves Hot Springs to resume her Southern tour.

Ground Breaking

L ate in January or early February in 1917, when
workers break ground in Irvington, Madame's
probably in Texas. By now, people up and down Broadway have heard
the rumors, but the Tiffanys and the Rockefellers and their neighbors
react to this outlandish news by means of the conventional wisdom,
which dictates that no colored woman can afford to live among the
wealthiest Americans in the country, therefore no colored woman will.

Vertner Tandy writes that he's just been to Indianapolis to discuss
estimates with Ransom, and reminds her that in their last conversation
they had agreed to start at the top, with the best builder and materials,
then scale down if they had to. The heftiest bid came in at $96,800;
the lowest, by the Miller Reed Co., at $79,997. Not surprisingly, they
choose the latter and will have a revised budget in hand by the end of
the week, when a number of decisions have to be made. Tandy
strongly urges her to come immediately to New York, to confer with
Mr. Miller in person and, after inspecting his figures, sign off on his
plans, instead of delegating the responsibility. Most likely, Tandy
would rather work directly with the woman with the bank account and
the more extravagant tastes, but Madame refuses to change her schedule and refers him to Ransom. The frustrated architect wires the
lawyer to come to New York, commanding him to "Answer Immediately," and he does, at which point the deal with Miller Reed is
finalized. Lelia, interestingly enough, does not appear to have been
consulted. Tandy may have made her exclusion a requirement, given
all the dunning and confusion caused by the 136th Street renovations.

Later in February, the foundation is laid and the construction of
Madam Walker's mansion begins while she motors from Texas to
Ohio, back to Texas, then on to Baton Rouge and Nashville. . . .

In April, Woodrow Wilson takes the country to war after Germany declares submarine warfare on all ships. "The world," he famously proclaims, "must be made safe for democracy," and America becomes a potential international superpower.

From the road, Madame buys more real estate: a five-story, fifteen-family apartment house at 374 Central Park West in a neighborhood thought to be declining, principally because it skirts a "colored settlement." Like other buildings on the block, this one is well designed and maintained, and looks directly onto Central Park. Trolley tracks run past, on the side of the street closer to the park. The purchase of this and another apartment building in New York may relate to a letter Ransom received from John Nail, informing him that in order for people of the race to move up in the world in terms of housing, there had to be a desire among philanthropists and business people to "lift up the fallen." And, describing this enterprise as "business in the name of philanthropy," he enclosed a *New York Herald* article citing the lack of decent housing for Negroes in Harlem as a reason for their stalemated position in American life and society. This address on Central Park West isn't particularly attractive to the general public; it's on the wrong side of the park and too far uptown, not to mention that colored settlement. (When Madame dies, the Harlem town house will be valued at only $16,000, because its location is deemed "very poor for residential purposes; district occupied by colored people.") But it's a fit place to live, and people of her race can move in without fear of discrimination. That's what Madame's looking for, that and a sound investment. In her will, she reiterates the desire to use her wealth to help the people of her race acquire modern homes.

By now this particular migration of Southern blacks into the North has reached its peak, and on Proclamation Day, May 15, when Wilson announces military conscription, thousands provided with free tickets north are jamming into railroad cars. Between April and November, 118,000 black people—95 percent of them men—will move from the South to West Virginia, Pennsylvania, New York, New Jersey, Ohio, Indiana, Missouri, Illinois, Michigan and Connecticut, drawn by jobs vacated by laborers suddenly turned soldiers. They have plenty of other reasons to flee the South, and since the fare's on industry, they have nothing to lose.

In May 1917, exactly two years before her death, Madame decides it's time to write her will. She dictates her wishes to Ransom from New York and, later that month, travels to Indianapolis to enter into the Marion County Probate Court the fully executed last will and testament of Sarah Walker, better known as Madam C. J. Walker. Considering her recent hospitalization, in all probability she's been thinking about this for a while.

Item 1 requests that her debts and funeral expenses be fully paid before any other assets are distributed, while item 2 leaves to Lelia all title to and interest in *one-third* of the Madam C. J. Walker Manufacturing Co. and one-third of the income and profits that flow therefrom, to have and enjoy for the rest of her natural life. At Lelia's death, her portion of the business goes to her issue and their heirs. But if Lelia dies without issue, her portion of the income and business reverts to Madame's estate. (Now, assuming adoption counts, Lelia already has issue, but Mae is not mentioned, and Madame essentially maintains control over the company after her own—and even Lelia's—death.)

Item 3 concerns Alice Kelly. If she is still in Madame's employ at the time of her death, she is to receive $10,000 cash and a life position at $2,000 a year as long as she honestly and faithfully performs her duties for the company. This is an extraordinary gift, and that her name appears so highly on this list of beneficiaries indicates her significance in Madame's life, as teacher, forelady and indefatigable companion.

Item 4 provides the beloved Parthenia "Grandma" Rawlins, maker of those Dixie biscuits, with $5 a week for the rest of her natural life, as well as enough money to pay for her funeral and burial expenses, presumably because, at her age, she has no other way to support herself.

Breedloves don't do so well. Big sister Louvenia gets $50 a month for the rest of her life, and $200 to be set aside for her funeral expenses, while her son, Willie Powell, gets a flat $1,000 so that he might have "a decent start in life." Fifty dollars a month must seem like a slap in the face to Louvenia, considering that her little sister has four cars, two mansions, a factory, real estate all over the country and a wildly thriving business. Presumably, Madame's paltriness when it comes to family is intentional. She leaves $1,000 and the house in Los Angeles to Thirsapen Breedlove and nothing to Anjetta, Lucy, Mattie or Gladys, though upon Thirsapen's death the property falls to Lucy and her heirs, who are not mentioned by name.

Madame's been straddling the line of ancestry and its obligations ever since she left Denver and went on the road. In her early life—in St. Louis and Denver—she searched out family, reconnected with them, used them, provided for them. But once she became Madam Walker, she began writing her own story. And when she says she got her start by giving herself a start, she believes it.

In the next item, she says she's still "exceedingly anxious" to establish a good industrial and mission school in Africa, and that if she has established such an institution at the time of her death, she bequeaths "all shares of stock of every kind of which I may die possessed and not otherwise disposed of for the support of said school." If she hasn't established the school, she gives $10,000 toward its creation and whatever stock is necessary to support it.

After the cash dispersals, the other two-thirds of her business and the profits that accrue from it, along with the investments she has made, are to be deposited into a trust fund, the proceeds of which should be used for the upkeep and maintenance of the Irvington property. Decisions concerning the trust fund are to be made by "five colored citizens of Indianapolis," Freeman B. Ransom and four others to be appointed by the judge of Marion County Probate Court. Bearing in mind that she has owned the Irvington property for less than a year and that a house hasn't yet been built on it, this request indicates that she considers it almost as important as her business as a testament to her accomplishments.

She's also somewhat tightfisted toward men. The only adult male besides Willie Powell to whom she bequeaths anything at all is her chauffeur, Lewis Tyler, who gets $5,000. Any other domestic help who have been in her employ for five years get that same amount; those who may have worked for her for a shorter period of time are to be provided for as Lelia thinks wise and just. A number of children receive bequests of between $500 and $1,000, the biggest of which goes to Ransom's oldest son, Frank, her godson, to whom she leaves a house and lot in Chicago. C. J.'s sister, Agnes Prosser, gets $1,000; he gets nothing. Many other women are remembered with small bequests. Her friend Maggie Wilson of St. Louis gets $1,000. Violet Davis Reynolds gets $2,000. Charities include the Colored Orphans' Home of St. Louis, the Colored Alpha Home of Indianapolis, the Tuskegee Institute and the Mite Missionary Society of St. Paul's AME Church in St. Louis.

Lelia gets all personal and household property and any real estate not otherwise disposed of. Upon her death, the real estate will revert to Madame's estate. Once again, Mae is not mentioned, nor are Lelia's wishes as to the disposal of what by rights will be *her* property after her mother's death. Instead, from beyond the grave, Madame manages her daughter's living arrangements: "It is my express wish and desire that my daughter occupy the Irvington property as a home, and that the same property be forever maintained out of said trust fund as a monument to my memory." This is a tall order indeed, to occupy a house, consider it home and simultaneously maintain it—forever—as a monument to your mother's memory. Lelia does, however, get to decide where her mother is buried, and Ransom is to continue as her adviser and as attorney for the Mme C. J. Walker Manufacturing Company. Even in a will notable for its improvisational quality, the provisions for Ransom are shocking. For his unstinting loyalty; for the complaints he's fielded from Lelia, Tandy and Singerman, from agents wanting free products and newspapers wanting money, from everyone pressing him for Madame's time and attention; for the letters he's written and favors he's asked for in her name; for the divorces he's arranged and the tributes he's composed—for all this he receives no cash, no percentage of the company, no guaranteed salary. What he does get is a one-fifth vote in the administration of two-thirds of the business and the joy of working with Lelia the rest of his life.

You have to wonder how this man who once compared her to Joan of Arc felt as Madame dictated to him the terms of her will. Didn't he deserve at least as much as Alice Kelly or Violet Reynolds? Wouldn't he have said something? Being Ransom, probably not. Knowing Madame's position on brain work versus manual labor, I wonder if perhaps she felt that as a lawyer, Ransom could write his own ticket without any help from her. Or maybe she just felt slightly peculiar about extending a helping hand to him in particular. Whatever her reasons, Madame signs the document and that, officially, is that.

In early July, a shameful race riot occurs in East St. Louis, Illinois. Given the industry-funded black migration and simultaneous threat of union busting, white workers cite job security as the initial provocation. But rightful protest quickly gets out of hand when marchers unite into a racist mob and all black people become fair game. In the long, merciless attack, thousands of African-Americans are driven from their homes. Hundreds of homes are burned, some with people inside. When forty-four railroad cars are burned, scores of black people flee on foot across the Eads Bridge to St. Louis. On the third day, mangled bodies float to the surface of the Mississippi. One week later, when W. E. B. DuBois and Martha Gruening, a white social worker and NAACP associate, travel to Illinois to investigate, they report that whites have driven six thousand blacks from their homes and murdered one hundred twenty-five by shooting, burning or hanging, with no guarantee that more bodies might not yet turn up in the river or Cahokia Creek.

In New York, when the NAACP holds a preliminary meeting to plan a protest, board chairman Oswald Garrison Villard (grandson of the abolitionist William Lloyd Garrison) comes up with a concept that emphasizes drama over political machinations: a parade to be conducted in total silence down the middle of Fifth Avenue, a procession the likes of which the city has never seen. The key is turning out the numbers, and to make sure of that, the planning committee is chosen carefully. Rev. Hutchens Bishop, pastor of the toney St. Philip's Episcopal Church in Harlem, is appointed director, and the roster of names includes DuBois; James Weldon Johnson and his brother, the composer J. Rosamond Johnson; John Nail; Fred Moore; and such ministers as J. W. Brown and Adam Clayton Powell Sr. Only two women are asked to serve, and Madam C. J. Walker is one of them.

She has friends on the committee who'd have submitted her name. John Nail's her realtor; Fred Moore courts her advertisements. They are considered close enough friends to serve as pallbearers at her funeral, as will J. Rosamond Johnson and her minister, Rev. J. W. Brown of the Mother Zion AME Church. Madame, who can contribute both money and people, readily accepts.

The Silent Protest Parade takes place on Saturday, July 28, when ten thousand black people march down Fifth Avenue to the roll of muffled drums. Children in white lead off, followed by women in white and then men in dark clothes. No one speaks, not even bystanders. Black Boy Scouts pass out leaflets saying, "We march because we want to make impossible a repetition of Waco, Memphis, and East St. Louis by rousing the conscience of the country and bring the murderers of our brothers, sisters and innocent children to justice. . . . We march because we deem it a crime to be silent in the face of such barbaric acts. . . . We march because we are thoroughly opposed to Jim Crow cars . . . segregation, discrimination, disfranchisement, LYNCHING and the host of evils that are forced upon us. . . . We march because we want our children to live in a better land and enjoy fairer conditions than have been our lot. . . . We march in memory of our butchered dead" and "because the growing consciousness and solidarity of race coupled with sorrow and discrimination have made us one. . . ."

A banner asks, "Mr. President, why not make America safe for democracy?" A child's sign reads, "Mother, do lynchers go to Heaven?" Behind the American flag flies a streamer reading, "Your Hands Are Full of Blood." A placard quotes "All Men Are Created Equal" and then notes that African-Americans need not apply.

It's unlikely Madame's up to marching in a parade in the dank city heat of late July when the concrete streets and buildings never cool off. But even if she walks only a block or two and then drops out—or doesn't participate at all—she has contributed plenty.

The circular passed out by the Boy Scouts represents an extraordinary statement of unified concern by all black people for their civil rights, the first in the country's history. But while such unanimity hasn't been possible before, these sentiments have been in the Harlem air for a while. The month before the parade, the Jamaican Marcus Mosiah Garvey arrived in the U.S. and has been delivering speeches about the need for unity. He has also organized the first American branch of the Universal Negro Improvement Association, which advocates economic improvement and independence for all African-Americans and proposes to create a fraternity of Negroes worldwide. In 1918, Garvey will begin publication of a newspaper, *Negro World,* whose slogan will be "Africa for the Africans." No one fails to notice Garvey's presence, and in his grand uniform and plumed hat he attracts thousands of disciples, including Madame—despite his vigorous campaign against the "Anglocizing" of African hair.

Four days after the parade, Madame goes to Washington with a delegation of black people to present to President Woodrow Wilson a petition urging him to support legislation that makes lynching a federal crime. Afterwards, Fred Moore writes in the *Age,* "On Wednesday of last week, I went through an unusual ordeal at the White House which might be entitled, 'not seeing the President.' " Wilson refuses to receive the delegation, instead sending his secretary, Joseph Tumulty, to inform the group that while the events in East St. Louis are personally revolting to him, he's too busy to admit them, because of, as Moore reports it, "the great importance of the feed supply bill."

And so the delegation—W. E. B. DuBois, Moore, John Nail, Adam Clayton Powell and others—deliver their petition to Congress and then return home.

The Road, the Times

In August, she mails a memo to her agents, announcing the time and place of her first national convention, set for Philadelphia on August 30–31, at which time "many important matters with reference to the future plans of the company will be discussed and explained." She then issues the teasing prospect of turning her business into a cooperative venture, so her agents can share in its profits, and then reminds them, as well, not to forget the contests currently in progress, which will close on August 1. Those unable to enter this year are urged to make arrangements to do so in 1918. She closes the memo with a swift, somewhat hypocritical sermon: "THE VIRTUE LIES IN THE STRUGGLE NOT THE PRIZE."

Of course, there isn't the remotest possibility she'd actually turn her lucrative enterprise into a cooperative venture, but you have to wonder how she came up with this idea in the first place. The fact is, since the Wizard's death, her move to New York, the Illinois riots and her trip to D.C., she's been listening to new ideas—some bordering on socialism—and might even have heard Garvey's disciples spouting theories of social responsibility on Harlem street corners. Sensing a change in the mind-set of her people—most of whom have given up on Washington's philosophy as being too passive and gradual, even regressive—she's shifting her own priorities as well. Determined to be taken seriously as a race woman, she's trying out theories, some of which she announces a little precipitously. And in the case of profit sharing, she realizes as much and doesn't mention it again. As for the agents' union, she clearly stated in her earlier memo that the basic reason for its creation was the need to protect her company from fraud and outside, unregistered agents.

Come August, some two hundred of her agents—waving the hot,

still air with paper fans and convention programs—gather in the Union Baptist Church on Fitzwater Street. Ransom has worked tirelessly with Margaret Thompson, the president of the Philadelphia Hair Culturists' Union, to ensure that the event proceeds in an orderly fashion. A group photo of the occasion shows most of the women wearing white, either blouses and skirts or lightweight dresses. The only man in the picture is Ransom, in the front row, looking miserable in a white suit, with Madame next to him in an airy dress with a tiered skirt. Her hair's done simply, in the Diana style of the Scurlock photo, and she looks slightly thinner. A banner across the entrance of the church reads, WELCOME DELEGATES.

Calling them to order inside the sanctuary, Madame gets the meeting off to a jolly start by stating that "in a session composed of graduates of the Walker system, who [are] experts in all things pertaining to the hair, it should not be necessary to request that the ladies remove their hats." The hot, bonneted women quickly oblige, and then are welcomed by the mayor of Philadelphia and other local dignitaries. Ransom and Knox speak, as do representatives of the Monarch Talking Machine Company and the Progressive Business Association. Madame unveils a new speech, "Women's Duty to Women," in which she advises them to use their own success to advance the careers and lives of other women. This, too, indicates a shift in her thinking, away from the individualistic approach of "The Negro Woman in Business" and toward a sense of unity and obligation.

Later, she introduces international politics into her address when, "in a ringing message," she speaks of the present war, advising her people to remain loyal to their homes, their country and their flag because, after all, this is the greatest country under the sun. At the same time, she warns, love of country and patriotic loyalty must not stand in the way of protests against wrongs and injustice. "We should protest until the American sense of justice is so aroused that such affairs as the East St. Louis Riot be forever impossible." And she presents to the convention a resolution to be sent to President Wilson, declaring:

We the representatives of the National Convention of The Madam C. J. Walker Agents in convention assembled and in a larger sense representing twelve million Negroes, have keenly felt the injustice done our race and country through the recent lynching at Memphis, Tenn., and horrible race riot at East St. Louis, and knowing that no people in all the world are more loyal and patriotic than the colored people of America, respectfully submit to you this our protest against the continuation of such wrongs and injustice in this land of the free and home of the brave, and we further respectfully urge that you as President of these United States use your great influence that Congress enact the necessary laws to prevent a recurrence of such disgraceful affairs. Respectfully submitted.

Once everyone signs, this noteworthy resolution is duly sent to the White House. Then, before leaving Philadelphia, the delegates are given copies of the new "Hints to Agents," which contains the memorable "DRIVE THE NAIL HOME" exhortation.

Within the following week, Madame invites a number of manufacturers of hair goods to meet with her at the Harlem town house and form the National Negro Cosmetic Manufacturers' Association. At least twelve people attend, and when the meeting is over they issue a preliminary statement of purpose, namely: "to protect Hair Growers and Manufacturers of Hair Goods against fraud and false representation, to properly regulate prices, to encourage thrift, honest and fair dealing, to protect the honest and legitimate business against the dishonest and illegitimate, to develop and inculcate the spirit of value for value, to protect the uninformed and unsuspecting, to promote the spirit of business reciprocity among ourselves, to encourage the development of Race enterprises and acquaint the public with the superior claims of high class goods, the product of Negro business men and women. . . ."

The statement is pretty vague and unspecific; its tenets reflect both the fierce competition of the time and the current belief in scientific management. The minutes of the meeting also address the members' need to protect themselves from price controls, the tariff and white competitors, "wherein it has so often been the case that the white man who is not interested in Colored Women's Beauty only looks to further his own gains and puts on the market preparations that are absolutely of no aid whatsoever to the Skin, Scalp or Hair."

Conspicuously missing from the meeting are Madame's two biggest competitors, Anthony Overton and Annie Malone. Neither is there any mention of Lelia.

Madame's newfound politics often clash head-on with her continuing—and very public—desire not only to fill her own coffers but blatantly to show off the possessions she's come by. Whether she struggles with these contradictions, or even notices, is hard to say, but with so much going on—the country at war, her people at continued risk, her income moving at twice the pace of the previous year, her health deteriorating, Lelia in a constant sulk—such inconsistencies seem almost inevitable. When she talks about reciprocity, profit sharing and price regulation, she's speaking an unfamiliar language. Though she doesn't follow through, her mind is churning. Her inclination toward left-leaning politics will only increase during her last eighteen months, as she becomes involved with groups the government considers so radical that they send citizens of her own race to spy on her and, based on their evidence, name her a potential subversive.

But people don't become other people; they only change directions and rethink prior convictions. What we have here is the same Sarah Breedlove Walker as always, with the same burning desire to outsmart, outdo and outearn—basic impulses which often eclipse altruism altogether. There are so many things she still wants to buy, trips she wants to take. To accommodate these conflicts, she manages to convince herself that it's good for her *people* if she installs a gilded pipe organ in her Irvington house, and inspiring for them when she buys a Locomobile, the most expensive car ever made. Let others speak of contradictions and incongruity. Her goal is to have it all.

The convention season continues when, a couple of weeks later, the National Equal Rights League meets in New York. Madame attends as a delegate, as does Ida Wells-Barnett. While in the past Wells-Barnett has been consistently skeptical about Madame's presence in the movement—partly based on her lack of education and failure to have been "ashamed of having been a washer woman"—on this occasion she's completely won over. In her autobiography, she refers to Madame as a woman who "by hard work and persistent effort [gives] demonstration of what a black woman who has vision and ambition can really do," and whose phenomenal rise made her "take pride anew in Negro Womanhood." But the journalist does not altogether shed her patronizing tone. When invited to the Harlem town house, she expresses some surprise that Madame has "learned already how to bear herself as if to the manner born. She gave a dinner to the officers of the Equal Rights League and left the meeting a short time before it adjourned in order to oversee dinner arrangements. When we were ushered into the dining room, Madame sat at the head of her table in her décolleté gown, with her butler serving under her directions."

According to Wells-Barnett, Madame visits the Irvington site daily, and when asked what on earth she will do with a thirty-room house, she explains that she wants "plenty of room in which to entertain my friends. I have worked so hard all of my life that I would like to rest."

But she isn't resting yet, and by November she's in such poor health that in Chicago she visits a physician, Dr. George Sauer, who finally diagnoses the disease that's been slowly killing her for years: acute nephritis, an irreversible, usually fatal disease of the kidneys which in her case has been accelerated and aggravated by hypertension. Dr. Sauer recommends that she check into Battle Creek Sanitarium—not for six weeks, but indefinitely. When she arrives at the famous Michigan hospital, her blood pressure is so high and her condition so poor that the admitting physician makes an even more ominous recommendation: that she stop working and give up all social activities for the rest of her life. The consequences of ignoring this advice seem obvious, but no doubt Madame promises nothing.

Operated by cornflake magnate Dr. John Harvey Kellogg, Battle Creek—known to regulars as the "San"—is the most famous health facility in the country, and is known for its racial openness. Sojourner Truth spent her last days there and is buried nearby. Abolitionists had gone for reasons of health and hygiene and to discuss matters of racial heritage. When Booker T. Washington was admitted, Kellogg assigned a male nurse to attend to him personally, and after the Wizard's assault he wrote a letter of support.

Brochures discount reports that "The Battle Creek Idea" is a fad or a fallacy, and proclaim it as a *great truth:* "to keep well—to get well—keep the stomach right." Madame loves rich, tasty food and is loath to restrict her diet in any way, but at the San, she follows a regimen of vegetables and grains, strenuous exercise and baths in closed cabinets. Daily rations consist of cereals, fruits, juices, lots of water and such main courses as ground nuts and grains patted into clever shapes, then baked or sautéed and sprinkled with peanut meal. Menus deconstruct the dishes into protein, fat and carbohydrate counts. To harmonize diners' gastric juices, soft music is played during meals; looking up, they are reminded by a sign on the wall to FLETCHERIZE, or chew each bite of food thirty-two times, one chew for each tooth in the normal mouth.

While not exactly the life Madame's used to, she sticks it out for a month or so, but by her fiftieth birthday she's back in New York and making regular trips to Irvington. Still, she must have enjoyed at least one of Kellogg's treatments, because at some point she buys one of his electric-lightbulb-warmed bath cabinets to put in the basement of the Irvington house, where it will remain for eighty years or more. And at the end of January, she checks back into the San for another week.

B y coincidence, it's during her first Battle Creek stay that the *New York Times Magazine* makes her an even bigger celebrity by running the story entitled "Wealthiest Negro Woman's Suburban Mansion (Estate at Irvington, Overlooking Hudson and Containing All the Attractions That a Big Fortune Commands)."

Its authorship unattributed, the piece is mostly about otherness and race: how remarkable it is that an uneducated colored woman has come so far, how bold of her to build in such a ritzy neighborhood, what a stunning thing to trust a Negro to be your architect. And when the reporter drops in on some locals—whose race goes unmentioned but is obvious—they want to know if the woman actually intends to *live* there or if she's speculating. They find their answer in the *Times,* which quotes her intention to live in and furnish her home in accordance with her tastes, while giving details of her current live-in staff, including a butler, a sub-butler, a chef, several maids, a social secretary and a nurse. Other employees include a chauffeur and gardener. The *Times* writer reports four cars in the garage, including her electric runabout; however, later this year Madame will have scaled down to one, the custom-made Locomobile limousine.

At the bottom of the article are pictures of the five best-selling Madam C. J. Walker products: Wonderful Hair Grower, 50 cents; Temple Grower, 35 cents; Vegetable Shampoo, 50 cents; Tetter Salve, 50 cents; and Glossine, 35 cents. The boxes are round, and the three larger ones feature a photo of Madame on the lid, the face-forward, long-haired one which took the middle position in the original triptych. This must further irritate the locals, seeing not a light-skinned, white-looking black woman but an honest-to-God *Negro* with a broad nose and dark skin—and she's predicting large-scale entertainments for her friends! For the *Times,* and subsequently for her white audience, she revives the dream theory, this time without the black man. "One night," Madame tells the reporter, "I had a dream, and something told me to start the business in which I am now engaged. This I did."

After christening Madame the Hetty Green of her race—for the woman known as the "Witch of Wall Street" because of her wealth and tightfistedness—the article cranks up the cost of her house to $250,000 and quotes "friends" as saying if she's not worth a cool million, she's close. When asked to respond, Madame demurs. "I am not a millionaire, but I hope to be some day, not because of the money, but because I could do so much then to help my race."

In the *Times*'s Brown Brothers photograph, the house looks finished. Yet home building never goes smoothly, and in October the garage—which Miller Reed intended to renovate—burns down. Fortunately, their insurance covers the rebuilding, but now they have to draw up designs and start from scratch—more money. Tandy frets when Madame buys furniture on her own instead of letting the decorators he's hired do it for her, and so he asks Ransom to insist that she consult the experts and "evade the danger into which she is likely to fall"—presumably, being overcharged by merchants who've heard the millionaire stories and, like those involved in the Flushing sale, take advantage.

There are many tedious skirmishes: one involving light fixtures for exterior gates that Ransom thinks should cost far less, another about the library accessories, which *Madame* thinks are too expensive. Ransom assures decorators that if they approach her in the right way, matters can quickly be settled—when, that is, she returns. Soon he hears from Tandy about squabbles involving the builder and the decorators and the ornamental-plaster contractor. Tandy feels called upon to say that Mr. Miller is unreasonable and exasperating—possibly a fair characterization, since in the course of three days the builder writes him thirty-two letters. Then, when the end is in sight, Madame weighs in with a request for an extra bedroom and storage room to be built *under* the terrace. (Tandy gently suggests that perhaps ten bedrooms will suffice.) Meanwhile, business is skyrocketing, and letters pour in, from agents, club women and fans from all over the country. People write directly to Madame—just as they do to the long-dead Lydia Pinkham and the fictional Betty Crocker—and imagine her sitting down at her desk to personally respond.

Lubertha Carson writes from Landrum, South Carolina, that "all my friends ask me to take the trade so that they can get the treatment from me." After Grace Clayton teaches her sister the system, she writes, "I am shore she is all right now and ready to receive your papers." After Beatrice Crank of Des Moines hears Madame speak, she writes, "I told you when you were in Des Moines that your talk inspired me so that I was determined to see what good I could do in this world and for my people." While her brother fights in Europe, Annie Bell is charged with the care of his child. Unable to find work as a maid, she becomes a Walker agent. Taking to heart Madame's admonition about getting around among people, Belinda Bailey decides not to commence work as an agent until she gets better acquainted with her neighbors, because right now, she says, "it is hard for me to catch on to the ways of them." A registered agent gets down to the heart of the matter when she proclaims that Madam Walker has "enabled hundreds of colored women to make an honest and profitable living where they make as much in one week as a month's salary would bring from any other position that a colored woman can secure." Maggie Branch of Chuluota, Florida, finds she can sign up as many as six customers after canvassing her neighborhood for only a few hours. And so, she testifies, "I am confident this wonderfull remedy will sell like hot cakes."

And it does. By the end of this year Madame's gross sales are reportedly up to $275,000. She's got thousands of agents. And yet incredibly enough, an auditor from the Internal Revenue Service reports in August 1919, her business operates as it has from the beginning, "on a cash order basis" with minimal inventory and very little capital.

While Ransom, Violet Reynolds and others stamp her signature on answers to her fan mail, Madame motors around Kansas making speeches for the NAACP. And she's said yes to an engagement in Pittsburgh, where she'll be the featured attraction at a fund-raiser for an old folks' home. Now that she's in such demand, she's decided to charge twenty-five cents a head for her lectures, and on one occasion reports having netted a hundred and fifty dollars. From afar, she instructs the home office on arrangements for her second national convention, this year to take place in Chicago. In response, the Walker press machine outdoes itself by proclaiming that "every age has its great men or women and this is true of every people. No unbiased historian can chronicle the history of the Negro without weaving the name of Madam C. J. Walker into the warp and woof of its life and institutions here in America." After guidelines for the annual contests are announced, one woman writes in to say that in the hopes that she'll win a prize, she's "both day and night with my hair work."

Madame and Lelia seem a bit broody toward one another at this point, perhaps as a result of their continuing dispute over the Harlem operations. When Lelia gives a coming-out cotillion for Mae, Madame apparently doesn't attend. But profits rise, and by spring the company has been granted two new patents. One is for a logo that will serve as a seal on every box of her products, to guarantee certification by the Walker Company. Oval in shape, the trademark resembles a picture frame, with a narrow rim around the outside and a larger black one inside. Diagonally across the oval is a scroll inscribed with the official Mme C. J. Walker signature, which the U.S. Patent Office says is a facsimile of the signature of the applicant. The other is for a product the patent office calls "Hair Tonic," which presumably is Wonderful Hair Grower.

On her way north from St. Louis to give an important speech in Chicago, Madame stops by Indianapolis and gathers up Alice Kelly to ride with her. Speaking under the auspices of the Pastor's Aid Society at the Olivet Baptist Church, she tells her illustrated stories with the assistance of a technician from the local Y, who operates the stereopticon projector. Skipping politics and heavy messages, she covers her gift to the Y, the glory of Booker T. Washington—here described as an "Angel of Mercy"—and her other philanthropic activities. In addition to the usual slides of the Delta cabin and her factory, she also shows off her new possessions and real estate holdings.

She tours the *Defender* plant, gives another talk, returns to Indianapolis and three weeks later is in Pittsburgh to address the local Madam Walker Beneficial Association, an organization "interested in community betterment activities as well as cooperatively assisting its members." After opening with her standard bootstrap advice, she moves on to larger issues. "This is your country," she reminds her audience. "Your home. What you have suffered in the past should not deter you from going forth to protect the homes and lives of your women and children." DuBois and the NAACP also urge support for the war, in a strategic move to remind the country that if black men are ready to make the ultimate sacrifice, they deserve the benefits of full citizenship, including protections guaranteed them in the Constitution.

Within a week, Madame is in Washington, where she speaks at an anti-lynching rally. Then, she returns to Harlem and, in May, solidifies her connection with the NAACP by running a full-page ad in the *Cri-*

sis for the five most popular Walker products. She's only a month away from moving into her new home, but even so she again heads west, to Akron and Chillicothe, Ohio; then to Indianapolis and to Idlewild, Michigan, a well-known black resort, where she buys more property to add to her growing real-estate collection, which now contains two more tenement buildings in the Bronx. She'd like to buy a house on Riverside Drive, but Ransom objects and this time she acquiesces. By the end of the month she's back in New York, in time to move into her new home, which by now has acquired a name. Having been to the house with Lelia, the famed tenor Enrico Caruso—enchanted by the look of the place—christens it Villa Lewaro: "Villa" for its Italianness, "Lewaro" for Lelia, using the first two letters of each of her names: Lelia Walker Robinson. Madame goes along with this, and in June, around about her daughter's thirty-third birthday, she moves in. Ironically, she'll live there—on and off, in her customary fashion—for less than a year, and the daughter for whom the property is named will spend as little time there as she can get away with, and after her mother dies, almost none at all—thus defying her "express desire and wishes."

In Europe, 278,000 U.S. troops have landed, and thousands are killed the first week. In a *Crisis* editorial, DuBois contends that since the war's ultimate purpose is civilization and loyalty, its cause is the Negro's as much as anyone else's. That same month, as if in mocking response, race riots occur in Philadelphia and Chester, Pennsylvania; in Estill Springs, Tennessee, a black man is tortured with hot poker irons and then burned to death. And although lynchings decline in 1917, they'll almost double in 1918.

Madame's plan to rest at the villa will have to wait. Within a week she's heading to New Haven and then to Denver, where from July 7 to 10 she'll play a starring role at the NACW meeting. Afterwards, she'll return to Chicago for her convention, make a few speeches in the area, have perhaps two weeks at home before the NNBL convention in Atlantic City, on the heels of which she's giving her first big Irvington party, in honor of Emmett Scott, whom Wilson has appointed special assistant to the secretary of war for Negro affairs. And in the fall? More speeches, an open house and, in early December, the National Equal Rights League convention. Maybe she can rest later in the month, around her birthday and Christmas . . . if, that is, nobody else wants a piece of her she feels compelled—obliged—to give.

A Simple, Visible Act

She arrives in Denver visibly ailing, according to NACW president Mary Talbert, but as determined as ever to pull through, especially since no other meeting has mattered more. On opening night, she'll make a brief address; the next day she'll preside over a round-table discussion about business, give a short talk on "Her Hair, the Glory of Woman" and discuss job opportunities for hardworking women. This will enable her to comment on the Walker Clubs' association with the NACW and announce her $500 donation to the mortgage fund to benefit Cedar Hill, Frederick Douglass's home. Then she'll sneak in an appeal to her sometimes snobbish colleagues to "get in touch with our women in the factory." All this in one afternoon session.

But the next night's the big one, the convention's finale. Nettie Napier (wife of NNBL president J. C. Napier) will give an itemized financial report on Cedar Hill, after which there'll be a tribute to the black soldiers in Europe. Madame's friend Elizabeth Carter will then stand and read the Douglass mortgage in its entirety and hand the paper to Mary Talbert, who in turn will pass it to Madame. The next few moments will be worth whatever effort she needs to get through them. She'll move to the pulpit—they're meeting in the sanctuary of her old Denver church, the Shorter AME—with a candle hidden in the folds of her skirt. "I am glad," she will say to the packed house, "to be able to show the world by this simple, visible act that the mortgage so long threatening this historic home has been reduced to ashes." She'll then draw out the taper to be lit and, while her St. Louis friend Victoria Clay Haley sings "Hallelujah, 'Tis Done," will apply the flame to the paper, then lift it high, burning, for all to see. The audience will gasp and cheer and sing "Hallelujah," Madame holding the blackening mortgage aloft until it's on the verge of blistering her fingers, then dropping it into a bowl and letting it burn out. Then she'll take her seat, the audience watching this woman who in Mary Talbert's opinion came because she wanted to see Denver one last time. The sanctuary is silent until a Philadelphia delegate rises to pledge $100 toward the renovation and upkeep of Cedar Hill. And after a musical finale, Mary Talbert gavels the meeting closed.

The women will make Madame a lifetime member of the Cedar Hill board of trustees, her name inscribed on a parchment that hangs in the house still. A few years hence, when the restoration has been completed and Mary Talbert is asked for details, without mentioning names she'll explain that several men's groups had taken up the cause twenty years earlier, but failed. Who, then, made it happen? "Our women, of course," she snaps. "Inspired by pride and love for this fearless and loyal American." And when she mentions Madame's name as the largest contributor to the fund, she bows her head in tribute.

On her way east from Denver, Madame makes personal appearances in Fort Dodge and Omaha, and in Des Moines gives a speech under the auspices of the NAACP in which she traces the history of the bravery of "our boys," from Crispus Attucks to those in Europe now, when "black hands are still holding high the flag. We see them as they come, 12,000,000 [*sic*] strong, marching, their faces wreathed in smiles, going over the top in No Man's Land. . . . Can you longer doubt the valor, loyalty and patriotism of the black man? . . . He has gone over there to mingle his blood with the blood of other nations, that the world may be safe for democracy, which has been so long denied him." She's performing a tricky maneuver, stirring social protest into fire-eating patriotism, even tossing in Wilson's "make the world safe for democracy," perhaps on the advice of DuBois, whose sense of irony is stronger than hers. "Now and then," she continues, "but seldom, you hear someone say, 'This is not my country. I have no right to fight for a flag that does not protect me.' But let me say to you that this is our home and whether we have that protection . . . or not, all we have is here and the time will come and it is not far distant until we must and will receive every protection guaranteed to every American citizen under the American Constitution."

Since she's new to political speaking, I take it as a given that the NAACP assisted her with strategy and ideology. But the most felicitous phrase in her speech is that simple and very moving "all we have is here." The language is so effortlessly straightforward (the prose style so similar to the "simple, visible act" of her NACW speech), I tend to believe it's her own, possibly even spontaneous.

Afterwards, back to Indianapolis. Her Chicago convention opens in two weeks, so she probably works on her keynote speech, checks out press releases and the convention program, dictates memos and letters to agents. Since she engages in no social activities, I assume that either she's told Ransom that she needs to lie low or, noting her frailty, he insists upon it. In the foreword to the program, they turn the Malones' $5,000 contribution to the St. Louis Y to their own advantage when they chastise those friends and supporters who have downgraded Madame's $1,000 donation as a "mere gift." The greatness of Madame's act, they explain, rests "in the fact that [she] was the first of her Race to give so largely," and this "unselfish act" then inspired those "who otherwise would not have given at all, certainly not as generously as they subsequently did." It was Madam Walker who "blazed the way." Thus, the Walker Company makes use of its competitor's language—"Poro blazed the way and it still leads" (1909)—as well as Annie Malone's claim that every hairdresser in the country learned from and copied her. The rift between these two women has never healed, and over the past few years, as each of them became more successful, the carping has occasionally turned nasty, particularly from Malone. In these instances, Madame has made public attempts to bridge the gap between them, which peace offerings Annie Malone has dismissed, thus yielding the point.

There is nothing in the foreword about Delta or her early struggle, no dream, but education and Christian charity come in for heavy play. Villa Lewaro is mentioned by name and is said to have cost a quarter of a million dollars to build and is "conceded to be the finest home owned by any member of the Race in this country." On the reverse side of this handwritten page, Madame makes an editorial comment: "O.K. You might add, aside from this home and stating its cost, I have a town home in N.Y. costing $275,000—together with the Indianapolis holdings—also that I own a bungalow in Los Angeles, where my brother's widow lives with her family free of rent."

Less than a week before the start of the convention, the *Defender* announces Madame's first appearance, at Grace Presbyterian Church, where she will give a "short and spicy" address to the women of the Windy City on leadership. But Annie Malone scores a coup when the paper runs her photo and press release on the same page, in the lead position. Above a head shot, the headline reads, "COMING!!! Mrs. Malone, Founder of 'Poro' College, St. Louis, Mo." A brief article heralding her appearance on Friday, July 26, at a meeting of agents from Chicago, Evanston, Aurora, Joliet and Gary, notes the enthusiastic meetings Mrs. Malone has previously conducted in Chicago and urges everyone to show up on time.

On Sunday, when Madame's scheduled to speak, the skies open and a drenching downpour reduces her Grace Church audience to a skimpy clump. She repeats a portion of the Des Moines speech and talks about patriotism and honors the war dead among the race. After a musical program, Robert Abbott speaks appreciatively of her success, and in a moment of rare solidarity, her competitor Anthony Overton lauds Madame for her "work all over the country."

The Second Annual Mme. C. J. Walker Convention takes place at the Olivet Baptist Church on the South Side of Chicago, with three hundred agents reportedly in attendance. On opening night, Madame mounts the platform to a "tremendous ring of applause" and welcomes her agents, reminding them that even though they are all passing through a great crisis, they must be grateful for what they have, and that they are here together, well and happy and full of good cheer. Their purpose this year, however, must be not just to inspire one another but "to pledge anew our loyalty and patriotism, our love for our common country and to say to the President that the Colored women of America are ready and willing to undergo any hardship and to make any sacrifice necessary to bring our boys home victorious."

She encourages them to avoid the appearance of narrow self-interest by letting the world know that the Walker Company rewards benevolence and that they are ready to do their part "to help and advance the interests of the Race." Then—of particular relevance in Chicago—she turns toward migration and the national concern about "the influx of Colored people into our northern and eastern cities and the effect of the same upon the economic life of the communities in which they find homes." What, she asks, are we going to do about the young boys and girls who turn up in our cities? Personally, she subscribes to the belief that we are all instruments of God's will and of the "greater and larger adjustments of our Race." She suggests it is her duty and theirs "to go out in the back alleys and side streets and bring them into your home and . . . into your clubs and other organizations where they can feel the spirit and catch the inspiration of higher and better living."

Narrowing her focus, she says, "You are doubtless aware that these conventions are a great expense to me. . . ." After the altruistic buildup, this statement comes as something of a surprise. But, she vows, if she can "make permanent the determination to make good, to build up a successful business, a desire to be of some real service to the Race," then her money will have been well spent. Then, continuing in this vein, she engages in some dirty pool, claiming that owing to the "unusual cost of material, heavy taxes, etc." her business this year was running almost at a loss—this after announcing the cost of her new house and the value of the Harlem town house in her program. But she has not raised the price of her products because she doesn't want her agents to suffer. "You have been loyal to me and, by the help of God, I am trying to be loyal to you." Then she abruptly switches directions again and concludes in her crowd-pleasing, hard-selling mode: "My advice to everyone expecting to get into business is to hit often and hit hard; in other words, strike with all your might."

The reference to her sacrifices in the name of loyalty is a coy way of responding to her agents' complaints about selling to drugstores. And while Ransom has to some extent taken their side, Madame refuses not only to give them the exclusive rights they've demanded but also to deal straightforwardly with their grievances, instead questioning their constancy and gratitude.

The membership re-elects her as president. In response to Woodrow Wilson's recent address on the "disgraceful evil" of mob violence, the convention votes to send him a telegram commending his "strong and vigorous" stand against lynching, even though his speech made no mention of race.

After the closing ceremonies on Sunday, Madame gives one more NAACP speech and then heads home. Naturally we'll go with her, but from time to time will leap forward as well, and by examining the future of Villa Lewaro, hope to discover what it is like now, as she moves toward it.

VIII · *Villa Lewaro, 1918–1919*

A Negro Institution Purchased
with Negro Money

It would be swell if we could walk through a wholly preserved Villa Lewaro and see it as she did in August of 1918, if we could go room to room and imagine her lounging on her curvy settee, holding court at her walnut dining table, cranking up that gold-plated phonograph. The house, of course, still stands, but except for the Estey pipe organ and the Battle Creek Electric Light Bath and Chair, everything is gone, the furnishings sold off in 1930 at an auction primarily attended by white people. And so we need to refer to an appraisal made after her death by the Astor Audit and Appraisal Corporation, Louis Bliss doing the real estate and Charles Bard her personal possessions. And since the estimate establishes the value of Madame's holdings in New York State as of the day she died—less than ten months after the Chicago convention—we can construct a pretty accurate picture of what the house, grounds and furnishings looked like upon her return.

But first we have to get there, following her route from Harlem, going a few blocks west from the town house and making a right turn north onto Broadway, which to this day holds the title as the nation's longest named city street. We run parallel to the river, past the Cloisters, through the Bronx and, many blocks to our east, past Woodlawn Cemetery, where Madame and Lelia are buried. After Yonkers we cross into Westchester County's suburban eases. After Ardsley-on-Hudson, where Madame's white neighbors play tennis and golf, we segue almost without notice into the next town, Irvington-on-Hudson. To our left is the steep, narrow downtown, and beyond it, the railroad station. Just past a dowager-gray Presbyterian church is

Fargo Lane, where we turn through stone pillars inscribed VILLA LEWARO into the half-circle drive which leads to Madam Walker's front door.

With the current owners I have sipped champagne in her front parlor while Leontyne Price sang Puccini in the background. I've chopped vegetables in her kitchen for an elegant meal, have walked through her halls and onto her fabulous veranda overlooking the Hudson and have seen the Battle Creek bath cabinet in her basement, even walked into her private stand-up shower with water jets up and down the walls. In her bedroom I tried to imagine it as it was then, rose with moss-green accents, with Madame in it—the bed perhaps over there, where she slept and died. The current occupants of Villa Lewaro, Harold and Helena Doley, are the first black people to have owned and lived in the house since the early 1930s, when A'Lelia's boundless extravagance and the Depression brought the Madam C. J. Walker Company to its knees, forcing a quick sale of the house that *Chicago Defender* columnist and friend Bessye Beardon called Madame's dream of dreams.

In the bland language of the professional assessor, Louis Bliss describes Lewaro as a modern country home with two and a half stories and a basement, made of stucco, about fifty by sixty feet, situated on the west side of Broadway on 3.80 acres, with two hundred feet of road footage and a modern three-car fireproof garage with, upstairs, an apartment. Bliss estimates land and buildings as worth $75,000. What he does not say is that Villa Lewaro is unlike any other house in the area. Because of its keen sense of history, Westchester County has formed a committee to oversee the preservation of its finest homes and trees, and so most of the original houses still stand. Because fewer people now can afford to live as the Tiffanys and Rockefellers did in the early 1900s, many of them no longer function as residences but serve as headquarters for various organizations. From the street Lewaro has an open, airy look, in welcome counterpoint to the forbidding, darkly turreted Tudor castles along Broadway. Its stucco turns rosy in the early morning and blinding white by noon, softening again as the sun sets behind the Palisades. With its red-clay roof and many windows, balustrades and balconies, the villa looks as if it had been floated into Irvington from a seaside perch on the Mediterranean.

In Madame's time, on weekends people promenaded up and down Broadway—first in carriages, then in fancy touring cars—to see who was in town and what kind of outfits everybody was wearing. From a car, all you can see of the other houses lining the street are gravel driveways curling into walls of thickly planted shrubbery and leafy trees, pruned precisely to ward off the prying eyes of strangers. But Madame's house is *right there,* close enough to the street for all to see. A showplace, not a snooty hideaway, since she meant for people to know she was there. Otherwise, why bother?

The drive skims the roots of two magnificent trees—a 300-year-old American beechnut and a rare 250-year-old Chinese gingko—which, in monetary value, challenge those at Bishop's Court. Flanking them are elms, oaks and a Japanese prayer tree Madame particularly loved. Cars pull right up to the front portico, with its wrought-iron grilles, its red tile floor and six white columns clustered in a tight semicircle, as if protecting the two-story French doors behind them. These open directly onto a narrow reception hall with a small fireplace at one end, its hearth busily decorated with gold-leaf froufrou, and a stately marble staircase at the other. Above our heads, the ceiling comprises a checkerboard of hand-painted wooden squares, each with a rosette in its center. From a center square hangs a brass chandelier lit with electrified candles.

The Doleys are from New Orleans and they have furnished their home sparingly, allowing its beauty to speak for itself. They've left the tile floor of the reception hall mostly uncovered, relishing its warmth and soft shine, and the windows gloriously bare as well, to allow the light to flourish. The previous owners of Lewaro restored the ceiling tiles, and the Doleys have recreated some of the original design work as well, but they don't think of Villa Lewaro as a monument or a museum. It is, they insist, their *home.* But I'm not sure they entirely believe that, and I know *she* wouldn't.

Madame, on the other hand, in accordance with the tastes of her time, filled every space with rugs, artwork and furniture. In the reception hall, an oak library table stood opposite the front doors, holding two sterling silver monogrammed calling-card salvers, an electric table lamp and the marble figure of a black child. Around it were arranged three oak chairs described by Bard as "after the Italian Renaissance," a tapestry side chair with two matching rockers and a large oak hall chair with a red-cushioned seat. The appraiser's list continues thusly:

Green marble pedestal and figure.
Red upholstered settee, split cushions, five pillows.
Bench, 18″ × 30″, covered in red cloth.

Anatolian table, square with long fringe.
2 music hall cabinets, 2 busts of women.
4 pair portieres, silk brocade.

And, covering the floor, an 18 × 24 Tabrios rug, a 4 × 6 Karabagh prayer rug, a 4 × 5 Bokhara and a 2 × 3 Anatolian mat. The rugs were valuable, especially the Tabrios, at $1,500.

Because the front doors are mostly glass, with a fan of windows above and long ones on either side, light floods into the room. Opposite the front entrance, one pocket door leads into the dining room, another to a butler's pantry. From her dining room, Madame could walk—or look—directly out double French doors onto three large terraced verandas, descending like layers on a cake to a swimming pool fed by a gently spitting fountain. Beyond, in her time, a pergola entwined with flowering vines graced a formal garden overlooking a wide sweep of the Hudson Valley and the tall craggy bluffs on the west side of the river. In our world of electronic thrills, the Palisades have lost their magic, but in Madame's day they were a sightseeing attraction, like Pikes Peak and the Royal Gorge.

The swimming pool has been out of commission for years, a crucial leak making repairs expensive and perhaps impossible. The pergola collapsed a long time ago. The formerly clear view of the Hudson is interrupted by another house, as well as the trees along the bank, now higher and thicker.

Beyond the small fireplace lies Lewaro's show-stopper room—eighteen by forty-five feet with pale gold parquet floors and windows on three walls—variously called the music, gold or drawing room. A large oval has been set into the ceiling, hand-painted in soft blue with gray-white cloudy puffs, like a cutout of the sky. A spangled crystal chandelier hangs at either end of the oval, beyond which are two more sky-colored insets, but these are speckled with gold-leaf chips, as if the sky had exploded, slicing the sun into bits.

From the beginning, Madame insisted on a genuine pipe organ, the kind that could be switched from manual to automatic, with music rolls to choose from so that she could hear her favorite songs any time she liked, night or day. She also asked for speakers to be installed all over the house, so that her overnight guests could waken to the strains of "The Blue Danube," "Holy, Holy, Holy" or "Communion in G."

Originally covered in gold leaf, the Estey still hunkers in the northeast quadrant of the music room, and probably always will, because as Helena Doley says, the house was practically built around it. But the gilt overlay has been stripped off and it's now white with natural wood trim. Along the north wall, beside a set of speakers, the pipes seem ready to pump out a chord, but the organ doesn't work anymore.

Although her decorators ordered furniture custom-made, Madame insisted on keeping the rugs, artwork, wall hangings, settees and tables she'd purchased in Indianapolis. And in Bard's inventory they're all there: the Chickering piano, the onyx tables and curved upholstered settee, the life-sized marble statues, one of a woman holding a globe-like sphere, the other of a seated girl.

Beyond the music room, the solarium sits curvily casual and glass-walled. With its undulating tile floor, wicker furniture and aquarium, it seems oddly out of place in this formal setting and can perhaps best be understood as a reflection of Madame's love of the tropics and sunlight.

Making our way back through the reception hall to the marble stairs, we come to the library, a small, rectangular room on the northeast corner with two sets of double doors, each leading to a small balcony. Today, this room is painted a soft lavenderish gray, which Doley thinks might be original. In Madame's time, there was a four-piece walnut suite—a library table, a six-foot slipcovered couch and two matching armchairs—as well as a five-by-five Chippendale mahogany bookcase and a mahogany side chair. There were also several mahogany lamps and jardinieres, a rug and a number of small decorative figures, including the plaster of Paris bust of Shakespeare from Indianapolis and the books she had in her library there, among them a sixteen-volume set of the Foreign Classical Romances, the twenty-four-volume Redpath Library of Universal Literature, the twenty-volume 1911 Dodd, Mead International Encyclopedia, nineteen volumes of *Messages and Papers of the Presidents* and a twenty-four-volume Alexandre Dumas collection in green buckram binding. Just outside the library on the landing there used to be a carved teakwood chair with inlaid mother of pearl, perhaps purchased from one of her island journeys, or in San Francisco after her visit to the Panama-Pacific Exposition

Opposite the library, the breakfast room was furnished with a six-piece polychrome dinette set—breakfast table, buffet and four chairs—and a rose-and-purple Turkish rug. The windows were covered with light-green velvet draperies. Between it and the dining room is a butler's pantry with a dumbwaiter, a floor-to-ceiling glass-fronted cabinet for glasses and dishes, a window overlooking the back, and an icebox.

The icebox is still there and the dumbwaiter still works.

Bard sets the worth of Madame's extensive walnut dining room suite—ten-foot marble-top table with leaves, twelve chairs, marble-top buffet, glass-fronted corner china cabinet—at $1,500. There's also an oval mirror, a Chinese rug and two electric candles. The dining room itself is warm and inviting, its barrel-vaulted ceiling hand-painted in a watery design in Madame's favorite colors, rose, buff and moss green.

Mounting the stairs to the second floor, Madame would have passed her eight-foot Tiffany hall clock and a reproduction of the Walker crest Lelia had had designed for the town house. In front of her she'd have seen, past the sewing room and a balcony, a long hall to the bedrooms. To her left, Lelia's wing is complete with sun parlor and a sizable bedroom in shades of baby blue and ivory, the same as in Harlem, with a wall safe for her jewelry and a bidet in her large bathroom.

There are three more guest bedrooms, one furnished with a mahogany four-poster, matching highboy, dressing table and mirror, valued at $1,250, compared to $300 for Lelia's bedroom suite and $175 for Madame's. This room also contains a number of rugs, another dresser, an upholstered armchair—a veritable furniture showroom.

Madame's suite takes up the entire south wing of the house and includes a sunporch and a bathroom, which, while not as large as Lelia's, features that stand-up shower. Madame furnished her sunporch sparsely, with a single bed, a writing desk and chair, a folding card table and a small dresser. Perhaps her nurse slept there, or maybe, on warm nights, she liked to rest there herself.

Her bedroom is familiar rather than fancy, nothing elaborate or expensive. The rose damask upholstered armchair from Indianapolis, the rose-cushioned mahogany rocker, the rose silk chaise lounge and matching silk damask draperies, the Turkish rug in rose and brown. Her bedroom set is of a lighter shade of ivory than Lelia's and there are a couple of rugs, lamps, a writing desk and chair, a wall safe and three paintings by William Scott, Madame's dancing partner at the 1914 musicale. Another bedroom adjoins it, furnished with single beds, a dressing table, dresser, mirror and matching chairs, possibly meant for a nurse or traveling companion.

The third floor, in Madame's time, was empty but for half a dozen folding cots and some old linens; A'Lelia will refurbish it, to use for card games and parties, with a custom-made billiards table and handsome cue racks built into the wall.

Lewaro's kitchen is large, with two big sinks, ground-level windows along the back wall and, in the center, a long wooden worktable. It is a warm and inviting room in which to sit, swap stories, laugh, chop vegetables and—as I did with the Doleys—eat an excellent meal prepared by a friend of theirs who was once a New Orleans chef. As we enjoyed the red wine, crown roast of lamb and fresh mushrooms, onions, locally grown squash and zucchini, I thought of Madame serving a meal for her Indianapolis boarders from a single pot, and of Parthenia Rawlins rolling out her Dixie biscuits. When A'Lelia entered any house, she is said to have headed straight for the kitchen to see what was cooking. These women liked to eat and to cook, and unlike many of their neighbors, they probably spent a lot of time in this room.

Madame equipped the laundry room with an electric washing machine and mangle, along with an unusual steam dryer that at first glance looks like four metal floor-to-ceiling drawers installed in the walls. When the drawers are closed, only the handles are visible. But then Helena Doley pulled one out to show me how the thing worked. Iron pipes serve as clotheslines, and after the damp laundry is hung over them, the drawers are pushed back into the wall and a steam blower is switched on, to blow the clothes dry.

Also next to the kitchen is a sizable pantry. Madame's set of Limoges, 112 pieces, was valued by Bard at $75, and 147 pieces of Haviland at $50. There were any number of cut-glass tumblers, cups and saucers, fruit plates, finger bowls, trays, beer mugs, assorted Japanese pieces including a tea set with tiny cups and saucers, Sheffield mugs, Charlotte russe servers . . . the list goes on and on. In addition to the regular pantry there's a closet-sized pantry-safe, but, according to the appraisal, Madame's silver is all plate, or Sheffield steel, including the punch bowl, the trays and the famous tea set. Doley suspects foul play here and says anybody might have made a switch, plate for sterling.

The servants' dining room adjoining the kitchen is small, and had oak furniture, a round table, a buffet and five chairs. Bard called the big room beyond it a gymnasium, where she installed the Battle Creek Electric Light Bath and Chair.

Walking through Villa Lewaro, I marvel at the gifts this woman allowed herself, the visual beauty, the music and light. For a woman born in a sharecroppers' cabin in backwoods Louisiana, these comprise nothing less than a new way of being.

By mid-August she's home and by all accounts having a wonderful time, puttering about the house and the garden, pulling weeds and gathering vegetables. A bucolic interlude is exactly what she needs, but it doesn't last long. Within two weeks, she leaves Lelia and her staff to make final arrangements for the star-studded event she's staging here a week later and departs for the NNBL meeting in Atlantic City. There, she's recognized on several occasions, including a tribute by her architect, Vertner Tandy, who calls her the "greatest woman this country has produced." She also helps rally support for a commendation of San Antonio newspaper publisher George Breckenridge, who has pledged $100,000 to help convict lynch mobs in Texas.

By the time she gets home, formal invitations have been sent to a guest list of one hundred friends and notables: "Mme C.J. Walker requests the pleasure of your presence at an afternoon with Hon. Emmett J. Scott, Assistant Secretary of War. Sunday August twenty-fifth, from three until six, at her residence, Villa Lewaro, Irvington-on-Hudson. R.S.V.P. Conference of interest to the race." After they gather on her veranda to enjoy a late lunch and admire the view of the Hudson and the Palisades, the "leaders of their respective races" will adjourn to the "great salon," for a chamber concert of modern and classical music, with J. Rosamond Johnson at the Estey.

Attendees include people from Madame's near and distant past: Thomas Taylor, former secretary of the Indianapolis Y, now in the same position in New York City; Will Lewis, who wrote so effusively of her in the *Freeman;* her old friend Jessie Robinson from St. Louis; a number of NAACP board members, including Mary White Ovington and John Shillady; philanthropist William Jay Schieffelin, who introduced Bayer aspirin to the nation; W. S. Scarborough, president of Wilberforce University; Fred Moore and Mary Talbert; J. C. Napier; several residents of the all-black town of Mound Bayou, Mississippi; Lelia's great friend Edna Thomas, now Madame's social secretary; Vertner Tandy; Lelia, of course, and Mae.

After he concludes the musical program, Johnson introduces Ransom, who in turn introduces Madame. She welcomes her guests and explains that she has invited them to meet the Honorable Emmett Scott to confer with him about the role being played in the war by the American Negro and to discuss the likely consequences of their valor when they return home. And she reissues the call she made in Chicago for people to stand together behind the high principles of the war, ending the speech on this note of national solidarity. The *New York Age,* which runs extensive coverage of the event, says that Ransom then introduces Scott, a slight and narrow-shouldered man in rimless spectacles and a bow tie whom many remember as a mouthpiece and spy for Booker T. Washington, and as now playing the same role for Wilson and Secretary of War Newton Baker. DuBois, Trotter and other NAACP leaders consider him the perfect subordinate to power, therefore an ideal white man's choice for an important job. But since the president has otherwise made a clean sweep of African-Americans in the federal government, most black people feel they have little choice but to support him.

As for Madame—who's already come in for a good deal of criticism simply for hosting this soiree—her demeanor is that of the objective moderator. Without heaping praise on the honoree, she merely invites her guests to meet Scott, pose questions and conduct a general discussion. But then when she suggests that the time has come to forget differences and join together in mind and spirit behind "higher principles," some in her audience interpret this as a signal not to ask the guest of honor tough questions—a strategy that may have originated with Lelia, who has been particularly concerned about the guest list.

Madame's not the only one pushing for a common cause beyond race. In the summer issue of the *Crisis,* DuBois published an editorial, "Close Ranks," in which he urged "Negroes and all the darker races" to forget their special grievances during the war and "close our ranks shoulder to shoulder with our white fellow citizens and the allied nations that are fighting for democracy." Some simply disagree with the editorial, while others accuse DuBois of currying favor with the government at what many feel is the perfect time for African-Americans to stir the national conscience and keep their special grievances before the public eye.

Scott stands, receives his applause, pays tribute to his hostess, then brags about the accomplishments he and the War Department have made, such as the dismantling of prejudicial draft boards and the investigation of reported ill treatment of Negro soldiers. According to the *Age,* the audience finds Scott's remarks "exceedingly pleasant," and he states that colored women will soon be sent overseas as Red Cross representatives, that a board of health will be established to study sanitary conditions affecting colored soldiers, that a special correspondent will soon be selected to report on black activities and achievements in the war.

For the most part, a congenial afternoon, even though neither Monroe Trotter nor Ida Wells-Barnett seems to attend, and afterwards, Schieffelin complains publicly about the "militancy" of Madame's remarks when she suggests that black soldiers should be treated differently when they return, as an acknowledgment of their sacrifices and bravery.

In November, Germany surrenders, an armistice is signed and the peace conference arrangements are made in France. In an effort to seize the moment and force Wilson to come face-to-face with racial inequities at home, African-American leaders hope to send their own delegates to Paris. At the National Equal Rights League meeting in Washington, Madame and Ida Wells-Barnett are selected as alternate delegates but with the understanding that they will pay their own travel expenses. Wells-Barnett gratefully declines, explaining that the years she has spent working on behalf of her race have left her financially strapped. Perhaps the NERL feels embarrassed, because an amendment is passed to cover both women's expenses.

Meanwhile, however, Woodrow Wilson and his wife have made a triumphant tour to Brest, Paris, London and Italy, the huge crowds waving American flags and hailing "the God of Peace." The last thing Wilson wants is for a delegation of Negro malcontents to show up at his peace conference and sabotage his Fourteen-Point Plan, his international League of Nations and his place in history. And so the State Department denies the NERL delegates travel clearance, and in the end nobody from the League goes except Trotter, who will eventually arrive—too late—disguised as a cook.

Madame's at home for Christmas and her fifty-first birthday, enjoying nice meals and the company of close friends, wrapping presents for her staff and entertaining little Frank Ransom, who's there for the holidays. Still, she's also preparing for a meeting she's agreed to hold at Villa Lewaro in January, to help organize the International League of Darker Peoples. Freeman Ransom in particular is distressed about this, since he considers some of those involved to be strictly opportunists, after Madame's money. He says as much, warning her that, unlike herself, the people with whom she's aligning herself have nothing to risk, give or lose. But she moves ahead anyway.

Those "special grievances" that DuBois referred to in his editorial have received little or no attention, despite African-Americans' support of and participation in the war. Of the two hundred thousand black men who shipped out to serve their country, the majority were allowed only to dig foxholes and string barbed wire, and those assigned to combat never received equal or fair treatment. After white soldiers refused to fight alongside them, the all-black 369th Infantry Regiment—who performed heroically enough to be renamed the Harlem Hellfighters—were brigaded with a French division. Moreover, the French were requested not to treat black Americans with "familiarity and indulgence," because such treatment might invite aspirations that white Americans might consider "intolerable." When peace was declared, the black Ninety-second Division was confined to muddy encampments, to safeguard the virtue of French womanhood. And now that the war is over, there is a general rush to strip African-American officers of their ranks and to discredit their achievements and heroism. Wilson will send Tuskegee president R. R. Moton to Europe to caution African-American soldiers to exercise self-control on their return and not to expect changes.

Meanwhile, back home, sixty blacks are reported lynched in 1918.

Last Days

Diabetes is like a good pet, dutiful and consistent. Hypertension provides the counterpoint, issuing alarms and then backing off. Once the two collaborate, things happen: channels collapse, openings seal, poison doesn't flush but instead eats through pliant tissues like rust through a tailpipe. And when the kidneys start to fail, mystery vanishes. No one knows how slow or fast the end will come, only that it will. As one, Madame's doctors advise her to make no more public appearances, throw no more parties, to relinquish all business responsibilities; in a word, to simply stop living the life she's used to. After all, she has a beautiful home to enjoy; she can tend her garden, listen to music and look at the river.

There's no way this would ever suffice. Yet she knows she can't travel as before, and that in order to secure the health and continuation of her company she has to make some changes. Since she can't single-handedly oversee the whole operation and is certainly unwilling to leave it up for grabs—or in Lelia's hands—she reportedly asks Freeman Ransom what it will take to convince him to give up his practice and work full-time for her, as general manager of the Indianapolis, Harlem and branch offices. Ransom names a figure he worries is too high, but Madame doubles the amount, perhaps to make up for the will's oversight. He closes his office, sets up full-time on North West Street and hires an advertising manager.

But he's not in charge of *her*, and neither he nor anybody else can change her mind once she's made it up. Despite his vigorous objections, she moves ahead with plans for the Lewaro meeting of the International League of Darker Peoples. With Adam Clayton Powell Sr., A. Philip Randolph and Marcus Garvey initially expected to participate, the organization's stated purpose is to unify people of color from all over the world so as to confront racism and governmental prejudice. And in direct contradiction to the positions she's taken over the past two years, as well as the ones she'll support in the immediate future, Madame aligns herself with those who believe that skin color counts more than nationality or even race. In January, when asked how the Japanese racial question relates to the concerns of African-Americans, she emphatically, if somewhat vaguely, states that the darker peoples of the world must amalgamate for racial rights the world over, and then she slides away from internationalism slightly, adding that if she could afford it, she'd give a "million dollars to help my race fight for its rights."

And so the meeting takes place—but without Garvey, who has abandoned the ILDP for his own program—and within days the organization announces that it will send Negro delegates to the peace conference in Paris, after which they will tour major European cities to spread "psychological propaganda." The ILDP also intends to help secure passports for delegates and supporters, maintain a headquarters in Paris, issue a newsletter and stage a conference at Carnegie Hall. There's no indication of how they mean to finance these plans.

A week later, the ILDP conducts another meeting, this time at the Waldorf Hotel, and in the very formal photo taken there, Madame—in a severe black dress with prim white collar and cuffs—sits surrounded by six men, including one of the founders of the organization, a man who sometimes calls himself Brother R. D. Jonas and occasionally the Prophet Jonas; A. Philip Randolph; an unnamed delegate from Japan; and Louis George, who, oddly enough, now assists Ransom on the drugstore campaign. Madame's fond of George—calls him "Louie" and "my boy"—but he seems decidedly apolitical, and I wonder what he's doing there: perhaps seeing after his employer's interests, especially once she's elected treasurer. Or maybe Madame asked him to come keep her company.

Considering the causes she's been involved with and the general direction she's been heading over the past five years or so, it's not that surprising that Madame would get caught up in an organization like this—even after Ransom points out that the self-styled minister Jonas has been run out of Indianapolis, among other places, and can't be trusted. DuBois and the NAACP are planning their own Pan-African Conference in Paris, and she's already allied herself with them, so why go off on this other tangent and support what can only be seen as a rival organization? Two possibilities quickly arise: the generosity she's displayed, somewhat indiscriminately, toward groups that sponsor causes she either believes in or *wants* to; and her ambivalence about money, how much to give and to whom, when to give or withhold it and how to decide who's worthy or only taking advantage. Randolph is a Shakespearean scholar and an eloquent speaker whose wife, Lucille, runs a lucrative Walker parlor; that alone might have convinced her to join up. At any rate, within a couple of weeks, when the French government sanctions the NAACP's Pan-African Conference—representing North and South America, the West Indies and Africa—and the U.S. State Department denies passport clearance to ILDP members, she's off the hook. The *Age* approves of the government's decision, since money that would've been used to send delegates abroad will now be "applied in a practical way toward bettering conditions for the Negro in the United States." And in years to come, at least one of Ransom's suspicions will prove justified when the Prophet Jonas is unmasked as an undercover agent for the Military Intelligence Division of the War Department, hired to provide information about his black colleagues.

Four days later, Madame issues her own statement. "To the officers and members of the International League of Darker Peoples: Owing to the fact that I do not expect to be in the city this winter and to the further fact that my physician has advised against my participation in public affairs, I herewith tender my resignation as treasurer and member of the above-named organization, to become immediately effective. I do, however, wish the league every success." And she follows the advice of the *Age* by redirecting her energies and resources toward the anti-lynching campaign.

In her Madison Parish chronicle, Minnie Murphy connects Madame to Delta and the Burneys one last time. In the conclusion to her story, she writes that Anna Burney Long's daughter Lillie Mae had signed up to go overseas for canteen duty, and that while staying at the Martha Washington Hotel in New York, waiting to be shipped out, she called Madam Walker's Harlem shop. The next day, Madame herself phoned from Irvington and arrived that afternoon at the appointed time "in a handsome Locomobile, a liveried driver in the chauffeur's seat and a colored trained nurse in attendance."

According to Murphy, Madame then took Lillie Mae on a tour of the Harlem town house and her country home, both of which Miss Long found "in no wise overdrawn by newspaper descriptions." She describes the Harlem apartment as the last word in comfort and luxurious appointments, and deems the Westchester home an estate, with its "beautifully tended grounds . . . a liveried footman to greet them at the door . . . maids in sharp black dresses with crisp white collar and cuffs gliding about in silent and efficient attendance." Murphy further reports that according to Lillie Mae, while all the servants were black, none were distinctly so, but with the "smooth light skin of the mixed breed." She also claims that Madame told Lillie Mae of her accomplishments and said that in the next year or so she would like to pump up her bank account from a half-million to a round million, then admitted that might never come to pass. "I am," Murphy quotes her as saying, "on the downward path of life, a sick woman. I keep my nurse with me always."

Some of this account is probably accurate, though there's no telling how much. Murphy has Lillie Mae describe a nonexistent elevator in Villa Lewaro, and I find it highly unlikely that Madame would confide details of her declining health to a young white girl she hardly knows. But the gist of it is certainly possible, and it's hard not to *want* to believe that Madame had a chance to show off her grand life to the granddaughter of the white man who once owned her parents.

On a bright, sunny day in February, Madame's been invited to sit on the reviewing stand with Governor Al Smith when the returning 369th Infantry Regiment—accompanied by James Reese Europe's Hellfighters marching band—parades up the length of Fifth Avenue and then, at the north end of Central Park, turns on Lenox Avenue. When the band reaches Harlem, Jim Europe changes the music to "Here Comes My Daddy Now," and the thousands of African-Americans waiting along Lenox go "wild with joy" as the Hellfighters march between "two howling walls of humanity." It's a great day, a superb occasion, and surely Lelia—who has done volunteer work for a number of war relief agencies—is there, watching. Madame, however, stays home, having issued an open invitation to the returning soldiers to drop in at Villa Lewaro whenever they feel so inclined.

People respond to chronic conditions in various ways, and Madame simply takes a stand against hers whenever possible, and even in her last days finds ways to believe that her desperate condition is a temporary crisis that might well pass. And so she distracts herself with ideas and possibilities for cures, such as going to France to take the waters. Later that month, she has her chauffeur drive her to Tiffany's, where she buys $1,755 worth of jewelry, perhaps planning to wear her new diamonds to Paris. Sometimes she complains of a nagging cold she can't seem to get rid of.

In Indianapolis, business is booming and Ransom's trying out new ideas. In March, he announces that in response to "the demands of the times and the requests of our many agents," the Madam Walker Company is introducing five new products: cleansing cream, cold cream, vanishing cream, witch-hazel jelly "for the hands of those who work in the open and women who put their hands in hot water," and face powders in white, rose-pink and brown. Because white cosmetics firms are pouring out competing products, Ransom's working with Louis George and his advertising manager to make certain the company keeps up with current trends and that the new products are publicized coast to coast, not only in black newspapers but also in farm journals and religious periodicals. Madame's been anxious to move into the white market for some time, and now it seems the company's doing exactly that. She also adds a personal note, to "correct the erroneous impression held by some that I claim to straighten hair," insisting that she has always presented herself solely as a "Hair Culturist" who grows hair. She also replies to a "noted white speaker" who has admonished Southern black women to improve their personal appearance, saying that that's exactly what *she's* been preaching all along. She concludes with a prediction that "in the next 10 years it will be a rare thing to see a kinky head of hair and it will not be straight either." Odd, her use of the word "kinky," if she is indeed the one who wrote this.

S oon afterwards, there's an even more significant development. The disputations between mother and daughter have come to a head, and since Madame can't stop interfering in—or rescuing—the Harlem operation, especially now that her traveling's been curtailed, Lelia's left the country. Either she got fed up and simply sailed away or Ransom said she ought to or she persuaded her mother to send her; maybe Madame recommended a vacation—one way or another, she goes. Once she's safely shipboard, Ransom issues a brief statement announcing that Madam Walker is assuming entire control of her Harlem business, including Lelia College and the Walker Hair Parlor, in order to permit her daughter to travel to South America and the West Indies in the interests of her company.

Some of Lelia's friends dispute this. According to them, Lelia snatched Mae out of school, gathered up the company's Spanish-market agent and simply stormed off. There are many complicating components to this story, including an argument between mother and daughter over a potential suitor of Lelia's. Clearly, with her own health failing, Madame would like her daughter to remarry right away, but not the handsome, arrogant Wiley Wilson, a licensed pharmacist from Pine Bluff, Arkansas, who'd recently finished medical school at Howard University and now practices in Washington. Wilson's tall and stylish, and while he's certainly captured Lelia's attention, Madame doesn't trust him. Her choice for a son-in-law is another pharmacist-physician, also from Arkansas, James A. Kennedy, a staunch, upright disciple of J. H. Ward's, a war hero and, according to Lelia's friends, a pious and boring gold digger whom Lelia frankly despises. Once again, mother and daughter squabble, with independence and autonomy the underlying issues.

I tend to think, also, that Lelia's starting to party more vigorously and to spend more time pursuing an inappropriate nightlife, her interest in the business waning. When she leaves in March, Lelia says she won't be back until August, which is a long time to stay gone, even on a business trip. But by then, Ransom's takeover will be complete and she'll be spared the interim embarrassing questions and sly insinuations.

Maybe there are other reasons. Rumor has it that Lelia got drunk one night and gave away the formula for a Walker product. There's no proof of this, but it seems fair to wonder why the thought occurred to anyone. Is she drinking that heavily now? Might there be a liaison that needs hushing up? After Lelia's death, members of her partying clan will tell of a ménage à trois involving Edna and Lloyd Thomas and Edna's British girlfriend Olivia Wyndham, whom members of her Harlem posse term a "big lesbian," and A'Lelia Walker herself will be pictured in *The Advocate*—a magazine for gay men and women—as one of the many Harlem Renaissance homosexuals. But who knows. And while it's odd that she took Mae out of school to go with her, Mae's twenty now and maybe a more interesting companion than she was as a teenager.

We can only speculate. And wonder. Knowing how little time her mother has left, I can't help dreaming of a different ending to this story, and wishing that Lelia would turn around and come back home.

After her death, friends will claim that Madam Walker would often stand on her veranda and, looking out, say that here she felt at home for the first time in her life. Sometimes she'd talk of building a tennis court by the swimming pool, so her people would have a place to play in Westchester County. Somebody says she was even thinking about getting some chickens to raise out by the pergola. But in dark times, none of this matters. Landscape offers no comfort; on the contrary, beauty only rankles. Life is movement, or so it seems, and Madame—now ailing and lonely—has never known anything else.

So when Jessie Robinson invites her to spend Easter in St. Louis— as she did last year—and to give a talk at the Coliseum, despite all advice to the contrary Madame agrees. En route, she spends some time in Indianapolis, seeing her faithful friends and, perhaps, looking over the ads designed by Ransom's advertising man. And I wonder if her heart dips a little, knowing she will play no part in selling the new skin products, noting that her publicity department is now an all-male operation. Then she heads to St. Louis, arriving April 25. Still complaining of the cold, she warns the Robinsons to keep their distance and goes to bed. The next day, when Madame does not, cannot rise, Jessie Robinson cancels the speech and asks her St. Louis physician, Dr. William Curtis, to make a house call. After an examination, Curtis calls in a kidney specialist. The doctors prescribe complete bed rest and constant care, nothing more.

But Madame knows she's dying and she wants to go home. Like the Wizard when he was near death, she can talk of nothing else. When the Robinsons summon Ransom, he communicates with J. H. Ward—now serving out his medical military stint at Fort Upton—then travels to St. Louis. Ward having agreed that Madame's too ill to return to New York by automobile, Ransom proposes a private railroad car in which she can lie down the whole trip. He'll hire a private nurse and Dr. Curtis can accompany her.

As these plans are being set in motion, Madame subscribes $4,000 to the Victory Bond campaign, then issues a statement to African-American newspapers: "May I take advantage of your valuable paper to urge upon my agents and customers the importance of purchase of Victory Bonds at this time? To my mind it cannot be too strongly emphasized that our boys have done their bit; brought home victory to our great cause and have finished the job; leaving it clearly up to the great army back home to make the victory complete and go over the top on this side of the water. . . . We were loyal and patriotic during every stage of the great struggle and because of that loyalty we will go down in history as one element of American citizenship that did not shirk or balk when duty called." And she urges other African-Americans to subscribe promptly and liberally to this last campaign, so that there will be no uncertainty where the Negro stands in these, the closing days of "this great crisis."

Confined to the Robinsons' bed, she has ample time to rethink her priorities, and at some point she calls in Ransom to prepare a codicil to her will. Once Ward and Curtis give their consent, and a drawing-room car on the Twentieth Century Limited from St. Louis to New York has been reserved, they leave: Ransom, Madame, Dr. Curtis and his nurse, Antoinette Howard. By the time they arrive in New York, the codicil's witnessed, signed and ready to submit to probate. Tyler's driven the car ahead and is on hand when Madame is transferred from the train to an ambulance. It's said that immediately upon arriving at Lewaro, she asks for music, and so somebody turns on the Estey and it plays all over the house as the patient is assisted into bed.

When the town house was finished, Madame confessed to Ransom that however beautiful it was, she could never be happy living in somebody else's house, even her daughter's. Exhausted as she now is, she must feel comforted to be home once again, surrounded by all her familiar possessions. Old things soothe the heart, and so do the presence and love of her friends, staff and doctors; J. H. Ward has taken an emergency leave from the Army and will arrive soon; Ransom's there, and her loving staff and friends. But there is only one person who truly matters and she isn't there. According to Ransom, Lelia hears of the gravity of her mother's condition in Colón, Panama, but neither he nor anybody else says when that is, or at what point a cable was sent. All we know is, Madame's dying and her only child isn't there. Even as her condition worsens—according to the people who are with her to the end—Madame will ask that Lelia not be alerted, in case the "crisis" passes.

But some of this has been invented, after the fact and for obvious reasons, and the truth is, Ransom would've sent word by now, no matter Madame's wishes. Professional to the bone, he understands that his job description has changed and that it now includes making decisions *for* his employer. Odds are, he began tracking down Madame's daughter from St. Louis and that cables for Lelia Walker Robinson lie waiting for her in various cities and countries, all saying the same thing: COME HOME IMMEDIATELY, MADAM WALKER GRAVELY ILL.

Four weeks will pass between the day Madame is helped into the railroad car in St. Louis and the moment of her death at Villa Lewaro. Another five days before funeral services in the Grand Salon. Ample time for a distraught and wealthy daughter to make arrangements to sail to New Orleans, take a train to New York and be driven to Irvington.

Assuming she got word. Assuming she bothered to check for messages.

Deathwatch

In part, the codicil to her will reinforces Madame's ongoing commitments by simply increasing the amounts she's already bequeathed to such causes as the Mite Missionary Society, Mary McLeod Bethune's Daytona Normal and Industrial Institute and the "Old Folks Home" of St. Louis. She doubles some of these bequests, adds new ones and augments her bequests to some of the children—godsons Frank Ransom and Hubert Barnes Ross (son of a Denver friend), as well as R. L. Brokenburr's daughter, Nerissa. Mae Robinson, who was not included in the original will, is now to receive $10,000, even though, unlike the Ross boy's, her connection to Madame is not specified. And this time she includes Ransom, who is to receive a raise of $1,000 a year until his annual salary is up to $10,000. She also directs that Brokenburr's salary be raised to $5,000 a year once he's been in her employ for five years, even though he's already been working for her longer than that.

Lelia's one-third share of the business is left unchanged, but the other two-thirds is to be divided into two separate trust funds, one for charities, the other for the upkeep of Villa Lewaro. Lelia is still included as one of the five trustees who are to administer these funds, but in the codicil, Madame names Ransom and Brokenburr as two others to serve in this capacity, presumably to prevent Lelia from stacking the deck in her favor. She still leaves Lewaro to her daughter, but the disposition of the property after Lelia's death reflects Madame's intensified political awareness as well as a growing distrust of Lelia's intentions and her own need to maintain control over her home beyond the grave.

Item 3 of the codicil directs that "if at the death of my daughter, Lelia W. Robinson, the National Association for the Advancement of Colored People is measuring up to the satisfaction of the committee named, I direct that my residence, Villa Lewaro, and the trust funds set aside for its maintenance and upkeep to be turned over to such Association for its use and benefit. If not, the Committee will select such organization as in its judgment is doing the most for Racial uplift and benefit and turn said residence and trust fund over to the organization so selected." It's not clear exactly who will serve on this "Committee," but assuming she is referring to the same trustees who will handle her trust fund, this obviously rules out any opportunity for Lelia herself to determine what happens to Lewaro after her death. By April 29, the will's been filed in Marion County, Indiana, Probate Court.

Within a week of Madame's arrival in Irvington, the Walker Company launches its new ad campaign, to introduce the toilet articles and unveil its revised style of marketing. There's no picture of Madame and none of her products, no illustrations, no stories to educate and convince. The ad takes up a full page and the printing is reversed so that the background is black and the lettering white. Squeezed between two large number tens, the ad lists "Madame C. J. Walker's VERY BEST Hair and Beauty Preparations": the five standard hair preparations, plus the new face products. Down below which is "the testimony of millions" attesting that "once you use Madame C. J. Walker's, nothing else will satisfy." A smaller version of this same ad boasts, "Worth More Than They Cost. Sold Everywhere." Now that the market's been saturated with hair products and information, and women already believe in the products, there's no longer a need to extol their efficacy. Another change is the spelling of Madame's name with the *e* at the end for the first time in years.

A couple days later, on May 5, a two-day meeting is convened at Carnegie Hall, dedicated to the anti-lynching cause. Some twenty-five hundred attend, including members of the City Bar Association, former New York governor and future Chief Justice of the U.S. Charles Evans Hughes, and Emmett O'Neal—a white man who, once governor of Alabama, has spoken out against lynching. "Little can be done," says

Hughes, "in the cause of international justice unless nations establish strongly and securely the foundations of justice within their own borders. . . . You cannot dethrone justice in the South and let lynching go unpunished there and expect to be secure in the metropolis of New York." Eloquently succinct as always, James Weldon Johnson suggests that "the race problem in the United States has resolved itself into a question of saving black men's bodies and white men's souls."

Madame has sent a $5,000 donation by way of Mary Talbert, the money to be used to "further the propaganda against lynching." When this contribution is announced from the stage, illness is cited as the reason for Madame's absence, though her condition is said to have improved.

Her cause has always been education, to spread the learning process throughout both races until the best people understand and then change. But the word "propaganda" indicates a loss of faith in the process, implying that education alone isn't enough and issuing a call to action—perhaps borrowed from the ILDP.

That's a cool $9,000 she's donated in a couple weeks' time, not to mention the codicil's extra ten thousand or so to charities. One reason the estimates of Madame's worth vary so wildly may be that she doesn't actually *know* what she's worth, or how much she has to give away. Her will and especially the codicil read like the documents of a woman reaching into a bottomless basket, pulling out a handful of dollars and like Johnny Appleseed planting trees, tossing them hither and yon. Reaching back in, scooping up some more.

In Irvington, the deathwatch continues. Her caretakers do a layered duty, tending to the patient's basic needs while telling lively stories, cooking special meals, switching organ-roll tunes, responding to Madame's wishes. When kidneys fail, vision diminishes. By now, it's likely she can barely make out who's at her side. Hours crawl, nobody sleeps. The Tiffany clock chimes four times an hour, forty-eight times during the day and ninety-six times a day. Edna Thomas—an actress who knows music—plays Madame's favorites. Ward stays on and so does Curtis. When Antoinette Howard is exhausted, another nurse is brought in, to spell her. Traveling companion Lulu Thompson arrives, stays. Other specialists are called.

There is nothing to do but keep on. Wait.

On May 16, Madame rises up in bed to write or dictate a letter to her daughter, addressing it to "My darling baby." She was delighted to learn—apparently from letters read to her by Edna and Lou—that Lelia had decided to marry James Kennedy, because while she never said as much, he, and not Wiley Wilson, was always her first choice. Her only desire now is for Lelia to marry quietly at Lewaro and then take off for France, where she can get the chateau she wants and Kennedy can study for a year. Madame, after completing her anticipated trip around the world, will join them there, making France her headquarters. Closing with a poignant admission—"I never want you to leave me to go this far again"—she then sends love from Nettie and the girls and herself, with "kisses and kisses and kisses" from "Your devoted Mother."

Lelia might not, in fact, read this until she arrives in Irvington. And when did she write the letters read by Edna and Lou, *if* in fact she did? Or did her friends compose the notes for her, knowing how desperate Madame was to receive word? In either case, what message convinced Madame that Lelia was going to marry James Arthur Kennedy? In a six-part series that in 1931 will run in the *Inter-State Tattler*—a spicy Harlem gossip and society sheet—columnist Edgar Rouzeau suggests that "knowing her mother was near death," Lelia "wrote from South America to announce her decision to marry Dr. James Arthur Kennedy," who was Madame's choice for Lelia but "not the man [she] loved."

That the source of this theory may well have been A'Lelia herself—who cooperated with Rouzeau—complicates the situation even further. To begin with, there's the implication that she wrote a convenient lie to her mother on her deathbed. And then there's the more troubling question: if she wrote because she knew her mother was dying, why didn't she come home? I'm trying to give Lelia the benefit of the doubt here, but sympathy comes hard. Even if somebody wires Lelia and says that while her mother's seriously ill, there's no need to rush home, she should keep pushing for business in Latin America, it's what her mother wants, common sense holds that the patient's not in charge, and if any loved one—much less your own mother—is sick unto death, you don't listen to others' admonitions, or even her own; you buy a ticket (or, considering the size of her fortune, a boat if necessary) and go home. In the end we come face-to-face with the fact that *nothing* justifies a delay if Lelia has even an inkling that her mother might die before she returns. And there's little doubt that she had more than that.

Additional contradictions arise in that same Edgar Rouzeau story when he describes A'Lelia's 1919 trip as an "indefinite vacation" through Cuba, Jamaica, Haiti, Trinidad and the West Indies. Having grown "weary of toiling" in the 136th Street office, Rouzeau says, she was having such a wonderful time on her trip that Madame begged her doctors not to notify her unless they " 'thought it best.' " But as in the case of Minnie Murphy, we have to wonder whose story this is and why he felt compelled to put "thought it best" in quotation marks, and just whom he's quoting, anyway. It's important to remember as well that the *Tattler* is filled with juicy and spirited information about A'Lelia—her whereabouts and new dresses, her blowouts at Villa Lewaro, what kind of whoopee she's making at all hours of the morning. But to give due credit, A'Lelia Walker wasn't a liar. At the time of the interview, she was nearing the end of her own life, and if she'd wanted to polish up her behavior, wouldn't she have said she was toiling for her mother's company in the Caribbean instead of having the time of her life?

When Minerva Breedlove died, we've surmised, she left seven-year-old Sarah with a legacy of constancy, resoluteness and the ability to work long hours without complaint or letup. *Learn to read. Stay out of white people's way. Mind no business not your own.* These lessons served Sarah well, allowing her to live her own life, to believe in her own possibilities and to do great things. But her legacy to her own daughter is far more complex, as it was bound to be. As Ransom's daughter, A'Lelia Ransom Nelson, will say with a shrug, "Madame came from scratch, her daughter had everything." Is it any wonder they had differences and difficulties?

While we don't know *how* Madame came to the conclusion that her daughter is planning to marry Dr. Kennedy—whether from a delirium-induced revelation or her daughter's own declaration—obviously she finds a way. And in a wild overreaction, she summons him to her bedside. Once there (according to Edna Thomas), when not attending to his future mother-in-law—who has, reportedly, *asked* him to marry Lelia—Kennedy skulks through Villa Lewaro like a boy prince, assessing his future dowry.

As for the chateau and the trip around the world, Madame's been telling her daughter from the beginning that whatever she wants is hers, and nothing has changed. When she writes that last letter, she is within three days of falling into a coma from which she will never return. Surely another cable is sent to Lelia: COME HOME IMME-DIATELY.

End

It's hard to know how much truth a dying person wants or needs, but in the end Madame's friends decide to tell her about the death on May 9 of a friend, thirty-eight-year-old James Reese Europe, who, after surviving the war with the 369th Infantry, and only three months after his band's triumphal march through Harlem, has been stabbed to death in Boston by his own drummer, whom he'd reportedly instructed to "put more pep in his sticks." Apparently, Madame takes the news hard, and some of the people tending to her believe this shock contributed to the accelerating downturn in her condition. Europe—who is credited with bringing jazz to the Continent—is laid to rest in Arlington Cemetery.

As if a harbinger of trouble to come, his murder signals the beginning of a season so violent and filled with racial terrorism, it will come to be known as Red Summer. In Vicksburg, on the very day of Europe's burial, a twenty-three-year-old black man named Lloyd Clay is burned to death while the sheriff stands idly by and wives shout to their husbands and little boys to their daddies to bring them a finger. Clay has been accused of entering the room of a white woman, who later apologizes for having yielded to her own fear when a crowd brought Clay to her and insisted that she identify him.

Racial backlash to African-American participation in the war makes for a nonstop wave of murders, arson and intimidation, even as black men and women continue campaigning for Victory Bonds in Harlem. Moorfield Storey, chairman of the NAACP, warned of this possibility when the war ended, because "Negroes will come back feeling like men and not disposed to accept the treatment which they have been subjected." In a similar vein, a Chicago paper suggests that what white terrorists fear is that the "Negro is . . . beginning to bask in the sunlight of real manhood." DuBois goes a step further and predicts, in addition, the assertion of a new African-American womanhood. Meanwhile, violence erupts in other quarters, and in one day only, a New York City postal clerk uncovers thirty-six bombs addressed to government officials and capitalists, including J. P. Morgan and John D. Rockefeller.

Woodrow Wilson is wrapping things up in Versailles, getting ready to come home and make sure Congress passes his League of Nations bill. And in all of the commotion about world peace and how parity with nations of darker-skinned peoples will affect the white man's historical belief in his right to dominate and own, Congress takes time to consider the Eighteenth Amendment, outlawing the sale of liquor.

B eginning Monday, May 19, the basic functions of Madame's life shut down, one by one. On that day, states the *New York Age*, she "became unconscious and remained in a coma" until her death the following Sunday. But the *Chicago Defender*—which runs a fuller coverage of her last days, and actually sends a journalist to Lewaro on Thursday night, the twenty-second—reports that she went through alternating periods of stillness and delirium until the last seven hours of her life on Sunday, when she slipped into a coma. The truth is, there are two states people call a coma. One can be described as unrousable unconsciousness, the other a deep stupor into which the patient falls but from which she may be roused. Perhaps Madame suffered the latter.

The weather had turned cold on the Thursday night the *Defender* reporter arrived. Rain was falling in a steady drip, and gloom pervaded Villa Lewaro. According to the journalist, the weather only "added to the melancholiness of the whole thing." Madame was "conscious, though speechless, due to the paralyzing of the muscles in the throat." Also, she had lost the sight in both eyes, and her condition was described by her loyal caretakers as "pitiful." While she has no desire to take nourishment or breathe through an oxygen mask, Ward convinces her to eat some pureed food, and he reattaches the oxygen tent "in a vain hope that her daughter . . . might see her alive." On Monday the nineteenth, the *Defender* reports, Lelia had cabled to say she was on her way.

Villa Lewaro fills up. Agnes Prosser, Madame's former sister-in-law and C. J. Walker's sister, arrives from Louisville. Freeman Ransom's wife, Nettie. Three of the Breedlove nieces—Anjetta, Mattie and Thirsapen—from Los Angeles. Another Harlem friend of Lelia's, Beatrice "Bee" King. Louis George. Edna Thomas's husband, Lloyd. With the doctors Kennedy, Curtis and Ward, Ransom, Edna, Louise and the two nurses, this comes to sixteen guests, and there are probably more, so perhaps someone brings out the half-dozen folding cots stored on the third floor.

By Friday, Ward informs the household that Madame Walker cannot last longer than Sunday. On Saturday night, about midnight, she slips into unconsciousness. And her faithful friends and doctors and family gather around her bed; they are religious people who also believe in love and company, and that no one should pass from this life into the next alone. And so they wait, hushed, whispering, watching her, waiting.

Sunday dawns warm and clear, and early rays of the sun crack through the drawn damask curtains and perhaps fall in splinters across the rose silk coverlet on Madame's bed. At seven o'clock her people are still there, but no one feels her go and no one knows when she dies until Ward turns and says, "It's over."

And if they weep it is with relief, for the end of her suffering. Her dying words, Ward later reports, were "I want to live to help my race."

R ansom announces that funeral services will be private, and held at ten-thirty on Friday morning, May 30, at Villa Lewaro. They are waiting, he explains, to give Madame's daughter time to arrive. In the meantime, the remains will be kept in a vault at Woodlawn Cemetery, where Madame is to be buried, and in any case, there will be no interment until Lelia is present.

Sunday. Monday. Tuesday. Wednesday. Thursday. Time between a death and the funeral drags like a weight around the neck. You wake up, do things, people come, you talk or don't talk, eat, walk around, tidy up, straighten books on a shelf, thinking surely it's noon, time for lunch. But the clock reads ten-fifteen. Hours left. Hours to walk through endless minutes.

Florists' trucks deliver huge bouquets, enormous baskets. Edna Thomas keeps the list. She will be the one to write the thank-you notes for Lelia to sign.

By Wednesday some of the petals have curled, and there is still no word. Nor on Thursday.

Edna Thomas says Dr. Kennedy's air of entitlement during these days made her skin crawl. Nobody knows when Lelia's planning to show up, much less whom she'll marry, if anybody, once she gets there. But Edna, Lulu Thompson and Bee King are certain about one thing: she might well marry Dr. Kennedy, but she will never like him.

On Friday morning, as reported by the *Defender,* the casket is returned to Villa Lewaro. Mourners arrive, and the service begins. Though the funeral is "private," a thousand people are said to crowd into the downstairs rooms of Villa Lewaro. The circle drive is packed with cars, and others are parked down Broadway all the way to the Presbyterian church. There are several buses. The Irvington chief of police stands in the middle of Broadway directing traffic and signaling gawkers to pass on by.

Inside, the metal casket has been placed in the center of the music room, under the sky-painted ceiling between the crystal chandeliers. To accommodate the crush, the pocket doors between the music room and reception hall and the veranda have been slid into the walls, and the portieres thrown open. The staff has been briefed on crowd control, and several young women from the Women's Motor Corps have volunteered to help. The casket is open, and the crowd files by. Madame's wrapped in a simple white satin shroud, a bouquet of orchids on her chest.

The Harlem-based Adolph Howell Funeral Home is in charge of the services. Chairs have been set up for friends, family and participants in the service on the east end of the room, facing the Estey. The young women of the Motor Corps have kept a path clear from the staircase through the reception hall and into the music room, and at eleven o'clock, the funeral party marches in a formal parade down the marble stairs and into the big room. Leading it is Reverend J. W. Brown, pastor of Madame's church, the Mother Zion AME in Harlem, and master of these ceremonies, followed by the ministers Richard Bolden, William Sampson Brooks, F. M. Ellegor and Adam Clayton Powell Sr. Then come the pallbearers—presumably chosen by Ransom—J. Rosamond Johnson, Fred Moore, Eugene Kinckle Jones, Vertner Tandy, John Talbert and John Nail. Finally, a few friends and "the relatives," presumably the Breedlove nieces, for without Lelia who else is there? Louvenia Powell doesn't come and doesn't send flowers; neither does her son, Willie. (One obituary has Madame leaving two unnamed sisters behind; there certainly might be another, but if so, she isn't here, and more than likely the reference is to Lucy

Breedlove, her sister-in-law. Another obituary notes both a sister—Louvenia Powell of Akron, Ohio—and an unnamed brother in St. Louis, but he doesn't show up, either.)

One of the ministers opens the ceremonies with the reading of the Twenty-third Psalm, followed by a prayer by a different minister. Edna Thomas plays Madame's beloved "Communion in G" on the Estey, and Thomas Taylor, secretary of the West 135th Street YMCA, reads a number of telegrams and resolutions. Another minister reads other resolutions. Then the well-known singer and composer Harry Burleigh sings a hymn, and Adam Clayton Powell reads an obituary which ends, "She has crossed the bar with malice toward none."

Rosamond Johnson sings his own composition "Since You Went Away," after which Rev. Brooks, one of Madame's St. Louis ministers, preaches the sermon and tells of his last meeting with Madame, when she was ill in St. Louis, when they read the twenty-first chapter of Revelations together. He ends his sermon with the line "Farewell, farewell, a long farewell." In a brief nod to Madame's politics, Assistant Secretary of War Emmett Scott and John Shillady of the NAACP speak briefly, and the services conclude with a musical version of Tennyson's "Crossing the Bar."

During the ceremony, a telegram arrives from New Orleans saying that Lelia will arrive at four-thirty that afternoon. At two-thirty, the casket is returned to Woodlawn Cemetery, where the satin-shrouded figure of Madame waits for interment. Night falls. No Lelia.

DAUGHTER FAILS TO ARRIVE shout the headlines of the *Chicago Defender*.

Daughter Arrives

She shows up on Saturday afternoon, the thirty-first, bringing with her stories of missed boats and trains and getting the news mid-ocean and the officers on board sending a radiogram to New Orleans to secure Pullman reservations from there to New York, and she was hoping Saturday afternoon wouldn't be too late.

The attentive Kennedy is at the station to meet and console her, possibly to accompany her to Woodlawn to view her mother's remains. But much to everybody's surprise, Lelia postpones her trip to the cemetery, traveling instead to Lewaro, where she soon takes Kennedy aside to inform him that she is not in love with him and will not marry him (anyway, according to some, his divorce from his first wife is not yet final). And the scorned doctor—who more than likely had not considered love a binding element in this particular contract—pulls himself together and is driven to New York to board the train back to Chicago. By then, Lelia has invited her other suitor, the handsome Wiley Wilson, to Irvington.

On Monday morning, when she goes to Woodlawn, the caretaker has slid the casket from its vault into a viewing room. Who is with her? Mae? Ransom? Both, probably. That night or the next morning, Wiley Wilson arrives, and on Tuesday, Madam Walker is buried. Only Lelia, Ransom and "members of the household" attend. Presumably this means everybody staying at Lewaro, including Edna Thomas, the Breedlove nieces, Nettie Ransom, Mae, and the Lewaro staff. Lelia orders a lush blanket of roses to cover the grave.

Three days later, she gets married. Fred Moore, editor of the *New York Age* and one of Madame's pallbearers, chooses to announce the nuptials in front-page scandal-sheet fashion: "WEDS THREE DAYS AFTER BURIAL OF HER MOTHER . . . Mrs. Lelia Walker Robinson Becomes the Bride of Doctor Wiley Wilson on June 6th." Indeed, on her thirty-fourth birthday.

The ceremony's performed at St. James Presbyterian by Rev. Frank M. Hyder. Lelia's matron of honor is Edna Thomas, while Wilson chooses a fellow doctor for his best man. Among those present are Louise Thompson; Louis George; Lewaro housekeeper Sara Everett and her daughter, Estelle; the Breedloves of Los Angeles; Edna Thomas's husband, Lloyd; Bee King; "Miss Mae Robinson, adopted daughter of the bride"; and Nettie Ransom, whose husband pointedly does not attend. There's no formal reception afterwards, but the "contracting parties" do have a luncheon at Wanamaker's, Madame and Lelia's favorite department store. This story's repeated word for word—including the crassly precise "contracting parties"—in a couple of papers and on several wire services, so obviously it has been written by the Walker Company and issued as a press release, which also reports that when the newlyweds met about a year ago, a strong attachment sprang up between them, culminating in a romantic courtship and marriage. After spending their wedding night in the city, the couple will reportedly travel to Villa Lewaro, where the bride will take up her abode as mistress, "which was in accordance with the desire of her mother." Within two weeks, Dr. and Mrs. Wilson will leave on a three months' honeymoon in the Canadian Rockies, California and Honolulu, after which they will live in Irvington-on-Hudson and Dr. Wilson will begin the practice of medicine in New York.

Later in 1919, Andrew Carnegie dies. Having given $350 million away in his lifetime, in death he still has $30 million left for foundations and causes, servants and old friends, not to mention Scottish tenant farmers on his estate. The Senate fails to approve Wilson's League of Nations. Red Summer lingers, and in a Chicago race riot twenty-three Negroes are killed in five days. When the Boston police go on strike, Governor Calvin Coolidge steps in and, after breaking the strike, becomes an instant hero. Steelworkers strike, mine workers and railroad workers strike. The cost of living goes up. The Yankees purchase Babe Ruth for $125,000.

At the Walker Company's third annual convention in Muskogee, Madame is given a memorial sermon and the new "editress" of the company-published *Woman's Voice* magazine is introduced, but Lelia, who's still on her honeymoon, does not attend. The president suffers a debilitating illness, probably a stroke, though details are withheld. After being declared insane, the drummer who murdered Jim Europe has pled guilty to manslaughter and receives a ten-to-fifteen-year prison sentence. In Paris, a uniformed African-American soldier is murdered by a white officer for "bumping" into him. The *Defender* issues an EXTRA! giving the details of Madame's will. A marble stone is placed at the head of her grave, with no message or date, only her name: MADAM C. J. WALKER. And there she lies, under a sheltering oak, in her bronze casket, wrapped in white.

IX · *Afterwards, 1919–1931*

A'Lelia Walker was the great Harlem party giver. . . . Big-hearted, night-dark, hair-straightening heiress, she made no pretense at being intellectual or exclusive . . . at her "at homes," Negro poets and number bankers mingled with downtown poets and seat-on-the-stock-exchange racketeers. . . . She had an apartment that held perhaps a hundred; she would issue several hundred invitations. . . . Her parties were as crowded as the New York subway at rush hour.

LANGSTON HUGHES, *THE BIG SEA*

The Joy Goddess of Harlem

The year after Madame dies, the nation goes a little crazy. In January, the Eighteenth Amendment outlaws liquor, which, according to the Commissioner of Prohibition, will not henceforth be "sold, nor given away, nor hauled in anything on the surface of the earth or under the earth or in the air." Most citizens accept this as a challenge and an encouragement to drink more than they ever had before. Eight months later, women get the vote, then fashion goes berserk, with skirts up to the knee, flesh-toned stockings, bobbed hair. Corsets are flung in the trash, replaced with flimsy silk and rayon. The twenties: Louis Armstrong blows in a new music, Josephine Baker shakes her bananas in Paris and Eugene O'Neill's *The Emperor Jones,* staged at the Provincetown Playhouse, features a *Negro* actor playing the title role. Shocking novels are published about ugliness in small bourgeois towns, about girls who dance and kiss and go wild, and the emptiness and futility represented in those books suggest to some an end to romance altogether.

Obviously, Madame's time was so different that she might as well have lived on a different planet, but her sense of entrepreneurship far outweighed any attachment to the past, and if she'd lived, she'd have not only dealt with the new craziness but exploited it. Still, she'd have been hard-pressed to predict that her daughter's untethered ways would become the norm, replacing uplift, temperance and the work ethic entirely. According to the English writer Osbert Sitwell, Prohibition was "a national obsession. Love of liberty made it almost a duty to drink more than was wise. In this respect, intellectuals vied with socialites. . . . Most festivities depended on supplies of synthetic gin and whiskey and the strength of them was formidable."

As the gin flask circulates and Harlem gangs gather to deal cards, gossip and dream up trouble all night long, Lelia Walker Wilson adds an A-apostrophe to her name. This doesn't happen until about 1923, two years after her marriage to Wilson is over but for the lawsuit (hers, over furniture) and final decree, and three years before she chases down the supremely available *other* pharmacist-physician and, like a prodigal daughter gone straight, weds the man of her mother's choice, Dr. James A. Kennedy.

No accounts explain where she came up with that *A'*. Azalia Hackley, the singer and author of *Colored Girl Beautiful*? Her trip to Addis Ababa? Her parties don't get started until past midnight, when her gang gathers to drink illegal gin, champagne and spiked iced tea. Maybe, dealing out a bridge hand at four in the morning, one of her pals says, "Lelia's a *boring* name," and they all chip in, shuffling possibilities until somebody comes up with it.

At thirty-six, the Joy Goddess of Harlem, the Mahogany Millionairess and "queen of the colored squirearchy of the planet WORLD" is too old to be a flapper, but that *A'* cuts the last thread to her beginnings as the daughter of a washerwoman. She is, after all, like her mother, an institution. And as such, she requires a memorable designation. Just as Sarah Breedlove McWilliams changed when she became Madam C. J. Walker, the newly baptized A'Lelia McWilliams Robinson Wilson Kennedy seems compelled to run faster, fly higher, go wilder. As one of her running buddies would later say, "A'Lelia had so much, and it was the days of feathers and plumes and sometimes she wore them all."

Harlem Scrapbook

When Lelia and Wiley Wilson come home from their honeymoon, they settle on 136th Street and Wilson works in a Manhattan hospital. Madame's wishes go unheeded as the newlyweds barely visit Villa Lewaro, much less think of it as home, though when the census enumerator comes around in February, they're counted as residents of Westchester County, town of Greenburgh, village of Irvington. The doctor is named head of household, Lelia as his wife and Mae Robinson his stepdaughter. Only five servants now reside at Lewaro—one of them the loyal chauffeur Lewis Tyler, who lives in the garage apartment with his wife and four children. And there is a boarder, Verna Hawkins, a single mulatto woman, thirty-one years old, with no job or profession listed. A'Lelia Walker will come to be known for her fleet of light-skinned women, their only job to remain gorgeous, stylish and gay, always within earshot of A'Lelia's latest whim. Might Ms. Hawkins fit this bill?

By the end of 1920, Lelia's off to Europe, while Wilson stays home. Ransom runs the company, and he claims to have tripled 1919's profits of $250,000. Fearful of the still-increasing competition from white drug and cosmetics companies, he decries firms "operated by colored but . . . financed by white capital" and, in a stunning departure from Madame's lifelong stand against such products, introduces a skin bleach called Tan-Off, which sells even as the demand for hair products falls off.

Women vote in the 1920 presidential election, and the affable Warren Harding is elected. Langston Hughes writes the poem that made him famous, "The Negro Speaks of Rivers," during a train ride to Mexico. James Weldon Johnson becomes the first black executive secretary of the NAACP. *Shuffle Along,* a Broadway musical written and produced by Negroes and starring Florence Mills, is a big hit. White artists and bohemian types flock uptown from Greenwich Village to Harlem, where Carl Van Vechten—one of A'Lelia's closest running buddies—is known as white master of the colored revels. After her death, he'll write novelist Chester Himes, "You should have known A'Lelia Walker. Nothing in this age is quite as good as THAT . . . !" Except for the occasional event or weekend blowout, Villa Lewaro doesn't feature in Lelia's new life. When the president of the Liberian Republic comes to New York, she does arrange a weekend of entertainment there: lavish meals, fireworks and even a visit to Teddy Roosevelt's grave. Her estranged husband joins in, as does Mayme White, her future housemate and traveling companion, known for wearing bracelets to her elbow.

At the Walker Company convention (in Boston that year) Lelia is not mentioned, but by then her marriage is over. To save herself from embarrassing rumors and attention, she once again sails for France, spends a month in Paris, celebrates Christmas and then goes on to Nice, Monte Carlo, Spain, Portugal, Liberia and Egypt. On a Suez Canal steamer, she journeys the length of the Red Sea, disembarks in Djibouti, heads overland to Ankober and then Addis Ababa, where, according to the *Chicago Defender,* the empress Waizeru Zauditu admires her costumes and jewelry. Lelia chronicles her journey in a relentlessly boring travel report ("Now we come to the Mount of Olives . . .") appearing in *Woman's Voice,* which the Walker Company is now publishing and using as a selling tool, exactly as Madame had planned. Reading her travelogue, it's hard not to feel sympathy for this lost, overindulged daughter, who—unlike her mother, the croppers' child—was given books and an education, yet can't come up with one original idea, much less turn it into a graceful sentence.

The nonsense tune "Yes! We Have No Bananas" tops the musical charts. Jean Toomer's novel *Cane* is published, Paul Robeson makes his debut singing the role of a voodoo king, Bessie Smith records "Down-Hearted Blues," mobster Owney Madden has opened the Cotton Club in Harlem and Columbia University anthropology professor Franz Boaz declares in a speech that there is no evidence whatsoever that the white man is inherently superior to any other race.

Back home, contemplating the many charitable requests pouring in, A'Lelia makes choices more by who's asking and how she gains socially than out of any sense of mission. And when invitations are sent out to a 1923 benefit for the Ethiopian Art Players to be held at the Harlem town house, she signs them with her new name, A'Lelia Walker. In Indianapolis, the company announces a contest among agents for the best essay on the Americanization of the Negro, and then a Holy Land Contest, the first prize a trip there and $250. (The latter is open to pastors, bishops, presiding elders and general officers of any religious denomination; in other words, men.) The new ads turn misty-magical, one featuring an Art Deco fairy (white) waving a wand, another the Fountain of Youth. No trace of Madame, no issues of womanly pride. Ransom says the company now employs forty thousand agents. In California, Warren Harding dies mysteriously in a hotel room, perhaps poisoned by bad crabmeat.

In November 1923, A'Lelia pitches a wedding for Mae Robinson the likes of which Harlem and much of America has never before seen. The ceremony is thoroughly publicized as costing $42,000 and takes place in the church that broke the Harlem color line, the renowned St. Philip's Episcopal, with the well-known Rev. Hutchens Bishop officiating. And A'Lelia's found the perfect husband to serve her social ambitions, if not her daughter's happiness. Gordon Henry Jackson is a notably stiff-spined, unhandsome, bald fellow many years older than the bride. Known for his explosive temper, he nonetheless makes up for his deficiencies by being a light-skinned doctor from an old and prominent Cincinnati family (known, ironically, for its frugality).

Looking perfectly miserable, the bride wears a crown of seed pearls and a very pretty dress of chiffon, lace and satin. Except for the one worn by the mother of the bride, the dresses of the wedding party have been designed by African-Americans. No racial stickler when it comes to fashion, A'Lelia's in metallic gold from Paris. There is no mention of Mae's blood relatives, the Bryants and the Hammonds. Freeman Ransom, a stand-in, gives the bride away. Extra police are sent to Harlem to contain the crowds, and the publicity is phenomenal. Newspapers slant the story in various ways:

> "9,000 Guests Invited to a Colored Wedding . . . Of the 9,000 invited, 1,000 are the personal friends of Madame A'lelia Walker."—*New York Times*
>
> "Heiress to Become Bride . . . An attractive young lady, demure, socially prominent, a graduate of fashionable Spelman Seminary."—*St. Louis Argus*

"Marriage of NY Heiress to Chicago Physician is a Most Elaborate Function . . . Streets are jammed with people wanting to get view."—*New York Age*

"Negress Gave Daughter $42,000 Wedding to Show Her Race What It Could Do."—*New York World*

"The Negro 400 Strutted!"—*Kansas City Star*

And from Jervis Anderson, in his book *This Was Harlem:* "134th Street, from Seventh to Eighth Avenues, was jammed with thousands of people, colored and white . . . hundreds of automobiles of every type and description. . . . Admission to the church was entirely by card and so great was the interest, it is reported that many not having invitations expressed a willingness to pay $50 if one could be obtained. . . ."

Another invitation is required to attend the reception at Villa Lewaro, which A'Lelia has had spruced up at a cost of $17,000. Afterwards, the newlyweds move to Chicago, where Mae buys cookbooks and, in an effort to become a dutiful doctor's wife, takes a class in domestic science. Dr. Jackson claims he knows nothing of his wife's riches and has no interest whatsoever in the cosmetics business. By the end of 1925, Mae is pregnant with the couple's first child and A'Lelia has received her final divorce decree.

When Ransom offers concrete proof of financial setbacks in the company, A'Lelia economizes by selling whatever cars remain in the Irvington garage and making do with one big Lincoln. Early in 1926, she spends six weeks under a doctor's care for an unexplained malady, perhaps to do with her nerves, which she often describes as "shot." And in May, to settle her life somewhat, she takes a last stab at conventionality by marrying Dr. Kennedy. This time Ransom approves, and the wedding takes place in his home in Indianapolis. Kennedy's finances are a mess and he needs a new start, so through the good graces of her mother's old friend and physician J. H. Ward, A'Lelia secures for her new husband an appointment at Tuskegee, working in the hospital.

On her wedding day, A'Lelia sends a poignant telegram to Carl Van Vechten and his wife, Fanya: "Married twelve o'clock today. PRAY FOR MY HAPPINESS." From Chicago, less than a week later, she pens a note in purple ink on her new lavender bread-and-butter stationery, assuring them she is quite happy because, she reasons, "what bride isn't?" But her underlying doubts come through when she writes of being "stationed" in Chicago and closes with a wistful "Gee, I'll be glad to get back to New York," adding in a P.S. that she's keeping her "maiden" name.

That same month, an eight-months-pregnant Mae leaves Dr. Jackson and moves into her own apartment. By December she's filed for divorce and taken herself back to New York with her six-month-old son, Gordon Walker Jackson. But in the end, A'Lelia does a better job managing Mae's life than Madame did hers. Appearing in August 1927 is Pittsburgh attorney Marion Perry, rumored to have been on the lookout for an heiress for some time, having only a few years earlier lost out to a fraternity brother on a bid for an Oklahoma oil queen. In New York, he fares better and is invited to an evening at Villa Lewaro. On a whim, A'Lelia takes her guests into town for a tour of Harlem nightclubs. Mae's not invited, yet within months is married to Perry. He'll adopt little Gordon, whose name will become Walker Gordon Perry, called—as C. J.'s contribution to this family continues—Walker.

The 1926 convention is held in Kansas City, and A'Lelia's scheduled to attend; if she does, the company doesn't say so and she doesn't make a speech. Discussions among agents focus strictly on business—general efficiency, and the latest vogues of beauty culture here and abroad. No politics, no visionary talk of great things ahead for proud women of the race. Back home that fall, she makes a quick trip to Villa Lewaro, throws a few parties and stages a ball at the town house for two young "nieces," possibly Wiley Wilson's, about to make their debut. Osbert Sitwell says a Dr. X, known as the Negro Lenin, accompanies A'Lelia, that she wears an elephant-gray Greek ballgown and her hair up with strands of gold braided through it. And that late in the evening, she takes him upstairs and opens a real bottle of champagne, which they proceed to drink down as she complains about her feet. They spoiled her honeymoon twenty years ago, she tells Sitwell, and they still hurt.

A'Lelia makes another couple of trips to Tuskegee, but by the spring of 1927 she's rented an apartment on Edgecomb Avenue in Harlem's Sugar Hill as a refuge from the town house and the business and a hideout for big parties and a more private life. Mayme White makes frequent trips from Philadelphia, and stays over; two male pals live across the hall; everybody pursues pure endless fun, its intensity only heightened by the illegality of the refreshments. ("Ah," exults *Inter-State Tattler* "Social Snapshots" columnist Geraldyne Dismond, "the flowing bowl!") A'Lelia orders elegant new stationery with "Le Charmant Secret" at the top.

She returns to Indianapolis to participate in the groundbreaking of the next big post-Madame mistake, and it's a whopper. She and Ransom have collaborated on the construction of a four-story, 48,000-square-foot building, with a 1,500-seat theater for both live events and movies; there's also plenty of room for factory and office space, a beauty parlor and coffee shop. The cost of the site alone is $68,000, and the design and building estimates run as high as a million. It's a beautiful structure, which from the outside somewhat resembles the Flatiron Building in New York. But the timing couldn't be worse.

A'Lelia shoots on back home, takes her friends to Atlantic City, attends the opening of Club Ebony, goes to Chicago to sit ringside when Gene Tunney gets a long count and defeats Jack Dempsey for the heavyweight championship. In October of 1927, having decided she'll make it into high society by means of culture, she turns her town house living quarters into a salon she calls the Dark Tower after Countee Cullen's column of that name in *Opportunity*, the National Urban League's periodical. Dedicated to "the aesthetes," the Dark Tower, she promises, will be a "quiet place of particular charm. Members only." A *salon*, it's to be, where art and ideas will hatch and A'Lelia will hover, angel-like, in the background.

Imagine the aesthetes' surprise, then, when they present their engraved invitations to the grand opening and step inside only to discover that to check their hats they'll have to pay fifteen cents. If they manage to push through the mostly white crowd to the kitchen, a cup of coffee goes for a dime, sandwiches for a half-dollar and lemonade for a quarter. One artist is nearly refused admission for not wearing a tie. Painted on the walls of the Dark Tower are the poems of Langston Hughes and Countee Cullen, but to save money A'Lelia hired a sign painter instead of giving the job to an artist.

Bruce Nugent—an artist, writer and self-proclaimed homosexual—later said that artists didn't like the place because it was mostly a "place for A'Lelia to show off her blackness to whites." And that when they did have meetings, mostly people sat around discussing uncertain plans until somebody produced a quart of gin "like some immaculate conception," and in these lush, lavish early days of the Harlem Renaissance nobody could turn down a good time because it was richly deserved and too important to ignore. Thus do art and ideas fly out the window. As Geraldyne Dismond will say in her "Social Snapshots" column, at A'Lelia's gatherings, the "whoopee was Grade A."

But A'Lelia launches even more soirées to which white social New York and visiting royalty are invited, and soon the Dark Tower no longer serves her purposes and begins to fail. The sulky patron blames the artists for letting her down and closes the Dark Tower after less than a year. Her social secretary, Sari Price Patton, runs ads in the *Tattler* announcing the availability of the "newly Renovated Walker Studios" for weddings, banquets, receptions, club meetings and all social occasions. And so the Dark Tower reopens as a classy watering hole.

A'Lelia leaves for what she calls "the interior"—Alabama—for maybe a week, to visit Kennedy at Tuskegee. Then she's back, giving another party. Geraldyne Dismond: "Had the best time at the Dark Tower from around 2–4 A M . . . Ralph Banks sang 'The Man I Love,' Uncle Tom McCleary Stinette did a too bad tango . . . oodles of bumping by the rest of us . . . and A'Lelia Walker of course was there and by the way she had on a metal brocade gown with thousands of dollars of Russian sable on it. . . ." Six nights later, the gang meets at the Dark Tower for turkey sandwiches and "A'Lelia iced tea," and the next night they all go to the Cotton Ball and a few nights later to sit in A'Lelia's box at the Renaissance Casino's debutante ball. Two weeks after that, there's a photograph taken of them all at a Dark Tower party, and at five foot nine—six feet in heels—and a hundred ninety pounds, she's by far the biggest of these women; for once she's wearing neither turban nor wig, and her hair is either cropped to her skull or she simply doesn't have much. The overall effect, considering her size and the flouncy dress, is not pretty. The party then moves two doors down to the Rosebud Tea Room, and when they crawl out at five in the morning into a snowstorm, they whoop with what Dismond reports is surprise and delight. In Indianapolis, the Walker Theater opens with the showing of *The Magic Flame,* a film with Ronald Colman, Vilma Banky and an all-white cast. And when, two days after Christmas, the *Tattler* runs a "Their Favorite Sports" column, A'Lelia says hers is bridge and so does Edna Thomas, but Geraldyne Dismond prefers the sport of dieting.

Somewhere along in here, the whoopee starts to get tedious. This becomes obvious when Dismond describes a Harlem evening's festivities as "the usual routine of pleasure. . . . Talk, drink, talk, drink, eat, drink, talk." Nothing satisfies, the imagination goes stale, A'Lelia Walker's life is clearly at a standstill. And yet she and her pals keep partying—it's all been so much *fun* and besides, what else are they supposed to do?—as if waiting for some major event to come along and tell them enough is enough and maybe they should think about doing something else.

"Strangest and gaudiest of all Harlem spectacles in the twenties and still the strangest and gaudiest, is the annual Hamilton Club Lodge Ball at Rockland Palace Casino. . . ." So wrote Langston Hughes of the event he once attended as A'Lelia's guest. The two of them sat in a box and looked down on the dance floor to see men in gowns and feathers and women in tuxedoes, doing the lindy hop, the new dance craze introduced at the Savoy Ballroom. Hughes also writes about the Scandinavian prince who couldn't get into one of A'Lelia's parties at her Sugar Hill apartment, so she sent refreshments down to his car; and about Nora Holt, the blond Negro entertainer from Nevada who sang "My Daddy Rocks Me with One Steady Roll"; and about the annual birthday party Carl Van Vechten gave for his publisher, Alfred A. Knopf, and the writer and statesman James Weldon Johnson.

Sometimes A'Lelia Walker's nerves go whizzy on her and she'll take off into the interior. She's in Indianapolis for the 1928 dedication of the Walker Building and the eleventh annual convention of agents. The next year she plans to go to Alabama but thinks better of that idea, instead traveling to Indianapolis and Chicago, then to Hot Springs, Arkansas, to recover from depression, doubt and general ill health. From there, she writes openly to Carl Van Vechten: "Ever so pleased to have a line from you, found me worlds better . . . but saddled with a million doubts, that go for the rest of my life which proceeds to make me hot and hostile I can tell you. When I go over this list of doubts there isn't nothing much left for me to do but pass on. . . . I wish you would stay put for a long while so I can see you. . . ." She spends a long six months away from New York, and by the time she gets home, it's early fall, 1929.

Something had to give, financially and personally. But no one's paying attention or wants to take the time to notice—except of course Freeman Ransom, who's overplayed his doomsday cards so many times that by now nobody listens.

After A'Lelia reopens the Dark Tower, an attempt to restore her confidence and spirits, she returns to her usual routine. At one party, she serves black guests haute cuisine and the white ones chitterlings and watermelon. The night after having her picture made in furs and a cloche hat at the annual Howard-Lincoln Thanksgiving football game, she swans into the Odd Fellows Ball in a Russian court costume with silver palanquin and a deep sable flounce. Madame's friend Bessye Beardon is there too.

When the stock market crashes in October, there is no noticeable reaction in Harlem, and the night crawling continues. Mayme White moves into the Edgecomb Avenue apartment for good. Mae has her third child. In his annual address, President Herbert Hoover assures the nation that the country is fundamentally sound. In Alabama, Dr. Kennedy divorces his wife on grounds of desertion because of her refusal to live at Tuskegee. In public response, A'Lelia says her own physician advised her not to move there, and she further declares, "I will always live in New York and I never intend to marry." By the end of the year Kennedy has married a Mrs. Bessie Battey of Tuskegee.

By spring, factories are shutting down all over the country. Bread lines lengthen. Hoover says the worst is over. In hard times, how can a beauty business survive? The Walker Company starts to go down.

Midway through 1930, having read in the *New York World* that Villa Lewaro is for sale, Walter White of the NAACP writes Freeman Ransom a friendly letter. Didn't Madame give A'Lelia a "life interest in the property," and after her death weren't they supposed to be given first shot at owning Lewaro? In his rather terse response, Ransom explains that indeed the company is considering selling the property subject to A'Lelia's life interest, but that whatever happens, the NAACP shouldn't expect a grand bequest because after the mortgage and taxes have been paid off, there won't be much left. Anyway, he adds in a decidedly aggrieved tone, the company has had to take money from other funds for upkeep of the villa, which hasn't been used for anything other than weekend parties and "serves no purpose whatsoever—even the colored people do not appreciate it." Once the debts are paid, he assures White, the Walker Company will donate the balance of the proceeds to the organization doing the most for "Negro uplift," as stipulated in Madame's will.

In light of these developments, A'Lelia writes Carl Van Vechten to ask if he'd be interested in buying Lewaro, because as he can probably guess she's been holding on to it only out of sentiment for her mother, but in the end has concluded that since she feels no family ties to the house and spends all her time in the city, this is silly. House and property, she informs him, have been assessed at $190,000, but they are prepared to let it go for $150,000. Van Vechten declines.

In November, all pretense crumbles. Ransom turns down a bid on the house for $50,000 and the *New York Times* runs an ad for an auction to be held at Villa Lewaro. "Magnificent Works of Art, Furniture and Furnishings. The Entire Contents of the Palatial Home of the late Madame C. J. Walker. Under the supervision of the well-known auctioneer, Benjamin Wise, who served in the same capacity when the furnishings of the Waldorf went under the gavel. By order of F. B. Ransom, Esq., Attorney. And other parties in interest."

Her Dream of Dreams

A nd so everything goes. The Persian rugs, the gold-plated phonograph, the china and the leather-bound books. White people flock to Villa Lewaro. Broadway's lined for a mile with parked cars; additional policemen are brought in to contain the sightseers and bargain hunters who swarm the house. Covering the event for the *Chicago Defender,* Bessye Beardon casts a sad eye around the music room, where the organ sits, immovable, at one end. "It was," declares Mrs. Beardon, "her dream of dreams."

When somebody makes a low bid for the grand piano, A'Lelia ups the bid so as to hold on to it, at least for a while. And she refuses to sell the furniture in the bedroom where her mother died.

A 'Lelia Walker lives for another eight months or so, then dies at that birthday shindig in New Jersey after eating that lobster and cake and drinking that bottle of champagne. She's in a guest-cottage bedroom when apoplexy takes her, and Mayme White is with her when she goes.

Her funeral in Harlem is yet another jam-packed event, by invitation only. In her silver casket, A'Lelia wears a shiny dress and necklace. Rev. Adam Clayton Powell Sr. conducts the service. The Four Bon-Bons sing the Noël Coward song "I'll See You Again." A Langston Hughes poem, "To A'Lelia," is read as a kind of Dark Tower postmortem. And at Woodlawn, when the silver casket is lowered into the grave next to Madame's, the daredevil parachutist Herbert Julian jumps from an airplane down, down, down onto the green, green turf. As Langston Hughes remarked of A'Lelia's funeral, "That was really the end of the gay times of the New Negro era in Harlem, the period that had begun to reach its end when the crash came in 1929 and the white people had much less money to spend on themselves and practically none to spend on Negroes, for the depression brought everybody down a peg or two. And the Negroes had but few pegs to fall."

Ransom holds another auction, for the remainder of Madame's furniture as well as A'Lelia's. The city of New York buys the town house to convert into a health center; and within the year, the Companions of the Forest of America—an all-white insurance and social organization, formerly the women's auxiliary of the Ancient Order of Foresters— buy Villa Lewaro for $47,000 and transform it into the Annie E. Poth Home for tired mothers, convalescents and the aged. After the NAACP issues Ransom a quit-claim deed releasing the company from any obligation to their organization, the white women start moving in.

Ransom keeps the Walker Company afloat, but it's difficult. In time, he and Mae have their legal troubles. All of that, however, is in the future, and has nothing to do with Madame.

In the end, everything goes except the incorporated company and the new building.

And the triumph of Sarah Breedlove Walker. Which remains.

Notes

ABBREVIATIONS

AB: A'Lelia Bundles, *On Her Own Ground: The Life and Times of Madam C. J. Walker* (New York: Scribners, 2001).
AW: Lelia (A'Lelia) Robinson Walker
BTW: Booker T. Washington
CD: Chicago Defender
CJW: C. J. Walker
FBR: Freeman Briley Ransom
IF: Indianapolis Freeman
IR: Indianapolis Recorder
LoC: Library of Congress
MW: Madam C. J. Walker
MWC, IHS: Madam Walker Collection, Indiana Historical Society
NNBL: National Negro Business League
NACW: National Association of Colored Women

1. WHERE SHE CAME FROM, 1867–1878

12   "bounded on the East and West": Madison Parish Conveyance Records, Volume C, p. 266.
13   "booming the town": testimony of F. P. Stubbs, *Heirs of Burney v. Towne, Ludeling et al.,* 1895.
20   "quagmire, never thoroughly dry": "Madison Tensas" (Henry Clay Lewis), *Odd Leaves from the Life of a La. "Swamp Doctor"* (Philadelphia: T. B. Peterson and Bros., 1846), p. 112.
20   "colony of men and women": Arthur Vernon Girault, "The Patrician Days of Madison County," *Banner County Times,* Canton, Mississippi, n.d.
21   "a long and painful illness": Betty Couch Wiltshire, *Marriages and Deaths from Mississippi Newspapers,* vol. 3 (1813–1850) (Bowie, Md.: Heritage Books, 1987).
23   "for the purpose of cutting": Indenture Act and Agreement, *Heirs of Burney v. Towne, Ludeling et al.,* 1895. From the law offices of Sevier, Yerger, and Bishop, Tallulah, La.
25   "the depot at Mr. Burney's": John Q. Anderson, *Brokenburn: The Journal of Kate Stone, 1861–1868* (Baton Rouge: LSU Press, 1972), p. 103.
25   "freedom came": Vernon Lane Wharton, *The Negro in Mississippi, 1865–1890* (Chapel Hill: University of North Carolina Press, 1970), p. 47.

II. VICKSBURG, 1878–1887

44 "Madam Walker could be": *Two Dollars and a Dream,* dir. Stanley Nelson, Half Nelson Productions, 1987.

44 "preparation to meet": James Weldon Johnson, *Along This Way: The Autobiography of James Weldon Johnson* (New York: Penguin Books, 1990), p. 66.

46 "Oh, that's all right": *Two Dollars and a Dream.*

70 "I am not ashamed": Records of the NNBL. Washington, D.C.: University Publications of America, 1912.

III. ST. LOUIS, 1887–1905

123 "the principal figure": Frances L. Garside, "Queen of Gotham's Colored 400," *Literary Digest* 55 (Oct. 13, 1917); originally appeared in *Kansas City Star.*

136 "in justice to Madam C. J. Walker's memory": FBR to George Stewart, George Stewart Papers, MWC, ISH.

137 "fussy, mean and dangerous": Ida B. Winchester affidavit, Dec. 26, 1919; AB, p. 51.

151 Annie Turnbo (Malone) quotes from "Woman Says Poro College Is Hers to Last Penny," *St. Louis Post-Dispatch,* n.d. (probably 1928).

160 "told her if you can get": *Two Dollars and a Dream,* dir. Stanley Nelson, Half Nelson Productions, 1987.

IV. DENVER, 1905–1906

195 "It is somewhat trying to me": CJW to FBR, Oct. 17, 1922; AB, p. 90.

196 "All you have to do is": From "Hints to Agents," MWC, IHS.

V. PITTSBURGH, 1907–1910

224 "Honorable Booker T. Washington": BTW papers, Walker folder, container 531, reel 400, LoC.

226 "My dear Madam": Ibid.

VI. INDIANAPOLIS, 1910–1916

231 "My heart went out to [Madame]": Agnes Prosser to FBR, Oct. 2, 1922; AB, p. 101.

246 "We had a quarrel": *Robinson v. Robinson* official divorce papers, Allegheny County Court of Common Pleas.

248 "doing heads in another room"; "You understand she was struggling then to get a foundation": FBR to Edgar Rouzeau, Sept. 25, 1931; AB, p. 105.

255 Letter to Washington: BTW papers, MW folder, LoC.

255 "in the hands of Mr. [George] Stewart's committee": BTW to MW, BTW papers, MW folder, LoC.

262 details of incorporation: MWC, IHS.

267 Washington letter: BTW to MW, BTW papers, LoC.

269 "joyous expectation": FBR to AW, Dec. 6, 1911; AB, p. 123.

270 Letter to Washington: MW to BTW, BTW papers, MW folder, LoC.

271 "I have talked with Mr. Washington": BTW papers, LoC.

271 "the habit of unnecessary moving": Ibid.

272 "I feel like that": "The Workers Convention," *Cleveland Gazette,* Feb. 24, 1912, p. 1.

272 "big, sensible, strong businessman": "Louise" to CJW, Jan. 11, 1912; AB, p. 124.

273 "master of the situation" and quotes on pp. 272–73 re: CJW and Dora Larrie: *IF,* Mar. 21, 1914.

276–79 NNBL meeting information and all Madam Walker quotes: Report of Thirteenth Annual NNBL Convention.

283 "designing evil woman"; "keep sober and build up a big business": FBR to CJW. "My heart is changed"; "Say, Mme": CJW to FBR. "spend every penny": FBR to CJW; AB, pp. 138–39.

287 "You should have seen": MW to FBR, 1915; Noliwe M. Rooks, *Hair Raising: Beauty, Culture, and African American Women* (New Brunswick, N.J.: Rutgers University Press, 1996), p. 90.

291–92 "Your business is increasing here everyday": FBR to MW, May 2, 1913; AB, p. 145.

292 "Madam is in a fair way": FBR to AW, May 27, 1913 and May 30, 1913; AB, p. 146.

292–93 Information on Cole Motor Company from *Cole Bulletin,* vol. 4, no. 2, and from *The Cole Blue Book.*

293 "Oh, it's the latest thing": FBR to AW, May 27, 1913; AB, p. 146.

297 Mrs. William James letter: quoted in Walker Company advertisement.

299 "Am dodging behind you": AW to FBR, Dec. 7, 1913; AB, p. 170–71.

300 "perfectly beautiful": FBR to MW, June 30, 1913; AB, p. 146.

303–5 All quotes from NNBL meeting: Report of the Fourteenth Annual NNBL Convention, LoC.

307 Letters between MW and BTW: BTW papers, Walker folder, LoC.

308 Divorce: *Robinson v. Robinson* official divorce papers, Allegheny County Court of Common Pleas.

309 "tired of fooling with these ungrateful Negroes": MW to FBR, June 3, 1916; AB, p. 159.

312 "responsible upbringing"; "Madame wanted me": Violet Davis Reynolds interview, *Nine Leaves on a Sprig,* dir. Tom Alvarez, WRTV, Indianapolis, 1973.

315–16 Letter to Dr. Washington: MW to BTW, BTW papers, LoC.

318 NACW quotes: NACW 1914 convention minutes, LoC.

319–22 All quotes from NNBL meeting: Report of Fifteenth Annual NNBL Convention, LoC.

326–27 Letter from S. A. Singerman: Nov. 5, 1914, MWC, IHS.

327 "As you know": FBR to AW, Nov. 30, 1914; AB, p. 175.

328 "As regards my coming back": MW to FBR, June 3, 1916; AB, p. 176.

332 Quotes regarding harpist: *IR,* Feb. 27, 1915; *CD,* May 8, 1915.

332 "People know that he has been": MW to FBR, June 26, 1916; AB, p. 159.

332 "sassy letter": MW to FBR, Mar. 20, 1916; AB, p. 159.

332 "I do not care to have": MW to FBR, Feb. 16, 1916; AB, pp. 159–60.

334 "Now in regards to": MW to FBR, Oct. 20, 1915; AB, p. 164.

337 Special agents' contract: MWC, IHS.

338 "I was born in the South": Louis Harlan, *Booker T. Washington: The Making of a Black Leader, 1856–1901* (New York: Oxford University Press, 1972), p. 454.

339 "of course I have": BTW papers, LoC.

341 "the building has cost": Gust Ericsson to FBR, Jan. 23, 1916, MWC, IHS.

342 "It is just impossible": MW to FBR, Jan. 22, 1916; AB, p. 169.

344 "created news": Rooks, *Hair Raising,* p. 82.

345–46 Margaret Joyner quotes: interviews in *Chicago Tribune,* Feb. 4, 1987; *Shoptalk* 3 (Spring 1984): 52–57; and Jessie Carney Smith, *Notable Black American Women* (Detroit: Gale Research, 1992), pp. 366–70.

345 Nettie Johnson quote: *Two Dollars and a Dream,* dir. Stanley Nelson, Half Nelson Productions, 1987.

VII. HARLEM, 1916–1918

356–57 Information on beauty course in schools: Noliwe M. Rooks, *Hair Raising: Beauty, Culture, and African American Women* (New Brunswick, N.J.: Rutgers University Press, 1996); AB; Kathy Peiss, *Hope in a Jar: The Making of America's Beauty Culture* (New York: Metropolitan Books, 1998).

357 Exchange with Robert Russa Moton: Moton papers, LoC.

357 "as you know": MW to FBR, June 18, 1916; Rooks, *Hair Raising*, p. 105.

359 "Bishop's Court is not": Vertner Tandy and John Nail to FBR, MWC, IHS.

360–61 Sale of Irvington property: Westchester County Courthouse files.

361 Mae and Spelman: Spelman College archives.

361 Minnie Murphy story: unpublished, Madison and Ouachita Parish Libraries.

362 "richest Negro woman in the world": newspaper clipping cited in AB, p. 195.

363 "a bone of contention": MW to FBR, Dec. 1, 1916; AB, p. 197.

364 "I know mother is": AW to FBR, Nov. 6, 1916; AB, pp. 198–99.

365 "all but grazed"; "the doctor told me": MW to FBR, Nov. 24, 1916; AB, pp. 196–97.

369 "lift up the fallen": John Nail to FBR, Dec. 11, 1916, MWC, IHS.

379 "ashamed of having been"; "by hard work": Alfreda M. Duster, ed., *Crusade for Justice: The Autobiography of Ida B. Wells* (Chicago: University of Chicago Press, 1970), p. 378.

382 "evade the danger": Vertner Tandy to FBR, MWC, IHS.

382–83 letters from agents: Peiss, *Hope in a Jar*, pp. 90–91.

383 "on a cash order basis": Ibid., p. 73.

386 Details of NACW meeting: NACW Annual Report, 1918.

VIII. VILLA LEWARO, 1918–1919

393 Astor Audit appraisal: Westchester County Historical Association files.

400 "greatest woman this country has produced": NNBL papers, LoC.

405–6 Information on R. D. Jonas: Theodore Kornweibel Jr., *Seeing Red: Federal Campaigns Against Black Militancy, 1919–1925* (Bloomington: Indiana University Press, 1998), p. 80.

406–7 Minnie Murphy account: Madison Parish and Ouachita Parish Libraries.

413 codicil to Madame's will: Marion County Courthouse, Indianapolis.

415 "My darling baby": A'Lelia Bundles, "Madame C. J. Walker to Her Daughter A'Lelia Walker—The Last Letter," *Sage: A Scholarly Journal for Black Women* 1, no. 2 (Fall 1984): 34–35.

IX. AFTERWARDS, 1919–1931

427 "A'Lelia Walker was": Langston Hughes, *The Big Sea* (New York: Knopf, 1940), p. 244.

432 "Now we come": *Woman's Voice*, Madam C. J. Walker Co., Oct. 1922, p. 18.

434 "134th Street, from Seventh to Eighth Avenues": Jervis Anderson, *This Was Harlem, 1900–1950* (New York: Farrar, Straus and Giroux, 1981), p. 228.

434 "Married twelve o'clock today": Carl Van Vechten papers, Beinecke Library, Yale University.

438 "Strangest and gaudiest": Hughes, *The Big Sea*, p. 273.

438 "Ever so pleased": Carl Van Vechten papers, Beinecke Library, Yale University.

439 "serves no purpose whatsoever": FBR to Walter White, NAACP Collection, LoC.

441 "That was really the end": Hughes, *The Big Sea*, p. 247.

Selected Bibliography

NEWSPAPERS

Newspapers helped me create the day-to-day world of Madam Walker. These are only some of the ones I depended upon.

Baltimore Afro-American
Chicago Defender
Colorado Statesman
Concordia Eagle (Concordia, Louisiana)
Indianapolis Freeman
Indianapolis Republic
Indianapolis World
Madison Journal
Natchez Democrat (Natchez, Mississippi)
New Orleans Weekly Pelican
New York Age
New York Times
Pittsburgh Courier
Pittsburgh Press
Richmond Compiler
Statesman (Denver)
St. Louis Argus
St. Louis Palladium
St. Louis Post-Dispatch
St. Louis Republic
Vicksburg Daily Commercial
Vicksburg Herald

Particularly useful newspaper collections include:

Indianapolis Recorder. Indiana Historical Society, Indianapolis.
Inter-State Tattler. Schomburg Center for Research in Black Culture, New York Public Library.
Madison Journal, Centennial Edition, Tallulah, La. From the collection of Geneva Rountree Williams, Tallulah, La.
Pittsburgh Press. Specifically, "African American Notes" column, Library and Archives Division, Historical Society of Western Pennsylvania, Pittsburgh.

Statesman. State Historical and Natural Historical Society, Denver.

Vicksburg Daily Commercial, 1877–1883. Natchez Trace Collection, Center for American History, University of Texas at Austin. (On yellow fever in Vicksburg.)

Also, *African-American Newspapers and Periodicals: A National Bibliography,* ed. James P. Danky and Maureen E. Hady (Cambridge, Mass.: Harvard University Press, 1998), was an invaluable and exhaustive guide to the history and present location of African-American publications.

BOOKS

Allen, James. *Without Sanctuary: Lynching Photography in America.* Santa Fe, N.M.: Twin Palms, 2000.

Altman, Susan. *The Encyclopedia of African-American Heritage.* New York: Facts on File, 1997.

Anderson, Jervis. *A. Philip Randolph: A Biographical Portrait.* New York: Harcourt Brace Jovanovich, 1973.

———. *This Was Harlem, 1900–1950.* New York: Farrar, Straus and Giroux, 1981.

Anderson, John Q., ed. *Brokenburn: The Journal of Kate Stone, 1861–1868.* Baton Rouge: LSU Press, 1972.

———. *Excerpts from The Richmond Compiler, Richmond, Louisiana, 1841–1844.* Tallulah, La.: Madison Historical Society, 1996.

Asher, Louis E., and Edith Heal. *Send No Money.* Chicago: Argus Books, 1942.

Ayers, Edward L. *The Promise of the New South.* New York: Oxford University Press, 1992.

Baker, Ray Stannard. *Following the Color Line.* New York: Doubleday, 1908.

Batterson, Jack A. *Blind Boon: Missouri's Ragtime Pioneer.* Columbia: University of Missouri Press, 1998.

Beaton, Gail M., and Lynda F. Dickson. *Women's Clubs of Denver: Essays in Colorado History.* Denver: Colorado Historical Society, 1993.

Bennett, Lerone. *Before the Mayflower: A History of the Negro in America.* Chicago: Johnson Publishing, 1962.

Berlin, Edward A. *King of Ragtime: Scott Joplin and His Era.* New York: Oxford University Press, 1994.

Biggart, Nicole Woolsey. *Charismatic Capitalism: Direct Selling Organizations in America.* Chicago: University of Chicago Press, 1989.

Bodenhamer, David J., and Robert G. Barrows, eds. *Encyclopedia of Indianapolis.* Bloomington: Indiana University Press, 1994.

Bodnar, John, Roger Simon, and Michael P. Weber. *Lives of Their Own: Blacks, Italians, and Poles in Pittsburgh, 1900–1960.* Urbana: University of Illinois Press, 1982.

Bontemps, Arna, and Jack Conroy. *They Seek a City.* Garden City, N.Y.: Doubleday, 1945.

Booker, Robert J. *And There Was Light!: The 120-Year History of Knoxville College, Knoxville, Tennessee, 1879–1995.* Virginia Beach, Va.: Donning Co., 1994.

Breitbart, Eric. *A World on Display: Photographs from the St. Louis World's Fair, 1904.* Albuquerque: University of New Mexico Press, 1997.

Brooks, Tilford. *America's Black Musical Heritage.* Englewood Cliffs, N.J.: Prentice-Hall, 1984.

Bruce, Robert V. *1877: Year of Violence.* Indianapolis: Bobbs-Merrill, 1959.

Bundles, A'Lelia. *On Her Own Ground: The Life and Times of Madam C. J. Walker.* New York: Scribners, 2001.

Buni, Andrew. *Robert L. Vann of the Pittsburgh Courier.* Pittsburgh: University of Pittsburgh Press, 1974.

Cash, W. J. *The Mind of the South.* New York: Knopf, 1941.

Cayton, Horace R., and St. Clair Drake. *Black Metropolis.* London: Jonathan Cape, 1946

Christian, Charles. *Black Saga: The African-American Experience.* Boston: Houghton-Mifflin, 1985.

Clamorgan, Cyprian. *The Colored Aristocracy of St. Louis.* St. Louis: Continental Printing Co., 1894; reprint, Columbia: University of Missouri Press, 1999.

Clevenger, Martha R., ed. *"Indescribably Grand": Diaries and Letters from the 1904 World's Fair.* St. Louis: Missouri Historical Society Press, 1996.

Corbett, Katherine T. *In Her Place: A Guide to St. Louis Women's History, 1764–1965.* St. Louis: Missouri Historical Society Press, 1999.

———, and Howard S. Miller. *Saint Louis in the Gilded Age.* St. Louis: Missouri Historical Society Press, 1993.

Corliss, Carlton J. *Main Line of Mid-America: The Story of the Illinois Central.* New York: Creative Age Press, 1950.

Dennett, John Richard. *The South as It Is, 1865–66.* Baton Rouge: LSU Press, 1965.

Dolzall, Gary W., and Stephen F. Dolzall. *Monon: The Hoosier Line.* Glendale, Calif.: Interurban Press, 1987.

Dorsett, Lyle W., and Michael McCarthy. *The Queen City: A History of Denver.* Boulder, Colo.: Pruett Publishing Co., 1977.

Douglas, Ann. *Terrible Honesty: Mongrel Manhattan in the 1920s.* New York: Farrar, Straus and Giroux, 1995.

Downer, Debbie, ed. *African American Associated Historic and Architectural Resources of Vicksburg, Mississippi.* Vicksburg, Miss.: Vicksburg Foundation for Historic Preservation, 1993.

Dray, Philip. *At the Hands of Persons Unknown: The Lynching of Black America.* New York: Random House, 2002.

Drury, George H. *The Historical Guide to North American Railroads.* Waukesha, Wisc.: Kalmbach Books, 1994.

Dry, Camille N., and Richard J. Compton. *Pictorial St. Louis, the Great Metropolis of the Mississippi Valley: A Topographical Survey Drawn in Perspective.* St. Louis: Compton and Co., 1876; reprint, Hazelwood, Mo.: McGraw-Young, 1997.

DuBois, W. E. B. *Black Reconstruction in America, 1860–1935.* New York: Harcourt and Brace, 1935.

———. *Dusk of Dawn.* New York: Schocken, 1940.

———. *The Souls of Black Folk: Essays and Sketches.* Chicago, 1903; reprint, New York: Signet, 1982.

Dudden, Faye. *Serving Women: Household Service in Nineteenth-Century America.* Middletown, Conn.: Wesleyan University Press, 1983.

Duster, Alfreda M., ed. *Crusade for Justice: The Autobiography of Ida B. Wells.* Chicago: University of Chicago Press, 1970.

Early, Gerald, ed. *"Ain't But a Place": An Anthology of African American Writings About St. Louis.* St. Louis: Missouri Historical Society Press, 1998.

Eaton, John. *Grant, Lincoln and the Freedmen.* New York: Longmans, Green, 1907.

Foner, Eric. *Freedom's Lawmakers.* Baton Rouge: LSU Press, 1996.

———. *Reconstruction: America's Unfinished Revolution, 1863–1877.* New York: Harper and Row, 1988.

Fox, Stephen R. *The Guardian of Boston: William Monroe Trotter.* New York: Atheneum, 1970.

———. *The Mirror Makers: A History of American Advertising and Its Creators.* New York: Morrow, 1984.

Fox, Tim, ed. *Where We Live: A Guide to St. Louis Communities.* St. Louis: Missouri Historical Society Press, 1995.

Franklin, John Hope. *From Slavery to Freedom: A History of Negro Americans.* New York: Knopf, 1967.

———. *Reconstruction After the Civil War.* Chicago: University of Chicago Press, 1994.

Freedmen and Southern Society Project. *Freedom: A Documentary History of Emancipation, 1861–1867.* New York: Cambridge University Press, 1982–1993.

Fuller, Alfred C. *A Foot in the Door.* New York: McGraw-Hill, 1960.

Genovese, Eugene D. *Roll, Jordan, Roll: The World the Slaves Made.* New York: Vintage, 1975.

Gibbs, Wilma L. *Indiana's African-American Heritage: Essays from Black History News & Notes.* Indianapolis: Indiana Historical Society, 1993.

Gottlieb, Peter. *Making Their Own Way: Southern Blacks Migration to Pittsburgh, 1916–1920.* Urbana: University of Illinois Press, 1987.

Gould, E. W. *Fifty Years on the Mississippi.* St. Louis: Gould Publishing, 1889.

Graff, Polly Anne, and Stewart Graff. *Wolfert's Roost: Portrait of a Village.* Irvington-on-Hudson, N.Y.: Washington Irving Press, 1971.

Gutman, Herbert G. *The Black Family in Slavery and Freedom, 1760–1925.* New York: Pantheon, 1976.

Guy-Sheftall, Beverly. *Daughters of Sorrow: Attitudes Toward Black Women, 1880–1920.* Brooklyn, N.Y.: Carson Publishing, 1990.

Hall, Gwendolyn Midlo. *Africans in Colonial Louisiana: The Development of Afro-Creole Culture in the Eighteenth Century.* Baton Rouge: LSU Press, 1992.

Handy, W. C. *Father of the Blues.* New York: Macmillan, 1955.

Harlan, Louis. *Booker T. Washington: The Making of a Black Leader, 1856–1901.* New York: Oxford University Press, 1972.

———. *Booker T. Washington: The Wizard of Tuskegee, 1901–1915.* New York: Oxford University Press, 1983.

Hermann, Janet Sharp. *The Pursuit of a Dream.* New York: Oxford University Press, 1981.

Hine, Darlene Clark. *When Truth Is Told: A History of Black Women's Culture in Indianapolis.* Indianapolis: National Council of Negro Women, 1981.

———, Elsa Barkley Brown, and Rosalyn Terborg-Penn, eds. *Black Women in America: An Historical Encyclopedia.* Brooklyn, N.Y.: Carlson Publishing, 1993.

Hoge, Cecil C. *The First Hundred Years Are the Toughest: What We Can Learn from the Competition Between Sears and Ward's.* Berkeley, Calif.: Ten Speed Press, 1988.

Hughes, Langston. *The Big Sea.* New York: Knopf, 1940.

Hunter, Tera W. *To 'Joy My Freedom: Southern Black Women's Lives and Labors After the Civil War.* Cambridge, Mass.: Harvard University Press, 1997.

Israel, Fred L., ed. *1897 Sears, Roebuck Catalogue.* Philadelphia: Chelsea House, 1968.

Johnson, James Weldon. *Along This Way: The Autobiography of James Weldon Johnson.* New York: Penguin Books, 1990.

———. *Autobiography of an Ex-Colored Man.* Boston: Sherman, French and Co., 1912.

———. *Black Manhattan.* New York: Knopf, 1930.

Jones, Jacqueline. *Labor of Love, Labor of Sorrow: Black Women, Work, and the Family from Slavery to the Present.* New York: Basic Books, 1985.

Katzman, David M. *Seven Days a Week: Women and Domestic Service in Industrializing America.* New York: Oxford University Press, 1978.

Kellogg, Paul Underwood. *Wage-Earning Pittsburgh.* New York: Survey Associates, 1914.

Kellner, Bruce. *The Harlem Renaissance: A Historical Dictionary for the Era.* Westport, Conn.: Greenwood Press, 1984.

Kiple, Kenneth F., ed. *Plague, Pox and Pestilence: Disease in History.* London: Weidenfeld & Nicolson, 1998.

Kleinberg, S. J. *The Shadow of the Mills: Working-Class Families in Pittsburgh, 1870–1907.* Pittsburgh: University of Pittsburgh Press, 1989.

Knox, Thomas W. *Campfire and Cottonfield: Southern Adventure in Time of War, Life with the Union Armies and Residence on a Louisiana Plantation.* Philadelphia: Jones Brothers, 1865.

Kornweibel, Theodore, Jr. *Seeing Red: Federal Campaigns Against Black Militancy, 1919–1925*. Bloomington: Indiana University Press, 1998.

Lerner, Gerda. *Black Women in White America: A Documentary History*. New York: Vintage, 1973.

Levine, Lawrence. *Black Culture and Black Consciousness: African-American Folk Thought from Slavery to Freedom*. New York: Oxford University Press, 1978.

Lewis, Alfred Allan, and Constance Woodwroth. *Miss Elizabeth Arden: An Unretouched Portrait*. New York: Coward, McCann & Geoghegan, 1972.

Lewis, David Levering. *W. E. B. DuBois: Biography of a Race, 1868–1919*. New York: Henry Holt, 1993.

———. *When Harlem Was in Vogue*. New York: Knopf, 1979.

Litwack, Leon. *Been in the Storm So Long: The Aftermath of Slavery*. New York: Knopf, 1979.

———. *Trouble in Mind: Black Southerners in the Age of Jim Crow*. New York: Knopf, 1998.

Logan, Rayford. *The Betrayal of the Negro: From Rutherford B. Hayes to Woodrow Wilson*. 1954; reprint, New York: Collier Books, 1967.

Lorant, Stefan, ed. *Pittsburgh: The Story of an American City*. New York: Doubleday, 1964.

Lynch, John Roy. *The Autobiography of John Roy Lynch*. Chicago: University of Chicago Press, 1970.

Mackie, Dr. George. *Appletons' Cyclopedia of Drawing, Designed as a Text-book for the Mechanic, Architect, Engineer, and Surveyor*. New York: D. Appleton & Co., 1857.

McDill, Robert McKee. *The Early Education of the Negro in America, with Emphasis on the Work of the McKee School in Tennessee*. Hastings, Neb.: Edmonds Brothers, 1943.

McFeeley, William. *Frederick Douglass*. New York: W. W. Norton, 1991.

———. *Yankee Stepfather: General O. O. Howard and the Freedmen*. New York: W. W. Norton, 1970.

McKay, Claude. *Harlem: Negro Metropolis*. New York: E. P. Dutton, 1940.

———. *Home to Harlem*. New York: Harper & Bros., 1928.

McKee, Homer. *The Cole Blue Book*. Indianapolis: Cole Motor Car Company, 1912.

McMurry, Linda O. *To Keep the Waters Troubled: The Life of Ida B. Wells*. New York: Oxford University Press, 1998.

Meier, August. *Negro Thought in America, 1880–1915: Racial Ideologies in the Age of Booker T. Washington*. Ann Arbor: University of Michigan Press, 1963.

Mollison, M. E. *The Leading Afro-Americans of Vicksburg, Mississippi: Their Enterprises, Churches, Schools and Societies*. Vicksburg, Miss.: Biographia Publishing, 1908.

Moore, J. Mack, and Gordon A. Cotton. *Vicksburg Under Glass: A Collection of Early Photographs from the Glass Negatives of J. Mack Moore*. Vicksburg, Miss.: Vicksburg and Warren County Historical Society, 1975.

Morgan, Thomas L., and William Barlow. *From Cakewalks to Concert Halls: An Illustrated History of African-American Music from 1895 to 1930*. Washington, D.C.: Elliott & Clark, 1992.

Murphy, William M. *Notes from the History of Madison Parish, Louisiana*. Ruston: Louisiana Polytechnic Institute, 1927.

Norris, James D. *Advertising and the Transformation of American Society, 1865–1920*. New York: Greenwood Press, 1990.

Northrup, Solomon. *Twelve Years a Slave*. Baton Rouge: LSU Press, 1968.

Oshinsky, David M. *"Worse than Slavery": Parchman Farm and the Experience of Jim Crow Justice*. New York: Free Press, 1996.

Osofsky, Gilbert. *Harlem: The Making of a Ghetto*. New York: Harper Torchbook, 1971.

O'Toole, Patricia. *Money and Morals in America: A History*. New York: Clarkson Potter, 1998.

Ottley, Roi. *Black Odyssey: The Story of the Negro in America*. New York: C. Scribner's Sons, 1948.

Painter, Nell Irvin. *Exodusters: Black Migration to Kansas After Reconstruction*. New York: Knopf, 1977.

Panati, Charles. *Panati's Parade of Fads, Follies and Manias: The Origins of Our Most Cherished Possessions.* New York: Harper Perennial, 1991.

Patterson, Orlando. *Rituals of Blood: Consequences of Slavery in Two American Centuries.* New York: Civitas/Counterpoint, 1998.

Peiss, Kathy. *Hope in a Jar: The Making of America's Beauty Culture.* New York: Metropolitan Books, 1998.

Penn, I. Garland *The Afro-American Press and Its Editors.* Reprint, New York: Arno Press and the *New York Times,* 1969.

Pennsylvania Negro Business Directory 1910, Industrial and Material Growth of the Negroes of Pennsylvania. Harrisburg, Pa.: James H. W. Howard & Son, 1910.

Porter, Gladys L. *Three Negro Pioneers in Beauty Culture.* New York: Vantage Press, 1966.

Potter, Janet Greenstein. *Great American Railroad Stations.* New York: John Wiley & Sons, 1996.

Primm, James Neal. *Lion of the Valley: St. Louis, Missouri, 1764–1980.* St. Louis: Missouri Historical Society Press, 1980.

Rawick, George P. *The American Slave: A Composite Autobiography.* Westport, Conn.: Greenwood Press, 1979.

Reid, Ira De A. *Social Conditions of the Negro in the Hill District of Pittsburgh: Survey Conducted Under the Direction of Ira De A. Reid, Director, Department of Research, the National Urban League.* Pittsburgh: General Committee on the Hill Survey, 1930.

Reid, Whitelaw. *After the War: A Tour of the Southern States, 1865–1866.* New York: Harper Torchlight, 1965.

Ripley, C. Peter. *Slaves and Freedmen in Civil War Louisiana.* Baton Rouge: LSU Press, 1976.

Rooks, Noliwe M. *Hair Raising: Beauty, Culture, and African American Women.* New Brunswick, N.J.: Rutgers University Press, 1996.

Santino, Jack. *Miles of Smiles, Years of Struggle: Stories of Black Pullman Porters.* Urbana: University of Illinois Press, 1989.

Schafer, Judith Kelleher. *Slavery, the Civil Law, and the Supreme Court of Louisiana.* Baton Rouge: LSU Press, 1994.

Schlereth, Thomas J. *Victorian America: Transformations in Everyday Life, 1876–1915.* New York: HarperCollins, 1991.

Schoener, Allon, ed. *Harlem on My Mind: Cultural Capital of Black America, 1900–1978.* New York: Delta/Dell, 1979.

Schroder, Joseph J., Jr., ed. *The Wonderful World of Ladies' Fashion, 1850–1920.* London: Weidenfeld & Nicolson, 1998.

Severa, Joan. *Dressed for the Photographer: Ordinary Americans and Fashion, 1840–1900.* Kent, Ohio: Kent State University Press, 1995.

Sewell, George. *Mississippi Black History Makers.* Oxford: University of Mississippi Press, 1977.

Slavitt, Todd. *Medicine and Slavery: Diseases and Health Care of Blacks in Antebellum Virginia.* Urbana: University of Illinois Press, 1978.

Smith, Jessie Carney. *Notable Black American Women.* Detroit: Gale Research, 1992.

Spears, Timothy B. *One Hundred Years on the Road: The Traveling Salesman in American Culture.* New Haven, Conn.: Yale University Press, 1995.

Stage, Sarah. *Female Complaints: Lydia Pinkham and the Business of Women's Medicine.* New York: W. W. Norton, 1970.

Steffens, Lincoln. *The Shame of the Cities.* New York: Hill & Wang, 1963.

Sterling, Dorothy. *The Trouble They Seen: The Story of Reconstruction in the Words of African-Americans.* New York: Doubleday, 1976.

Stevens, Fred P., and Harry David Smith. *Denver the Coming City: A Collection of Forty Instantaneous Photographs of Life in Denver.* Denver: F. S. Thayer, 1902.

Stevens, Walter B. *St. Louis, the Fourth City, 1764–1909.* St. Louis: S. J. Clarke Publishing, 1909.

Strasser, Susan. *Never Done: A History of American Housework.* New York: Pantheon, 1982.

Sullivan, Mark. *Our Times: The United States, 1900–1925.* New York: C. Scribner's Sons, 1926–1935.

Summers, Mark Wahlgren. *The Gilded Age, or The Hazard of New Functions.* Upper Saddle River, N.J.: Prentice-Hall, 1997.

Taylor, Joe Gray. *Louisiana Reconstructed, 1863–1877.* Baton Rouge: LSU Press, 1977.

———. *Negro Slavery in Louisiana.* Baton Rouge: LSU Press, 1963.

Thornbrough, Emma Lou. *The Negro in Indiana Before 1900: A Study of a Minority.* Bloomington: Indiana University Press, 1993.

Tourgée, Albion Winegar. *The Invisible Empire.* Reprint, Baton Rouge: LSU Press, 1989.

Trelease, Allen W. *White Terror: The Ku Klux Klan Conspiracy and Southern Reconstruction.* Baton Rouge: LSU Press, 1971.

Vincent, Charles. *Black Legislators in Louisiana During Reconstruction.* Baton Rouge: LSU Press, 1970.

Walker, Peter F. *Vicksburg: A People at War, 1860–1865.* Chapel Hill: University of North Carolina Press, 1960.

Washington, Booker T. *The Negro in Business.* Boston: Hertel, Jenkins & Co., 1907. Reprint, Wichita, Kans.: DeVore and Sons, 1992.

———. *Up from Slavery.* New York: Penguin, 1986.

Wharton, Vernon Lane. *The Negro in Mississippi, 1865–1890.* Chapel Hill: University of North Carolina Press, 1970.

White, Howard A. *The Freedmen's Bureau in Louisiana.* Baton Rouge: LSU Press, 1970.

White, Shane, and Graham White. *Stylin': African American Expressive Culture from Its Beginnings to the Zoot Suit.* Ithaca, N.Y.: Cornell University Press, 1998.

Williamson, Frederick W. *The History of Northeast Louisiana.* Monroe, La.: Historical Record Association, 1939.

Williamson, Joel E., ed. *The Origins of Segregation.* Boston: D. C. Heath, 1968.

Woodward, C. Vann. *Origins of the New South.* Baton Rouge: LSU Press, 1971.

———. *Reunion and Reaction: The Compromise of 1877 and the End of Reconstruction.* Boston: Little, Brown, 1951.

———. *The Strange Career of Jim Crow.* New York: Oxford University Press, 1954.

———. *Tom Watson: Agrarian Rebel.* New York: Macmillan, 1938.

Wright, George C. *Life Behind a Veil: Blacks in Louisville, Kentucky, 1865–1930.* Baton Rouge: LSU Press, 1985.

Wright, John A. *Discovering African-American St. Louis: A Guide to Historic Sites.* St. Louis: Missouri Historical Society Press, 1994.

Yeatman, James E. *A Report on the Condition of the Freedmen of the Mississippi.* St. Louis: Western Sanitary Commission Books, 1863.

ARTICLES, PAMPHLETS, UNPUBLISHED MANUSCRIPTS

"The Afro-American Almanac, 1987, and What Colored People Say." Pamphlet. Brooklyn, N.Y.: Lyon Manufacturing Co., 1897.

Anderson, Albert. "The Amazing Inside Story of the Malone Case." *The Light and Heebie Jeebies,* Feb. 19, 1927, pp. 15–22.

Bacon, Elizabeth Mickle. "The Growth of Household Conveniences in the United States from 1865 to 1900." Ph.D. diss., Radcliffe College, 1942.

Bercovici, Konrad. "The Black Blocks of Manhattan." *Harper's Monthly,* vol. CXLIX, p. 612.

Black History News and Notes, various issues 1990–2002. Published by the Indiana Historical Society.

Brandt, Lilian. "The Negroes of St. Louis." *American Statistical Association,* no. 61 (March 1903): 203–68.

———. "The Negro in the Cities of the North." *Charities: A Review of Local and General Philanthropy* 15 (October 1905): 7–11.

Burroughs, Nannie. "Not Color But Character." *Voice of the Negro* (July 1904): 277–79.

Bushman, Richard, and Claudia Bushman. "The Early History of Cleanliness in America." *Journal of American History* 74, no. 4 (March 1988): 1213–38.

Christensen, Lawrence Oland. "Black St. Louis: A Study in Race Relations 1865–1916." Ph.D. diss., University of Missouri, 1972.

De Bow, J. D. B., ed. *De Bow's Review.* New Orleans.

Dickson, Moses. *Laws Governing the Knights of Tabor.* 1891. Pamphlet on file at Missouri Historical Society, St. Louis.

Evans, J. W. "A Brief Sketch of the Development of Negro Education in St. Louis, Missouri." *Journal of Negro Education* 7 (October 1938): 548–52.

Fletcher, Ralph, and Mildred Fletcher. "Some Data on Occupations Among Negroes in St. Louis from 1866 to 1897." *Journal of Negro History* 20 (July 1935): 338–41.

Goldman, M. R. "Hill District of Pittsburgh, As I Knew It," *The Western Pennsylvania Historical Magazine* 51, no. 3 (July 1968): 279–95.

"Graduating Exercises, Sumner High School," June 17, 1901. Pamphlet on file at John D. Buckner papers, Black History Collections, Western Historical Manuscript Collection, University of Missouri at St. Louis.

Herr, Kincaid. "The Louisville and Nashville Railroad: 1850–1927." *L&N Magazine* (December 1960): 66–67, 89.

Higbee, Mark David. "W. E. B. DuBois, F. B. Ransom, the Madam Walker Company and Black Business Leadership in the 1930's." *Indiana Magazine of History* (June 1993): 101–24.

"Human Interest Story: Madam Walker," unsigned, reportedly written by Minnie Murphy as part of WPA project. Ouachita Parish Library Special Collections, Monroe, La.

Interview with George Schuyler, *The Messenger* (July 1924).

Kiple, Kenneth F., and Virginia H. Kiple. "Black Yellow Fever Immunities, Innate and Acquired, as Revealed in the American South." *Social Science History* 1, no. 4 (Summer 1977): 429–36.

Latham, Charles, Jr. "Madam C. J. Walker and Company." *Traces* 1, no. 3 (Summer 1989): 28–37.

Louisiana: A Guide to the State. Compiled by the Writers Program of the WPA, 1941. Sponsored by the Louisiana Library Commission, Baton Rouge.

The Madame C. J. Walker Beauty Manual. Indianapolis: Mme C. J. Walker Manufacturing Co., 1925.

"Madison Parish." Unpublished manuscript, Monroe Project of the WPA, 1937. Ouachita Parish Library Special Collections, Monroe, La.

Moore, N. Webster, comp. "St. Paul A.M.E. Church, 1841–1981, Oldest A.M.E. Church West of the Mississippi River." Unpublished papers on file at Black History Collections, Western Historical Manuscript Collection, University of Missouri at St. Louis.

Morrow, Willie. *Four Hundred Years Without a Comb.* Undated pamphlet on file at Schomburg Center for Research in Black Culture, New York.

Nelson, Jill. "The Fortune that Madame Built." *Essence* (June 1983): 84–89.

Newsom, Elizabeth Young. "Unto the Least of These: The Howard Association and Yellow Fever." *Southern Medical Journal* 85, no. 6 (June 1992): 632–37.

" 'Poro' in Pictures, With a Short History of Its Development St. Louis." Poro College, 1925. Pamphlet on file at Missouri Historical Society, St. Louis.

"The Proceedings of a Mississippi Migration Convention in 1879." *Journal of Negro History* 4 (January 1919): 51–92.

Santiago, Chiori. "It All Comes Out in the Wash." *Smithsonian Magazine* (September 1997): 84–92.

Scott, Emmett J. "The Louisiana Purchase Exposition." *Voice of the Negro* 1 (1904): 305–12.

"Secrets of the Court of Queen Victoria." Pamphlet. Brooklyn, N.Y.: Lyon Manufacturing Co., 1910.

"A Short History of Sad-Iron Manufacturing." Pamphlet. Seneca Falls, N.Y.: Downs and Co., c. 1880.

Vail, Mary Beals. "Approved Methods for Home Laundering." Pamphlet. Cincinnati: Procter and Gamble, 1906.

Wetmore, Claude H., and Lincoln Steffens. "Tweed Days in St. Louis." *McClure's Magazine* XIX (May 1902): 577–86.

Young, Kenneth M. "As Some Things Appear on the Plains and Among the Rockies in Mid-Summer." Pamphlet. Spartanburg, S.C.: Herald Printing Establishment, c. 1890. On file at Daniel A. P. Murray Collection, Library of Congress.

OFFICIAL DOCUMENTS AND REPORTS

Allegheny County Court of Common Pleas Records, October 1913, July 1914. Allegheny County Courthouse, Pittsburgh, Pa.

Bureau of Refugees, Freedmen and Abandoned Lands Records, RG 105, Locater #M1027, MF 7-34. National Archives, Washington, D.C.

Cedar Hill Marriage and Cemetery Records, Christ Episcopal Church, Vicksburg, Mississippi. On file at Warren County Public Library, Vicksburg, Miss.

"Estate of Robert W. Burney vs. the United States," Claim No. 20441, *Southern Claims Commission*. National Archives, Washington, D.C.

Fisher Funeral Home Records, 1864–67. Mississippi Department of Archives and History, Jackson, Miss.

"Investigation into the 'Vicksburg Troubles,' " Report No. 265, *House of Representatives*. Washington, D.C.: U.S. Government Printing Office, 1874.

Madison Parish Agricultural Schedules, Conveyance Records, Deeds, Notarial and Probate Records, and Slave Schedules, 1845–1878. Madison Parish Courthouse, Tallulah, La.

Madison Parish Marriage Records and Wills, 1869–1874. Madison Parish Courthouse, Tallulah, La.

Marion County Probate Records, June 1919. Marion County Courthouse, Indianapolis.

Marion County Superior Court Records, September 1912. Marion County Courthouse, Indianapolis.

Regulations of the Secretary of the United States Treasury, "Providing for the employment and general welfare of all persons within the lines of National Military Occupation within Insurrectionary States, formerly held as Slaves, who are or shall become free." Series, July 29, 1864. On file at Center for American History, University of Texas at Austin.

Report of the Committee on the Yellow Fever Epidemic of 1873 at Shreveport, Louisiana. Shreveport, La.: The Howard Association, 1874.

Scott County Deeds, 1840–1862. Scott County Courthouse, Meridian, Miss.

St. Louis Marriage Records, 1894. St Louis City Hall, St. Louis.

United States. Army Corps of Engineers, Vicksburg District. *Cultural Resource Investigations, Delta Mat Casting Field Additional Lands, Madison Parish, Louisiana*. Vicksburg, Miss.: U.S. Army Corps of Engineers, 1993.

United States. Bureau of the Census. *Census Returns, 1840–1920*. Washington, D.C.: U.S. Government Printing Office.

Washington County Marriage Records, 1909. Washington County Courthouse, Washington, Pa.

Washington County Orphan's Court Records, 1909. Washington County Courthouse, Washington, Pa.

Warren County Marriage Records and Wills, 1846, 1881. Warren County Courthouse, Warrenton, Mo.
Westchester County Surrogate Court, Affidavit for Appraisal, 1919. Westchester County Historical Society, Elmsford, N.Y.

ANNUAL REPORTS

Minutes of Biennial Conventions, National Association of Colored Women, 1912–1918. Manuscript Division, Library of Congress, Washington, D.C.
Records of the National Negro Business League, Part I, Annual Conference Proceedings and Organizational Records, National Negro Business League 1900–1919. Manuscript Division, Library of Congress, Washington, D.C.

CITY DIRECTORIES

Vicksburg, 1877, 1886.
Gould's St. Louis Directory, Gould Directory Co., St. Louis: Acme Publishing Co., 1881–1906.
Denver, 1904–1908.
Pittsburgh, 1908–1910.
Indianapolis, 1910–1913.

SPECIAL COLLECTIONS

Archives Center, American History Museum, Smithsonian Institution, Washington, D.C.: Warshaw Collection of Business Americana.
Amistad Research Center, Dillard University, New Orleans: American Missionary Association Papers.
Beinecke Rare Book and Manuscript Library, Yale University, New Haven, Conn.: James Weldon Johnson Papers; Carl Van Vechten Papers.
Chicago Historical Society, Chicago: Claude Barnett Papers.
Hermione House Museum, Tallulah, La.: history of Madison Parish.
Hill Memorial Library, Louisiana State University, Baton Rouge: Carson Papers; George M. Marshall Papers; Alonzo Snyder Papers; Rowland Chambers Papers; Mercer Papers; Montgomery Family Papers.
Indiana Historical Society, Indianapolis: George Stewart Papers; Madame Walker Papers.
Madison County Library, Canton, Miss.: James Arthur Thomas Papers.
Mississippi Department of Archives and History: Caroline B. Poole Diary.
Schomburg Center for Research in Black Culture, New York Public Library: David Levering Lewis Papers, "Voices from Harlem"; Madam Walker clipping file.

AUDIO- AND VIDEOTAPES

Nine Leaves on a Sprig. Dir. Tom Alvarez. WRTV, Indianapolis, 1973.
Re-oration of Booker T. Washington speech originally given at Cotton States Exposition of 1895. NBC Blue radio network program "Echoes of History," 1940. Recorded Sound Collection, Library of Congress, Washington, D.C.
Tresses of Triumph: Hairstyling in Twentieth-Century America. St. Louis Cosmetics Museum, n.d.
Two Dollars and a Dream. Dir. Stanley Nelson. Half Nelson Productions, 1987.

MAPS

City of St. Louis with Choteau's Pond Superimposed. N.d.

Gould's Official Map of St. Louis. 1892.

Insurance Map of Denver. New York: Sanborn Map Company, 1887–1904.

Insurance Map of Vicksburg, Mississippi. New York: Sanborn Map Company, 1886.

Madison Parish. c. 1850. Reprint, New York: DeBeers, 1961.

"Plot of Vicksburg District for Leasing Abandoned Plantations." 1864. Mississippi Department of Archives and History Maps Collection.

St. Louis. 1904.

The Trek Northward. Hand-drawn by Beane Everett, showing locations of African-American neighborhoods in Manhattan. Schomburg Center for Research in Black Culture, New York. Microfilm.

Acknowledgments

Many people rendered considerable aid during the time it took for this book to emerge. During its early days, when I wasn't even sure what it would turn out to be, a number of people went along with the uncertainty and offered help anyway. I would like to thank them, in particular, for sticking with me as I figured out what I was up to. In Madison Parish, Louisiana, Geneva Rountree Williams, Ed Hill, Eudora Hill, Burney Long; in Vicksburg, Yolande Robbins, Tillman Whitley, Dorothy Whitley, Gordon Cotton; in St. Louis, Karla Frye; in Indianapolis, Wilma Gibbs; in New York City, Patricia O'Toole; in Irvington, New York, Harold Doley and Helena Doley. In New York also, Amanda Urban, who first introduced me to Madam Walker, and Gary Fisketjon for his unstinting loyalty and friendship, the occasional use of his apartment and his uncanny ability not just to read but *listen* to what I'm trying to say, then help me say it right.

During the research and writing of the book, I lived all over the country, from Montana to D.C. to Montana again, then back to D.C.; from there to Tuscaloosa to Austin, then a return to D.C. A number of people offered accommodations friendly to this road-warrior approach to life and work. To them I extend warmest gratitude: Ann Patchett for the house in Sewanee and the apartment in Nashville; Susan Shreve and Tim Seldes for one home in D.C., Celia Morris for another; Rob Weiner for an open-ended stay at the Chinati Foundation in Marfa, Texas; Wilma Gibbs, again, in Indianapolis; Charlotte Norman in New Orleans; John and Mel Evans in Jackson; Colin Lowry and Andrea Ariel in Austin. A special piece of my heart goes to Mary Ross Taylor and Ginny Galtney, whose guesthouse provided shelter at particularly difficult times. In the initial stages of research, I did especially useful work in D.C. while staying at the Lenthal House during my year at George Washington University holding the Jenny McKean Moore chair. And in Tuscaloosa, in the Coal Chairholder's house while holding the Coal Royalty chair. Columbia University's Hertog Research Assistantship Program bestowed much needed help. I'd also like to thank Keith Buckley for his support during those early days. Research assistants who worked diligently, precisely and with fine good humor are Nelly Rosario, Jeff Giambrone, Mary Ross Taylor, Christy Zink, Alice Leaderman, Julie Polter and Alyssa Trzeszkowski. Special thanks to Karl van Devender for medical information.

I spent a lot of time, of course, in courthouses and libraries. I'd like to make special mention of some of them. In Louisiana: Gay Yerger and the Madison Parish Library staff and the Special Collections staff at the Ouachita Parish library; also, the people working at the Madison Parish courthouse; the Hill Memorial Library at L.S.U.; the Dillard University library and the New Orleans Historical Society. In Mississippi, the Jacqueline House (for tea and conversation as well as archived materials concerning African-American life in Vicksburg), the Old Courthouse Museum and the Warren County courthouse and library. Also helpful were the staff of the Mississippi

Department of Archives and History, and the Madison County, Mississippi, special collections in Canton. In St. Louis, the wonderfully housed Missouri Historical Society, the Archives Department at City Hall, the University of Missouri at St. Louis, the Cosmetics Museum and the St. Louis County Library. Denver's Western History Collection at the County Library is particularly well-organized and informative; I also found a great deal of information at the Colorado Historical Society and at the Black American West Museum and Heritage Center, also in Denver (and thanks to Toni Haynes for the photos of Madame's block). In Pittsburgh, the Carnegie Mellon University library and, especially, the Historical Society of Western Pennsylvania and its fine, friendly staff helped enormously, especially with the "Afro-American Notes" column and the maps. In Indianapolis, of course, I practically lived at the Indiana Historical Society and also worked at the Marion County Library and the county courthouse. At I.H.S., Becky Renz, Susan Sutton, and Glenn McMullen provided answers to many questions. At Fisk University, in Nashville, I located a number of the Walker Company's *Woman's Voice* magazines; the librarian at Tuskegee was particularly helpful; in the Claude Barnett papers at the Chicago Historical Society are letters to Freeman Ransom and information about Annie Malone and Poro. The Center for American History in Austin contains the excellent Natchez Trace Collection, including some personal papers of Robert Burney and all of those Vicksburg newspapers, which I found thanks to the guidance of Sally Leach. Others who offered needed help in Austin were Bob Abzug and Shelley Fisher-Fishkin. In New York, the Schomburg Center for Research in Black Culture contains a veritable wealth of information concerning African-American life and history. Preservationist Michael Adams helped me a great deal with the A'Lelia Walker years in Harlem; Tom Worth, executor of the Bruce Nugent estate, kindly sent some requested papers; and Daryl Williams gave me a professional tour of the area. I'm grateful as well to Stanley Nelson for the loan of his videotape production, *Two Dollars and a Dream.* Also in New York, I spent time at Columbia University, studying their Oral History Project and the Gumby Collection, located in their Special Collections, and I made frequent use of the 42nd Street New York Public Library in a number of different departments. The Westchester County Courthouse provided documents dealing with the history and purchase of Villa Lewaro. The Westchester Historical Society houses a number of Madam Walker documents, including the appraisal of Villa Lewaro. In Washington, the staff at the National Archives gave needed assistance tracking down BRFAL papers, as well as census information; at the Library of Congress, I was much helped by the staff in the periodicals room, as well as in the special collections, the prints and photographs room and the map collection. Leroy Cole sent me a wealth of information on the Cole automobile without having any idea who I was. Vincent Virga sharpened my sense of pictorial possibilities. Shane White gave the book a good historian's read. At Knopf, I've been very well cared for, and wish especially to thank Amber Qureshi, Ellen Feldman, Rebecca Heisman, Jon Fine, Steven Amsterdam, Carol Carson and, of course, Sonny Mehta, for his constancy and support.

We look to books and writers who come before us for information and direction. For family material and an especially generous bibliography, I'd like to extend my appreciation to A'Lelia Bundles. Finally, endless thanks to Tom Johnson, who entered my life and took his place in my heart in the later stages of the writing of this book, then read it thoroughly and well, providing invaluable suggestions, opinions and encouragement and, mostly, belief in what I was doing and steadiness when I had big doubts.

Photo Credits

Index

Page numbers in *italics* refer to illustrations.

A NOTE ON THE TYPE

This book was set in a typeface called Bulmer. This distinguished letter is a replica of a type long famous in the history of English printing which was designed and cut by William Martin about 1790 for William Bulmer of the Shakespeare Press. In design, it is all but a modern face, with vertical stress, sharp differentiation between the thick and thin strokes, and nearly flat serifs. The decorative italic shows the influence of Baskerville, as Martin was a pupil of John Baskerville's.

Composed by North Market Street Graphics,
Lancaster, Pennsylvania

Printed and bound by Berryville Graphics,
Berryville, Virginia

Designed by Iris Weinstein